I0796109

SCATTERED FAR AND WIDE

Four years together by the Bay
Where Severn joins the tide
Then by the Service called away
We're scattered far and wide
But still when two or three shall meet
And old tales be retold
From low to highest in the Fleet
We'll pledge the Blue and Gold

—"Navy Blue and Gold," verse 3

SCATTERED FAR AND WIDE

The Naval Academy Class of '38 at War

Justin Laborde

NAVAL INSTITUTE PRESS
Annapolis, Maryland

Naval Institute Press
291 Wood Road
Annapolis, MD 21402

ISBN: 978-1-68247-664-2 (hardcover)
ISBN: 978-1-68247-665-9 (eBook)
Library of Congress Cataloging-in-Publication Data is available.

♾ Print editions meet the requirements of ANSI/NISO z39.48-1992 (Permanence of Paper).
Printed in the United States of America.

33 32 31 30 29 28 27 26 25 9 8 7 6 5 4 3 2 1
First printing

Unless otherwise noted, all photographs are from *The Lucky Bag* '38.

CONTENTS

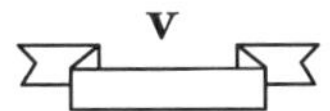

ILLUSTRATIONS

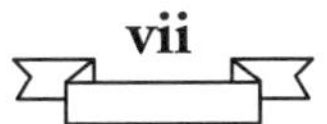

PREFACE

Over the years I spent researching and writing this book, telling anyone about the subject invariably spurred a number of questions. The ones I received most often from well-intentioned family and friends had to do with why I chose this class among all the others at the Naval Academy. "Why '38?" "Why not the Class of '37 or '36?" "Why not '39 or '40?" The questions were fair, for those classes too are replete with stories of young men serving through the dangers of the twentieth century's bloodiest conflict. Graduates of those classes and others also had tales to tell, tales of heroism and tragedy, selflessness and sacrifice.

To be sure, other classes suffered as much as '38 did. The losses experienced by the Classes of 1934, 1935, 1936, and 1937 were 12, 14, 16, and 14 percent, respectively. The Class of '38, by comparison, experienced roughly 10 percent fatalities during World War II. The Class of '39 saw the largest group of graduates in the Academy's ninety-nine previous years, 581, and 11 percent were lost. The Class of '40 also lost 11 percent. It was not the casualty rate the Class of '38 suffered that prompted my choice for this book's subject.

Nor was it the presence of true legends in naval history. The Class of '38 certainly had future bright lights in its ranks—Frank Lynch, Norman Kleiss, Ben Pickett, and Mike Rindskopf, to name just a few—but so did other classes near in time. Edward "Butch" O'Hare and George Street were members of the Class of '37, and both were Medal of Honor recipients. Eugene Fluckey, Class of 1935, sank more tonnage as captain of the submarine *Barb* than any other sub in World War II and received a Medal of Honor and four Navy Crosses while doing so,

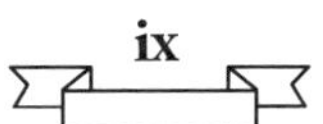

a feat unequaled by any living American. Richard O'Kane, also of the Class of '34, has come to be remembered as the most successful submarine commander of the war, and George Davis ('34) was captain of the USS *Walke* on January 6, 1945, when, while covering minesweeping operations in the Lingayen Gulf in the Philippines, she was struck by a kamikaze, an attack that enveloped her bridge in burning gasoline. Commander Davis, though horribly burned, remained on his feet conning the ship and supervising damage control operations until the *Walke* was out of danger. Only then did he relinquish command and allow himself to be taken to sick bay, where he soon died. He too was awarded a Medal of Honor. Stories like these and those of so many other graduates from the late 1930s, men like Milton Ricketts ('35), John Powers ('35), Kenneth Schacht ('35), Paul Riley ('37), Thomas Edwards ('37), Willard Holdredge ('39), and William Hogaboom ('39), fill the annals of the U.S. Navy and its Naval Academy.

So, why '38? Two reasons, chiefly. First, by virtue of when they graduated the members of the class had unique opportunities to be on the front lines at the war's start, to experience the conflict from day one. And second, the interconnections of these men throughout the war presented something special, I felt: shared experiences and yet personal and varying perspectives that contributed immensely to a more thorough (and entertaining) retelling of these events.

I obtained an old copy of *The Lucky Bag* from 1938 after realizing I wanted to write about the experiences of a class of graduates during World War II. As I flipped through my immaculately well-preserved edition of the thick, dark, leather-bound book, staring at the faces and reading the biographical sketches of each of that year's graduates, I was amazed by the possibilities of each of the fantastically young men in the years to come. These First Classmen were graduating, unbeknown to them in those formal portraits, at such a historically dangerous time. They were so blissfully unaware as they smiled ever so slightly for the camera. Yet, because they would have three and a half years of service before the Japanese attacked Pearl Harbor, they would be relatively experienced new officers in the war's early days, and ship captains in its later years, as well as pilots in leadership positions and submariners in charge. The Class of '38 would serve as young ensigns, lieutenants, and lieutenant commanders in perfect positions to experience the war up close and firsthand, to be tested as young leaders of men in real combat. These men were old enough to bear the burdens of command, yet young enough to be on the ships and in the planes at the front lines of the war's biggest and bloodiest battles and campaigns. They would be there with the wind and the spray in their faces, with the percussion of ship guns and depth charges knocking them off their feet at what I felt was the ideal moment in time, at a pivotal point of their lives and their careers, to make their experiences unusually compelling, awe-inspiring, and most assuredly heartbreaking.

What also resonated with me was the number of times these men crossed paths with each other during the war, the number of times they fought together in battles, affording opportunities to tell stories from alternative points of view. These young men were scattered across Pearl Harbor on December 7, 1941, served at the Coral Sea and Midway together across ships and squadrons, watched each other die during 1944's Typhoon Cobra from various vantage points. These moments of coming together provided unique lenses through which to write about these events. What's more, these classmates served together in squadrons and on surface vessels in combat, yes, but they also ran into each other aboard ships headed toward the South Pacific, on Hawaiian beaches after combat cruises, in wardrooms testifying before naval boards. It was these chance meetings and heartfelt conversations during the war, often purely serendipitous, that created moments of enormous poignancy and emotion.

Perhaps nowhere is this better exemplified than in a story that did not make the final version of this book. It is the tale of Ray Calhoun, Class of '38, and his chance encounter with classmate Frank Case in the North Atlantic in the weeks after the Japanese attacked Pearl Harbor. Calhoun was serving aboard the destroyer *Sterett* ferrying troopships across the freezing North Atlantic to and from England, hunting for U-boats, green water breaking over the main deck with each passage through whirling white flakes of snow. The North Atlantic in wintertime was and is a dangerous place to sail. On February 23, 1942, the *Sterett* steamed off the East Coast of the United States in the company of the aircraft carrier *Wasp*, the Maine shoreline not far to the west. The *Wasp* was engaged in flight operations, some aircraft landing and others taking off again, while the *Sterett* screened ahead for submarines. Calhoun stood on deck watching the distant operations above the carrier when he saw a plane in a returning group crash into the icy water several miles ahead of the *Wasp*, evidently from engine trouble. The *Sterett* immediately broke station and sped to the spot on the sea where the aircraft had gone down, arriving not more than ten minutes later. But there was nothing of the plane left. No fuselage, no wreckage, no life raft or pilot. It had all simply slipped beneath the waves. The *Sterett* searched the water for several more hours with another destroyer in the division, but they found nothing. Eventually the destroyer was forced to abandon its search and resume her position in the *Wasp*'s screen. It was not until several days later, when he was back ashore, that Calhoun learned who the missing pilot he had watched crash into the sea had been: Frank D. Case Jr., USNA, Class of 1938.

This book is about remembrance, about telling stories too long left untold, about lauding men too often ignored because they were mere junior officers when an event occurred and lacked the star power of the admirals who commanded the ships and the planes. But just such a claim could be made about the other classes that graduated from the Academy before and during the war. Perhaps down the road I will tell their tales too. They would be no less interesting, I am sure. In any event, the Class of '38 is an excellent place to start.

1938
USNA

FLOYD BRUCE GARRETT JR.

Little Rock, Arkansas

Small in size, but full of fight and determination, Bruce came all the way from Little Rock to learn this naval trade. He has become the most seagoin' fellow in the class, and some of the yarns he spins would turn the "Old Navy" green with envy. Always ready to have a good time, but serious enough to stand well in the upper third, his knowledge of the academic side of life has made him more than helpful as a roommate. His cheerful, level point of view is always dependable. His activities have been limited to holding down the radiator and complaining about the food. Seriously, we would have been lost without him. Our suite could never be complete without li'l Brucie's helpful, encouraging, and determined companionship.

The Lucky Bag, 1938

Prologue

AT THE MERCY OF THE SEA

Early on the morning of December 18, 1944, on the Pacific Ocean roughly five hundred miles east of Luzon in the Philippines, a *Farragut*-class destroyer named the USS *Monaghan* wallowed in the sixty-foot waves and screaming hundred-knot winds and paint-peeling spray of a vicious storm. The destroyer—small, low to the water, and top-heavy even in calm seas—yawed and leaned as wave after crashing gray wave pummeled the vessel, driving her out of formation in the screen of Admiral William F. Halsey's Task Force 38 and off to the west. Battered and exhausted sailors clung to whatever handholds they could reach.[1] In troughs, the men on her bridge could not see over the tops of the waves. The heaving ocean spun the ship like a toy. The *Monaghan*'s captain and crew were bearing the brunt of a massive typhoon's leading edge; the storm, Typhoon Cobra, would become famous for its violence, sheer size, and awesome destructiveness.

The captain of the *Monaghan* that morning was F. Bruce Garrett, a boyish-looking officer who was small of stature but who possessed a quiet dignity and a winning smile. He had graduated from the United States Naval Academy in Annapolis, Maryland, six years earlier, in 1938. He had been in the *Monaghan*'s captain's chair for a mere seven days, and as he desperately called out rudder and screw combinations to get his ship pointed south and back to her position in the fleet, he quickly realized that there were bigger problems than the ship's location. Desperately, Garrett reasoned that the only way he could keep his ship upright in the mountainous waves and gale force blasts of wind was to ballast her aft bunkers with seawater.[2] Garrett hollered the order, but the dangerous maneuver was unsuccessful, and soon thereafter the young ship captain transmitted a fleet-wide general distress signal reporting that his generator and steering had failed. His ship was out of control, bucking up the waves, crashing back down into the troughs on the far side, rolling severely in the wind gusts, and quickly taking on water.

Not far from where the *Monaghan* foundered, C. Raymond Calhoun, like Garrett a captain of a *Farragut*-class destroyer, the USS *Dewey*, and a fellow member of the Naval Academy's Class of '38, heard the distress call over his TBS (Talking Between Ships) radio and reached for his own microphone. He tried to reassure Garrett that he too was taking on major rolls in the waves and in danger of falling out of formation, but Calhoun could not get through to his friend.

Garrett did not reply because by then his ship's communications system had temporarily failed and he had lost all contact with the other vessels around him. With his ship in dire straits, Garrett sent a runner to his chief oilman, Watertender Second Class Joe McCrane, with an order to open the valves to two of the destroyer's empty fuel tanks and connect them to the main waterline attached to the bilge pumps. His ship was being torn apart, and getting her properly ballasted was their only chance at survival.

Once communications had been restored, Garrett quickly broadcast another message, this one to Captain Jasper Acuff, the commander of the task force's tankers, oilers, and support vessels. Shouting over the wind, Garrett reported he was unable to steer the base course of 180 degrees and was on a heading of 330, the storm pushing him directly for other ships in the task force, who were likewise foundering in the seas. At 0936 Garrett radioed an update: "I am unable to come to the base course. Have tried full speed, but it will not work."[3]

Calhoun again overheard Garrett's message. Hoping once more to reassure his classmate, he tried to establish a new connection with the *Monaghan* so he could tell Garrett that he had given up trying to maintain station or even return to the formation. Merely turning the ship in these conditions was challenging enough. Calhoun's radarmen had tentatively identified the *Monaghan* on their scope; she was only three thousand yards away. But before he could reach Garrett, Calhoun screamed for right full rudder as the light carrier *Monterey* suddenly loomed in front of him out of the rain squalls and the darkness. The massive aircraft carrier slid by his small ship at a distance of a mere fifty yards. Calhoun tried to get his destroyer back on a course of 180 degrees but noticed on the gyro repeater that they were changing headings very slowly. His quartermaster called out, "She's not answering, Cap'n."[4] Calhoun had never experienced such a thing before. He ordered port ahead full, but there was still no answer from the *Dewey*. He decided to try a turn in the other direction, asking for left full rudder, port stop, starboard ahead full. This time the ship turned a few degrees, then refused to turn any farther. She sat in the trough of a wave and could not break free. Calhoun thought of stopping where he was but could not be sure where the other big ships were located, so he kept trying. Soon he too placed a call to the rest of Task Group 30.8: "This is Achilles. I am out of control, crossing through the formation from starboard to port. Keep clear!"[5]

The *Dewey* corkscrewed through the other ships. Calhoun knew that even if the lookouts on the other vessels could see him, there was little the helmsmen could do to turn away if he crossed their paths. Suddenly, out of the rain, another huge black hull loomed in front of his ship. Both vessels rose atop a cross swell, and it appeared to Calhoun that the *Dewey* would come down right on top of the ship, but as they descended the wave's crest the oiler ahead of them was itself picked up and she was pushed clear. Said Calhoun, "I could have thrown a spud at her."[6]

He knew there were more ships across his path and that if he collided with any of them, it would be the end, but he had no other options save to continue on his course. More ships loomed up and slid past, one so close Calhoun felt he could have reached out and touched her. Somehow they made it through the formation. The ship was by now consistently rolling 50 degrees to starboard and as much as 40 degrees to port. Each time, the top-heavy *Dewey* slowly righted herself before she was smacked again by another wave and sent rolling anew. Capsizing, in Calhoun's mind, was very much a possibility. His eyes stayed glued to the inclinometer, and he watched as it registered 55, 56, 57, then 60 degrees. Calhoun had never rolled more than 50 degrees in all of the rough weather he had faced before. The maximum roll the *Dewey* could recover from was supposedly 72 degrees, but that data was years old, prepared well before the Navy had added more armament and radar systems to his destroyer's deck, thereby changing her stability characteristics significantly. Though it seemed unbelievable to Calhoun that any modern destroyer could ever capsize, he knew well, as he watched the inclinometer readings climb past 60 degrees, that the limits of what his ship could endure were rapidly being approached. The wind continued to increase. "It drove spray and spume with the force of a sand blaster. Capillary bleeding was etched on any face exposed directly to it. When the lookouts and signalmen turned away from it, their cheeks and foreheads were pocked with a bloody tattoo."[7] The wind stripped the paint off the superstructure and hull and drove into every crevice on the ship. The forward fireroom airlock hatch blew off, and seawater flooded the main distribution board. Her antenna wires flapped in the wind and dragged in the water when she listed. The *Dewey* leaned so close to the sea that waves began cresting her gunwales and her starboard weather deck was submerged for minutes at a time.

The *Monaghan*, not far away, was now locked in irons, without power, and drifting. She was dead in the water and "completely at the mercy of the wind and sea."[8] Despite Garrett's lack of command experience, he had done a magnificent job up to that point of directing her through the storm.[9] Garrett was well-liked by his crewmen, and he had calmly and adroitly kept his ship running before the wind, like a veteran destroyer captain rather than the newcomer he was. He had refused to leave the flying bridge all morning. After a time, few of the officers on board the *Monaghan* spoke, all well aware of the danger the destroyer was in. Garrett's ship was literally being torn apart as below, in the engine and fire rooms, the overheads started ripping loose from the bulkheads. Still, his biggest problem in such horrendous seas was that he had been unable to ballast the ship's empty aft fuel bunkers. Not one of his attempts had worked. Garrett and his crew quickly sensed the inevitable.[10] By 1045 the *Monaghan*'s rolls were approaching the ship's limits and the generators and steering motor had failed again. Communication between the bridge and the steering motor room was no longer possible. With each roll, men in the after gun shelter hollered out prayers like they never had before: "Don't let us down now, Dear Lord. Bring it back. Oh God, bring it back." When the ship came back, they would shout, "Thanks, Dear Lord!"[11]

It is believed that the failures of the ship's integrity soon caused massive flooding in the engineering room, and the *Monaghan* rolled for the last time around 1230, her inclinometer at 78 degrees as she sideslipped down a mountain of water onto her starboard quarter before her steel frame tore apart and she was driven under. Some sailors, maintaining good order, were able to heave themselves into the sea through the deckhouse's portside hatch, while other men clung to what they could of the ship, but the *Monaghan* bobbed on her side one last time and then was gone beneath the roiling wave tops, "battered under by a foe more relentless than any human agency," and taking Bruce Garrett, USNA '38, and more than 250 of his ship's officers and crew with her.[12]

Part One

THE TIME IS COMING

HERBERT IRVING MANDEL

Brooklyn, New York

From well-earned prominence in his large high school, Herb came directly to the humble confusion of a Plebe. Regulations and routine he earnestly adopted, even to the point of turning back his mattress at home on his first leave. Academics weren't so readily absorbed, but trials of his first two years revealed an amazing capacity for work. Cheerfully, if sheepishly, Herb admits that he likes all the girls, but he denies having made any choice. In music, reading, and informal athletics his tastes strike an enviable combination. We don't remember how many times he has been dimmed down flat in tussles with a man twice his size. However, we can't forget the keynote to his character in Herb's invariable treatment of the situation: "Well, ya big stiff, have ya had enough?"

The Lucky Bag, 1938

Chapter One
ON THE YARD

On a midsummer's day in June 1934, at 8:30 in the morning, a gaggle of young men, teenagers mostly, stood before the Main Gate of the U.S. Naval Academy in Annapolis, Maryland. These "nominees" were boys who milled about speaking with the accents of Richton, Mississippi; Passaic, New Jersey; and Portland, Oregon; who had left behind families in San Juan, Puerto Rico; Kenosha, Wisconsin; and San Francisco, California; who carried ticket stubs from Grand Forks, North Dakota; Beaumont, Texas; and Oskaloosa, Iowa. They had all lobbied for and earned the necessary appointments from their state's senators, had passed the required entrance exams, and had received their orders to appear at the Academy on this day and "be prepared to remain there permanently."[1] Singly and in groups the new arrivals entered through the gate and "came aboard" the Yard, where old, blue-uniformed men nicknamed "Jimmylegs" glided around the roads on bicycles and pointed the boys to the Administration Building. "Just keep on walking straight down this Maryland Avenue for a few paces until you come to the mounted naval gun . . . then turn right—and there you are!"[2] Some of the boys may have noticed as they started the walk past the green, gently sloping lawns that the roadway beneath their feet ran, both literally and symbolically, straight to the water in front of them.

In those days the Yard was 250 acres of wide commons, evergreen holly trees, granite lecture halls, white-faced brick buildings, athletic fields, and seven miles of roadways beyond which stretched the blue waters of the Severn and the white-sailed pleasure craft that were ubiquitous on its chop. It was a beautiful place, but one with a formal purpose—to indoctrinate, to focus the Navy at the center of each midshipman's world, to direct his attention to the water beyond and to make him sea-minded, and single-minded at that. Boats lay along the seawall. Nautical terms replaced the familiar names and verbiage of civilian speech. Time was told in ships' bells. Everywhere the new arrivals looked were naval guns, flags, relics, and statues. The Yard was designed to be a place apart, a place for controlled training and teaching, a place of few distractions. The historian Ian Toll labeled it "an austere, inward-looking, highly regimented social order, hermetically sealed off from the cacophonous civilian society in which [the midshipmen] had been raised."[3] The Academy was endowed with a clear and firm purpose, but it was dressed beautifully for the job.

The Administration Building served as the headquarters of the superintendent of the Naval Academy, and the boys reporting that day gathered in one of its hallways and waited for the chief clerk behind his temporary table to signal them forward. Historian Kendall Banning, in his descriptions of Annapolis at the time, described the new arrivals as "rich boys, poor boys, tall and short, from all walks of life" and from "every state of the Union." They were "sons of financiers and farmers, of merchants and mariners, of teachers and tailors, of soldiers and scientists, of bakers and bankers. . . . They constitute[d] a genuine cross-section of American life."[4] One by one the new arrivals were checked against a call list and their papers were time-stamped to go into the Academy's official files. Their presence now formally reported, the boys received instruction sheets that explained in exact detail what steps they had to take, when, and where each act was to be performed. It was their first introduction to the regimentation the Academy would impose so severely, and the very beginning of the process through which the Naval Academy shaped into proper midshipmen the raw material that arrived at its gate each summer.[5] It began that first day, that first hour, and would continue for the next four years until a distant June afternoon when some (but not all) of these boys would throw their hats into the air as newly commissioned officers of the United States Navy.

After their brief interactions with the chief clerk, the prospective midshipmen lined up outside the building in columns of twos and marched across the Yard to Bancroft Hall, where they were to begin the procedures laid out on the paper in their hands. For many it may have been their first view of it, the "mecca of all midshipmen,"the low, wide, and thoroughly imposing dormitory in front of them.[6] Named after former Secretary of the Navy George Bancroft and designed in Beaux Arts style by architect Ernest Flagg, the hall was home to the entire Regiment of Midshipmen for eight months out of the year, its massive masonry symbolizing the "common bonds" among the men inside.[7] As Robert Sleight, a midshipman in the 1930s, described it, "It is called a hall, but is in fact a city."[8] Within its walls were twenty acres of floor space; four wings with five decks to each; three miles of long, hard cement corridors layered with linoleum; and all the necessities for the housing, clothing, and feeding of the Regiment.

The young nominees walked across the sweeping approach to the building, more than one hundred yards of terrace inlaid with slippery brown promenade tile, past the four medieval French and Spanish cannon that flanked the broad, gentle two-tiered steps, and up to the massive bronze front doors inset into ornate granite frames. Upon entering the high-ceilinged marble Rotunda, the candidates ascended a staircase into "Sick Bay," their leather heels echoing. They proceeded through the various groups of doctors and their lab tests over to the station where personal and often uncomplimentary observations about general posture, bearing, proportions, scars, and physical peculiarities were made. Some boys were failed and sent home. The lucky ones blessed with good health, keen eyes, and sound bearing were then sent to a row of tables off the Rotunda where executive officers sat with more forms, including a "Personal History Sheet" that ascertained, among other things, whether the nominee was, or had ever been, married. A "yes" answer meant automatic disqualification, for there was not and had never been such a thing as a married midshipman.

From here, the decks of Bancroft Hall now swarming, the new arrivals ate lunch and then received their room assignments and laundry numbers; drew boxes containing sheets, blankets, towels, and laundry bags; and received their shoes, underwear, work uniforms, shirts, bathrobes, raincoats, caps, and leggings. They were handed a set of Naval Academy regulations, instruction folders, pamphlets, books, and placards. They quickly learned how to organize their lockers, walk down the decks, turn square corners, brace their shoulders, and "sound off" whenever entering a room.

Among the new students that day was Herbert Mandel, from Brooklyn, New York. Mandel had first come across a mention of the Naval Academy in grade school when, as part of a class in elementary physics, he had read a paragraph in his textbook about the man who first measured the speed of light, Albert Abraham Michelson, a Polish-born 1871 graduate of the institution. Intrigued by the idea of such a place, Mandel spent many a following Saturday afternoon in the public library looking up every reference he could find. Of course, growing up in Brooklyn, Mandel would often spot West Point cadets in their gray half-capes sauntering around the Theater District on liberty, but, as he wrote, "It did not sway me. I went for the Navy blue."[9] At the start of his senior year of high school, Mandel began searching for ways to obtain an appointment and was assisted by his father, who had numerous contacts among the naval officers stationed at New York City's Third Naval District. After some quick discussions about the difficulty of the algebra and geometry classes at the Academy, Mandel, his commitment resolute, took a leave of absence from James Madison High School and enrolled in the Naval Academy Prep Class for four months before passing the exams and earning his appointment.

Brinkley Bass too worked his way down the halls and through the crowds. He was born on the Fourth of July 1916 in Chicago, the only child to loving parents who raised him in Beaumont, Texas. Bass' home was a happy one, and the strong family ties his parents engendered had a profound influence on his development. Self-confident, energetic, and smart, Bass made friends easily, with his lively spirit, sense of humor, and outgoing personality.[10] At fourteen and a member of Troop 6 he was awarded the rank of Eagle Scout, and at the ceremony Bass remarked, "They should give the badge to Mamma. She is the one who had to get up at 4:00 in the morning and drive me out to camp so I could pass requirements."[11] He grew up to be a pragmatic young man: if there was something to be done about a situation, he did it; if not, he simply moved on. After graduating from Beaumont High School, Bass attended local South Park College for a year before, in the fall of 1933, deciding on the Naval Academy. He soon had nineteen prominent citizens of Beaumont writing letters in support of his nomination, including businessmen, attorneys, a judge, doctors, bankers, his high school principal, the publisher of the *Beaumont Enterprise*, and the minister at Westminster Presbyterian Church. After all of that, however, it was not Texas congressman Martin Dies who awarded him an appointment (all of Texas' were taken) but the Honorable D. D. Glover of the Sixth District of Arkansas after his uncle, who lived in the state, "adopted" him. Another letter, this one from Arkansas governor Harvey Parnell, certainly did not hurt matters. By then Bass was attending West Point–Annapolis Coaching School in Columbia, Missouri, and after passing his entrance exams, he received his notification to report to Annapolis as a prospective member of the class of 1938.

Throughout that first day on campus the matriculation process had been systematic, perfunctory, and rapid-fire. At 1700 that evening, however, an event took place that was not rushed, that was anything but perfunctory, and that the boys would remember well wherever their future careers took them. They were assembled in a ground floor corridor in their new sailor's uniforms, then marched once more through the Rotunda and up a gradually ascending central stairway into the marbled grandeur of Memorial Hall. This was a hallowed place of memory and reverence, with parquet floors, crystal chandeliers, and a sweeping view of the Chesapeake Bay through the windows. On the walls were years of naval history: trophies and battle standards and portraits of the legends who had come before and whose names still evoked images and tales of unsurpassed heroism and courage—John Paul Jones, Stephen Decatur, Oliver Hazard Perry, David Glasgow Farragut, David Dixon Porter, Edward Preble, George Dewey. The room was a "Valhalla" to all the graduates of the Naval Academy who had given their lives for their country since its inception.[12]

In this place the prospective midshipmen were lined up facing the most treasured of the relics possessed by the Naval Academy: the original eight-and-a-half-foot blue flag, once dark, now faded, that had been raised aloft by Commodore Perry during his engagement with the British at the Battle of Lake Erie. On its surface was crudely lettered the famous words of the mortally wounded Captain James Lawrence, who, dying from small arms fire on board his frigate *Chesapeake* on June 1, 1813, instructed his men, "Don't give up the ship." There, with the banner above them, the boys were instructed to raise their right hands by Captain Forde A. Todd, the Commandant of Midshipmen, who appeared in a starched white uniform, four gold stripes on his black shoulder boards, and told them to repeat the oath of office:

> I, (name), of the State of (state), aged (age) years, having been appointed a midshipman in the United States Navy, do solemnly swear (or affirm) that I will support and defend the Constitution of the United States against all enemies, foreign and domestic; that I will bear true allegiance to the same; that I take this obligation freely, without any mental reservation or purpose of evasion; and that I will well and faithfully discharge the duties of the office on which I am about to enter: So help me God.[13]

Captain Todd then paused, looked them over, and congratulated them on becoming as of that moment officers of the U.S. Navy, "if only in a qualified sense."[14] He told them they were now men of whom much was expected and on whom their country was relying. He talked of the great tradition of those who had come before, both in war and peace. He pointed to the paintings on the walls and recited the words spoken in the heat of battles prior: "Damn the torpedoes—full speed ahead" and "Surrender, hell—we have not yet begun to fight." He reminded them of their duty moving forward, which was to prepare themselves to become fully commissioned officers.

Of the 612 men sworn in that summer evening in 1934, 438 would graduate four years later (72 percent, which was roughly average), and 421 would serve in World War II.[15] They would be stationed on ships around the world and participate in the battles of Pearl Harbor, Coral Sea, Midway, and Okinawa as well as the Java Sea, the Atlantic, Solomon Islands, Savo Island, Kahili, and others. They were on board the *Wasp*, *Cisco*, *Amberjack*, *Houston*, *Pope*, *Pillsbury*, *Grampus*, *Yorktown*, *Monaghan*, and *Pickerel*, among others, when those ships and submarines were sunk. They flew planes and blimps. They spent years in prison camps. Twenty-six would become second lieutenants in the Marine Corps. They would win Distinguished Flying Crosses, Bronze Stars, Silver Stars, and Navy Crosses by the dozen. Forty-two would die from enemy action.

Ending his speech, Captain Todd once more looked over the new men arrayed before him. He said, "What you do from now on will reflect credit or discredit not alone upon yourselves but upon the naval service. . . . When the work . . . seems hard, when the future looks dark, when you get homesick, come up here and take a look at that flag. Don't give up—ever!"[16]

Though a fraction the size of West Point, the Naval Academy in the 1930s exuded a sense of "quiet dignity, simple elegance, and strength," its buildings hunkering on the south bank of the Severn River, at the tip of a peninsula that juts into the sparkling blue waters of the Chesapeake.[17] Piled up behind the Yard, on two hills overlooking the water, is the old city of Annapolis. While from the bay the Academy looks like a series of low, squat, severe buildings with the domed capitol in the distance, "a person would have to have decidedly negative characteristics not to be affected by the beauty and landscaping *par excellence* that is everywhere evident."[18]

The institution had been founded in 1845 as the Naval School by the historian and statesman George Bancroft, who, while Secretary of the Navy under President James K. Polk, discerned a distinct lack of preparedness and intellectual rigor among the U.S. Navy's emerging young officer corps of the time. Overcoming the opposition of the Navy's senior officers, who scoffed at the notion of a school for naval education situated *on land*, Bancroft selected Commander Franklin Buchanan as the institution's first superintendent and secured an old army post, Fort Severn, on which to establish his campus. The school formally opened on October 10, 1845, with seven faculty and approximately fifty acting midshipmen. Initially the course of instruction proffered by the Academy took five years to complete, of which only the first and fifth were spent on the Yard, the intervening three spent on board naval ships on active service. In 1850 the course of study was reorganized to four consecutive years, and the summer practice cruises were instituted. By 1851 the success of the school had been assured, and it was renamed "The Naval Academy."

What followed over the next four years for the members of the Class of 1938 was an endless array of mess hall meals and formal dinners, theater productions and musical performances, long bull sessions with roommates, daily formations and weekly parades, lonely shifts on guard duty, dances in the gym with young ladies affectionately called "drags," Army-Navy contests in every sport, boxing matches and basketball games (players were known as "basketeers"), two summer cruises to Europe and back (including prewar visits to Kiel and Berlin, Germany), holiday leaves, and hour after hour after hour of class time, coursework, study sessions, and instruction. The Naval Academy was determined to turn out men whose life's work was to be the naval profession, and that is just what it did.[19] Not just its course of instruction and educational techniques but its very character and culture had been organized around that objective. As such it was markedly unlike the civilian colleges and universities of the day.[20] Historian Ronald Spector wrote that "symmetrical general education there was lacking."[21] The Academy featured an academic program consisting of English, mathematics, history (mostly naval history), government, and languages but also seamanship and navigation, ordnance and gunnery, hygiene, and physical training. A separate executive program, headed by the Commandant of Midshipmen, was tasked with upholding the students' interior discipline, drills, and tactical instruction. In the 1930s the majority of the academic work was devoted to mathematics and the sciences (one of the better-known exam questions of Second Class year was "sketch and describe a torpedo"), while the rest of the students' attention was divided between so-called cultural subjects (referred to as "bull" by the midshipmen) and the more professional courses (marine aviation, electrical engineering, and the like).[22] The key to doing well in class was rote memorization. There was little need and few opportunities for deep analysis, creativity, opinion, or independent thought. Nevertheless, for "First Classmen" in their final year, lessons in the humanities were augmented by a series of Friday evening lectures by prominent educators on topics primarily concerning world affairs and their political aspects. No one was allowed to deviate from the established curriculum.

But training a midshipman for a career in the United States Navy was, to the Naval Academy, not solely about academic instruction. The Academy emphasized character, too. Honor, reliability, patriotism, integrity, sound judgment, loyalty, as well as being "well-liked" and "fitting in," were all deemed vital to a midshipman's ultimate success during their Academy careers, and these virtues were inculcated in the Class of '38 from the very beginning. As John

Paul Jones, the Academy's guiding light, said, "It is by no means enough that an officer of the Navy should be a capable mariner. He must be that of course, but also a great deal more. He should be as well a gentleman of liberal education, refined manners, punctilious courtesy, and the nicest sense of personal honor."[23] The Academy did not want to turn out officers who were merely smart. They wanted graduates who also looked and acted the part. Critics of the institution decried its function as an "engine of assimilation," one that pushed out the nonconformists, the nonbelievers, and the nontraditionalists, and while that may have been true in some instances, those who remained and thrived left as more than just heirs to the institution's "proud warrior tradition"; they left as men "bonded to each other and to the Navy, with a deeply felt *esprit de corps*, overpowering and for life."[24]

Each year's classwork at the Academy was rigorous. By the start of their fourth and final year in the fall of 1937, the members of the Class of '38 had progressed in every subject to the point that they now learned more advanced and more difficult concepts. In Seamanship & Navigation, for instance, what had started out as rowing lifeboats and semaphore in their first year now involved the "never-to-be-forgotten P-work" involving the practical application of navigational techniques using position plotters, dividers, enormous charts, and Bowditch.[25] They had started out in the Ordnance & Gunnery Department on the rifle range learning how to shoot. In their final year they studied the finer points of ballistics, fire control, and naval gunnery. They used "log log duplex" slide rules in the Mathematics Department; carried their leather "steam kits" down long halls strewn with motors, generators, and switchboards in the Electrical Engineering building; and sketched feedwater systems and the "dismal expanse of bilges" in their marine engineering classes.[26] In their English, history, and government coursework, their instructors detailed European history and its effects on current events and polished their oratorical skills over cigars as part of the After Dinner Speaking exercises designed to give these older midshipmen "the training to meet and greet the world."[27]

Despite the hard work that was required, being a First Classman at the Naval Academy was a mostly pleasant experience for those who could attain it. Throughout their first three years, the Class of '38 had been told that rank had its privileges, and by the start of their fourth year, as Herb Mandel wrote, "Life in Bancroft Hall was completely different from the fall of 1934 when we were Plebes."[28] By the latter part of 1937 they were at the pinnacle of the Regiment, one of the chosen few, and their status as First Classmen was denoted by a single horizontal stripe around the bottom of each jacket sleeve.[29] They were in unquestioned command of all other midshipmen, evaluated differently, disciplined differently, and treated differently at every turn. Truly they had become the Yard's "top dogs."[30]

In the fall of 1937, in Washington, DC, while Secretary of the Navy Claude A. Swanson was asking President Franklin Roosevelt to increase appropriations in order to strengthen the numbers of enlisted and officer personnel and bring several construction projects to completion on the Yard the midshipmen of the Class of '38 were engrossed in making sure they kept their grades up. Constantly updated aptitude ratings determined the quota named officers of the "First Group" (those with marks from 3.4 to 4.0), the "Second Group" (3.0 to 3.4), and so on, and these ratings ultimately determined each man's professional rise or fall in the Navy; they also formed a "personal estimate that [followed] him for the rest of his life."[31] In addition to academic and conduct marks, each midshipman was being scored on initiative, tact, attention to duty, reliability, interest, cooperation, military bearing, and attitude. In effect, each man was under surveillance twenty-four hours a day, watched and evaluated in and out of the classroom; in and out of the mess hall; on and off the athletic field, the rifle range, and the drill ground. Each month lists of all midshipmen who had less than a 2.5 in any subject were posted. The difficult academics continued to delay, and often even derail, many a promising naval officer's career. But there was no changing the system or hoping for leniency. The demands were ruthless, the rules ironbound, and exceptions nonexistent, even for those set to graduate in the spring.

One member of the Class of '38 who had already run afoul of the Academy's rigorous academics was Raymond Calhoun. By the winter of 1938, he had been at the Academy for four and a half years, unable to graduate the previous summer due to a failing grade in mathematics that had turned him back. Things were now looking up, though, and he was on course to finish with the class. Calhoun was born in Philadelphia in 1913. His father, a skipper in the Merchant Marine, had been gone for long stretches of his youth, but the time away did not dissuade Calhoun from an early interest in the seafarer's life. As a young boy he would often wander down to Delaware Avenue with a few friends and gaze at the ships tied up in their slips, sometimes even sneaking on board one or two for a closer look. When World War I began, Calhoun's father accepted a commission as a lieutenant commander in the Naval Reserves. In October 1918, roughly two weeks before the Armistice, he made his first trip overseas and, while docked in a harbor in France, was asked to make an official call on the commanding officer of a U.S. destroyer moored behind him. As he walked over, a crane unloading matériel from his ship broke, and an entire sling of cargo fell on top of him. Young Raymond was five years old when his dad died.

Though he grew up without a father, Calhoun had been blessed with a loving mother and generous grandparents who raised him in Kensington, a tough part of Philadelphia peopled by mill workers and blue-collar laborers. In high school he was told of a law stipulating that because of his father's death in World War I, he was entitled to an appointment at the service academy of his choosing, no political influence needed. It was an easy decision for Calhoun; he had wanted to attend the Naval Academy since the age of twelve. To prepare himself physically and mentally, Calhoun attended Valley Forge Military Academy until he was twenty. There he gained twenty pounds, became a starting guard on the football team, and, after two years, entered the Academy in the summer of 1933.

Every two months the students' aptitude ratings were tabulated afresh and the positions of each midshipman in the Regiment reestablished. The Regiment was led by the First Classman who, based on his aptitude ratings, earned the role of regimental commander (a midshipman commander or "five-striper"). Each of the four battalions had at its head a battalion commander (midshipmen lieutenant commanders, or four-stripers), and each battalion's two companies were led by company commanders (three-stripers; midshipmen lieutenants). There were four platoons per company, each led by a platoon commander (two-stripers, midshipmen lieutenants junior grade) and subcommander (one-stripers, midshipmen ensigns). Every single one of these positions of responsibility, from regimental commander on down to ensign, was filled by a First Classman, and a First Classman only. They were the bosses. Any First Classman outranked any underclassman. It was all about instilling in them the trappings and experiences of command.

In late January 1938, a new superintendent took over at the Academy. Rear Admiral Wilson Brown was a stern, severe-looking man with thinning hair, jutting ears, and a wide boxer's nose. In his official Academy portrait, Admiral Brown appeared hale and hearty, as well as tough, almost pugnacious. He looked set to get things done, and there were issues that demanded his attention. The politicians in Congress were steeling themselves to deny any funds for building up a Navy that could be used in an "offensive" war. They saw the funds as simply about "pacifism vs. aggression," when, in reality, appropriating sufficient funds to keep the Navy strong was a much more nuanced matter. According to the Navy's experts, even if the question was only about the country's isolation, naval strength was required to maintain it. If that power was nonexistent, they argued, the need for self-preservation would surely and irrevocably spur America's involvement in foreign wars. As writers in *The Log* wrote that February, "Only sufficient thorns can keep the rose from being plucked from its place on the bush. The thorns of the rose of American isolation are ships—fighting ships. Isolation as a national policy demands a superior navy."[32]

The rains came that March, heavy storms that sopped Farragut Field and sent gulls wheeling over the basin and eventually caused a blanket of yellow forsythia to emerge below the seaward mess hall windows and in other beds around the Yard. In Europe Adolf Hitler sent his Wehrmacht across the border into Austria, the "latest home run in the year 'round game played between the statesmen of Europe," according to *The Log*. "Hitler has definitely taken from Mussolini the batting championship of the Totalitarian-Democratic League."[33] Despite the violation of international law and national sovereignty it represented, the ultimate result of the invasion was, at least to the magazine's editors, uncertain. They could not tell whether the move would be for good or ill for the other democracies of Europe; nonetheless, they challenged Germany's rather ruthless methods.

"From an entirely detached point of view," the editors wrote begrudgingly, "one cannot help but be impressed by the impotency of democracy, even if the totalitarian states are divided." The article closed with the first mention of a possible war to come that appeared in the pages of *The Log* that academic year, saying rather ominously, "Of course men change. . . . But unless [Hitler and Mussolini] change very radically, it looks from this corner as if munitions stocks will be paying war dividends."[34]

Four years after their first day on the Yard, "June Week" arrived for the Class of '38. It started rather dissonantly on the last Friday in May as the Academy was converted from a stern, hard-walled, and severe place of study and discipline, slide rules, and demerits, into, as Kendall Banning wrote, a "pleasure ship."[35] The midshipmen could be forgiven their whiplash.

> For six triumphant days youth [rode] into the quaint old community of Annapolis to participate in a pageant of celebration and romance. For six days the Yard [was] filled with starry-eyed lovelies, with ecstatic young sisters and brothers and proud fathers and mothers from back home. For six days the schedule [was] replete with athletic sports, with parades and ceremonies, with exhibition boat and gun drills, with the sounds of martial music by day and of dance music by night, with cannonades, with garden parties and water carnivals under the glow of colored lanterns and with all the delights ever dear to the hearts of men and maids. It [was] June Week.[36]

The academic careers of the First Classmen had ended the week before in a celebration known as "No More Rivers." During the week of final exams, called "rivers" at the Academy, the men had marched to and from class singing in their deep baritones, "We are almost out of the wilderness, we are almost out of the wilderness, we are almost out of the wilderness, only four (or three, or two, or one) rivers to cross." When the last exam had been taken and the last pencils put away and the last booklets turned in, the lyrics changed: "Thank God we are out of the wilderness, thank God we are out of the wilderness, thank God we are out of the wilderness, and there are no more rivers to cross!"[37]

For the Class of 1938, as for every class before it and every one to come, June Week was the "ending of the old, [and] the beginning of the new."[38] It would see the graduation of the First Classmen and their commissioning as officers in the United States Navy. Wrote Kendall Banning, "The sands of the midshipman year [had] run their course; once again the hourglass [was] turned."[39]

Around the Yard there was an uncontainable spirit, a pulsing energy, bursts of excitement, and a palpable and heady mixture of happiness and anticipation and romance and fraternity. For Mandel, Bass, Calhoun, and the others it was the culmination of four (or in some cases longer) years' work; the realization of desperate hopes and dreams; the settling of doubts; and the proof of the graduating midshipman's mettle and intellect, his solidity and perhaps, in his eyes, his worth. There was a sadness to it, certainly, and a nervousness, but for most of the First Classmen graduation meant a new and boundless freedom, one they had rarely known during their time in Annapolis, a freedom from constraints and strictures and from the taut anchors of youth.

The rooms and boardinghouses of the city were overflowing. From every state, by automobile, bus, train, and trolley, the families, friends, and "One and Onlys" of the First Classmen arrived for the week's occasions. The First Classmen strolled languidly down the pathways and in and out of the academic buildings and the Chapel, taking their time, with parents and families and friends in tow or, even better, hand in hand with girlfriends. On the Monday morning of June Week, the wealthier First Classmen began receiving their preordered "Annapolis Salutes," elaborately shipped from Gemsco in New York in seasoned wood cases with their names engraved on top. Inside the boxes were a pair of ensign's shoulder marks, one imported navy sword knot, one complete set of gilt buttons with bodkin fasteners and studs, one pair of trimmed French epaulettes, one complete full-dress belt, and one beaver-covered chapeau.

On Tuesday, June 1, the Presentation of the Colors Parade took place on Worden Field. It was a sunny, breezy afternoon, and at exactly 1700 the bounce of distant drums began to throb from the south and rise over the murmurs of the large crowd in the grandstand that lined the grass. Brasses quickly picked up the tune, and the crowd rustled and hushed. Soon the

Regimental Staff, followed by the Drum and Bugle Corps and the rest of the Regiment, emerged from under the trees at the field's edge and out into the open in a column of squads. The white caps and trousers of more than two thousand men caught the sun while they marched in cadence down the field, the blue Severn behind them, their steel bayonets glinting next to their heads. After they formed into battalions, the music stopped, and orders were shouted up and down the line. The Regiment was brought to "present arms," and the national anthem was played, the crowd rising to its feet while the colors in front were dipped in salute. To the excitement of those in attendance, the adjutant then put the Regiment through a few movements of the manual of arms. Afterward, the commander of each battalion stepped forward in turn, flashed his sword, and loudly proclaimed the number missing: one man from First Battalion, nine from Second, three from Third, and eight from Fourth. It was all part of the tradition woven into the steps and rhythms of the ceremony. In reality, no men were missing; the numbers made up the year of the graduating class, "1938," and were shouted out by the Regiment's leaders to recognize those among them who were marching for the last time.

The Farewell Ball was held on Wednesday night in Dahlgren Hall. It was the First Classmen's last hop at the Academy. For this event the Armory was plastered with flags, and a pair of mock naval guns extended out over the dance floor. Plebes, heretofore unable to attend the hops, were allowed in, signifying their status as near-Youngsters. The Regiment wore their white coats and navy pants; the women wore long cocktail dresses that swayed when they moved. The superintendent's wife, the ranking lady of the station, served as hostess; she and her husband greeted each guest as they entered. The Armory was a huge room, six hundred feet long and one hundred feet wide, but on this night was so crowded with midshipmen and their dates that the big doors at the south end had been thrown open, allowing guests to mingle out on Thompson Field, lit up for the occasion, and to roam the grandstand and the seawall, catching the breezes. Couples also walked inside around the balcony, serving as a promenade for those pairs who could find no room on the dance floor below. The NA Ten provided the music, and each of the ladies carried a dance card. It was up to her midshipman date to see that it was filled.

The morning of Thursday, June 2, 1938, had a different energy for the First Classmen, who would graduate in a few hours. They removed from their closets something new—sparkling officers' whites provided by "Jakey" Reed & Sons, with matching shoes that fit better than their midshipmen footwear ever had. One can imagine them feeling like all manner of lords and kings and chieftains, like the chosen ones, like the heavyweights, like young admirals. The day would be theirs.

Graduation was to begin at 1100 in Dahlgren Hall, and tickets were at a premium—no one was allowed through the doors without one. At the ceremony's start the midshipmen of the lower classes walked in first and took their seats in a grandstand with loose boards that had been hurriedly erected. Families, friends, and proud dates found their seats across the rest of the floor's expanse and in the balcony above. Then, the room buzzing, the superintendent entered through a door behind the platform, accompanied by the commandant and assorted other admirals, generals, and public officials. Once these luminaries were settled, the doorway opposite the platform opened, and the white-clad members of the Class of 1938 marched down the central aisle in a single file, the crowd on its feet now, loud. The men of '38 carried rather dilapidated caps for "throwing away" purposes later. Each First Classman went to his assigned seat, the twenty-odd "star men" occupying the front row, the rest arranged in the chairs alphabetically. When things had quieted, the chaplain stepped forward to deliver a brief prayer, a new one he had written for the occasion, and the superintendent rose to welcome all. It was hot in the crowded Armory. Many in the seats waved homemade fans in front of their faces and fidgeted. The First Classmen sat directly in the sunbeams that blasted through the windows in solid yellow rails.

When the preliminary speeches and invocations had concluded, President Franklin Delano Roosevelt stepped to the dais. Presidents had spoken at the event before, but his attendance at this ceremony was especially meaningful. He had served as Secretary of the Navy in Woodrow Wilson's administration and, in that role, had assumed responsibility for preparing the American Navy for war. When he became president, he signed major expansion bills, the possibility of simultaneous wars in the Atlantic and Pacific on his mind. At the dais he read from pages in front of him in his usual slow, clipped manner, hesitating after every three or four words. He kept his address short and chose not to spoil the occasion by speaking of the troubles in the wider world beyond.

He opened with a story of a previous time he had sat on such a platform at the Academy, when, as Secretary of the Navy and exhausted from strenuous work, he had fallen firmly asleep in a chair next to the superintendent and before the entire graduating class. "I think indeed my mouth fell open," he said. "I slept ungracefully but soundly. . . . Could anything be more un-military, more humiliating and, at the same time, more completely satisfactory?"[44]

President Roosevelt then spoke of "citizenship" and what it meant to him personally. He advised the First Classmen to broaden their minds and remain always well rounded, regardless of their particular specialty. He urged them to obtain "national knowledge," specifically knowledge of "the problems of farming . . . the problems of labor and . . . the problems of capital." He said,

> You will need to know intimately the geography and the natural and human resources of the United States. You will need to know the current operations of federal and state and local governments. You will be called on for decisions in your line of duty where such knowledge will be of at least daily desirability—daily help to you in coming to your own conclusions and carrying out your own assigned tasks. Preliminary knowledge of that kind you have; but the best of it, the most important part of it, will come to you through the passing years.[41]

In other words, the midshipmen's days of rote memorization were over. What came next, what they were now expected to do, was to make informed decisions using their reason, their training, their experience, and their best judgment.

The president ended his speech with a joke of sorts that earned an amused chuckle and an embarrassed rustling of feet from the First Classmen: "And now there will be no more speaking, there will be something more important. Before you actually become Bachelors of Science, let me stress that in the days to come you do not place too much emphasis on the word 'Bachelor.'"[42]

As their names were called, each First Classman strode up the ramp to the speaker's stage, shook hands with the president, and grasped his diploma. Roosevelt stared hard at every graduate as if personally taking his measure and crushed their right hands with his immensely strong grip.[43] Clapping for each individual was permitted, and the company commanders in particular were greeted by roars from the Plebes who had served under them. Once all the names had been called, the cheerleaders led the class in the singing of "Navy Blue and Gold," and then one of the brand new First Classmen from the class of 1939 rose and said loudly, "I propose three cheers for those who are about to leave us!" After those three cheers, the Number One of the Class of 1938, John Dacey, stood from the sea of white and returned the honor: "I propose three cheers for those we leave behind us."[44] After the third cheer, with a wild, triumphant cry and before all of their guests and girls, Herbert Mandel,

Graduation ceremony for the Class of 1938

Ray Calhoun, Brink Bass, and their classmates threw into the air as one the weather-beaten old hats they had brought with them, "creating the impression of a white cloud of gargantuan snowflakes."[45]

The day's denouement occurred, for those who had chosen to be commissioned in the U.S. Navy, in Memorial Hall beneath Commodore Perry's old blue flag. The twenty-six who had selected the Marine Corps were sworn in elsewhere. After taking their oaths and stepping outside, the graduates stood in the shade of Bancroft Hall, near the Japanese Bell, and each man's mother or serious girlfriend affixed ensign's stripes, "which looked to be a foot wide next to the old middie ones," to her new officer's shoulder boards.[46]

In the back of the 1938 edition of *The Lucky Bag* is a two-page ode to the class. The passage begins with Lewis Carroll's words from *Through the Looking-Glass and What Alice Found There*, written in 1872:

"The time has come," the Walrus said,
"To talk of many things:
Of shoes—and ships—and sealing-wax
Of cabbages—and kings—
And why the sea is boiling hot—
And whether pigs have wings."[47]

It is a playful poem about the oddities and absurdities of fate and was perhaps meant to remind the graduates of life's capriciousness and ever-present humor. What followed the excerpt, however, was a well-written piece that seemed to counterbalance the levity of Carroll's words with sentences that were more somber—that were sad, even. Like all such summaries found in every yearbook ever crafted, it spoke of hope and optimism, wished for a rich and fulfilling life to each graduate, and included undeniable stabs of melancholy. It was a farewell to those moving on to unknown seas and skies over the horizon. It ended, "For four years we have lived by the sea—and now we shall go down to [it]. Poets have called the sea fickle, disarming, seductive, treacherous, fierce, and again calm, placid, friendly, and beautiful; but to us the sea will always be a friend. It has its troughs, as life has its pitfalls; and as the waves roll on forever, so our duty never ends, and our loyalty never falters.... In days to come may our voices keep tune while our oars keep time."[48]

ROBERT WARING McNITT

Perth Amboy, New Jersey

Having spent literally all his time before coming to Uncle Samuel's School of the Sea sailing on Raritan Bay, Waring brought with him an enviable fund of sea-going lore. Occasionally being of a serious turn of mind, he finds plenty of time to devote to the important consideration of academics and is well-known as a savoir. The rest of the time he is sailing, dragging, sailing, engaging in any one of the number of sports in which he excels, or sailing. If there is a respectable breeze and boats available, the choice is sailing. Get it? Robespierre will share his last apple or pipeful of tobacco, and his cheerful nature makes it easy to win friends that stick. Here's to the success of one fine fellow—Bottoms up!

The Lucky Bag, 1938

Chapter Two

FUSES

On June 21, 1938, a fuse was lit and a gun boomed in front of the Cruising Club of America in Newport, Rhode Island, setting a line of yachts sprinting off on a 635-mile southeasterly course for Bermuda. The Newport–Bermuda race was hosted by both the CCA and the Royal Bermuda Yacht Club and had been created by the organizations to "encourage the building and sailing of small sea-worthy yachts suitable for offshore cruising and racing, the development of seamanship, and proficiency in deep sea navigation."[1] Making its debut among the ranks of racers was a team from the U.S. Naval Academy.

The ship was the *Vamarie*, a 72-foot-long overall yacht that had spent more than a year tied up in an Academy slip, unused and neglected. On that early summer day, however, wind filled her sails and she bit into the water at the echo of the gun's report, the active naval officers in command shouting orders to the eager new ensigns of the just-graduated Class of 1938 who crewed her. Among those selected for a spot on board was Robert W. McNitt.

Born on July 29, 1915, McNitt grew up in Perth Amboy, New Jersey, where he learned to sail as a child. He entered the Naval Academy from Perth Amboy High School and boxed and played football at Annapolis. He was also a member of the Radio Club, the Class Ring Committee, and, naturally, the Boat Club. While serving on the Academy's Race Committee, McNitt organized and sailed in regular "knockabouts" on a triangular course off Greenbury Point.

Robert McNitt was not the only one putting to sea that summer after graduation. Assignments for the Class of 1938 had been tacked to a bulletin board in Bancroft Hall, and Raymond Calhoun and fourteen others, ensign's boards still fresh on their shoulders, had been ordered to the USS *Tennessee*, a battleship homeported out west in Long Beach, California. Herbert Mandel and five others from the class had been posted to the aircraft carrier *Wasp*. The new ensigns went to the *Idaho*, *Oklahoma*, and *Portland*. Robert McNitt, when his deep-sea race was completed, would join five members of the class on board the USS *Chicago*. Others had been sent to the *Mississippi*, *Vincennes*, *Phoenix*, *Savannah*, *Chester*, and a host of other ships.

Overseas, matters were taking a turn for the worse. In the spring of 1939, Hitler triumphantly strutted into Prague to take possession of an area he claimed was Germany's "historic destiny" even while, around him, Czechoslovakia lay in ruins.[2] By then Hitler had completely rebuilt the Fatherland's armed forces, in obvious violation of the Versailles Treaty, which he regarded as so much scrap paper. In addition to its Wehrmacht infantry armies, Germany could field six Panzer armored divisions, supported by over three thousand advanced warplanes, five battleships, and fifty-five submarines.

At 0445 on the morning of September 1, 1939, German heavy Panzers crossed the dark Polish border and, with screaming Stukas overhead, made violent and quick work of the country's forward defenses. Two days later President Roosevelt, under pressure from politicians on Capitol Hill and large numbers of his country's German American and Irish American populations, announced over the radio the continued neutrality of the United States.

Rumors were filtering back to the Academy's new ensigns on the West Coast that their classmates in the Atlantic were already bouncing over the north seas in destroyers, sailing what were officially termed "neutrality patrols."[3] Even though the United States was a noncombatant, these patrols were still dangerous. By that time, Britain was already engaged in a sea war with the German Navy, almost immediately losing close to 150 merchant ships to the Kriegsmarine's U-boats, as well as a battleship and an aircraft carrier.[4] Losses continued to rise as Germany quickly turned to total unrestricted mining and U-boat warfare, Hitler decreeing that a "concentrated attempt must be made to cut Britain off."[5] Into this tempest American patrol vessels sailed and scouted, all the while exposing their hulls to German periscopes.

Despite these global uncertainties, the Naval Academy's recent graduates and most of the men of the U.S. Navy were still not overly concerned with what the future held. Regarding the actions of Hitler in Europe, most "did not dwell upon it much of the time."[6] And as for the Japanese, a rising threat in the Pacific, conventional wisdom in the wardrooms of the U.S. fleet held that the Imperial Japanese Navy (IJN) was insignificant, of little threat, and would never be foolish enough to start a scuffle with the United States. Even if it did, the men of the Pacific Fleet believed "we could wipe them out in a few weeks."[7]

While the Navy's new ensigns and sailors were mentally glossing over the war clouds that appeared to be gathering, President Roosevelt and his generals and admirals were very much considering the future. They realized in short order that the armed forces of the United States had been allowed to deteriorate, so a slew of rebuilding initiatives were launched. Among them, Roosevelt passed legislation authorizing a 70 percent expansion of the country's Navy, at a cost of $4 billion.[8] For Robert McNitt and his classmates, this removed any doubt that their destinies lay with the Fleet. Previous classes at the Academy had seen graduates furloughed or assigned to the reserves, as there simply were not enough assignments in the smaller Navy of the time. For the Class of 1938, there was plenty of room, and they were desperately needed.

Not all of McNitt's classmates had ship duty in mind for their careers. If they had 20/20 vision and still wished to do so after serving the required two years on a vessel, new officers could apply for admittance to the Naval Aviation Training School in Pensacola, Florida, and a relatively large number of 1938 graduates did so.

Pensacola was at the time "the acknowledged Jerusalem and Mecca of U.S. Naval Aviation."[9] Receiving one of its open slots was difficult—the waiting list was lengthy, and even top-ranked men in their classes had to wait for spots to become available. But these were sailors with a yearning to fly, with wings and clouds and speed in their blood. They were men who wanted to be above the waves, not on them; to feel the wind on their face, not the salt spray.

In those years there were more than seven hundred students training to fly in Pensacola at any one time. The fourteen-month course included "the most comprehensive aviation schedule of all the world's air forces."[10] Trainees progressed through distinct squadrons, each entailing a special type of instruction and involving its own planes and flying-hour requirements. The program began with the study of airplane design, engines, radios, navigation, and gunnery, then moved to training in seaplanes, lumbering behemoths as graceful as freight cars in which the trainees learned the general principles of safe flying and soloed for the first time. In the final phase, the men flew everything from biplane scouts to large patrol planes, fighters, bombers, and torpedo planes. Men were weeded out along the way. Their ultimate assignments once they graduated were based on the cold needs of the Navy. Some were sent to fighter squadrons, others to bomber squadrons, and still others to scout or torpedo units.

It was an exciting and glamorous service, to be sure, and lured to the Gulf Coast a slew of First Classmen from 1938, including Wilmer Rawie, Eric Allen, Richard Crommelin, Osborne Weisman, Ralph Weymouth, Norman Kleiss, and Marion Dufilho. It also led to the first death of a member of the class, when Pete Howard was killed on March 24, 1941. While Howard was flying a Grumman Wildcat near Norfolk, Virginia, the flotation gear on his plane abruptly popped open, instantly pushing it out of control. The plane crashed before Howard could recover. In the blink of an eye, one of their number was gone.

Another man from the Class of 1938 who decided he wanted to attend flight school was Brink Bass. After some time in the surface fleet, he and another of his 1938 classmates serving with him, William L. Lamberson, wrote letters requesting admittance to flight training. After testing and some anxious months of waiting, they were informed through a handwritten order from the Bureau of Navigation that they had both been accepted.

Bass arrived in Pensacola in late August 1940 feeling confident. As his biographer put it, "He . . . had something new and exciting ahead of him. He was full of life . . . and knew where he was going."[11] Knowingly or not, Bass was headed to war, as events in Europe continued to deteriorate rapidly. In May 1940 British prime minister Winston Churchill sent a highly secret cable to Roosevelt stating unequivocally, "The scene has darkened swiftly. . . . The small countries are simply smashed up, one by one, like matchwood. . . . We expect to be attacked here ourselves . . . in the near future. . . . You may have a completely subjugated Nazified Europe established with astonishing swiftness, and the weight may be more than we can bear."[12] The Germans had commenced bombing London in early July, and while outwardly Roosevelt continued to assert America's neutrality, in private he was doing everything he could to aid Britain without being impeached. Hitler's confidence and optimism, as well as his delusion, reached their peaks in these months. On July 19, 1940, he made a triumphant speech at Berlin's Reichstag during which he predicted Churchill would soon be in exile in Canada and declared himself the war's victor. Churchill promptly broadcast a sharp rebuttal to Hitler's claims, and later that fall he sent Roosevelt another long letter reiterating how concerned he was that German submarines would continue to inflict unbearable losses on the British merchant fleet trying so desperately to keep the island supplied. Churchill told Roosevelt, "We need ships both to hunt down and to escort."[13]

To the Class of 1938, scattered about various oceans and ports and training centers, it was becoming increasingly obvious that formal American involvement overseas was "only a matter of time."[14]

Immediately after graduation from the Academy, Raymond Calhoun boarded the *Tennessee* and spent the bulk of his time belowdecks in the engineering plants and electrical stations of the battleship. These were important positions; nonetheless, he hated the assignments. Calhoun wanted to be out in the sun, where he could watch what was going on and be a part of it.[15] In the battleship's innards he submitted weekly hull reports and taught correspondence courses to sailors, but to him at least, his responsibilities appeared trivial. He was incurably bored and, within seven months, put in a request for a transfer to the "little-ship" Navy.[16] He yearned for destroyer duty.

The Navy sent Calhoun to the *Sterett*, one of the brand-new *Benham*-class destroyers that was then being constructed in Charleston, South Carolina. When he first saw her tied up at the pier, looking lifeless and still, Calhoun felt a twinge of regret. He was expecting one of the "greyhounds of the sea" that he believed filled the "tin can" Navy, not this unattractive pile with a cluttered deck, stubby stack, and severe, ungraceful bow.[17] Yet Calhoun did have to admit she looked rugged and seaworthy, and he and the other six new officers assigned to her got along well as they familiarized themselves with the ship's systems and designs and began putting a crew together. As time went on, Calhoun and his fellow officers grew excited by the vessel. She was undeniably new and modern, with advanced armaments, sonar, and depth charges, and the most torpedoes of any other destroyer class (sixteen). She would prove strong, fast, and dependable.

Calhoun was busy those first three months. He served as the assistant engineer as well as the mess treasurer, welfare officer, and officer in charge of the landing party. Each day he checked the installation of equipment, the loading of supplies, and the organization of personnel. He also traced the steam, oil, and water lines and verified the operation of all pumps, valves, boiler tubes, and reduction gears in the engineering department. Despite his workload Calhoun was having fun: as he put it, he was "raising hell ashore and doing my best to be a good officer aboard," but not always succeeding.[18]

One day, after a particularly "hairy" evening, his commanding officer on board the *Sterett*, a fine Virginia gentleman, sat him down in a chair.[19] "I want to talk to you on a man-to-man basis and I want you to know that I wouldn't talk to you about this at all if I didn't think you were worth the effort," he told Calhoun. "I'm telling you that you had better straighten up and fly right or I'm going to kick your ass out of the Navy." According to Calhoun, "He really got the message across."[20]

Subsequently Calhoun turned his attentions away from raising hell and toward Ginny, a dietician who lived up the road in Winston-Salem, North Carolina. No longer did he spend weekends in King Street bars. He wanted only to be with her. As he put it, "I had fallen in love. . . . Once that was accomplished, that [was] the end of my hell-raising."[21]

The *Sterett* went to sea as a commissioned ship for the first time on September 6, 1939, for a series of shakedown cruises. In the clean new wardroom, Calhoun and the crew talked about how dangerous Hitler seemed and surmised that "we were probably going to end up having a war with him."[22] They sailed neutrality patrols in the North Atlantic and down shipping lanes along the East Coast through the Caribbean to South America, difficult duty made miserable by bad weather. But it made them better officers and sailors. In the rough seas, particularly in the North Atlantic that winter, where crewmen were in danger of being washed overboard every time they went out on deck, Calhoun and the rest of the crew learned what kind of ship they truly had, and what sort of men made up her crew. They bonded, as so many ships' crews had before them, in the shared experience of struggling to survive on a hostile sea.

In the middle of 1940, the *Sterett* assumed station in Pearl Harbor as part of the Navy's Pacific Fleet. Pearl Harbor was a hive of activity. Among other things, Calhoun noticed crowds of Army Air Corps personnel descending on Oahu's Hickam Field. The men regarded anything at sea that was Japanese with suspicion. Fishing boats were all thought to be crewed by Japanese surveillance agents, and the *Sterett* even went so far as to board a few, though nothing of interest was ever found. Calhoun enjoyed the warm, sunny weather and the gentle swells of the Pacific—such a far cry from the blustery cold and the crashing green waves of the North Atlantic. "It was like moving into another world," he wrote.[23]

A year later, after months of patrols, surface gunnery shoots, shiphandling tests, man overboard drills, damage control exercises, and tactical unit training, the *Sterett* returned to San Diego for a refit and then sailed back to the East Coast. Calhoun took advantage of the opportunity to arrange to marry Ginny in Winston-Salem before the ship set off on yet another Pacific run. Marrying her, he wrote, "was the wisest move of my entire Navy career."[24]

After graduating from the Academy, Calhoun's classmate Lodwick Alford, USNA '38, had been assigned to the light cruiser *Phoenix*, and in the late summer of 1938 he sailed with her to Pearl Harbor. He was enjoying himself tremendously as he qualified for each department, from navigation and communications to engineering and gunnery. Early during his time on board, he achieved the most important and sought-after qualification for new ensigns, that of Officer-of-the-Deck Underway.

Alford said goodbye to his shipmates in August 1941, taking their leave in Panama and catching a Pan American clipper back to Miami and a train to Sylvester, Georgia, his hometown. On August 10 he married his fiancée and, soon after, received orders to proceed by first available transport to Manila in the Philippines, there to report to the commander in chief of the Navy's Asiatic Fleet. A request for his new bride to travel with him was denied.[25] Tensions were high and growing worse, and the U.S. government had decided that no more dependents would be allowed to travel to the South Pacific. Indeed, many spouses and children of military personnel in the region were already being sent home. Alford arrived in San Francisco and boarded the SS *President Pierce* for the long journey. Once on board, to his delight, he ran into two of his Academy classmates also headed to the Philippines: Howard Fischer and Bruce Garrett.

The Asiatic Fleet in the late 1930s and early 1940s was a motley collection of bearded, swarthy men and old ships that sailed warm waters and passageways on the far side of the world. There was a unique aura around its officers and men; they seemed to possess heavy doses of panache and worldliness and insouciance that often confused and irritated other sailors. It was said by many in the more mainstream and powerful Pacific and Atlantic Fleets that those posted to the distant South Pacific had gone "Asiatic," meaning they had become "free-spirited" "[men] of the world" who were "prone to [walking] on the wild side and who had adopted an offbeat appearance and the swagger and attitude to match.[26] It was commonly believed that everyone within the fleet's ranks was crazy: either that is why they were sent there, or they became that way once they arrived. Still, service in the Asiatic Fleet had its undeniable privileges. It was considered relaxed and exotic duty. The fleet anchored in old colonial ports where young officers could live cheaply. For the past twenty years, the ships of the fleet had wintered in Manila and spent the summers leisurely steaming in the waters off China's northern reaches. It beat the North Atlantic's rough black seas and ice storms.

As Alford, Fischer, and Garrett plowed through the deep Pacific ever closer to the Empire of Japan, they seemed to experience emotions "ranging from curiosity to apprehension. We had seen those photos and silhouettes of wicked-looking Japanese battleships with tall pagoda masts. We had [seen] the anger and the ruthlessness of Japan in dealing with any nation that got in her way. . . . And we were well aware of the rising tensions between the United States and Japan."[27] But the two countries were still at peace, at least officially, and the *President Pierce* arrived at the Japanese naval port of Yokohama on Friday, December 20, 1940. Alford and his two classmates caught a train for Tokyo and, in the late afternoon, toured the grounds of the Emperor's Palace and Frank Lloyd Wright's Imperial Hotel. They were amazed by the sights and sounds of the city and by the women who passed by in their kimonos and obis. No one was outwardly combative or unpleasant to the men, but they took note of the large number of Army officers who swaggered down the streets, swords clanking at their sides. The *President Pierce* soon left Japan and arrived in Manila late on December 28.

The next day Alford separated from Fischer and Garrett and reported aboard the old "four-stack" destroyer USS *Stewart*, anchored in the port just off the Army-Navy Club. He climbed the ladder to the quarterdeck, saluted the flag, and was given duty on the spot by the only other officer on board, who then immediately gave himself shore leave and disappeared over the side. Alford looked about, not knowing anyone and suddenly responsible for the ship and her crew. He quickly made himself known to the senior petty officers on watch and learned that the other officers were off hurriedly preparing wives and families for trips back home. The realization was settling in among the men of the Asiatic Fleet that war was quickly becoming likely, if not inevitable, and that the Philippines would be the first line of defense, and not a particularly stout one at that. The routine of the Asiatic Fleet had, unbeknown to Alford, changed suddenly, and each ship would soon be spending more time at sea training in division, squadron, and fleet exercises.

On board the *Stewart*, skippered by Lieutenant Commander Harold Page Smith, Class of '24, Alford's assigned job was first lieutenant responsible for maintenance, cleanliness, neatness, and the general appearance of the ship's sides and topsides. He "relished the job and had a great time doing it."[28] Though the *Stewart* was old, her keel laid in 1919, the crew was intensely proud of her. She was affectionately nicknamed the *Stew Maru*. As she too participated in the uptick in training exercises in the waters around Manila, Alford, though brand new, could not help but sense the increase in the crew's spirit and their "hell for leather" attitude.[29] In the weeks and months that followed his arrival, Alford and his new shipmates sailed the *Stewart* south into the central Philippines. They knifed through the Sulu, Sibuyan, Visayan, Samar, Mindanao, and Celebes Seas and other straits, gulfs, and bays where the water was green and chunky with flotsam and jetsam. In July 1941 they sailed the ship to Cavite Naval Shipyard, and the officers took a few days leave and went up to Camp John Hay, high in the mountains of Baguio about a hundred miles north of Manila, where it was cooler and where the pine trees reminded Alford of Georgia. Amid the breezes and the rustling tree branches, conversation inevitably turned to Japan. Certainly, they argued, Japan had been following a policy of expansion and a ruthless grab for power over the last few years, but the officers bandied about their beliefs that American politicians seemed bent on boxing Japan into a corner, particularly, they said, by restricting Japan's access to oil. Alas, Alford admitted resignedly, "these matters were not for us to decide."[30] Their only job would be to withstand Japan's opening attacks, for it was assumed they would be among her first targets.

Back in Manila the officers of the *Stewart* ate steak dinners on base and gambled at the Jai Alai Club. On several occasions Alford ran into Garrett, who had been posted to the destroyer *John D. Edwards*, and Fischer, on the *Pillsbury*. Others from the Class of '38 were in and out of the area too: Bill Spears on the USS *Pope*, Obie Parker on the *Parrott* in Alford's division, and Edmundo Gandia, already gray-haired, on the *Pillsbury* with Fischer. Leon Rogers and Hal Hamlin were on the *Houston*, and sometimes other classmates popped out of arriving submarines. The signs of an impending war were omnipresent. Manila Bay was mined, and destroyers constantly patrolled its entrance. Large PBY Catalinas from Patrol Wing Ten flew a regular schedule of reconnaissance flights over the South China Sea and the whitecapped waters north and east of the Philippines. Submarines continued to slip in and out of the harbor.

In November 1941 intelligence reached the Asiatic Fleet that the IJN was at sea with a powerful force, but no one knew where. Hurriedly, all ships were ordered out of Manila Bay and instructed to head south. The *Stewart* exited the bay on November 25, formed a screen with other ships, and sailed hard across the Sulu Sea. In the wardrooms the officers believed Admiral Thomas C. Hart, the commander of the Asiatic Fleet, was wise to get as many ships as possible out of Manila Bay. Though it was not a move popular with General Douglas MacArthur of the Army, it seemed prudent. Without air cover the fleet was defenseless, and if it was to have any effect whatsoever on the war, withdrawal was the only option. There was no doubt now: war was close, and no one wanted his ship to be hemmed in and unable to escape when the Japanese fleet arrived. On board the *Stewart* the men continued with their training exercises, Alford's promotion to lieutenant junior grade came through, and the ship sailed . . . somewhere. No one really knew where they were headed.

Two days after ordering his ships away, Hart received a message from the Chief of Naval Operations: "This dispatch is to be considered a war warning. Negotiations with Japan looking toward stabilization of conditions in the Pacific have ceased and an aggressive move by Japan is expected within the next few days. The number and equipment of Japanese troops and the organization of naval task forces indicate an amphibious expedition either against the Philippines, Thai, or the KRA peninsula, or possibly Borneo. Execute an appropriate defensive deployment." Hart, a patrician-looking man with crisply parted gray hair, heavy black eyebrows, and a full, strong nose, tightened security at Cavite Naval Base, though curiously the warning message left out any more specific directives about what shape and form the mandated "deployment" should entail.

By Friday, November 28, the *Stewart* and the other ships in her formation had left Filipino waters and, after entering the Celebes Sea, sailed on for Tarakan on Borneo's northeastern coast. With war imminent, Hart was ranging his fleet widely across the area. Once anchored, the destroyers took turns replenishing their fuel stores, patrolling off the harbor entrance, and drilling: General Quarters, gun exercises, fire and rescue drills, emergency landing force instruction, and practices organized around repelling boarders. Onshore, Alford listened to the Dutch skippers of K-class submarines tell stories over Bols gin in the dismal port town's bars.[31]

The men of the Asiatic Fleet were pragmatic, but they were not fatalists. They did not consider themselves martyrs. They did not believe theirs was some preordained suicide stand designed only to slow the Japanese down. They were in a dangerous position, certainly, but still believed help was on its way. The officers and sailors were told that if they could just survive the initial blows of the Japanese and fight a delaying action to the south, their brothers in the mighty Pacific Fleet would come save them. Some were dismayed, however, and others slipped into bitterness as the calendar flipped toward December, but most, including Alford, thought this strategy made sense and was at least roughly consistent with preexisting war plans as they understood them. As the early days of December rolled by, the *Stewart* waited in Tarakan Harbor and Alford and his shipmates passed the days in a sort of "suspended animation."[32]

While the Class of 1938 stood their watches, earned their qualifications, managed their personnel, learned to fly, married, raised hell, and generally settled in, the world moved inexorably toward a more horrific nightmare than they ever could have imagined, one in which the vast majority of them were destined to take part. By February 1940 Allied shipping losses in the Atlantic were approaching a quarter of a million tons, due primarily to the deadly efficiency of German submarines prowling the thermoclines in the sea-lanes to and from the United Kingdom and the European mainland. On May 15 English prime minister Winston Churchill was awakened by his bedside telephone: at lightning speed 134 German army divisions had attacked on a front extending from the Dutch border to the Ardennes. The call was from French premier Paul Reynaud, who, under stress and speaking in English, informed Churchill, "We have been defeated."[33] On the water Hitler granted his navy permission to lift all previous restrictions on U-boat operations around Britain and France.

The U.S. Army of this time was poorly equipped to contribute to the defense of Europe against Hitler's Blitzkrieg, but the Navy was in better shape. That said, Roosevelt's and the Navy's abilities to aid Britain in her struggle remained limited by a continually polarized American populace and government. Nevertheless, by June, Attorney General Frank Murphy was able to declare that Roosevelt and his administration could legitimately dispose of weapons deemed "surplus to requirements."[34] Quickly, the first batch of rifles was sent across the ocean just as Hitler's Wehrmacht launched its final push on the French capital.

The German navy referred to the months that followed in the Atlantic as its "Happy Time."[35] Forced to concentrate the bulk of its destroyer flotilla on anti-invasion duties, the British Admiralty left its merchantmen to fend for themselves on the deep seas, and U-boats picked off the slow, husky ships seemingly at will. Yet by the end of October, Roosevelt was still promising his constituents that he would not engage them in any overseas conflicts. Out of necessity, he was being distinctly two-faced. To American parents, he was saying, "Your boys are not going to be sent into any foreign wars."[36] In his own mind, however, Roosevelt believed America was already in the fight.

The growing alliance between Britain and the United States reached its prewar zenith in the spring of 1941 when, on March 11, the two countries signed the famous Lend-Lease Act, which mobilized American industrial might to support the democracies of Europe and led directly to the rearming of the United States. In effect, it put half of the United States' substantial economic and manufacturing assets at the disposal of the British, and it resulted in a not-so-veiled warning from Germany: "The American policy of pin-pricks, challenges, insults, and moral aggression has reached a point at which it is unsupportable."[37] Churchill, on the other hand, was understandably ebullient. In retrospect, as historian George Waller wrote, "the adoption of the Lend-Lease Act seem[ed] to be the most decisive of the series of moves which put America into an undeclared war in the Atlantic months before Japan struck at Pearl Harbor. The measure marked the end of any pretense of neutrality."[38]

For the American Navy, relations with Germany in the spring of 1941 were getting testy indeed. On April 11, its sailors fired their first shots of the war, one their country had still not formally declared, when, while rescuing seamen, the destroyer USS *Niblack* released a pattern of depth charges on top of what it suspected was a German submarine, to no apparent effect. Hitler was relieved, for he still had no wish to provoke the United States into declaring war, particularly on the eve of his invasion of Russia. Churchill, however, was disappointed the incident did not accomplish more. Nevertheless, the Kriegsmarine remained under strict orders not to attack U.S. Navy ships or otherwise provoke the Americans. Perhaps inevitably, they managed to anyway when, days later, the neutral Egyptian freighter *Zamzam* was sunk in the South Atlantic by a U-boat, killing American citizens. Then, a few weeks later, German submarines attacked and sank the clearly marked U.S. merchantman *Robin Moor*. At the end of the month, Roosevelt took yet another step toward formal hostilities, declaring the existence of an "unlimited national emergency" and announcing that he was extending naval patrols deeper into the North and South Atlantic.[39] The officers and crews of these patrols were under orders to keep an eye out for German ships and submarines, but not to shoot.

By August Roosevelt and his naval commanders were merely waiting for another spark with the Germans that would allow them to step up further activities in the Atlantic. It was decided to deploy the fleet farther east near Iceland, and, anticipating this would cause an incident between the two nations, Admiral Harold R. Stark, the U.S. Chief of Naval Operations, wrote, "We are starting considerable operations between North America and Iceland and the Good Lord knows, if the Germans want an excuse for war, they can have plenty."[40] After that shift the Atlantic Fleet was now ranging over most of the ocean, sailing aggressively and snarling for a fight. Captains had explicit orders to deal aggressively with any "threat of attack," no matter how slight, presented by German vessels.[41] On September 4, 1941, the American destroyer USS *Greer* was radioed by a nearby RAF Hudson and alerted to the presence of a U-boat that, the pilot reported, had crash-dived directly on her course. The *Greer* began to hunt and, not long after, found itself in the path of two German torpedoes, though both sides later claimed the other had fired first. The torpedoes did not strike, but it was enough for Roosevelt to declare six days later, in a broadcast to the nation, that the attack by the Germans was "piracy, legally and morally," and was part of a "Nazi design to abolish the freedom of the seas and to acquire absolute control and domination" of the Atlantic.[42] Upping the ante, he next declared that the U.S. Navy would now serve to protect all merchant ships of any flag engaged in commerce in its waters, calling the submarines a "menace to the free pathways of the high seas," a "challenge to [American] sovereignty," and, colorfully, the "rattlesnakes of the Atlantic."[43] Churchill was again delighted.

In October the inevitable happened. On October 17, five American destroyers were sent to reinforce convoy SC48, fifty slow ships sailing in autumn seas roiled by heavy weather. A day earlier eleven stragglers in the convoy had been sunk when they ran into a U-boat patrol line south of Iceland, and when the Americans arrived at sunset the next day, the U-boats, instead of slinking away, pressed their attacks, firing torpedo salvo after torpedo salvo. *U-568* released a spread of three torpedoes, and one of them hit the starboard engine room of the USS *Kearny*, killing eleven men. The *Kearny*'s captain managed to limp the grievously wounded ship back to port, but the sailors killed were the first American naval fatalities of what would become World War II. "We have tried to avoid shooting," Roosevelt said rather disingenuously on October 27, "but the shooting war has started. And history recorded who fired the first shot."[44] The first sinking of an American ship occurred days later, on Halloween, when the USS *Reuben James* was sunk near Halifax, Nova Scotia, while escorting a convoy eastbound. One hundred and fifteen American sailors died.

In the Pacific the storm clouds had become no less ominous. For practical purposes, Japan's role in World War II is said to have begun on September 18, 1931, when the Japanese government declared that Chinese soldiers were to blame for the sabotage of a South Manchurian Railway track north of Shenyang (Mukden), in China's northeast Liaoning Province. In truth, the "Mukden Incident" had been orchestrated by Japan to test the reactions of the international community to any aggressive actions it might take, in this case a subsequent invasion of Manchuria and the establishment of a puppet state there six months later. The invasion resulted in nothing more than words from the world's powers—some diplomatic notes, accusatory statements, and resolutions of protest that accomplished nothing save revealing to Japan that they had little to fear from other countries in the territorial land grab that would characterize their foreign policy for the next decade. Four months later Japanese marines landed at Zhabei in Shanghai, "setting alight flames that were to devour China" and, in effect, holding a match to the long, slow-burning fuse that would ultimately explode ten years later at a sleepy port in Hawaii.[45]

In the immediate aftermath of the Manchurian invasion, the American government's policy toward Japan was set as merely "firm but conciliatory."[46] They would refuse to recognize any of Japan's present and future conquests yet would also do nothing to provoke its leaders. As historian Ronald Spector wrote, "The U.S. would neither condone nor actively oppose Japan's actions," so as to avoid a "serious crisis" with them—a stance that did not, and would not, sway Japan from her ambitions.[47] What the United States did do, however, was begin to enlarge its Navy and reverse the deteriorations that had beset its ships, sailors, and officer corps in the 1930s.

The Japanese navy had been regarding the United States as its principal enemy since 1923, and America's expansion of its military and, in particular, its Navy in the 1920s had forced Japan to reassess its own war-making abilities. They found them wanting: they had neither the shipbuilding capabilities to equal what the United States would be able to put to sea, nor the oil reserves to match where the Americans could send their ships. That, plus their costly Manchurian campaigns, had made it evident to Japanese strategists that the country needed additional resources if they were to compete, so they cast their eyes on other mineral- and oil-rich targets in the area and began to develop plans for the establishment by force of what they called, almost comically, the Greater East Asia Co-Prosperity Sphere, a territory that would provide the raw materials Japan needed to continue its conquest of China and support the land grabs that were so critical to its plans.

Relations between the United States and Japan grew worse, out of the sphere of diplomacy and talk and into the sphere of blood, when, on December 12, 1937, Japanese bombers dropped their cargoes on the U.S. gunboat *Panay* anchored on China's Yangtze River. Roosevelt responded by imposing economic embargoes on shipments to Japan and granting millions of dollars of commercial credit to China. Undeterred, at the end of 1938 Japanese premier Prince Fumimaro Konoe announced his country's commitment to the creation of a "new order in East Asia."[48] The United States rejected this ambition as "counter to the provisions of several binding international agreements [Japan] voluntarily entered into."[49] To the Japanese these were just more words, frail responses that signified weakness and acquiescence. It became more than mere words, however, when, the following summer, the U.S. government officially informed Japan that it was terminating the Treaty of Commerce and Navigation signed between the two countries more than a quarter of a century before, resulting in Japan's economic isolation.

Though many Japanese wanted the embargo issue settled diplomatically, hardliners in and out of the military establishment were unwilling to give up the territorial gains they had already accomplished. They were also unwilling to suffer the humiliation and loss of prestige a withdrawal from China would entail. If they could not obtain what they needed—oil, tin, nickel, rubber—through trade, then they would take it. If war was the only solution, so be it.

In January 1941 U.S. Ambassador to Japan Joseph C. Grew came across an unsettling rumor, one that he wasted no time passing on to Washington. An employee at the Peruvian embassy had overheard talk that the Japanese military was actively planning a surprise attack on the U.S. Navy's Pacific Fleet at Pearl Harbor in the event of trouble with the United States. In his memo relating the intelligence, Grew urged caution and vigilance. He knew Japanese history and tactics, and surprise attacks were a part of both. Washington received, but ignored, Grew's message. The U.S. Navy had moved large elements of the Pacific Fleet to Oahu in May 1940 to serve as a deterrent to Japanese aggression. Since then, Pearl Harbor had become the nation's strongest military outpost, the "head and heart" of America's defenses; in addition to the Navy's ships and seamen, there were 45,000 Army personnel to protect them. [50] Roosevelt's military advisers and intelligence experts were anticipating a Japanese attack somewhere, but their intelligence, before Grew's message, had never indicated Pearl Harbor.

Days later, the commander in chief of Japan's Combined Fleet, Admiral Isoroku Yamamoto, offered his "Views on Preparations for War" to senior leaders in Tokyo. They were the plans of a gambler, which Yamamoto was. They called for secrecy and surprise and for "decapitating" the U.S. Pacific Fleet and leaving the entire U.S. Navy in that ocean "impotent, if not dead."[51] The plans could, if successful, result in a quick victory, which was absolutely critical to Japan's fortunes.

Yamamoto was in his late fifties, with close-cropped white hair, large eyes, and a bull neck. He loved women, poker, and Abraham Lincoln. Though he was skeptical Japan could win a war against the United States, he was also devoted to his duty and "as eager [as anyone] to see Westerners pay some long-overdue respect to the Empire's power and culture."[52] When his country chose to fight, he devised an opening attack that was breathtaking in its audacity and its ruthlessness. Colleagues advocated for leaving the U.S. Navy's Pacific Fleet alone, but Yamamoto would not hear of it. The mighty American fleet must be destroyed, and quickly, and at a time and place of his choosing.

The United States at least went through the motions of trying to secure a nonviolent peace during this time, even as Japan prepared its surprise attack, though most officials believed such efforts would prove fruitless. Cryptoanalysts had been reading secure Japanese diplomatic messages since late 1940 and were therefore well aware that the emperor's military leaders were preparing for war. Still, the Roosevelt administration was focused on Europe and the Atlantic theater and was not anxious to see war with Japan initiated until American forces were better prepared. They therefore continued with their diplomatic proposals. On August 17, 1941, Roosevelt conveyed to the Japanese ambassador to the United States, Kichisaburo Nomura, that if the Japanese government took any further political or military steps to dominate neighboring countries, "the Government of the United States [would] be compelled to take immediately any and all steps which it may deem necessary toward safeguarding the legitimate rights and interests of the United States and American nationals and toward insuring the safety and security of the United States."[53] Later in the year the U.S. government submitted a lengthy ten-point proposal for a wide-ranging settlement in the Far East but insisted on measures they once again knew the Japanese would never agree to, including the complete evacuation of its forces in China and Indochina. Surprising no one, the Japanese rejected it.

On September 3, 1941, at an Imperial Conference of Japanese senior leaders, it was reaffirmed that "if by the early part of October there is still no prospect of being able to obtain our demands, we shall immediately decide to open hostilities against the U.S., Great Britain, and the Netherlands."[54] In October Hideki Tojo forced the moderate Prince Konoe out of office and assumed the post of prime minister. The military was now in charge of the civilian government, and he quickly decreed there would be no compromise with the United States on the stationing of troops in China. On November 5 Yamamoto's "Top Secret Operation Order No. 1," outlining the attack plan for the bombing of Pearl Harbor, was distributed to fleet commanders. The gruff, small, fifty-five-year-old Admiral Chuichi Nagumo, not a friend of Yamamoto's and not in favor of the raid, was named the commander of the IJN's Pearl Harbor Striking Force on November 7, the same day Secretary of State Cordell Hull warned others in the Roosevelt administration that the United States should be prepared for military attacks by Japan "anywhere, at any time."[55] Most thought the strikes would occur in Southeast Asia, others north against Siberia. Ambassador Grew's earlier memo describing the Pearl Harbor rumors was still not seriously considered.

Talks continued between Hull and Nomura, but each side still found the demands of the other impossible to accept. On November 22, American cryptologists alerted Roosevelt that Tojo had imposed a deadline of November 25 for an accord to be reached. It was later extended by four days.

Roosevelt and his aides and advisers viewed U.S.-Japanese relations as desperate, though many others in Congress were less troubled, sharing the view of many sailors, airmen, and infantry that the Japanese were more of a menace than a threat. Speaking on December 4, 1941, at the Naval Air Station in San Juan, Puerto Rico, Senator Owen Brewster of Maine bellowed his belief that "the United States Navy can defeat the Japanese Navy at any place and at any time."[56]

A few days before, on December 1, the Japanese leadership had reviewed their final war plans before Tojo delivered an impassioned harangue. The emperor then nodded his head, conceding that every diplomatic option had been exhausted and giving his consent to all-out war against the Americans, to begin on December 7 (December 8 in Japan)—a date chosen for its favorable moonlight and good coordination with strikes planned for Malay, and because it was a Sunday in Hawaii, considered the best time to catch American ships in port and men off duty.[57] By then the six massive aircraft carriers of Admiral Nagumo's

First Mobile Striking Force, called the Kido Butai, as well as the warships and oil tankers supporting them, had already slipped out of their anchorages in Hitokappu Bay in the remote, windblown Kurile Islands. Observing strict radio silence, on a gray, pounding ocean shrouded in fog, beneath a worn sky and through temperatures just above freezing, the fleet sailed for Hawaii, heading eastward into the wild, empty stretches of the northern Pacific.

In Washington, DC, Roosevelt waited, two oceans and two war zones on his mind. Despite the blood already spilled in the Atlantic, by that point Roosevelt believed that the real first blow, the one that would compel the United States to declare war, would come from the west. As historian Robert Sullivan wrote, "The duel was engaged, with guns yet to be fired."[58]

Part Two

ON THE WAVES

MARION HUGO BUAAS

Bakersfield, California

Mar came to us from God's paradise—yes, that's California; just ask him. His fiery enthusiasm for his home state is exceeded only by his fervor for the service, which struggles with the academics and life within these cold gray walls have failed to dim. Although not outstanding in athletics Mar spends his spare time managing the football team, playing a mean fiddle in the orchestra, or in the heat of class elections campaigning for his friends. But not even these keep Mar from one of his favorite pastimes—dragging, for while not a confirmed snake, Mar seldom misses a hop. Loyalty, a warm sense of humor, and a pleasing personality have made Mar a great pal and a fine roommate. So here's to Bakersfield's favorite son and to the success he'll surely achieve.

The Lucky Bag, 1938

Chapter Three

SUICIDE MISSIONS AND OTHER ROUTINE DUTIES

The Class of 1938's involvement in the Japanese attack on Pearl Harbor began not on December 7, 1941, but six days earlier, albeit tangentially. On December 1 a small Navy yacht named the USS *Isabel*, serving with the Asiatic Fleet in the Philippines, received orders to set sail on a secret, potentially even suicidal, mission to the waters off Cam Ranh Bay, Indochina. Serving as that ship's executive officer was Lieutenant (jg) Marion H. Buaas, USNA '38.

The orders had originated not with the Asiatic Fleet's commander, Admiral Thomas C. Hart, but with President Franklin Roosevelt himself. The strange set of commands, destined to be one of the more controversial messages of the war, directed Hart to prepare three small surface ships, each with a minimum of arms, and send them out on "defensive information patrols" in the supposed paths of the large Japanese amphibious fleets thought to be sailing down the West China Sea and the Gulf of Siam, for radio traffic and observers in the Far East had earlier informed the Americans that Imperial Japanese Navy warships were then heading toward the Philippines.[1] Though the orders were not written as such, and it would be debated by historians for decades, there was little doubt in Admiral Hart's mind that these ships were to be intended as "sacrificial goats" meant to spy on and, in the process, provoke the Japanese captains.[2] Critics of Roosevelt's would claim he was trying a "baiting feint" with the Japanese, and putting American sailors in harm's way to do it, in order to spark an incident that would ensure he could join the war if the Japanese attacked the British or the Dutch.[3] His supporters would dismiss such devious notions and claim he was simply trying to conduct necessary reconnaissance that would keep him informed of Japanese fleet movements. Either way, the small ships were, in fact, unnecessary. Hart's land-based B-17 bombers were already searching the seas for Japanese warships and were doing so from a much less intrusive and safer distance, making Roosevelt's orders to Hart even more confusing, and the claims of his detractors at least somewhat plausible.

Hart was able to prepare only two vessels in time.[4] The *Isabel* was not a man-of-war, patrol craft, or intelligence-gathering vessel of any kind. She was Hart's personal yacht, his holiday flagship used for official ceremonies and for entertaining high-ranking foreign and domestic dignitaries in the Far East. She was two-funneled, painted a bright white, sleek, and small. Chosen to skipper the ship on her mission was Lieutenant J. W. Payne,

The USS *Isabel* in the Southwest Pacific, 1942

USNA '35, who received his orders in a meeting with Admiral Hart himself: to patrol off southern Annam between the entrance of Cam Ranh Bay and Cape St. Jacques and report back with any information about the location and direction of the Japanese fleet, if and when it was seen. If stopped and questioned by the Japanese, Payne was to say they were looking for the crew of a downed plane.

On December 3 Payne, Buaas, and the rest of the *Isabel*'s small, mixed Filipino and American crew set off. Unsurprisingly, while still quite far from Indochinese waters, she was spotted by Japanese scout planes, which shadowed and buzzed the small yacht but did not engage it, for even then the real Japanese threat, Nagumo's Kido Butai, was in the far northern Pacific on its way to Hawaii. No one in the IJN wished to see their hopes for a surprise attack on Pearl Harbor spoiled by a snooping American yacht plying the waters of the South China Sea. Because she had been spotted, the utility of the *Isabel*'s mission was immediately nullified, and after only two days on station, the yacht was recalled back to Manila.

On December 6, U.S. Secretary of the Navy Frank Knox released his annual report, which read, in part, "The American people may feel fully confident in their Navy. In my opinion, the loyalty, morale, and technical ability of the personnel are without superior. On any comparable basis, the U.S. Navy is second to none."[5]

On the Hawaiian island of Oahu, Admiral Husband E. Kimmel, the commander of naval forces in Pearl Harbor, and Lieutenant General Walter C. Short, commander of the U.S. Army's Hawaiian Department, granted the normal weekend leaves to their officers and men.

Neither officer was unaware of the potential dangers he faced. They both had been alerted to the possibility of a war with Japan and were told it was expected to begin imminently. Over the preceding months there had been fleet exercises, war games, studies, phone calls, briefings, plans, memos, and discussions about the dangers of a surprise air attack. The two men knew Japanese tendencies as well as their officers and men; they had conducted surprise alerts and drills to prepare for just such an occurrence. Yet they simply were not convinced the Japanese would start the war with a surprise attack on *their* base. Both Kimmel and Short believed an opening gambit would happen elsewhere, against other targets, in some other bay or harbor—not against the mighty Pacific Fleet. Not at Pearl Harbor. Earlier, Kimmel had received a war warning alerting him to the breakdown of negotiations with Japanese diplomats and ordering an appropriate defensive deployment, but in Kimmel's view, the message never explicitly mentioned Hawaii, so it portended no imminent threat to him. The two senior officers released their men to enjoy themselves.

In his office that afternoon, Kimmel and his chief of staff, Captain William Ward Smith, reviewed messages and discussed the latest news. Intelligence reported that the Japanese were burning their codes. The IJN had changed call letters not once, but twice in the past month. Their carriers had left their anchorages and disappeared. The two American officers debated whether to keep the units currently in the harbor, particularly the battleships, tied up or send them to sea. They would be easier to find if they were moored, they reasoned. But due to the absence of the Navy's aircraft carriers and the lack of available air cover for the ships if they did sortie, Kimmel decided not to release his heavy battleships. At least in the harbor, the Army's antiaircraft defenses could protect them. And the missing Japanese carriers did not overly concern the men. Naval Intelligence had already lost them a dozen times in just the past six months.

Admiral Nagumo's carrier task force was at that time continuing its steam through vacant northern Pacific waters toward the islands. It was what one aide remembered as "the most difficult and most agonizing period for every officer . . . who knew about [the raid]."[6] That morning, on board his flagship, the carrier *Akagi*, Nagumo had received a final report from the Japanese consulate in Hawaii stating that all nine battleships (in fact, there were only eight) and many smaller vessels were in the harbor—but that the American aircraft carriers were not. Nagumo was dismayed, wondering in front of his senior leaders whether they should even move forward with the attack. But he was urged ahead. Surely, his officers pressed, nine battleships ought to be worth at least three carriers.[7] Besides, they argued, perhaps one or two of the American flattops might return at the last minute. Ultimately, Nagumo agreed. There would be no turning back.

On Oahu that evening sailors, soldiers, and airmen headed out to play golf at the Fort Shafter course and grab some dinner at the Pearl Harbor Officer's Club. At the Army-Navy YMCA on Hotel Street in Honolulu, soldiers and sailors stepped out of taxis and buses that had brought them from the Harbor's Merry Point Landing and went looking for drinks, usually starting at the Black Cat Café across the street before working their way down the block, past the shaky wooden buildings and the mobs of people and the traffic that cluttered the road, through a heavy stink from the spoiled pork and overripe fish that wafted from the eateries. Christmas lights on Fort Street twinkled over the crowds. Historian Gordon Prange wrote, "Oahu moved serenely into a pleasant evening of routine duties and family life."[8] Kimmel's counterpart, Lieutenant General Short, gazed over the harbor and watched the twinkling lights atop the battleships. He thought ruefully, "Isn't that a beautiful sight? And what a target they would make."[9]

CHARLES O'NEAL AKERS

Nashville, Tennessee

"Why the South has more beautiful women—," "And the damn-yankees ran so fast—," "Now that's good music—that's opera!" Always at ease in slothful indolence, he's eternally late to everything everywhere. Lean and agile, clever—but he wears no stars and boasts no N, for his Southern temperament exacts of him nothing that smacks of labor. Yes, he's loved—and lost! Ah! And loved again! A typical bust: Long ago, as a Plebe, he lost his overshoes in the maddening Saturday tangle at the Circle only to "frap" on Youngster Cruise for resurrecting them from the Arky's Lucky Bag. Wrought of the steel that men are made of, blessed with the charm of a true gentleman, and endowed with the abilities of a gallant officer, he's locked in our hearts forever.

The Lucky Bag, 1938

Chapter Four

TIGER, TIGER, TIGER

Early on the morning of Sunday, December 7, 1941, the USS *Ramsay*, an old destroyer recently converted into a mine layer, was moored at berth D-3 in Pearl Harbor, across from Ford Island, off the Pearl City peninsula, in a row with the *Gamble, Montgomery*, and *Treve*. In the harbor around the ship were big, anchored, quiet hulks filled with sleeping men and the calm of light, early-weekend routines. There were 8 battleships, 9 cruisers, 29 destroyers, 5 submarines, a hospital ship, and assorted auxiliaries, some 185 ships in all, almost half the total complement of the U.S. Navy's Pacific Fleet. It had rained earlier, but after dawn the sky was flecked with cloud shreds and the harbor was sunlit.

Attached to the *Ramsay* that morning as chief engineer was Charles Akers from the Naval Academy's Class of 1938. Akers had been born in Nashville, Tennessee, in 1915. After a year of premed classes at Vanderbilt University, he unexpectedly secured an appointment to the Academy in 1934, taking the slot of a midshipman who had been reassigned after deciding to get married. Upon graduating he quickly earned a reputation as an outstanding leader and gentleman, one who was cool and confident under duress. Fittingly, his first posting was to the battleship *Tennessee*, anchored across the harbor that morning, but he had been a member of the *Ramsay*'s crew since 1940. On several ships scattered around him were his classmates from the Academy: on the battleship *Oklahoma*, on the *Zane* anchored off Pearl City, on the *Patterson* lying north of Ford Island between the *Henley* and the *Ralph Talbot*, attached to Mine

Division One in the repair basin, and on the *St. Louis* moored to the pier at the Navy Yard south of Battleship Row, next to the *Honolulu*, where she was having major repair work done and where men up early that morning played checkers on her deck.

Around 0600 Hawaii-Aleutian Standard Time, roughly 230 miles north of the *Ramsay* and Oahu, Admiral Nagumo's strike force continued its slog through heavy seas. Despite the unfavorable wind, clouds, and chop, the first strike wave assembled on the carrier deck below the admiral and on those of the five aircraft carriers arrayed around him: 183 planes, including 51 dive-bombers, each with a 551-pound bomb; 40 torpedo planes; 49 level bombers, and 43 fearsome Zero fighters. As the carriers turned into the wind and, rolling and dipping, increased their speed to twenty-four knots, spray from the high waves slapped the decks. Normally they would not have tried to launch in such weather, but at 0629 sailors on board the *Akagi* hoisted a red triangular flag with a white circle to the top of the mainmast, then swiftly brought it down again, and the first Zero rolled down the deck and lifted into the sky to the sailors' cheers. All six carriers launched at the same time. The pilots each waited for the takeoff signal, a green lamp waved in a circle, before gunning their engines and screaming into the air. After the Zeros had all taken off, they circled overhead and waited for the dive-bombers and torpedo planes to get airborne. Despite the conditions the launch was orderly and quick, and about fifteen minutes after they started the planes formed up over the ships and turned south while the dawn sun broke through.

After a short interval, about thirty minutes, a second wave lifted off the carrier decks and formed up under a now cloud-filled sky with a low ceiling. On the ships, crews stood at their battle stations in the chop, and radio operators tuned their equipment.

At 0700 two American radarmen on Hawaii spotted something approaching. They were trainees at the Opana Mobile Radar Site, high up in the blue-green hills of Oahu's northernmost tip, and they noticed something highly unusual on their scanner: a swarm of contacts, spikes rising from a baseline on their five-inch oscilloscope, which indicated airplanes, "the largest group . . . ever seen on the [scope]," at a range of 132 miles, a few degrees east of true north.[1] The operators were Privates George E. Elliott Jr., twenty-three years old, and Joseph L. Lockard, nineteen. After some debate among the two, Elliott picked up the phone and called the on-duty pursuit officer at Fort Shafter. Not to worry, they were told by Lieutenant Kermit Tyler; the blips were Army Air Force B-17s inbound from California. Shut the equipment down, Tyler told them, and go get some chow. The two operators stayed, however, and continued to watch and log what they saw: "looming, ever clear blips, constantly changing shape as [they] approached,"closing at two miles a minute, heading directly toward them until they disappeared at fifteen or twenty miles out, when their reflections merged with the nearby Hawaiian hills.[2] The two men then locked the doors to the mobile unit and waited outside for a ride back to camp, and breakfast.

For the fliers in the Japanese first wave, the cloud cover over Oahu had become so dense and impenetrable that the planes were almost directly above the island before any of the pilots saw it. But at 0740, the clouds split just north of Kahuku Point, and the lead pilot, Air Group Commander Mitsuo Fuchida, glimpsed white surf below him rolling into a green shoreline. He immediately held out his signal pistol and fired a flare indicating surprise had been achieved. In flurries of movement, the dive-bombers circled upward to 12,000 feet, the horizontal bombers dipped down to 3,500, and the torpedo planes dropped until their underbellies skimmed the wave tops.

Fuchida faced another issue, though. The clouds were still bulbous and heavy and so, thinking quickly, he made the decision to revise his approach path. He found a bearing on a Hawaiian radio station and improvised, leading the massive pack of high-level planes behind him through the sun along the island's west coast at nine thousand feet, over Kaena Point and past Waianae and Nanakuli, before rounding Barbers Point, turning northward, and flying into the harbor from the south. Other packs of torpedo bombers angled in toward the harbor from a southeasterly direction or split off to attack the American ships from the north. A group of fighters flew in down the broad central valley of Oahu between the parallel mountain ranges of Koolau and Waianae. Intermittently, various groups of Zeros peeled off gracefully to attack their assigned bases and airstrips: Wheeler Field, Marine Corps Air Station Ewa, Naval Air Station Kaneohe, and Hickam Field. The result was that when the first wave attacked, the planes wound up coming in from various directions all at once: they approached from off the water to the south, from the east, just to the right of the early morning sun, and from the north, from over the jagged, low, tree-packed hills of the Waianae Range.

The Pacific Fleet was caught unawares, on a slow peacetime Sunday morning during which there was nothing scheduled save to hoist colors at 0800 and, afterward, hold divine services on deck. Five of the battleship captains were ashore, along with half of the officers assigned to the various ships around the harbor. The morning had started quite normally. On board the battleship USS *Maryland*, it was quiet. Much of the crew was at breakfast, while others prepared for their upcoming liberty, set to begin at 0900. The *Maryland* was moored alongside the *Oklahoma*, with lines and gangways connecting them. Astern of her were the *Tennessee* and the *West Virginia*, and ahead was the *California*. As the men in the galley cleared their dishes, they heard shouting topside. Unhurried, they climbed up to investigate.

At 0751 the first bomb of the raid smacked onto Wheeler Field, the main fighter base, as dive-bombers sped in off Kolekole Pass and set about destroying most of the field's complement of planes in fifteen minutes. Sailors on Akers' ship, the *Ramsay*, saw a bomb land on the western end of Ford Island and, above it, twenty-seven dive-bombers flip over and plunge downward. They then spotted forty torpedo planes lining up for runs on the big ships sitting orderly in two rows, waiting almost patiently for what was to come. The *Ramsay* went to General Quarters immediately and, not long after, a few of the quicker-to-action sailors on board got the .50-caliber machine guns up and firing. They shot intermittently when the Japanese planes zipped into range. A liberty party full of the *Ramsay*'s crew, hitching a ride back in a boat from the *Montgomery*, was strafed by torpedo planes, and the men in the launch watched as those same planes then let four torpedoes loose into the water, three hitting the old battleship *Utah* in a quick succession of explosions that capsized her in minutes.

At 0755 seventeen Japanese dive-bombers and eighteen fighters hit Hickam Field, south of the Navy Yard, and strafed and bombed the B-17s, B-18s, and A-20s there, lined up so prettily in four parallel rows. They also bombed the runways, hangars, barracks, and mess hall. More Zeros roared in from the southeast and southwest, some just above the rooftops, their machine guns spitting bullets at whatever targets their pilots liked.

Commander Fuchida, watching his fliers' opening attack runs from the air off Lahilahi Point, waited only two minutes before he sent back to the Kido Butai by telegraph key the agreed-upon signal: *to-ra, to-ra, to-ra*, again and again. Nagumo passed it along to Japan. It meant both that total tactical surprise had been achieved on Oahu and that the myriad other attack operations planned against Malaya, the Philippines, and the Dutch East Indies could proceed.

The first torpedo to hit Battleship Row struck the USS *West Virginia.* The second blasted into the *Oklahoma*, a direct hit, and she keeled over to port, her bottom quickly exposed as her masts buried themselves into the shallow harbor bottom. Four more torpedoes would strike her. Five smacked into the *West Virginia*, along with two 16-inch bombs. The *Arizona*, even though she was inboard of the *Vestal*, would take two torpedoes. The *California*, well away from the other battleships, received two torpedo hits of her own. Her manholes and covers had been thrown open in preparation for an inspection that was to take place that day, and as she shuddered from the strikes, water flowed in and rushed unhindered through her passageways. On the *Maryland* the ship's bugler blew General Quarters over the public address system and her klaxon wailed. A bomb tore a large hole in an awning strung across her forecastle, damaging the compartments underneath, while another hit below the waterline, causing her bow to settle five feet. The boatswain's mate of the watch shouted, "Away fire and rescue party!" over the speakers. Above Ford Island a rainbow arced through the smoke.

By 0804 radio station KGMB in Honolulu, southeast of Pearl Harbor, had interrupted its Sunday morning classical music program with an urgent summons of all military personnel in the city and surrounding areas to report for duty. The voice repeated the call over and over, giving no immediate reason for the message.

Shortly thereafter, a 760-pound bomb specially adapted to penetrate armored decks struck the forward magazine of the already suffering *Arizona*, setting off a searing flash and a shock wave that pilots ten thousand feet above felt in their fingers, shoulders, and thighs. The blast lifted the battleship from the water and broke her back. Her captain, Franklin Van Valkenburgh, together with Rear Admiral Isaac Campbell Kidd and over a thousand other officers and men, were killed instantly. Three more bombs struck her seconds later. Debris showered the *Vestal* next to her, including the "arms, legs, and heads" of sailors.[3] Burning oil from the battleship sent black smoke skyward as she crumpled, canted to port, and settled on the bottom, her shattered upperworks still pointing through the water, the oil, and the fires. Only 337 members of her crew would survive. It was the worst single-ship disaster in U.S. Navy history.[4]

On board the destroyer USS *Patterson*, moored at berth X-11 in East Loch with the *Henley* and *Ralph Talbot*, Elvin Ogle, USNA '38, from Moscow, Idaho, manned his battle station with the rest of the crew as the bombs and torpedoes fell. They opened fire shortly after the *Henley* started pounding away next to her. The gunners spied a plane diving on the seaplane tender *Curtiss* across the water in Middle Loch and claimed a hit with gun No. 2 as the plane burst into pieces approximately four hundred feet above the chop. The *Patterson* was left undamaged that morning and would stand out to harbor at 0900.

On the far side of Pearl Harbor from Akers and the *Ramsay*, in the Navy Yard, Ben Pickett, USNA '38, had watched the entire attack unfold from the USS *St. Louis*, where he was by then a respected officer and leader. By 0810, as the backbone of the Pacific Fleet lay smashed, burning, sinking, and belching smoke around him, the commanding officer of the *St. Louis* reached the bridge. George A. Rood, a square-jawed ex-submariner, was well-liked by his crew. He had salt-and-pepper hair and eyebrows;

a high forehead; and dark, serious eyes. He arrived still wearing his pajamas, a Colt .45 around his waist. His ship was "cold iron," so Rood at once directed the engine room to "make preparations for getting under way. Full power. Emergency."[5] He ordered his engineering crews to raise steam under boilers 1, 2, 5, 6, and 7. When he sounded General Quarters, the men responded well, rushing to their stations without panic or confusion. All her 5- and 6-inch mounts were temporarily inoperative due to disconnected power leads, so men quickly set about reconnecting them. At 0810 gunners on the *St. Louis* fired at a large single-engine olive drab plane bearing the insignia of Japan, which had been seen approaching at low altitude from the direction of Barbers Point. About three hundred yards out the plane climbed slightly, banked to the left, and fluttered. It then erupted into flames and crashed behind the Navy Yard, into the dense smoke already billowing from there.[6]

The first wave of the Japanese attack, having lost only nine planes, flew away northward at 0815.

BEN BROWN PICKETT

Pocahontas, Arkansas

What makes a man give up his shoot'n an' cawn-likker for the rigors of the life of a sailor-man? What possessed Arkansas' favorite son to become "a fine specimen of young American manhood" will probably never be revealed. However, when Ben put on his first pair of shoes and looked out from under that many-sizes-too-large hat, he must have been inspired to greater things than "chuck hunting." Though he has been known to assume either side of an argument without apparent rhyme or reason, his ideas on the service have been as definite and as firm as his desire to join the Fleet. Bulldog tenacity to an ambition will delineate Buckshot's character. To Ben, upon whom I can depend for anything from stamps to a pair of shoes, happy landfalls.

The Lucky Bag, 1938

Chapter Five

THE LUCKY LOU

There would be a lull of less than half an hour between the first wave's departure and the arrival of the second cluster of Japanese planes, though it did not seem like much of a respite to the men of the Pacific Fleet on Oahu. In the harbor the battleships, once as neatly anchored as "a team of horses harnessed to a stagecoach," now lay charred, blackened, and burning, their masts and superstructures leaning out of the heavy black columns of smoke at odd, haunting angles.[1] Sailors, some blown off the battleships, others who jumped to escape the heat and the explosions, tried to swim through the oil to Ford Island. Not all made it. Trapped men screamed from inside the blackened hulks. The burned screamed where they lay. The smells of charred flesh and superheated paint were thick and unavoidable. Incongruously, while her gunners waited for the next attack, the *Maryland*'s band played music near a deck fire started by a 15-inch shell.

The second wave flew in from the north and down the eastern side of the island: fifty-four torpedo bombers, eighty-one dive-bombers, and thirty-six fighters. The Zeros split up over Kahana Bay, some strafing Naval Air Station (NAS) Kaneohe and Bellows Field before rounding Koko Head on their way to the harbor. The rest flew on to hit Ewa and Wheeler Field again. The bombers divided into groups to reattack Ford Island, Kaneohe, and Hickam. About eighty planes flew straight to the ships. The pilots of this second wave, as they flew over the island, took time to notice its features: "the green island, the blue sea, the white surf."[2] Its beauty amazed them.

This time the Japanese pilots would not have the benefit of catching the harbor, its airmen, or its sailors by surprise, and immediately the planes were given a "real reception."[3] Amid flak and machine-gun tracers that instantly reached up for them, and with the pall of smoke over the harbor obstructing their views, the dive-bombers searched for anything that lay undamaged. The pilots assumed that any ship not firing had been destroyed, so they attacked only those vessels that were lacing bullets and shells into the air. Already torpedoed in the first wave, the light cruiser *Raleigh* received a bomb hit aft. The seaplane tender *Curtiss* took a direct hit, silencing her guns. The *Zane* shot down a plane directly above her. A bomb landed close aboard the *Perry*'s stern. A trio of them bore into the innards of the destroyer *Shaw*, causing her forward magazine to explode in a gigantic fireball. At the Navy Yard and on Ford Island officers worried the air attack would be followed by an amphibious landing, so they set gangs of sailors to work digging trenches and setting up machine guns on tripods.

At 0909 six Japanese dive-bombers at an altitude of seven thousand feet flipped over and bore down in a shallow dive on Ben Pickett, USNA '38, and the *St. Louis*, but her crew was firing back furiously by then with their .50-caliber and 1.1-inch machine guns. Four of the incoming planes, after dropping their bombs in the water, gushed smoke and exploded in the harbor between the burning battleships and 1010 dock. The fifth plane also released its bomb, which exploded harmlessly one hundred feet off the *St. Louis*' deck, causing no damage. The sixth plane turned to the nearby *Honolulu* and dropped a bomb that exploded underwater with a loud *crump*, damaging the *Honolulu*'s oil tanks and jolting the *St. Louis*. The plane exploded as it tried to pull out of its dive. The 171-gun aft on the *St. Louis* shot down a seventh plane coming in from behind, sending it crashing down near a distant boat shed.

Ben Pickett was not the only First Classman from the Naval Academy's Class of 1938 assigned to the *St. Louis* that morning. Raphael "Rafe" Semmes, an aviator stationed to the ship and a great-grandson of the Confederate naval captain of the same name, was not on board when the attack began, but he managed to hitch a ride on a passing motor whaleboat to

Ford Island. He watched the *Oklahoma* capsize in front of him. When the *Shaw* blew up in an enormous blast, Semmes, by then on the airstrip with his unit's damaged planes, threw himself into a drainage ditch, where he lost the officer's cap his wife had given him.

By 0931 the *St. Louis*, with boiler power for twenty-nine knots, prepared to slip away from berth B-17 and stand out toward open sea. The power leads had all been reconnected to the guns, and they were now in full operating order. A shipfitter hung down over the starboard railing with an acetylene torch and quickly burned off the gangway. Another sailor chopped loose the water hose, leaving a foot-wide hole in the ship's side, but a crewmate stepped in and, in ten minutes, had a plate welded over it.

Captain George Rood began backing the 10,000-ton cruiser out into Merry Point Channel toward the capsized *Oklahoma*—a difficult job without tugs, but he was a good ship handler. Not wishing to reenter Southeast Loch and delay any potential sortie of the damaged *Honolulu*, Rood decided to clear the harbor via South Channel. It necessitated a hard turn to port, made even tighter by the wind, which by then had pushed the ship close to the burning battleships at their Ford Island moorings. Just able to clear them, Rood, Ben Pickett, and the *St. Louis* proceeded out of the channel at ten knots; all the while her 5-inch batteries pounded away at the high-altitude bombers still circling overhead. Off her starboard side the *California* belched flames, the black smoke a stark contrast to the sunny sky and the white clouds over the mountains. The heat from the battleships seared the men's cheeks.

After clearing the nets off Holehiki Point, the *St. Louis* accelerated toward the exit and was nearly through when lookouts at the railing spied a pair of torpedo tracks in the water, running shallow toward the ship from ahead at an angle of 45 degrees, on a perfect collision course. The lookouts were horrified, "frozen like rabbits caught in a headlight," for there was no time to do anything.[4] Rood happened to look off the starboard bow and saw the tracks as well. He thought all was over, that the ship was going to "get smacked good and proper."[5] He was faced with no good options: he could not stop, because his ship would block the channel if it sank, and he could not maneuver evasively, as the channel was too narrow. Quickly he ordered "Emergency Full!" and the cruiser leapt forward through the tight space. Those with the presence of mind to do so braced themselves. Resigned to the seemingly inevitable, Rood called out, "If you want to see a ship torpedoed, come take a look!"[6]

But the 18-inch torpedoes did not hit; instead they buried themselves in a small coral spit off the entrance to the harbor about two hundred yards from the ship's side, where they exploded harmlessly near Buoy No. 1 in a "blossom of water and coral" that drenched the ship with spray.[7] Whoever had fired the fish had done so too soon; had he waited another sixty seconds or so, he could not have missed.[8]

After passing Buoys No. 1 and 2, Rood turned the cruiser hard left. This port turn, however, put her in danger of either grounding or ramming a pair of minesweepers moving just beyond the channel, much too close to avoid. Thinking quickly, Rood kept the ship at full speed and, in a burst of good fortune, passed between the minesweepers, scaring the hell out of their skippers while smashing through their heavy sweeps and cutting across their tow lines before coming clear. Rood, Pickett, and the *St. Louis* then headed southward. She was the first and largest ship to escape the harbor that morning.

By 0945 the last of the second wave's planes flew away to the west, landing back on the Japanese carriers between 1030 and 1330. In total the Japanese lost twenty-nine planes and fifty-five airmen, well within their margin of "acceptability." The Americans, in that same time, lost some 2,390 dead and 1,178 wounded, eighteen ships sunk or seriously damaged, and 347 planes wrecked or in need of repair.

In Pearl Harbor the East Loch was awash with blackened debris and dead men. Millions of gallons of oil floated on the water, half a foot thick. Sirens still wailed. The heat from the fires was too intense for rescuers to get near Battleship Row. Dead and wounded were being pulled from the water and laid in rows on the piers. Sailors gathered in confused clumps, unsure what to do.

At 1130 a radio report was received alerting the *St. Louis* that there was an enemy carrier escorted by four vessels sailing thirty miles due west of their position. Aware of the risks, Rood changed course to 270 degrees to attack it, ordering the nearby *Perry*, *Phelps*, *Lawson*, and *Blue* to join up with him and serve as an antisubmarine screen. These other destroyers had "sortied and joined up with commendable alacrity," given the traumas of the morning.[9] Rood had his anchor chains struck below and the flammable stores, brooms, swabs, and paints thrown overboard as his men prepared for a possible fight. The ship's sailors spotted and fired on two groups of high-altitude bombers, though they hit none.

About forty-five minutes later the flotilla was directed by a signal from Admiral Kimmel's headquarters to divert again and attack a vessel with escorts reported five miles off Barbers Point. As he approached these new targets, Rood thought eagerly, "There are the Japanese!" He later said, "My boys were at General Quarters and itching to knock the hell out of them."[10] The vessel turned out to be the USS *Minneapolis*, however, with two destroyers alongside. Rood stood to and exchanged recognition signals with the ship from about 23,000 yards. At 1238 the *St. Louis* was ordered to join with the nearby *Detroit* and *Phoenix* and continue searching for targets together. The *Minneapolis* arrived soon after, and the ships formed Task Force 1, set Condition of Readiness II, and sailed through the waters around the Hawaiian islands for the next two weeks, American subs "thick as bees" the entire time as, together, the Navy ships waited and watched for another Japanese armada to appear.[11]

After collecting his second wave, Admiral Nagumo, still north of the Hawaiian Islands and unseen by the Americans, had a decision to make—launch a third attack or withdraw. By 1330 that afternoon the debate between Nagumo's senior officers had turned heated. Some, including his air commanders, thought there were still attractive targets to be found on Oahu, and virtually no defenses that could seriously harm them. Even more importantly, it was argued, another attack might draw the American carriers in and force them to reveal themselves. Eventually, Nagumo ended the matter, slowly announcing, "We may conclude that anticipated results have been achieved."[12] As historian Walter Lord wrote, Nagumo "had gotten away with it, but he certainly wasn't going to stretch his luck."[13]

Back in Hiroshima Bay Admiral Yamamoto's radio operators were corralling intercepted messages from the Japanese planes. From what they heard, they knew very early on that the attack had been a surprise and that the results had been outstanding. The officers around the admiral cheered at each new message, but Yamamoto refrained from any outward sign of emotion. He was disappointed Nagumo was withdrawing his carriers after only two attack waves, believing there was more in the offing. He was right. Undamaged during the attack were the harbor's two tank farms, with their 4.5 million barrels of oil, easily visible from the sky and critical to Pearl Harbor's function as a major naval base, as well as the harbor's ship-repair facilities and machine shops. Also neglected was the group of nine submarines parked out in the open. And, of course, the American carriers were untouched and out there somewhere.

By 1005 the islands' governor, Joseph Poindexter, announced a state of emergency covering the entire territory. Beginning at about 1430 on the East Coast, "White House Says Japs Attack Pearl Harbor" flashed over newswires, and announcers on the mainland began telling listeners what had happened.[14] To many, the names of the places referred to by the newsmen were not well-known. But most people understood that the U.S. military had been surprised and had been hurt badly and that the repercussions of the attack would be life-changing. On the West Coast there were more immediate fears of invasion, producing near panic in towns up and down the coasts of California, Oregon, and Washington.

December 7 found Brink Bass, USNA '38, serving as an aviator on the aircraft carrier *Lexington*, which was transferring Marine aircraft from Pearl Harbor to distant Midway Island. Knowing his parents would be concerned about his welfare once they heard of the raids, Brink wrote them a quick letter: "Well, it is here at last! We know very little more than you probably do. I am all right and expect to stay that way. . . . Can't say much. I feel fine and am getting plenty of sleep and good food. Please try not to worry much because it doesn't look like much cause for it. Brink."[15]

1938
US NA

ERIC ALLEN JR.

Manchester, Vermont

The Green Mountains lost another good Republican when Eric came to Annapolis. He admits he was headed for the ministry but finished by casting his lot with Uncle Sam and has not regretted his choice. An infectious grin and an irrepressible sense of humor put him at ease anywhere, and though self-styled a misogynist, he has always been ready to drag for a friend. Well known for his famed shower rendition of "Danny Deever," nevertheless he has a pleasing voice and choir and Glee Club always found him present. Around the pool, Eric and unorthodox dives were synonymous, but the sub-squad remembers him as the easiest man to save. Always a good roommate, even to his last clean gloves—may we someday be shipmates.

The Lucky Bag, 1938

Chapter Six

FRIENDLY FIRE

When the planes of Admiral Nagumo's Kido Butai winged in and attacked the Pacific Fleet at Pearl Harbor that Sunday, they were primarily looking for American aircraft carriers, and while there were none to be found in the harbor, one was not far away.

At the time of the attack, the U.S. Pacific Fleet had three aircraft carriers in its ranks. The USS *Saratoga* was moored on the West Coast of the United States on December 7, while the USS *Lexington* was sailing out in the vastness of the Pacific near Midway Island. The USS *Enterprise*, however, was nearing Oahu that morning as part of Vice Admiral William F. Halsey's Task Force 8 (TF 8). The carrier was returning to Hawaii after delivering additional aircraft to the small American base on Wake Island atoll.

She was a massive vessel, displacing 25,500 tons at war load, with a weather-hardened wooden flight deck that was 825 feet long. She accommodated an air group of over seventy aircraft, and among the squadrons on board that day was Fighting Six (VF-6), commanded by thirty-nine-year-old Lieutenant Commander C. Wade McClusky. McClusky was level-headed, direct, well respected, and personable. He ran his squadron well, and though it was filled with mostly new pilots still learning the ropes, McClusky had been blessed with good raw material in the men assigned to his unit. Of his nineteen pilots, nine were "trade school" graduates of the Naval Academy, including five classmates from the Class of 1938: Lieutenant (jg) Eric Allen Jr., Lieutenant (jg) Rhonald J. Hoyle, Lieutenant (jg) Frank B. Quady, Lieutenant (jg) Wilmer E. Rawie, and Ensign John C. Kelley.[1] The nineteen-man aviation cadre of Fighting 6, red comet insignia painted on their planes, was a tight group. The men slept, ate, trained, briefed, and traveled together, and the Grumman F4F Wildcats the men flew were the latest war machines in the military, the "U.S. Navy's hottest aircraft"—tough, fast, and maneuverable, with firepower to spare.[2]

At 0942 Admiral Kimmel sent a warning to Halsey, then about two hundred miles west of Oahu, as well as to the commanders of two other task forces in the area, that the harbor had been attacked. At almost the same time, Halsey's radio operators picked up panicked messages warning of Japanese carriers in the vicinity, as well as landing parties attacking ammunition depots on base, Japanese paratroopers and gliders heading for Kaneohe, and transports laden with invasion troops rounding Barbers Point. Halsey could not discern what was accurate and what was not, but he promptly spread the word to all his ships, ordered the "Prepare for Battle" signal flags hoisted up the yardarms, turned east, and immediately launched four fighters for combat air patrol and a group of seaplanes to search for the nearby Japanese forces. While some of the reconnaissance planes would fly as far as 175 miles to both the northwest and northeast, by Sunday evening, as Pearl Harbor burned, the Japanese flattops had still not been located. By then Halsey had grown gruff and impatient. An older man and one of the Navy's most seasoned carrier commanders, with a shock of white hair that lent him the air of a wizened old sage, he was in the dark about where the Japanese had come from and where they had gone. He did not know how many carriers there were or whether they would be back. He did not know if the Pearl Harbor raid had been one part of a larger series of attacks, if an invasion force was on its way to the Hawaiian beaches, or if the raid was the end of the Japanese military's opening gambit. But he knew he was not yet ready to give up. All day long he and the sailors and pilots in his task force had heard conflicting reports and wild speculation about the damage done and the casualties suffered on Oahu, and they were all eager to exact at least some measure of revenge.[3]

Shortly before 1700 that evening, long after the Japanese raid had been completed, six Wildcats of McClusky's VF-6 were assigned to escort a strike of eighteen TBD Devastator torpedo bombers (VT-6) and six

Dauntless dive-bombers of VB-6. This task was not a total fool's errand, as an enemy carrier had been reported one hundred miles southeast of TF 8 and sixty miles south of Oahu. After reaching the target area about one hour after takeoff, however, all they found was an empty ocean, and a black one at that, for there was no moon that evening to whiten the wave tops. After struggling to stay in formation in the dark, Lieutenant Commander Gene Lindsey, VT-6's commander, briefly flipped on his exterior lights, signaling the group to turn back.

While returning to the carrier, the six F4Fs of VF-6 were separated from the rest of the group. Commanding the fighters on their first combat mission that evening was twenty-nine-year-old Lieutenant (jg) Francis "Fritz" Hebel. Hebel was one of McClusky's oldest and most senior men, having earned his wings in 1937. His wingman was Ensign Herbert Menges, and among the other Wildcats spread out behind them were Ensign James Daniels, Ensign Gayle L. Hermann, Ensign David R. Flynn and, in plane 6-F-12, Lieutenant (jg) Eric Allen Jr., USNA '38, flying in the escort formation's "Ass-End Charlie" position.[5] Though separated from the other squadrons, Hebel knew his business, and he used his plane's quirky Zed Baker homing device, together with a plotting chart and dead reckoning, to navigate precisely back to the blacked-out Big E's position.[6] He blinked on his exterior lights for a moment, alerting his men behind him that they were over the carrier. Somewhat surprised by his fighters' prompt return, and not wishing to recover them in the dark, Halsey ordered Hebel and his flight group, including Allen, to instead fly the one hundred miles to Oahu and land at the naval air station on Ford Island. Though surely apprehensive, for they were already low on fuel and would be returning to a base in the dark that had just been devastated by a surprise attack, Hebel complied with the order and turned his squadron north around 1750. The Devastators and Dauntlesses who arrived above the carrier fifteen minutes behind VF-6 were permitted to land due to their near-empty fuel tanks. As the fighters flew off, signal operators on the *Enterprise* took the unusual step of breaking radio silence and notifying Ford Island that six American aircraft were on their way there.

At the Naval Academy, Eric Allen had been a strong swimmer and a talented choral tenor. He had played water polo and joined the Boat and Musical Clubs. On the night of December 7, twenty-five-year-old Allen was second in command of the six-plane fighter section, not by dint of his experience, for in fact he was the least-experienced pilot in the section—he had earned his wings only eleven months before—but, rather, because he was an Academy graduate. As the fighters approached Oahu from the south, Fritz Hebel, at the head of the formation, spotted the lighthouse at Diamond Head and fires in the darkness. He thought they had been started by farmers burning their cane fields before the harvest, so Hebel assumed he and his squadron were over Kauai and he headed east, hitting Molokai before he realized his mistake and turning back. The fires were the remnants of the morning's raids, and they were the only lights visible from the blacked-out island. Had it been lighter, he would have seen smoke still belching from the bombed cruisers and destroyers at their moorings, and the battleships lying turtle or tilted along Battleship Row. He would have seen the fireboats spraying water on the flames that still engulfed the *West Virginia* and the *Arizona* and men cutting into the hull of the upturned *Oklahoma* with acetylene torches. He perhaps would have spied the dead men in white canvas bags being lined up on the hospital lawn, or the other bodies that still floated in the water, not yet corralled by the men in launches, or the trucks even then driving coffins to island cemeteries where bulldozers dug 150-foot-long trenches to receive them.[7]

Hebel checked the fuel status of each of his planes and then led the flight back across the channel west to Oahu's Makapuu Point at the southeastern tip of the island. From there they hugged the coastline south before banking west over Waikiki toward the Pearl Harbor Channel Entrance, past the runway lights of Hickam. At close to 2100 hours, Hebel anxiously radioed Ford Island's tower for landing instructions. In the control tower at Ford Field was Lieutenant Commander Howard L. "Brigham" Young, the *Enterprise*'s air group commander, who had flown in earlier that day, in the middle of the attack. Blessed with good fortune, he had been able to land on Ford Island's runway in the midst of the Japanese swarms, climb out of his plane, and sprint to the tower. As Hebel and his fighters approached, Young took the microphone and told Hebel to fly over the field and break up for landing. He also told Hebel to have his men turn on their planes' running lights. At the command of Rear Admiral Patrick L. N. Bellinger, who was worried about a friendly fire incident, Navy aviation personnel left the building and hurried to the gunners scattered on the smoldering docks and damaged facilities, warning them about the incoming group of friendlies. The tower also broadcast two different messages to all ships and army antiaircraft units around Pearl Harbor, alerting them to the forthcoming arrival of the American planes. When Hebel notified the tower that he wanted to circle the island and land from the north, executing the usual left carrier break for landing, Young responded that Hebel should come straight in. Hebel either failed to hear him or ignored the order.

Allen and the others pushed back the canopies of their cockpits as they droned ever closer to the airfield, and the pilots could not help but smell the stench of burned oil, paint, wood, and flesh. It was "thick and sulfurous enough to be mistaken for Diamond Head's volcanic spew rather than the work of man."[8] Wheels dangling, green and red running lights clear, flying slowly in a loose right echelon formation, giving every appearance of friendlies on a routine night landing, the planes lined up for the airfield, in the process closely buzzing the nervous and inexperienced gunners on board the ships in Drydock Channel, in the Navy Yard's berths, and along Battleship Row.

A soft rain fell. A bugler that evening had sounded colors, and throughout the base men had stopped what they were doing to stand at attention and salute the American flag as it was lowered. The men at the gun sights that night were jumpy and scared, angry and beaten. Many had heard, and believed, shipboard rumors that the *Enterprise* had been sunk by the Japanese out at sea. Yet even in darkness, F4F Wildcats did not look like Japanese planes, with their "fastback" turtledecks behind the cockpits and their high tails, squared wingtips, and barreled fuselages. To the gunners in Pearl Harbor, though, they flew, and they droned, and thus they looked and sounded enough like Vals and Kates and Zeros, even as the real Japanese planes sat safely on their carriers hundreds of miles away. Men on board several warships in the harbor that night would claim they challenged the lighted aircraft for proper recognition signals but received no countersigns in return.

At first only a few scattered shots were taken at the American planes as they descended to an altitude of one thousand feet. It is believed that gunners from one of the aft antiaircraft batteries on board the battleship *Pennsylvania*, in Dry Dock One's caisson, were the first to fire. A gun ripped open and a line of red tracers arced toward the Wildcats. Hebel, spying the rounds, immediately aborted his landing, and instinctually the Wildcats behind him scattered. It was enough to convince the other gunners, all along wary and suspicious, to fire too. In a blast of light, sound, and fire, "every gun on the island seemed to open up."[9] One sailor said, "The sky lit up like daytime."[10] Captain James Shoemaker, the officer in charge of NAS Pearl Harbor that night, said, "I never saw so many bullets in the air—all tracer bullets at night."[11] According to James Daniels, in the plane beside Allen, "The sky was filled with so much metal you could have walked on it."[12] Even soldiers with Springfields raised their rifles and fired at the planes. Flashes of yellow from the starboard guns on the battleships winked, red tracers from small-caliber weapons arced, and many, many bullets whipped through the night sky toward the planes. The sailors shot whatever they had, whatever would shoot, at their countrymen. The control tower operators screamed into the radio for the crews to hold fire. "By God," said a Seaman Mason on board the USS *California*, "this time we were going to shoot back! . . . We were striking back at the foe who had so humiliated us."[13] There was so much fire that men on the ground were momentarily blinded.

Fritz Hebel shouted at the tower through his radio, "My God! What's happening?"[14]

He banked his Wildcat north toward Wheeler Field, but Army gunners north of the harbor got him, knocking out his engine on his final approach to the airfield. He glided the Wildcat into a sugarcane field near Aiea, bounced off the dirt, and skidded into the stubble, where the plane cartwheeled, broke into two pieces, and landed in a gulley, afire. Civilians nearby had watched the whole thing, and they pulled him out of the cockpit before he could burn up, but his skull was fractured, and he was unconscious. He was brought to the hospital at Schofield Barracks but never regained consciousness. He died the next day.

Hebel's wingman, Herb Menges, was either killed or severely wounded when bullets ripped through his cockpit. His F4F stalled and drifted beyond the Ford Island field toward Pearl City and the peninsula where, after a shallow dive, it crashed into the veranda of the Palm Lodge and exploded. The resulting fire eventually burned the waterside tavern to the ground. The twenty-four-year-old Menges became the first U.S. Navy fighter pilot to be killed in the Pacific War.

The main fuel tanks of Eric Allen's Wildcat were hit by gunfire, leaving him just seconds to bail out. As his plane dove out of control into Drydock Channel, Allen deployed his chute, but he was not high enough, and he struck the water hard. Gunners on the ships watched the planes go down and thrilled at the sight of their handiwork.

Gayle Hermann's plane could not get away either. A 5-inch shell tore into his Wildcat's engine, knocking it out, and, like Hebel, he was forced to try a dead stick landing on Ford Field. As he glided in, his plane was hit eighteen more times. The plane bounced off the runway and hurtled over the airstrip's apron and onto a nearby golf course east of the field. Unhurt, Hermann grabbed his parachute and jumped out of the cockpit as small arms fire pinged off his plane's fuselage and kicked up clumps of dirt around him. He sprinted to a nearby field hangar.

Whereas the fire gave Hebel, Menges, and Allen no time to react, the other two pilots, Jim Daniels and Davy Flynn, were able to take some measure of evasive action. Daniels alertly turned off his running lights and dove for the southern edge of the field, hoping the gunners would lose him in the floodlights. From there he cranked up his wheels and sped away west toward Barbers Point, where, unhit and relatively safe, he flew in circles. When he contacted the Ford Field tower again, Howard Young told Daniels to leave his lights off, come in low and fast, and land quickly. Daniels nearly clipped the foretop of the beached *Nevada* on his approach but landed safely despite taking more fire from three different directions. Even as he taxied, gunners took shots at him, and with a painful wrenched back, he had to explain who he was to a group of Army security officers about to shoot him. His loud cussing probably went the furthest in convincing the security personnel that he was not a Japanese pilot.

Davy Flynn, turning twenty-seven that very day, juked left and flew ten miles out to sea. He was the last of the six-man flight still airborne and understandably felt no inclination to return to Oahu. But Flynn's plane was perilously low on fuel, so he turned back toward the harbor. He made landfall at Barbers Point and, instead of flying to Oahu and Ford Field, turned north toward Ewa and the Marine airfield there. Still miles short of the runway, Flynn's gas ran out and his Wildcat stalled. At 2130 he parachuted out at twelve hundred feet. Flynn hit the ground, landing in a cane field, his aircraft exploding in the distance, and he was quickly picked up by nearby soldiers who brought him to Tripler Army Hospital with relatively minor injuries.

Alive but with grievous internal damage, Eric Allen, a strong swimmer, stroked in intense pain through the water, thick with oil and clogged with debris. Incredibly given his condition, he swam past the Drydock Channel and the wrecked battleship *California*, where, finally, sailors on the minesweeper *Vireo* spotted him and dragged him on board. They brought him to Ford Island, by then a frenzied, chaotic place where barracks and mess halls were serving as hospitals and morgues and where the wounded sat on the patios and steps and waited their turn. It was only later, when medics washed away the ooze and oil from Allen's torso, that they realized he had been hit by a .50-caliber bullet, machine-gunned as he hung from his parachute. One of his lungs collapsed later that night, and Eric Allen died at 0200.

At sunrise on Monday morning, December 8, the *Enterprise* sailed into Pearl Harbor. Seven destroyers trailed in a single file behind her. Once docked, fuel lines were immediately hauled on board from a waiting tanker, and reprovisioning began. From Halsey down to the youngest seaman, everyone wanted to be away from the place and back out to sea as quickly as possible.

Eric Allen was the first combat casualty from the Naval Academy's Class of 1938, but he was not the last of that group to die during the long weekend of the Pearl Harbor raid. James Ginn, USNA '38, hailed from Bayard, Nebraska, and was a member of the Quarter Deck Society during his time at the Academy, as well as a writer for *The Log*. At Pearl Harbor he was stationed on board the *Maryland*. A seaplane scout, Lieutenant (jg) Ginn took off from Pearl Harbor on Monday, December 8, 1941, mere hours after Allen's death, on a southwest heading in plane 4-0-2 with his radioman-gunner to conduct a pie-shaped search for the Japanese fleet, believed to still be out there somewhere. On their way back, the plane ran out of fuel and crashed into the Pacific roughly eight miles offshore of Oahu. The crash rendered both men unconscious, but Ginn's gunner, Radioman Second Class William R. Roberts, recovered quickly and freed Ginn from his belts as the plane sank around them. Repeatedly diving, and once almost drowning when he became entangled, Roberts pulled the plane's inflatable rubber life raft free and laid the unconscious Ginn on a wing float. He then paddled to shore, all the while towing Ginn behind him. Breakers near the beach capsized the two men, but Roberts continued to assist Ginn until they reached the sand. The two men were later rescued, and, for his actions, Roberts was awarded the Navy Cross. Ginn's injuries were too severe, however, and he died later that day.

LODWICK HOUSTON ALFORD

Sylvester, Georgia

Unk Alford—a real native Southerner with a good, old rebel drawl cultivated way down there in Georgia. Although inclined to be slightly redheaded, he is one of the easiest to get along with. He knows his football games from A to Z and is not averse to giving odds on a game he's doped out to be in the bag, is famous for his football predictions, the material for which he sacredly keeps in his circular files. He accepts a blind date now and then and swears he never will be so taken in again. Unk's not one of the star men, but he always gets the word. With a twinkle in his eyes, Unk looks confidently forward to the future.

The Lucky Bag, 1938

Chapter Seven

OPENING ONSLAUGHTS

At 0325 on the morning of December 8, 1941, the old flush-deck "four-piper" USS *Stewart* lay at anchor in Tarakan harbor, on the northeast coast of Borneo (far away across the International Date Line from Hawaii). On the bridge the petty officer of the watch stood at his station and looked forward to his relief in a little over half an hour. Just onshore were the dark black mountains of Kalimantan, and in the harbor, other ships of the U.S. Navy's Asiatic Fleet sat silent and still.

The morning's calm was shattered in an instant when an urgent alert reached the *Stewart*'s radio shack, broadcast from the commander in chief of the Asiatic Fleet to all his ships. Admiral Thomas Hart had received the news of the attack in his Manila hotel room just before 0300, when the Marine duty officer back at his naval headquarters telephoned him: "Admiral, put some cold water on your face. I'm coming over with a message."[1] When he arrived, the Marine officer handed Hart a sheet of paper with the words "AIR RAID ON PEARL HARBOR. THIS IS NO DRILL." Quickly Hart drafted a dispatch to his ships. The message was stark: "Asiatic Fleet. Priority. Japan started hostilities. Govern yourselves accordingly."[2] It offered nothing more.

The radioman on board the *Stewart* that morning rushed down to the quarters of her captain, Lieutenant Commander Harold P. Smith, USNA '24. The undoubtedly harried sailor also alerted the commander of Destroyer Division 58, Commander Thomas H. Binford, Class of '20, who was on board as well. Still in their bathrobes, Smith and Binford quickly conferred, then Smith turned and ordered the ship to General Quarters.

The USS *Stewart* before the war

"Man your battle stations, we are at war."[3]

The alarm that followed echoed through the ship's predawn passageways and sent the crew rushing to their posts in a frenzy of footsteps.

For Lodwick Alford, USNA '38, it was certainly an eerie feeling to be "startled out of a sound sleep . . . and to learn [so] quickly that the war had started."[4] When the alarm bellowed, he shuddered, rose from his bunk, pulled on some clothes, then climbed the three ladders to his battle station on the director platform, just forward of the wardroom, above the piloting and navigation bridge. From there he controlled the main battery of 4-inch and .50-caliber guns using his gunfire control director, as well as the machine guns on the galley deckhouse and the antiaircraft gun on the fantail. Hurriedly his men filled all the ready ammunition boxes. Warheads were installed on the torpedoes. The air flasks were charged, the depth charges were armed, and the recoil cylinders were topped off. All unnecessary lights were doused, and the ship soon hunkered in the quiet water, now tense and alert. In the blackness Alford felt his way to the main deck and started checking on his gun crews. His men were tense and apprehensive, he noticed, yet many appeared exhilarated, too. They had all been expecting war for some time, and now that it had arrived, they seemed to struggle with the sudden waiting. They needed something to do, he thought, something to fight. Certain crews acknowledged and talked to Alford as he appeared out of the black of the early morning. Others stared off into the water and the sky, lost in their thoughts. Alford tried to calm them when he could. If they did not want to talk, he moved on.

When Alford thought about the war's start himself, his mind's eye landed on moments from his life and images from his past. He wondered if the ship would be sunk and if he would survive. Would both his career and his life be over so soon? "Was my adorable and adoring young wife never destined for fulfillment? How did I get here, or more to the point, what the hell is Lodwick Alford doing here at this time, in this place?"[5] No one, not Alford or Lieutenant Commander Smith or anyone else on board the four-piper, had any illusions about their ship or its fleet. Other men in other fleets were cocky and bandied stereotypes and preconceptions about the Japanese back and forth. In the Asiatic, they thought differently. They were overmatched, both quantitatively and qualitatively. Their fleet was decrepit, broken down, past its prime. They would be plugging gaps and biding time and hoping to bloody the nose of the Japanese while they did so, but their chances of survival were best not considered, for the math was bad.

Admiral Hart in Manila wisely decided not to sit and wait for the Japanese onslaught he was sure was coming; rather, he took quick emergency steps to prepare his forces as best he could. He commanded a "fleet" in name only. In reality, it was a mere agglomeration of ships. Under his command, arrayed throughout the Dutch East Indies, were three American cruisers (the *Houston*, *Marblehead*, and *Boise*), thirteen old destroyers, a flotilla of small gunboats, yachts, yard craft, and auxiliary vessels, and one admiral's white party boat (the *Isabel*). He also had an assortment of slow PBY planes, half a dozen PT boats, and twenty-nine submarines of various sizes. He too knew the odds his fleet faced were appalling. Heading toward them, he soon learned, was an Imperial Japanese Navy armada with ten battleships; three cruisers; nine aircraft carriers; over a hundred destroyers; sixty-three submarines; and hundreds of land- and carrier-based fighters, bombers, and torpedo planes. Hart prepared orders for the ships of his fleet to head south where they could link up with the navies of the British and the Dutch. Safety, to him, seemed to be in numbers.

In Tarakan a few hours later, as the sun peeked up in the east and sailors could finally see again, the men on board the *Stewart* began stripping the ship of unnecessary wood and other flammables and made general preparations for getting underway. The *Stewart* slipped from her pier at 0531, through the light of early morning, and moved smoothly toward the harbor mouth. As they exited, Alford grew both scared and excited. He and the other officers had no real idea what they were sailing to face. Japanese surface ships could already be just beyond the harbor's entrance. There could be submarines in the waters offshore, listening and waiting. Or there could be enemy airplanes patrolling in the sky, glasses trained on the known harbors in the area. Still, no one on board had any wish to remain in Tarakan, with its lack of maneuvering room, when the Japanese ships, subs, or planes attacked.

The *Stewart* reached open sea safely and soon formed a column with other vessels of the Asiatic Fleet who were also departing the harbor. Lieutenant Commander Smith set a course south toward nearby Balikpapan, zigzagging with the *Marblehead* and *Parrott*.

The U.S. Navy was only one of several Allied fleets operating in the South Pacific at the start of World War II. Earlier, in preparation for hostilities, heterogeneous units of Dutch, British, Australian, and American forces, ranging widely over several thousand miles from Burma to Western New Guinea, from the Dutch East Indies to the Philippines to northwestern Australia, had been melded together into a single unified command, to be called ABDACOM (the sea forces were called ABDAFLOAT). But this did little to alleviate any of the serious concerns about or deficiencies in Allied military strength in the region in late 1941. The naval vessels lacked air cover, a massive disadvantage in any future battles to come. Their submarines were in short supply and featured defective torpedoes that rendered them, and thus the submarines themselves, virtually useless. Very few of the American and British naval officers could speak Dutch, nor could they understand the Dutch Navy's charts or sailing instructions or comprehend its signals and codes. Political agreements between the nations were, in the early days, nonexistent. Operational plans were makeshift. Communications were rudimentary. Beginning in the very first days of the war, errors and misunderstandings plagued the combined fleet's operations, critically curtailing its effectiveness. But ABDACOM was all the region had: its men could not count on reinforcements for several more months, if realistically even then, and each hour the fleets and strike forces of the IJN churned closer. That they knew.

By the early afternoon of December 8, the *Stewart*, *Marblehead*, and *Parrott* had rounded Cape Mangkalihat between the Celebes and Java Seas and headed southwestward, farther down Borneo's coast. On the *Stewart* the radio shack continued to pick up pieces of information emanating from Pearl Harbor that gave Alford and the sailors some hint of the damage that had been inflicted, and the officers and men began to suspect the suddenly obvious, that mighty Big Brother would not be coming to their aid anytime soon. There were other attacks that day too, on Allied airfields in the Philippines, on Wake Island, and on air bases in Malaya, Burma, and Hong Kong. Conversation in the wardrooms and in the galley aboard the *Stewart* that afternoon centered on the oil fields in the Netherlands East Indies, how important they were to Japan's survival, and the fact that ABDACOM was now the only thing blocking access to them.

At 0900 on December 9, the three American ships picked their way through mines and into the anchorage in Balikpapan Harbor. Alford and his fellow officers listened to the official reports and to the commercial radio in Manila for more news of what was happening elsewhere: at midday Japanese bombers struck Clark Field, the principal American air base in the Philippines, leaving not one of the base's structures undamaged. They heard that in Malaya a Japanese invasion force had already put ashore on the northeastern coast, and in British-controlled Singapore Japanese bombers had hit the base installations and runways. The bad news continued: on December 10, the mighty and venerable British battleship *Prince of Wales*, together with the cruiser *Repulse*, set sail from Singapore with no air cover, and the two ships were sunk in the South China Sea in the early afternoon by Japanese aircraft. The damage to the power and prestige of the Royal Navy in the area, and to the Allies' ability to slow the Japanese advance, was crippling. "With those ships," Alford thought, "we might have held them off for several months."[6] Now they were at the sea bottom.

The Philippines' Cavite Naval Shipyard was the U.S. Navy's principal base west of Pearl Harbor, and that same day, a pack of fifty Japanese bombers heeled over and, untroubled, bombed the shipyard, the waterfront, and the ships moored at the wharves. More casualties were caused by Japanese planes that strafed sailors as they carried their wounded to the dispensary. Strong winds swept off the bay and fanned the fires. Among those injured were two of Alford's Academy classmates, Don Hamilton and Howard Fischer. Admiral Hart watched the attack from the rooftop of his headquarters in the city.

On Friday more American ships crowded into Balikpapan: the *Holland* and *Otus*, the yacht *Isabel*, and the *Boise*, *Houston*, *Langley*, *Barker*, *Paul Jones*, *John D. Ford*, and *Pope*. The forces in the now-cluttered harbor represented just about everything the U.S. Asiatic Fleet had available. Alford and the Class of 1938 could have hosted a small reunion onshore. Its members were scattered across the harbor that afternoon, including Leon Rogers and Hal Hamlin on board the *Houston*, Marion Buaas still on board the *Isabel*, and Bill Spears on the *Pope*. For two days the ships reprovisioned in the harbor while the captains and commodores discussed among themselves what to do next. The commander of the American force, now designated Task Force 5, was Admiral William A. Glassford, and he called a conference of his captains on December 14 on board his flagship, the *Houston*. All of those present knew they were in "a hell of a situation," with few options that offered anything other than entrapment and destruction.[7] They could remain near Balikpapan and fight; or move south and east, fighting a delaying action as they made for Australia; or they could sail southwest for Java, there to join forces with a Dutch Navy that had decided it would flee no farther and would defend the island.

Alford was aware of the mortal danger the ship was in, but he was increasingly reluctant to discuss his feelings with any other members of the crew for fear of damaging already fragile morale. The officers on board refused to allow any fatalism or despondency to set in among the men. What they did do was train. They were determined to land as many blows as possible on the Japanese fleet when they inevitably met them. If they had to go down, they would go down throwing punches. Alford drilled his gunnery department repeatedly over the next few days. Their most lethal weapons were the dozen torpedoes they carried, but it would be his guns that would finish off anything the torpedoes damaged, so he overlooked nothing. He drilled his men in every action and procedure, and the morale of the men improved with their proficiency.

On Monday, December 15, one week after Pearl Harbor, Glassford determined that his ships were too exposed in Balikpapan, so he scattered them. The *Stewart* departed the next day and headed southeast for the port of Makassar in the Celebes, arriving on December 18. Four days later, General Quarters sounded at 0230. By 0600 all ships in Makassar had cleared the harbor, and word soon filtered down that they were headed south for Surabaya, on Java, the Allied locus of control in the Dutch East Indies. The men surmised that Hart was sending the Asiatic Fleet to link up with their friends in the Royal Netherlands Navy, where together they could stand against the Japanese in the nest of islands arrayed to Java's east and west. It had taken two weeks for the requisite commanders to decide what to do with the Asiatic Fleet, but finally a course of action had been chosen. The news spread through the ship. It steeled nerves left jangled by the continuing reports detailing more unchecked advances by the Japanese.

Though Alford and the other officers in the Asiatic Fleet did not know it, in Washington, DC, Admiral Ernest J. King had determined their fate. King, the commander in chief of the U.S. Navy, had finally decided that his Pacific strategy after the Pearl Harbor raid rested on two main objectives: Hawaii and Australia. Neither could fall. To those ends, King ordered Admiral Chester Nimitz, his new chief of the Pacific Fleet, to first secure the seaways between Midway Island, Hawaii, and the West Coast of the United States and, second, protect the lifeline between North America and Australia by holding the Hawaii–Samoa line. Shipping along those lines must remain open and secure to allow for an eventual counteroffensive from "Australasia." All other considerations in the region were secondary. Though it was not officially acknowledged, planners and administrators in Pearl Harbor and in Washington quickly understood that everything in the Pacific beyond those two secure lines would fall: the Philippines, Burma, the Dutch East Indies, and the islands of the Bismarck Archipelago, including New Ireland, New Britain, and New Guinea. That also included the ABDA forces and its American Army units and U.S. Navy ships. The ramshackle Asiatic Fleet was expected to do its best, to slow the rate of the Japanese advance, to inflict what damage it could, and to buy a few weeks' time. They were not expected to last long in these efforts.

To the men on board the *Stewart*, underway on December 22 with the bulk of the Asiatic Fleet, Surabaya in Java offered more than just the chance to join forces with the Dutch: it also offered a friendly port city and the chance to get some needed rest. There was the prospect of some Christmas liberty, some drinking and carousing. By 1400 on Christmas Eve, the *Stewart* was moored alongside the Rotterdam quay. Alford spent Christmas Eve subdued, his thoughts on home. He retired in the evening to his stateroom, wrote letters to his family, stayed awake until midnight, then opened a few presents he had received prior to the Pearl Harbor attack. On Christmas Day he went ashore and sent a cablegram to his wife, the first she had heard from him since hostilities had started. Then he joined other officers for a Christmas supper.

On December 28 plans changed again, and the fleet left the harbor and sailed eastward at twelve knots for the long haul to Darwin, Australia. They had yet to see a live Japanese enemy, but knew they would soon be nearby, and the *Stewart* investigated enough false alarms to suggest that the Japanese might in fact be lurking just over the horizon. The fleet swept past Bali and Lombok, Sumbawa, Sumba, and Timor, through the Flores, Savu, Banda, and Arafura Seas. To Alford it was an undeniable thrill to feel the ship slicing at high speeds through the waves, to see the islands come and go off the starboard railings. The *Stewart* spent New Year's Eve waiting off Booby Island in the Torres Strait. Alford wrote in his journal, "New Year's Day and a war to be won. On to Tokyo."[8]

The strategy of the Japanese in the early weeks of January involved a three-pronged drive south from their home islands toward Malaya and Sumatra in the west; the Philippines, Borneo, Celebes, and Java in the center; and the Bismarck Archipelago, including New Guinea and Rabaul, in the east. Early in the new year Japanese forces took Luzon and Mindanao in the central prong, advancing to Jolo in the Sulu Archipelago. It was this middle thrust against which Alford, the *Stewart*, and the rest of the Asiatic Fleet would be arrayed to defend.

Once in Darwin Alford and his fellow officers listened to whatever radio reports they could obtain. The broadcasts confirmed little but birthed seemingly new rumors every hour, and all suggested that massed enemy vessels were moving south. "We knew they would be after us soon," wrote Alford.[9] He and his crew were still hoping more U.S. warships would arrive to assist and growing increasingly itchy to get involved in some way.

By mid-January Admiral Thomas Hart had been designated commander of ABDA's naval forces. Up to that point the war had been "mostly a bad dream" for him, and Hart knew he had few tools with which to slow the Japanese navy down.[10] He still had no air cover, and the fleet he had was a mixed four-nation flotilla each with their own priorities (the British were focused on saving Singapore; the Dutch, Java). But neither Hart nor his captains and sailors wanted to hide and wait. On January 20 a big, broad-winged PBY Catalina spotted an enemy invasion force off Balikpapan, and Hart sent four American destroyers (the *John D. Ford*, *Parrott*, *Paul Jones*, and *Pope*) through Makassar Strait to engage them in Balikpapan Bay. The destroyers made several close approaches, sank three troop transports, and damaged several more. It was a tactical victory, but nine of the transports survived and the inexperience of the American sailors was revealed (as was the unreliability of their torpedoes). The Battle of Balikpapan was the first American naval battle of the war and the first time U.S. naval ships had gone to battle against an enemy force since the Battle of Santiago Bay in 1898. It was exaggerated for its public relations value back home, but in reality the raid "did nothing to check the speed of the Japanese offensive into the Dutch East Indies."[11]

The *Stewart* men heard of the battle as they settled into convoy duty a long way away, escorting maddeningly slow British troop ships and Dutch tankers to Batavia, Osthaven, and Surabaya. On January 18, a set of welcome orders finally arrived, and the *Stewart* left her convoys, opened up her engines, and roared north at twenty-five knots. By noon on January 28 they were moored once again in Surabaya harbor. The four destroyers that had participated in the previous week's battle were in the harbor too, and Alford and his fellow officers circulated around the docks and listened to the crews as they retold their stories about their roles in the scrap. Morale among the men rocketed. The sailors who had participated in the raid had been bloodied and battle-scarred. They were veterans now and lorded it over the others. The men from the *Stewart* hung on their every word, jealous. Alford found his classmate Bruce Garrett, who was also in the harbor on board the *John D. Edwards*, and together they went in search of Heineken beers and more stories at one of the local bars.

As more Allied ships entered and docked in Surabaya, rumors began circulating from ship to submarine to merchant vessel that something big was upcoming, finally a real challenge to the enemy invasion forces pushing ever southward. The rumors, as they intensified, seemed to hint that the *Stewart* would be involved in the initial attack, wherever it was. Alford's sailors started approaching him in the passageways and asking anxiously about which ships would be alongside them in the fight. As Alford put it, "When one is going into battle, you want the utmost confidence that the ship ahead of you or astern of you will give you maximum support as you expect to do the same for him. . . . If a captain of a ship is thought to be timid or aggressive, you don't want that ship with you in battle. . . . You want a ship you can depend on."[12] Already ships and captains and crews were earning reputations, not all of them good.

On Friday, January 30, the *Stewart* backed away from the pier, and at 0900 Lieutenant Commander Smith called the crew to quarters on the forecastle. He told the men about the presence of threatening Japanese forces in the area, including an enemy carrier group sailing south through the Molucca Sea, and informed them that the *Stewart* would be part of an attacking force of four other ships. He recognized that it was not much to throw at a carrier group but, he said, with the element of surprise they might be able to do some damage. It was an ambitious plan, to say the least, and caused Alford to wonder if perhaps the Allies' perceived success at the Battle of Balikpapan had clouded, or even warped, some judgments at Naval Headquarters. The five destroyers (the *Stewart*, *Marblehead*, *Barker*, *Bulmer*, and *John D. Edwards*) left the harbor at noon and settled on a fast run to the northwest, followed by a turn due east at midnight. Excitement built. The *Stewart*'s crew were almost desperate for a fight. They burned for the chance to become grizzled veterans themselves. By noon on January 31, the reconnaissance reports had changed: there was no carrier, but there were two light cruisers and at least seven destroyers with multiple transports located in the vicinity of Balikpapan. At 1600 the force increased speed to a pounding twenty-five knots. Lookouts scanned the clouds for Japanese airplanes, expecting them at any minute, but none were seen. Alford thought of home. He wrote letters. He was anxious, as were all the officers and men, but more than anything else he was grimly determined to "beat the hell" out of the Japanese.[13] That was what mattered most. Another scouting message arrived and reported three light cruisers and twelve destroyers. Later, yet another described the force as five light cruisers, twelve destroyers, and seventeen transports. At that point, the odds were considered too great. Five destroyers against a force of that size was foolhardy and stupid. The attack was prudently canceled on the evening of the 31st. As the force turned around, Alford described in his journal not a battle but the full moon over the water.

The Japanese amphibious and naval forces continued their surge steadily southward like a storm front through early February, taking island after island, establishing airfields, seizing ports, grabbing oil fields, and claiming prisoners. According to Alford, "You could see the inevitable coming."[14] Hart, ever aggressive, seized upon another opportunity to take the fight to the IJN. He organized a Combined Allied Striking Force on February 2, placing in overall command the Dutch Rear Admiral Karel Willem Frederik Marie Doorman. His orders were to take his flagship, the Dutch light cruiser *De Ruyter*, along with the American vessels *Houston* (with Leon Rogers, USNA '38, and Hal Hamlin, USNA '38, on board), the light cruiser *Marblehead*, the Dutch light cruiser *Tromp*, an American division of four destroyers, and a Dutch division of three more and hit the Japanese as they advanced on either Makassar City on eastern Sulawesi Island or Banjarmasin, the capital of South Kalimantan, inland on Borneo's southeastern coast. The American destroyer division, DesDiv 58, would include the *John D. Edwards*, *Barker*, *Bulmer*, and *Stewart*.

Hart thought the Allied force he cobbled together stood a better-than-even chance against the Japanese, but what most worried him and his ship commanders were Japanese aircraft, against which ABDAFLOAT had no defense. Admiral Doorman hoped to counter this by fighting a night action, but for that to happen they would all have to sprint across the Java Sea in daylight and hope they were not spotted.

The Combined Allied Striking Force sailed from Surabaya at 0000 on February 4, *De Ruyter* in the lead, *Stewart* and the other destroyers arranged in guard positions on the flanks. *De Ruyter*'s lookouts spotted the first aircraft later that morning at 0949 while the ships sailed through Madura Strait. The sky was overcast and the sea moderate, and the twin-engine silvery Nells that overflew them were naval bombers originating from Vice Admiral Ibo Takahashi's Eastern Force. There were thirty-seven of them, heading west for Surabaya in perfect formation, and they almost missed the Allied fleet but quickly turned when they spotted the ships and re-formed into three separate groups for their attacking dives. Doorman radioed the sighting to his captains, who scattered wildly behind him, every ship for herself. The Nells swarmed downward, commencing their bombing runs and tossing aside four courageous U.S. Navy Catalinas that were in the area, saw what was happening, and tried to intervene. All four were shot down for their efforts. The Japanese bombers dove first on the big Allied cruisers. To Alford, watching, it seemed difficult to believe that the beautiful, sleek planes that were droning in the air were trying to kill them. *Stewart* and the other destroyers tried to fend off the bombers with their antiaircraft guns, but the small ships were ignored, their guns ineffective. The destroyers were not big enough prizes; there was larger prey afoot. Stick after stick of Japanese bombs initially missed the cruisers, but the law of averages soon caught up with the big ships. As they dodged and twisted back and forth, their antiaircraft batteries alight, the *Houston* and *Marblehead* were soon damaged fearsomely. A 500-pound bomb hit *Houston*'s after turret, setting fire to powder bags and causing an explosion that killed forty-eight officers and men instantly and wounded more than fifty more (Rogers and Hamlin survived unhurt). Blackened by fire and smoking, she limped away to seek safety in Tjilatjap, a fever-ridden little port on the southern coast of Java. *Marblehead*'s blasting was even worse. Repeated bomb hits turned her into a mass of flames with a starboard list, a jammed rudder, flooding forward, and eighty-three killed or wounded.

The *Stewart* twisted and turned during the bombing, alternately slowed and sped up. When the Nells left, their bomb racks empty, Doorman called off the raid, as he now lacked sufficient firepower to press on, and the destroyers circled the burning *Marblehead* protectively before escorting her southward after the *Houston*. The Japanese Occupation Force easily took Makassar four days later, losing only five men. The *Marblehead* would be sent back to the United States for repairs; the *Houston*, however, was deemed still fit for service.

Perhaps everyone in the Asiatic Fleet, but certainly Alford, hit the doldrums over the next few days of February. The officers heard false report after false report. Their talk turned idle and seemingly purposeless. They were spoiling for a fight, but none came. They sailed to rendezvous with other ships, but the ships never appeared. They steamed aimlessly without a mission or a purpose. Singapore was set to fall, they sensed apathy in the United States regarding their troubles, and many sailors asked, "What's next?" They grew accustomed to bad news, so much so that they came to expect it. Alford grew pessimistic about their chances of surviving, or not winding up as prisoners of war. He worked hard not to pass his moods on to others in the crew, but there was already a prevailing feeling that the Asiatic Fleet was alone, and in serious trouble. "God help us," Alford wrote in his diary in mid-February.[15]

On February 12 the *Stewart* was tied up in Surabaya, fueling and taking on provisions, when word reached the fleet that Admiral Hart had been relieved of his command, ostensibly for reasons of health, though in fact due purely to political maneuverings and petty jealousies within the American-British-Dutch-Australian hierarchy. On board the *Stewart* and other ships throughout what was now called U.S. Naval Forces, Southwest Pacific, the American sailors and officers received the news angrily. They were already low, and losing Hart saddened and depressed them anew. Many could not hide their frustration and grew defiant. The Americans had unbounded confidence in Hart, but none in his successor, the Dutch Vice Admiral Conrad Helfrich.

Helfrich quickly put together a large multinational striking force once again under the command of the Dutch Rear Admiral W. F. M. Doorman and ordered it to sail the following morning to intercept a Japanese invasion force then bearing down on Palembang, the capital city of Sumatra, off to the west of Surabaya. The force included three Dutch light cruisers (HNMS *De Ruyter*, *Tromp*, and *Java*), the heavy British cruiser *Exeter*, one Australian light cruiser, four Dutch destroyers, and six U.S. destroyers of DesRon 29 (including the *Stewart*, Bruce Garrett's *John D. Edwards*, and the *Pillsbury*, with Alford's Academy classmate Edmundo Gandia on board). The ships of the force stood out westward from Surabaya at 0430 on February 13, and by the 15th they were anchored at the southern tip of Sumatra. Before dark that evening the armada was away again and formed into night cruising disposition, with the big ships in column (*De Ruyter* in the lead), the Dutch destroyers screening ahead, and the American four-pipers on the *De Ruyter*'s port and starboard quarters. Alford finished a late watch, the seas roiling and the weather dark and stormy, and, once relieved, wrote another entry in his journal: "Expect action tomorrow and welcome it."[16] On his mind was whether they would have air cover in the morning.

They would not, and Japanese bombers found them early. The Allied ships, milling on the water, were hopelessly exposed, and for six hours the Japanese launched repeated bomber strikes at the force, giving many a severe jolting, though no ships were sunk. The planes were well out of the *Stewart*'s range, but she fired her 3-inch antiaircraft guns anyway. At 1222 a group of seven Japanese bombers dropped on the fast-moving *Stewart*, and Lieutenant Commander Smith yelled for hard left rudder. The bombs struck five hundred yards abaft. In the afternoon Doorman signaled for the ships to retire to the east, another frustrating sortie called off.

But the Japanese would not let them go peacefully. The ships of the striking force broke into small groups and dodged the repeated aerial attacks and bomb drops as best they could, but at times the narrowness of the straits and passages through which they sailed made maneuvering difficult. The *Stewart* was bracketed by a stick of bombs in the afternoon, and only a timely backing down of the ship's full speed by Lieutenant Commander Smith saved them. Shortly after 1800 the Japanese planes departed, and the Allied force re-formed and headed south, fast.

The force returned to Teluk Betung on Sumatra on February 16 only to find the town burning and fat bulbous pillars of black smoke belching skyward from several burning oil tankers in the harbor. Teluk Betung was the terminus of the railroad from all points on Sumatra and had been hit by the Japanese to minimize its usefulness to the Allies. As the *Stewart* anchored, Alford watched trains discharging evacuees near the waterfront in the rain and the smoke, and the men, women, children, and soldiers dashing in a panic to the few waiting transports able to take them on board. Plans called for the removal of all civilians and evacuees to Java, the last stronghold of the Dutch in their East Indies. As Alford wrote, "These were people who had spent their lifetimes in Sumatra, and now were leaving, abandoning their homes . . . and businesses. They were also losing their way of life. The sights and sounds of the people ashore . . . with anxious looks on their faces, searching for any means of reaching Java, were enough to convince anyone this was an awful and terrible war."[17] The *Stewart* did not remain in the anchorage for long; it quickly sailed at fifteen knots for Ratai Bay and fuel. Word continued to filter to the *Stewart* that the Japanese were getting closer—there were reports of amphibious forces escorted by strong warship contingents coming down through the straits between Borneo and Sumatra.

The reality for Allied commanders was even worse than that. The Japanese were also sweeping down from Celebes. Army forces were marching into southern Sumatra. They were wading ashore in Bali, where they would take the airfield, then capture its larger sister island, Lombok.

Surabaya and its harbor were now within a scant hundred miles of Japanese bombers and attack planes. The entire front was crumbling, and Allied naval forces were widely scattered and therefore unable to oppose the Japanese in any concentrated manner.

On February 18 Allied leaders decided to try once again to take on the Japanese in yet another decisive battle. Though the Combined Allied Striking Force was separated, the operational plan, quickly devised, called for a multipronged attack to relieve the pressure on Bali and Lombok. According to the plan, Doorman, then on Tjilatjap, would sail with his flagship, several other Dutch light cruisers and destroyers, and the U.S. destroyers *Ford* and *Pope* and attack the Japanese invasion force first, approaching from along the southern coast of Java and arriving before midnight on February 19. A second group, consisting of the Dutch light cruiser *Tromp*, the *Stewart*, and three other American destroyers, would attack the Japanese two hours later from Surabaya, after Doorman's force had retired to the north. A third group of nine feisty Dutch motor torpedo boats would sprint in and attack last, hoping to take advantage of the expected battle confusion to create further havoc. Their specific targets were the Japanese transport ships and escorts landing an army at Sanur Roads, on Bali's southeastern coast. The three Allied waves would approach the landing site through the narrow channel of Badung Strait, a mere fifteen miles wide.

Stewart and the other three American destroyers, the *John D. Edwards*, *Parrott*, and *Pillsbury*, were underway after 1500 on February 19, 1942. Lieutenant Commander Smith electrified the crew on board the *Stewart* when he alerted them to their mission, and excitement only continued to build as the task force formed on the water and headed toward Bali. On paper the attack plan seemed sound. "At last, it appeared that we might have a good chance of getting in some good licks of our own against the Japanese."[18]

The problem, and Alford knew it, was that only Doorman's first attack wave would own the element of surprise. The succeeding two waves would sail at a fleet hopefully bruised and battered, but undoubtedly alert. There was also the unfortunate fact that no one really knew what the Combined Allied Striking Force was sailing against, and which enemy ships would be there to oppose them.

In any event, Doorman's first wave was bedeviled by bad luck. On the run over, the Dutch cruiser *Kortenaer* ran aground and was lost to the operation. Then *De Ruyter* and *Java* pulled too far ahead of the American destroyers that were screening them, such that when the attack was launched at 2225 with a brief exchange of gunfire from the *Java*, the American destroyers were not yet in the area and thus unable to provide support. After their initial sorties the *De Ruyter* (with Doorman on board) and *Java* sailed away through Lombok Strait, leaving the U.S. destroyers and the Dutch ship *Piet Hein* to attack a riled enemy of still-unknown types and numbers by themselves. Their attack turned into a melee, guns exploding, star shells drifting over the water, torpedoes skimming beneath the surface in every direction, shells landing, smoke belching, and, all the while, the morning darkness impenetrable, made even worse by a thick cloud cover. At 2235 the *Piet Hein* was lethally struck, exploded in a "volcanic burst of flames," and sank quickly.[19] The *Ford* and *Pope* let loose final volleys of their guns and torpedoes, made smoke, and sailed southeast, escaping with negligible damage and no casualties.

The Dutch light cruiser *Tromp* led the second Allied column in. Alford and the *Stewart* sailed behind her, followed by the other three American destroyers in a line astern. On board the *Stewart* the men had heard snatches of conversation between the *Ford* and *Pope*, enough to know they were in "hot combat," but could not establish contact with them and thus still had no information about how the first wave had fared or what Japanese ships they could expect to find in the target area.[20]

At 0110 the column changed course to make their run in. The night remained fully impenetrable. Any ships would be extremely difficult to make out; they would appear only as slightly different shades of black against the dark mountains and misty shorelines of Bali to the north. But they were close by in the blackness somewhere, that was certain, and Alford was one of those peering through large binoculars trying to spot them. At 0134 what appeared to be two small ships were seen on the port bow between two thousand and twenty-five hundred yards away. The hackles on Alford's neck rose, and "my adrenalin was flowing as I thought to myself, this is it, it's now or never."[21] The black ships challenged the approaching Allied fleet with signal lights, expecting friends. The American and Dutch sailors ignored the lights, and each of their gun crews stood poised and tense, shells cradled in their arms, ready to load. Two minutes later both the *Stewart* and the *Parrott* launched all six of their portside torpedoes at the distant Japanese ships in an effort to hit first. The twelve fish ran hot, straight, and normal, but they all missed or failed to explode, causing bitter disappointment. Lieutenant Commander Smith asked Alford through the talker on the sound-powered phone if the deck guns were ready. Alford had already checked in with his gun captains: No. 1 on the forecastle, Nos. 2 and 3 on the midship deckhouse, and No. 4 on the after deckhouse were on target and standing by.

"Commence firing," Smith ordered.[22]

Simultaneously the *Stewart* opened her searchlight shutters and fired a three-gun salvo. They hoped to tear up the topsides of the Japanese ships with their first shots and disable them before they could react. The *Stewart* fired multiple salvos at the vessels, and after the fourth, Alford could tell their shells were landing. But it did not take long for the enemy cruisers to shine their own searchlights on the *Stewart*, and their guns soon flashed in reply. At that point, the *John D. Edwards* sailed in and joined the skirmish, launching her own spread of six torpedoes. Again, they all missed. It was to be a gunfight, then, and a furious one. As Alford wrote, "The enemy had been aroused by our first wave of ships, were at their battle stations, and [were] mad as stinging hornets."[23] Airbursts exploded just off the *Stewart*, spraying the port side of the ship with fragments. Waterspouts from very near misses blossomed just off the rails and soaked the deck. One man practically at Alford's elbow was hit by a fist-sized fragment and killed instantly. Four 8-inch shells ultimately struck the *Stewart*: one exploded into the boats on her deck, one destroyed her torpedo racks, one struck her galley, and one hit the ship aft, below the waterline, rending her seams and quickly flooding the steering engine room.

Alford and his gun crews kept up their firing; he was not afraid, for there was no time to be. What damage they were causing was not often discernible, and after five minutes the Japanese ships drew well aft and the *Stewart*'s guns could no longer bear. Lieutenant Commander Smith stopped firing after twelve salvos, changed the *Stewart*'s course to 065, and increased speed, the other American destroyers following astern. The Japanese cruisers had kept the Americans from charging into the anchorage site, and soon the battle quieted into a lull. As his destroyer zigzagged to the northeast, Alford thought again of his classmates behind him.

At 0212 three Japanese ships appeared from broad on the starboard bow of the *Stewart*, about five thousand yards away, announcing their presence with a salvo and searchlights. Smith immediately answered with his full load of six starboard torpedoes and had Alford reply with a salvo of their 4-inch guns. After six salvos they stopped firing, unsure of the damage they had inflicted, but they believed one of their torpedoes might have hit. At 0241 two Japanese destroyers, the *Michishio* and the *Arashio*, rushed in on a southwest-by-west course to continue the fight, but the Japanese found themselves at close quarters, arriving in the middle of the *John D. Edwards* and the *Stewart* on one side, and the damaged *Tromp* and *Pillsbury* on the other. Searchlights blasted the darkness and torpedoes were quickly fired, and the *Michishio* broke off to the north to avoid the *Stewart*'s lights, only to sail directly into the sights of the *John D. Edwards*, who hit the Japanese ship repeatedly with her deck guns. Soon the Japanese destroyer was dead in the water.

By 0317 the *Stewart* secured from General Quarters and headed to Surabaya with the three other Allied ships arrayed loosely astern and on her starboard quarter. Dawn revealed small holes scattered throughout the ship and a main deck littered with shell fragments to go with two feet of water in the steering engine room. Alford and his crewmates were left confused by the action. Had they inflicted any damage or accomplished anything useful? They also remained ignorant as to the enemy's true size and location, given the darkness during the engagement. Ultimately, as historian Paul Dull wrote, "the box score of the battle [later dubbed the Battle of Badung Strait] was unimpressive."[24] One Japanese destroyer was severely damaged, two more suffered light damage, and two transports were hit but not sunk. Allied forces, on the other hand, lost the destroyer *Piet Hein* and saw the *Tromp* badly damaged. In truth, the Allies waged the battle poorly. The three-wave strike plan had been tactically questionable from the beginning and, once initiated, resulted in ships scattered on their approaches and chased off before they could harass the enemy transports trapped at anchor. The final attack wave of Dutch MTBs also amounted to little. The Allied ships could have, and probably should have, done much more. They had been simply outfought by the Japanese navy.

Nevertheless, as the *Stewart* sailed away, damaged but afloat and still capable, Alford felt and saw the pride of the men in the ship swell. Their morale once again "went sky high."[25] They had been bloodied, losing one man killed and three wounded, but had stood tall and slugged it out with the Japanese. "We hung in there and took it to them," Alford wrote with excitement.[26]

The *Stewart* required some fairly extensive repair work upon reaching Surabaya, so the decision was made to put her in a 15,000-ton lift floating dry dock owned by a private shipyard. While the water was being pumped clear of the dry dock and her crew set out to beg for and borrow spare parts and tools, Lieutenant Commander Smith called a conference of the ship's officers in the wardroom. Their discussion had just started when Alford and the officers felt the ship tip suddenly to port beneath them. The men were thrown against the port side of the wardroom and they scrambled to get out, rather indignantly hanging onto lifelines on the slanted decks as the destroyer leaned against the dry dock's walls at a 37-degree list. The dry dock's bilge blocks had been improperly fastened and the side supporters had broken, unable to carry the entire load. The *Stewart* had slipped down along the stocks and seen her hull plating punctured in several places. Both engine rooms now had leaks, and two fuel tanks were spilling oil. She looked like a "beached whale," wrote one observer. "The air became blue around little knots of crewmen," the Americans' curses and shouts aimed at the Dutch and the Javanese both.[27] Lieutenant Commander Smith stared at his destroyer, broken-hearted. She deserved better.[28] Though some suspected sabotage from the Javanese dockworkers, they were more likely accustomed to the flat-bottomed hulls of merchant ships and not the slim, curved underwater hulls of Navy destroyers and had improperly set the ship. Estimates for the time it would take to repair her ranged from one month to three. There was no time for that: air raids on the harbor had already started, and a Japanese invasion of Java was imminent. "Things looked bleak," Alford wrote.[29] The *Stewart*'s crew was parceled out to the *John D. Edwards*, *Parrott*, and *Pillsbury*, and Alford for one feared the *Stewart* would be lost, though he took care to conceal his pessimism.

Frustrated and angry, the men took time to lay to rest their dead shipmate, Seaman Eugene R. Stanley, a sailor Alford described as "one of the finest young men I have ever known—neat, clean-cut, friendly, likable, smart."[30] They took his body to the Kembang-Koenig Cemetery onshore, where he was buried in a common grave next to men from the Dutch light cruiser *Tromp*. Alford stood with his shipmates, not ashamed of the tears he shed.

The day after the mishap, the American and British combined military chiefs dissolved the whole of ABDA command. At 1330 on February 22, it was decided that the *Stewart* would be abandoned where she lay, tilted and forlorn. It was a necessary decision so as not to sacrifice her crew as prisoners of war, but a "terrible and gut-wrenching" one nonetheless.[31] She would be left to the Japanese. Alford and her crew removed her ammunition, stores, and vital equipment and gathered their personal gear and belongings, using mattress covers as sea bags and raking everything off desks and out of drawers, their feet unsteady in the sharp list. Demolition crews rigged her with high explosives, to be set off later. Alford was forced to leave behind his record player and good collection of jazz records. The crew moved with urgency, knowing the city and the entire island would not last much longer. They split up and boarded the other three American ships nearby, Alford climbing on board the *Parrott*, on which his Academy classmate Obie Parker, USNA '38, was stationed. As the *Parrott* pulled away from the dock, Alford cast one long, last look at his ship, lying ingloriously askew in the dry dock.

The *Parrott*, together with the *Pillsbury*, steered east toward Tjilatjap. The next few days, Alford wrote, would be the most terrifying of his life.

LEON WILLIAM ROGERS

Washington, DC

"Reveille already! What this place needs is longer sleeping hours." Awake, Lee conserves energy with a prize-winning efficiency. He is probably the only Midshipman that has walked to all formations. A lazy stride gets him places with minimum effort. With a mild interest, Lee views sports, academics, and current news. With a quickened interest, he views an apple. Apples, you see, are his weakness. For Lee there are no secret ambitions; he wants to become a naval officer. He has a fathomless reserve of good nature that makes friends of all who know him and keeps them. He will laugh at your jokes, stand your week-end watches, or give you his last cigarette. One can have no better friend. Happy voyages, Shipmate!

The Lucky Bag, 1938

Chapter Eight

A MATTER OF SURVIVAL

On Monday, February 23, as the *Parrott* approached the Sunda Strait, Alford watched a large force of Allied warships sail past him in the direction of the Java Sea. The ships were rumored to be heading for a rendezvous with a Dutch strike force, after which the combined group would seek out and attack yet another Japanese invasion fleet believed heading to the area. Among them were two warships of particular interest to Alford, the USS *Houston* and the USS *Pope*. On board both were Academy classmates of his.

Allied intelligence had earlier indicated that there were potentially two Japanese invasion fleets charging south toward Java at that moment. For the Dutch, losing Java was unthinkable. The Royal Netherlands Navy had been pushed as far back as they would go. They would retreat no more. To their Allied partners, the Dutch position, while both tactically and strategically unsound, was not difficult to understand. Not only was Java the heart of Dutch possessions in the South Seas, with its vast oil deposits, numerous refineries, and administrative and industrial working centers, but many of those in the Dutch Navy also had wives and children and homes on the island. Allowing any Japanese invasion force to land there was unthinkable. Nevertheless, the outlook for their intended last stand off Java's coast was, as historian Theodore Roscoe described it, "dead black."[1]

The strike force, in addition to the *Houston* and *Pope*, comprised the Dutch cruisers *De Ruyter* and *Java*, the Australian light cruiser *Perth*, the Dutch destroyers *Kortenaer* and *Witte de With*, the U.S. ships *Alden*, *John D. Edwards*, *John D. Ford*, and *Paul Jones*, and an assortment of

British cruisers and destroyers. The men were worn down, and the strain of the past few weeks was beginning to tell in the haggard features and taut nerves of the sailors.[2] Yet with this force lay the Royal Netherlands Navy's last and best hope of staving off the Japanese.[3] The strike force, commanded once again by the luckless Admiral Karel Doorman, turned eastward in the Java Sea before sailing along the north coast of Madura Island and making a large westward sweep of the area, hunting enemy transports from dusk till dawn. On the morning of February 27, a Friday, Doorman turned the formation back again toward the harbor at Surabaya and some much-needed rest for his men. At 1430, however, an aircraft reconnaissance report jolted Doorman back into action with its sighting of an enemy fleet with transports near the Bawean Islands, not one hundred miles north, and he promptly set his ship on a new course to the northwest at twenty-five knots. There was no time to devise a plan; Doorman simply sent a message to the ships behind him: "Am proceeding to intercept enemy unit. Follow me."[4] The prospect of action was immediate, and it quickened the pulses of the officers and crews. But the Japanese knew the Allies were coming, having been alerted by their own scout planes that were radioing back Doorman's positions.

The *Houston* was a 10,000-ton cruiser whose keel had been laid at the Newport News Shipbuilding and Dry Dock Company on May 1, 1928. She was subsequently launched in September 1929. Prior to the war she had been one of President Franklin Roosevelt's favorite ships; on more than one occasion he had observed fleet maneuvers from her bridge, and he liked to use her for his regular fishing expeditions. When the war started the *Houston* had been docked on the island of Panay in the Philippines and, earlier that February, had been bombed by twenty-seven enemy planes in the Flores Sea while part of a striking force bound for the Makassar Strait. When the ship reached Tjilatjap on February 5, the crew had gathered all available lumber in town and built forty-eight coffins through the night for their dead, laid out on the fantail and covered in canvas. The next day the men had carried the bodies through the hot town's streets, sarong-clad natives watching from the sidewalks, the ship's band playing the dirge, and buried them in a Dutch cemetery that looked out over the sea.[5]

The *Houston* went to General Quarters at 1535 on the afternoon of February 27, and Doorman's Allied force made contact with the onrushing Japanese fleet at about 1615: one of the British destroyers in the flotilla's van reported two heavy cruisers to starboard, part of Rear Admiral Takeo Takagi's 5th Cruiser Division. The Japanese ships opened fire two minutes later at an extreme range of nearly 29,000 yards. For Doorman, meeting any ships before the transports were sighted was terrible news, but of course, because of his aerial scouts, Takagi had known where Doorman's ships were, had known their speed and course, had known where to position his transports to keep them safe, and had known where to take his cruisers and destroyers to meet the Allies at a point on the sea most advantageous to him. Soon the British light cruiser *Electra*, also in the van, reported another enemy force of one light cruiser and several Japanese destroyers bearing 330 degrees, hulls down and heading toward them from over the northern horizon. Both groups of Japanese ships appeared bent on crossing the "T" of the Allied force, for centuries a decisive tactic in naval warfare, so Doorman chose a port turn to eliminate this tactical advantage while continuing to bring the enemy vessels closer, within range of his cruisers' broadsides of 6-inch guns. Soon a third enemy sighting was reported: a "forest" of masts also on the northern horizon.[6] At first they were thought to be the hoped-for Japanese transports, but, cruelly for the Allies, it quickly became apparent they were another force of six Japanese destroyers and the four-stack light cruiser *Naka*, heading south at high speed to line up a favorable position for a torpedo attack on Doorman and his ships.

The initial group of approaching Japanese cruisers continued their fire, followed at 1633 by other onrushing IJN destroyers carrying deadly Long Lance torpedoes. The British destroyers out ahead met the Japanese attacks first, responding with their own deck guns, but both groups of ships were still firing at extreme ranges, and no hits were scored. The Japanese cruisers adjusted their salvos and soon began to straddle the British vessels and the other Allied ships behind them, dyed plumes of water mushrooming from the sea. The Japanese, excellent gunners, were further aided by their spotter planes still loitering above.

Even so, the *Houston*'s opening salvo of the fight also struck close, with the foretop spotter calling "no change" in the range. She had the biggest guns in the Allied strike force and targeted the Japanese light cruisers about two points off her starboard bow. Her gun blasts tore her crews' steel helmets off their heads and sent them rolling along the deck. The *Houston*'s sixth salvo was a straddle, and she drew the engagement's first blood with her tenth, hitting a cruiser second in line in one of the Japanese attack columns sailing toward them, blowing up one of her forward turrets, sparking fires amidships, and sending the cruiser scurrying from the line behind a thick smoke screen (she would later return to the battle). The Japanese salvos were now concentrating on the first two big ships in the Allied column, the RNN *De Ruyter* and the HMS *Exeter*, and the *Houston*, despite the accuracy of her shooting, was initially ignored by the Japanese, allowing her to keep firing unhindered. Eventually though, straddles blossomed to port and starboard of her, indicating the Japanese had the range, and the *Houston* and the nearby *Perth* quickly came under concentrated attack. They were not the only ones. Soon both the *De Ruyter* and the *Exeter* were hit, and the *Houston* was struck twice, though by a pair of duds that did little damage save to cut the TBS radio, eliminating her communications link with Doorman. The U.S. destroyers on the port quarter of the column watched the battle unfold before them "goggle-eyed," yet puzzled at Doorman's tactics.[7] He seemed to have forgotten that the American destroyers were there, and the Allied column as a whole was zigzagging with no plan, simply mimicking the motions of the *De Ruyter* ahead as it repeatedly changed course every ten or fifteen minutes without signaling.

At 1713 the first real blood of the engagement was drawn. The Dutch destroyer *Kortenaer*, slowed by a bad boiler and desperately trying to change stations, was struck by a Japanese long-range torpedo in a tremendous explosion that sent debris one hundred feet into the air and caused her to turn bottom up, break in two, and sink beneath the burbling water in a mere two minutes. The *Houston* sailed by the *Kortenaer* as she went down about three thousand yards off her starboard bow. Sailors on the *Houston*'s rails reported seeing a man hanging onto the slowly turning port screw as the vessel sank, but no survivors were spotted in the water after the green and gray ship disappeared.

All was confusion, for Doorman in overall command of the Allied fleet and for individual ship captains too. A torpedo passed within feet of the U.S. destroyer *John D. Ford*. Heavy smoke screens obscured the ships ahead and behind. The sea was thick with oil and debris. There were reports of Japanese submarines in the area, also firing their fish. Signaling between ships often had to be done via flashing lights. Enemy bombers arrived over the battle and were diving on the Allied fleet, adding their bombs to the madness. Fuel bunkers were running low on some of the Allied destroyers. The sun was going down.

Doorman ordered the British destroyers to counterattack, and they raced forward to meet a squadron of Japanese destroyers lining up for torpedo runs. At 1730 the British destroyers *Electra* and *Encounter* emerged from a smoke screen to find themselves at point-blank range from seven enemy cruisers. *Electra* scored hits, but she was pummeled in return and soon reduced to a flaming wreck. She sank at about 1800. The *Encounter* ducked back into the smoke from which she had come as the Allied cruisers used their heavy guns to push the Japanese back, three salvos striking with loud explosions. While the *Houston* and the other cruisers re-formed, Doorman finally ordered the four restless American destroyers into the fight at 1806.

But the order was quickly canceled, and what followed has been the source of much investigation and criticism in the war's aftermath. At the time, the conflicting communication only heightened the confusion. Doorman sent a message that, as Lodwick Alford described it, was variously interpreted as "Follow me," "I am going to attack—follow me," and "Cover my retirement."[8] His intention was to break contact, head south, then turn back in the dark that evening and launch a high-speed surprise attack on the Japanese troopships.[9] But unaware of what Doorman had in mind, the commodore of the American destroyer fleet chose to press on with his torpedo launches, as his column of ships was now in between the American and Japanese cruiser battle lines, his men were spoiling for a fight, and, absent clear instructions, he reasoned that a torpedo attack by his destroyers was the most effective way to cover Doorman and the best contribution he could make to the battle. So Commander Thomas Binford led his American destroyer force northwest at twenty-eight knots to close the range with the enemy cruisers, about 22,000 yards away to starboard. Their objective was to sink the ships, if possible, but to distract and dissuade the Japanese captains at the very least, and the sailors on board the American destroyers "lay to their tasks with enthusiasm."[10] The batteries of the Japanese cruisers soon opened on them, but the U.S. destroyers were low in the water and presenting small silhouettes and were therefore devilish to hit. Enemy bombers made runs on them from the air trying to break up their attack, but the destroyer force pressed on. Binford signaled at 1817 for a starboard torpedo salvo once the range with the Japanese had been shortened to ten thousand yards, and after firing he quickly changed course so that the destroyers could all fire their portside spreads. Again no hits were scored, probably due to malfunctions in the torpedoes, but it was a classic destroyer combat maneuver nonetheless, and one executed masterfully. In the growing darkness Binford rejoined the Allied cruisers east of him and withdrew.

The Japanese pursued them. By 1930 enemy ships were sighted on the striking force's port beam, well in the distance. The Japanese were sailing parallel and keeping pace, and the planes in the sky reported back the Allies' every move. Doorman tried to shake the enemy ships but turns in the darkness to the east and again to the southeast were spotted by the Japanese aircraft. The enemy cruisers fired star shells and probed the distant water with their searchlights in hopes of sighting the Allied fleet, but Doorman and his ships stayed just out of range. At 2008 Doorman changed course again to due south and the ships sighted the moonlit mountains of Java about an hour later. Doorman released the four American destroyers and sent them back to Surabaya to refuel and rearm, but he was still intent on attacking the Japanese transports and keeping them away from the island, so later that night he turned north again with the *Houston* and the rest of his bigger ships with enough fuel to fight, steaming toward the Japanese cruisers that had been shadowing them.

Before they could get far, they were again spotted by the circling scout planes who dropped flares on top of their masts, and Takagi moved his ships in to engage. The *Nachi* and *Haguro* opened up with star shells and flares, followed by gunfire that straddled the *Houston* on either side of her fantail, then both Japanese cruisers launched a spread of torpedoes, their lethal Long Lances. Unlike the Americans' torpedoes, those of the Japanese worked well, but it was not just the cruisers' torpedoes that tormented the Allied ships so thoroughly. At 2332 the Dutch light cruiser *Java* was hit by a torpedo fired from a submarine and "was almost instantly enveloped in flames and dead in the water."[11] According to the *Houston*'s War Diary, it "seemed as though her whole foc'sle exploded. . . . There followed several [more] with each one looking like fireworks on July 4th."[12] Not two minutes later another torpedo struck the *De Ruyter*, exploding her magazines "with a mighty thunderclap" that, for a moment, lit up the seascape and set her alight from stem to stern.[13] The *Houston* was forced to swerve sharply to avoid colliding with her. The ships had run straight into the middle of a Japanese submarine nest. The *Java* sank twenty minutes later; only nineteen of her crew would survive. The HMS *Jupiter* was then torpedoed several miles astern of the *Houston*; the Americans saw the flash on the water. She sent the message "Am Torpedoed" and was never seen again. The *De Ruyter* burned for two hours before she went under at 0100. She suffered an appalling loss of life, including Admiral Doorman himself. The Dutchman's final message to the strike force's last survivors, the *Houston* and the Australian cruiser *Perth*, was to make no effort to pick up survivors but to head west to Batavia's port, Tanjung Priok. It was a brutal order and a dastardly business. As she was breaking away, the *Houston* sailed through "clouds" of swimming sailors who were blowing whistles and shouting at the cruiser from their life rafts amid the debris fields.[14] The *De Ruyter* burned fiercely behind them, lighting the darkness like a pyre.

The loss of the two Dutch cruisers eliminated whatever rationale the U.S. Navy's Asiatic Fleet had to stay in the area and fight. The fracas, to be called the Battle of the Java Sea, was a ghastly defeat, accomplishing little and leading to the deaths and capture of thousands. The Royal Netherlands Navy was beaten, and Java and her Dutch civilians would soon be faced with a Japanese invasion that could no longer be stopped. For the U.S. Navy's ships in the area, and whatever scattered remnants of the former ABDAFLOAT still sailed, the matter was now strictly one of survival, the mission purely about getting out of the death trap that the Java Sea had become. But exits were few. The Japanese controlled all outlets to the north. The Bali Strait, east of Java, offered the quickest route out into the Indian Ocean and safe passage to Australia, but the water was too shallow for the cruisers. They had to find another way free.

At 1430 on the afternoon of February 28 the *Houston* and the *Perth*, speeding at twenty-eight knots and zigzagging without any real plan, arrived in bomb-battered Batavia, where they refueled, shifted ammunition, repaired sprung plates, and welded patches onto the holes in their decks. The *Houston*'s skipper, Captain Albert H. Rooks, met with his counterpart on the *Perth*, and the two discussed their dwindling options. The Dutch reported Sunda Strait was clear, but Leon Rogers, his Academy classmate Hal Hamlin, and the rest of the ships' crews were worn out. They had had little to no rest over the last seventy-two hours, and many were already being treated in the sick bays. Seventy cases of heat exhaustion had decimated the ranks of the *Houston*'s engineering personnel alone.[15] Yet Japanese troops were even then coming ashore, some as close as forty miles away, so the men rested only briefly before departing for destinations unknown at 2000 that night, the pair of ships leaving through a quartering sea as the sun set.

It was a windless evening, clear except for a smattering of clouds and a full moon. The men on the *Houston* watched the "restful" green of the Java coast, thick with coconut and banana palms, slide by and disappear behind them.[16] They all wondered how they could get through the Sunda Strait, as Japanese cruiser planes were shadowing them even then, droning in the distance. What luck did they have left? The ship cruised in darkness, her heavy metal battle ports bolted shut and all interior lights extinguished.[17] She and the *Perth* sailing ahead soon passed the Toppers Island light off their starboard bows at 2315 before quickly sighting other ships in the night, which the *Perth* challenged, believing them to be an expected escort of Dutch patrol vessels. Instead, a Japanese destroyer responded with a red starburst and sped away making smoke, and the two Allied ships instantly went to General Quarters and opened fire on the vessel from five hundred yards.

What resulted was a melee, savage and sudden.[18] The *Houston* and *Perth* had stumbled across a Japanese force of at least three heavy cruisers and a swarm of destroyers (perhaps as many as nine) covering a landing operation on a nearby beach, and soon the *Houston*'s guns were engaged on all sides as she ducked behind the *Perth* to maneuver, her searchlights swinging wildly, the Japanese cruisers and destroyers flashing in and out of the beams. The *Houston* herself was quickly caught in the glare of three searchlights, Japanese destroyers lighting her up for the heavy cruisers to destroy, and the Americans tried desperately to shoot the lights out. The *Houston*'s main battery fired, then the 5-inch guns, then the 1.1s on the communications deck, and the .50-caliber machine guns up high in the foremast and mainmast, sending tracers zipping over the water. Both Allied ships tried swinging to starboard to break free.

The *Perth* was struck first, torpedo blasts leaving the Australian ship dead in the water before Japanese shells sent her under; she kept up her fire even as she sank. The first major hit the *Houston* sustained was a salvo

A Japanese painting of the attack on the USS *Houston*, 1942

in the after engine room that burst steam lines and immediately killed all of the men there. Another shell hit her forecastle deck and set the paint locker aflame. Others hit turrets 1 and 2, and three torpedoes struck both sides of the ship. Leon Rogers was at his battle station above turret 2 when it was hit. Flames surrounded him, but he continued to train the fire from his battery for as long as he was able. The ship lost power. Live steam hissed from the two boat deck exhausts. More fires raged belowdecks near sick bay and the brig, as well as on deck near the life jacket lockers, the marine compartment, and near the navigating bridge. The shell hoists lost power, so the *Houston* fired her machine guns and 5-inch guns until all the ammunition was expended. Finally, frantically, she fired her star shells as surface ammunition at the enemy ships that swirled in and out of the searchlights around her. All remaining communications systems were quickly overloaded "with reports of damage received, of approaching torpedoes, of new enemy attacks begun, of changes in targets engaged."[19] As the *Houston*'s firing decreased and her maneuverability was lost, lurking Japanese destroyers grew bolder, approached closer, and fired faster. Captain Rooks was fatally injured when a shell hit the communications deck passageway as he ran down from the bridge to get a look at the No. 2 turret; a Japanese destroyer killed scores of men when it raked the quarterdeck and port hangar with machine-gun fire. Very soon the *Houston* was completely encircled by enemy ships on all offshore bearings. Extensive damage had been suffered forward of the quarterdeck. The bridge was wrecked and the conning tower abandoned due to the heat from nearby flames. Slowly the ship listed to starboard, lost steerageway, and stopped. The order to abandon ship was passed down at 0025 over the battle telephone systems still in operation and the general announcing system. The "Galloping Ghost of the Java Coast" was lost.

When the first order to abandon ship was issued, Leon Rogers' classmate Hal Hamlin, USNA '38, was near turret 1, which by that time was already flooded and abandoned.[20] The men around him were forced to quickly extinguish a fire in the locker before they could pass out life jackets and go over the side. Hamlin stayed on the forecastle until the list of the ship underneath him increased to about 30 degrees, at which time he and four other men abandoned her over the port bow, the last to leave the forecastle. Around him, what men there were still alive clung to rafts, life jackets, shell casings, mattresses, and any other debris able to support their tired bodies.

From the oily warm water, Hamlin watched the *Houston* as she was hit one final time portside; the blow caused the ship to roll to her starboard beam, her yardarms dipping into the sea while the American flag still flew from the mainmast. The *Houston* would sink at about 0045 on the morning of March 1, approximately eight miles northeast of the Saint Nicholas Point Light. She sank slowly enough to allow many other unwounded men to get over the side.

Leon Rogers went into the water from the port side of the boat deck.[21] He started swimming in his life jacket for an island he spotted in the distance before, after two hours, joining a group of shipmates on a life raft and helping to paddle it in the direction of the Java coast. They faced a severe current and made slow progress. An hour before sunrise they spied Japanese ships on a course that would bring them very close by, so Rogers left the raft, thinking he could make shore before the ships came near. About two hundred yards from the beach, however, he realized why the ships were in the area: the Japanese were landing troops on the shore in front of him. Afraid he would trudge from the water into a battle, Rogers gave up trying to swim closer, lay back, and allowed himself to drift with the current through the anchored ships, sometimes floating within fifty yards of them. Amazingly, he passed through the clump unmolested and, when clear, spotted three other rafts from the *Houston* loaded with sailors and drifting on the sea. Rogers found the currents too strong to swim to any of the other nearby islands, so he joined one of the rafts where bedraggled survivors were using pieces of wreckage to paddle, and together they stroked their way to a Javanese beach thirteen miles south of the Anjer Kidoel light.

Hal Hamlin also began swimming for an island he could see in Bantam Bay. When he reached it, he found no habitation but came across other knots of men from the ship. They waited for about an hour before spying a landing boat approaching. The men split up, with some running inland and others, like Hamlin, trying to escape back into the sea. He did not make it far, however, and was captured while attempting to cross the beach. Hamlin was taken out to a nearby enemy merchant transport on which a regiment of Japanese sailors was stationed, arriving on board before sunrise. He was questioned extensively but treated well and given food and clothing. Two days later, he was transferred to the *Somedong Maru*, a transport on which he found ten more survivors of the *Houston* and roughly two hundred other assorted English and Australian sailors. The men waited six days until they were brought ashore, loaded onto motor trucks, and sent to Serang, where the group was locked in the local jail.

Leon Rogers and the men he had come ashore with slept in a native village that night, given water by the occupants but no food or dry clothing. In the morning they walked south for the town of Labuhan, along the way meeting up with several other *Houston* survivors and Australian sailors from the *Perth* at Tjarita. Pony carts were ferrying men to the town in shifts of four, and Rogers climbed on board one at 1400. The locals in the area soon grew agitated, however, muttering, "Japan was coming," and their nervous driver made Rogers and the others with him get off the cart before they reached the town.[22] They found another large group of Australian sailors along the road and sat in the dirt to decide what to do. Soon word reached them that the natives in Labuhan were "rioting," refusing to give the Allied sailors who had so suddenly and unexpectedly flooded the town all morning any food or places to rest. Rogers' group ultimately headed off to the inland town of Menes, where they believed they could find supplies and get directions to the Dutch army's campsite.

Progress was slow. The men were weak, the roads were blocked by fallen logs every twenty yards that had to be climbed, and the party began to spread apart and "straggle out."[23] Rogers reached Menes at 1000 on March 3 to find the city abandoned by the Dutch and looted by the natives. Exhausted, he slept in an empty hospital for a time and then started walking to Pandeglang, where the Dutch army was rumored to be establishing new lines. Along the road Rogers watched the natives hang Japanese flags from their homes and motion the Allied sailors along, murmuring, "Don't stop here."[24] With no shoes, weapons, maps, or friendly guides, the weary men knew they were in no position to try for the surrounding hills.

They had to stick to the roads. The men straggled apart again, and Rogers, now stumbling down the roadway with one Australian seaman, decided he would turn himself in to the first Japanese soldier he saw. On the outskirts of Pandeglang that evening, natives put them in another horse cart and rolled the two men to the local jail, where a Japanese flag fluttered over the front door. More survivors were brought in over the next few hours, and the men were kept there for seven days, other prisoners joining them throughout the week. They were given thin straw mats to sleep on, cotton shirts and shorts, and cold water, along with small bowls of rice and greens to eat. Covered wooden tubs served as toilets. They were allowed to walk in the stone-walled prison yard each morning and afternoon. Japanese soldiers stopped by intermittently for inspections but did not stay long, leaving the jail's operation to the local natives, whose treatment of the men was tolerable. Rogers joined Hamlin in the Serang jail on March 11.

Approximately 350 of the 1,008 officers and men of the USS *Houston* escaped the ship's sinking and were later captured. The U.S. Navy would not learn of the ship's fate, or what had happened to her crew, for another nine months. Only 266 would survive the prison camps and the years of abuse, forced labor, and depredations that followed.

When Leon Rogers first reached the *Houston* in September 1941, he had written his parents a letter. Among his musings: "It looks like a pretty dull routine, but I don't mind that, as the only thing I am interested in is getting back. . . . So now I am settling down to a long, long wait."[25]

That wait would be terribly long.

WILLIAM OSCAR SPEARS JR.

Chattanooga, Tennessee

Bill came to Navy via military school and Severn Prep. With him he brought his own motto of "Never do today that which you can put off till the day after tomorrow." A less talented man would have bilged long ago, but Bill rarely has trouble with mental specters. Navy's white hope in high jumping, he finds plenty of time to show the boys how Culbertson plays bridge. Willie is no snake, but he has such a pleasant disposition that he never says "no" to a classmate's entreaty to drag blind. Worlds of success to you, Bill, and here's hoping we are shipmates again when we reach the Fleet.

The Lucky Bag, 1938

Chapter Nine

GUARDIAN ANGELS

The destroyer USS *Pope* attempted its escape from the Java Sea in company with the wounded British cruiser *Exeter* and the destroyer HMS *Encounter*. By then the *Pope* had earned a reputation as a fighting ship, having performed well at the Battle of Balikpapan and during a scrape in the Lombok Straits. She and her crew had come through both fights unscathed. Some even considered her "charmed."[1] The three ships departed Surabaya on the evening of February 28 with orders to try for Colombo, on Ceylon (now Sri Lanka), in the Indian Ocean. Their plan was to sail during the daylight toward Borneo's southern coast, hoping to avoid any Japanese scout planes and, once the sun set, to make a run westward for the Sunda Strait.[2]

The plan fell apart early on March 1, a sunny day with a calm sea, light swell, and little wind. They were spotted by Japanese scout planes, which had bedeviled the Allied ships' escape attempts from the beginning. Once Admiral Takeo Takagi of the Imperial Japanese Navy learned where they were, he immediately gave chase. At 0730, while the three-ship column sailed on its westerly leg, the *Exeter* made first contact with an enemy flotilla of two heavy cruisers and a large destroyer. Lookouts reported the pagoda masts of the Japanese warships bearing down on them from the south-southwest. On the *Pope* the men left their breakfasts and sprinted to their battle stations. The *Exeter*'s captain, O. L. Gordon, signaled for a turn southwestward, but his course change helped little. The Japanese turned to match his course and launched more planes from their catapults to keep an eye on the Allied ships from above. In the dazzling sun there was nowhere on the sea for the Allies to hide. They were "as exposed as a caravan in mid-desert."[3] Captain Gordon ordered a northwesterly course change, but escape in that direction was blocked by more onrushing Japanese ships, this time the flagship group of Vice Admiral Ibo Takahashi, including two more heavy cruisers and another three destroyers. The Allied ships found themselves massively outgunned, out in the open, and quickly out of options.

The gunfire engagement started at 0935. Quickly the *Pope*, *Exeter*, and *Encounter* launched their portside torpedoes at Takagi's initial group and their remaining torpedoes at the reinforcing enemy ships that were approaching on their starboard beams. Hits were scored, and to Bill Spears, USNA '38, in charge of firing the torpedoes, it looked as though one of the Japanese cruisers was sunk. The Japanese fired back with their guns and Captain Gordon quickly made smoke and turned the three ships on a radical course change due east, intending to make a run along the Borneo coast. But IJN ships were everywhere, even then flying down through Makassar Strait, steaming between Celebes and Bali, and blocking Karimata Strait to the west with the aircraft carrier *Ryujo*. Gordon's group was trapped, and their eastward run bought them nothing but an hour. The Japanese were sailing faster and Takahashi's cruisers eventually overhauled the Allies, closing the range to 14,000 yards. Despite more smoke and salvos fired off the *Exeter*'s stern, the Japanese gunners were aided by their spotter planes and their shells hit the *Exeter* from the start.

At 1100 puffy clouds and rain squalls popped up east of the three Allied ships, and Gordon ordered his engineers to "pour on the coal."[4] It was a race they could not win, however. The *Exeter* was the first to be reeled in. Japanese destroyers drove in on her starboard beam, and though *Pope* and *Encounter* fired their guns in support to try to ward them off, the duel was one-sided. Quickly a shell blew apart the *Exeter*'s boiler room in a cloud of smoke and she slowed to four knots, then went dead in the water. Gordon ordered the *Pope* and *Encounter* to keep going as his now wallowing ship was struck again and again by Japanese shells and "murderous fans" of torpedoes.[5] Eighteen of them were fired at the *Exeter*, the last striking just after Gordon ordered his crew to abandon ship into the oil she was leaking. That last blow caused the British cruiser to capsize quickly and go down at about 1140. The *Encounter* lasted a few minutes longer: she quickly received her own fatal hit, a strike most likely to her ammunition magazine, and sank in a mass of smoke and flame not far from where the *Exeter* had slipped beneath the surface.

The *Pope* found herself alone on the water, now the last Allied ship afloat on the Java Sea. According to the historian Theodore Roscoe, "No ship in World War II or any war [before] was in a situation worse than that of this old 'four-piper' cornered in the sea below Borneo, with cannon to the right of her; cannon to the left of her; her crew ready to drop from exhaustion; her torpedoes expended; her nearest safe haven, Australia, a thousand miles to the east."[6] As Lieutenant Commander W. C. Blinn, her captain, wrote in beautifully understated fashion, "Her operations . . . had been such as to engender considerable psychological tension."[7]

But Blinn refused any talk of surrender, and according to Roscoe, the crew had full confidence in him. They were ready to "sweat it out and slug it out—to hell with the odds!"[8] For a moment it seemed as though the *Pope* might survive. She drove closer to the rain squalls, opaque on the approaching seascape, and Blinn ordered his engineers to squeeze every possible turn out of the engines as he blanketed the ocean astern with more smoke. Geysers from Japanese shells blossomed around them, but none hit, and the *Pope* flew into the safety of the squall's clouds and darkness, where they caught a thirty-minute breather. The Japanese faded away behind them. With the break the men rushed more ammunition to the handling rooms and ready boxes and performed quick emergency repairs in the dark cloud bank's rain. Soon the *Pope* emerged from the storm, spotted another in the distance, raced through the sun to it, and disappeared into the safety of rain clouds once again. Captain Blinn allowed himself to hope. Perhaps they could continue to elude the Japanese eastward along the Borneo coast and then, at night, race south through Lombok Strait.

But the second rain squall dissipated quickly, once again leaving the *Pope* beneath a merciless "noonday sky of tropic blue" and Japanese cruiser-carried spotter planes.[9] The pilots radioed their sightings, and very soon six dive-bombers from the carrier *Ryujo* to the west answered.

They arrived on the scene to dive-bomb the *Pope* at 1230. The Americans initially held the planes off with a single 3-inch antiaircraft gun, but it eventually jammed, leaving the ship's gunners with nothing for defense save their .50-caliber machine gun, which had little chance against the fast and diving Vals. Blinn had a seaman lie on his back with a pair of binoculars and call out when the planes dropped their bombs. The Japanese pilots made run after run, most of their bombs splashing harmlessly into the sea as Blinn turned aggressively. On the eleventh dive-bomb attack, a near miss damaged the *Pope* port side aft, punching a hole beneath the waterline, springing seams, and flooding compartments. The port engine had to be shut down before its vibrations shook the ship to pieces. Her time was expiring quickly.

More Japanese planes arrived, this time a swarm of high-level bombers that made their runs at three thousand feet and showered the limping *Pope*, which by now was visibly settling into the water by the stern, her afterdecks already awash. The ship's damage control officer informed Blinn the flooding could not be slowed, so the captain passed the order to stand by to abandon ship. His officers raced to destroy code books and rigged critical instruments for destruction. The depth charges were dropped on

The USS *Pope* under attack, March 1, 1942

their "safe" settings. Other men prepared to scuttle the vessel by opening watertight doors and ports. Word was then passed to abandon ship and the sea cocks were opened, magazines flooded, and ten pounds of TNT blown in the engine room. To add to the finality of her destruction, a final 8-inch round from one of the Japanese cruisers then hit with a blast, and the ship sank behind a pall of smoke and steam within fifteen seconds, stern first, listing to starboard.

By then, Bill Spears and the rest of the officers and men on board had quit the ship in good order, taking their assigned places in the motor whaleboat, a damaged wherry, and in her cork rafts. What happened next was inglorious, on both sides. As the survivors of the *Pope*'s sinking sat in the water, a Japanese seaplane skimmed the motor whaleboat, prompting one American seaman to shoot at the plane with a Browning automatic. Other Japanese pilots in the air then took advantage of the seaman's rashness and raked the survivors with machine-gun fire for the next thirty minutes. Improbably, no one was killed during the strafing. Soon the whaleboat, the wherry, and the three life rafts linked up in the water, the wounded were moved to the whaleboat, and a muster was taken: only one man had been killed in the battle and the subsequent sinking. Blinn, Spears, and the other officers divided into six watches, and they scanned the sea for signs of an American submarine that might pick them up, as the captain had sent out messages about their plight during the attack.

For three days the survivors drifted. At one point, the men were able to get the whaleboat puttering toward Java, towing the other boat and rafts, but the fuel ran out at noon on the third day. They rigged a sail and the strongest of them paddled, but over time more and more of the crew grew too exhausted in the sun and the heat and they gave up their seats, able to do no more. No American submarine came, but a Japanese destroyer eventually approached over the dark horizon at 2230 on the third night, and all hands, including Bill Spears, were picked up. The men were sprayed with carbolic acid and searched, then taken prisoner.

The Japanese crew treated them professionally. They were given corned beef, chipped biscuits, and a sweet tea, and then, two days later, landed at Makassar City in the Celebes, where their treatment quickly deteriorated.

After nine days in a squalid native jail, the officers and men of the *Pope* were transferred to an old Dutch camp with survivors from the *Exeter* and the *Encounter*. Blinn, with the other captains, was sent on to Japan. For Spears, his years long suffering at the hands of the Japanese as a prisoner of war began.

There were other escapes to be attempted. On February 28, back in Surabaya, Lodwick Alford, USNA '38, was now on board the *Isabel* serving as first lieutenant and gunnery officer (ironically, on a ship with no guns) with his Academy classmate Marion Buaas, still serving as the yacht's executive officer, and they watched the doomed USS *Pope* and the British ships *Exeter* and *Encounter* sail out for their escape attempts. Other ships departed on various courses for safety throughout the day. The *Isabel*, however, sat camouflaged with bushes and palm fronds and moored along the east bank of the Kali Donan River, which flows into Tjilatjap harbor. She was the last Allied ship in the port, ordered to stay behind and pick up any stragglers or last remaining staff people, and her small crew were growing increasingly anxious by the minute as the necessary orders to leave failed to arrive. At any moment Alford, Buaas, and the others on board expected overflights from Japanese spy planes. They listened glumly throughout the long hours of the day as more bad news poured into the radio shack. They learned of the disappearances of the *Houston* and the *Perth*, lost out there somewhere, and of the enemy landings taking place on both ends of Java. They heard that the *Exeter, Encounter*, and *Pope* had all been run down and sunk. Alford wrote in his journal, "Japs raising hell everywhere."[10] There was a rumor that an enemy convoy was also headed their way. All the while, they waited.

Finally the *Isabel* received her orders, and shortly after 2100 on March 1 she slipped her moorings and cleared the minefields. There was bright moonlight, and the men knew the yacht potentially presented a pretty target for enemy submarines, perched as she was on the bright sea. Near 0030 lookouts on the yacht spotted a torpedo wake to port. With no time to take evasive action, the men held their breaths, scared out of their wits, until the fish passed under the bridge without exploding. The captain turned the yacht away from the torpedo's track and asked for top speed. In his journal Alford noted, "Have a hell of a gauntlet to run."[11]

Throughout March 2 the men on board "lived in mortal fear of bombers and warships with hardly anything to fight them with."[12] Alford had never been so scared in his life. At one point during the day, the captain called all hands to the main deck and gave the men a talk. He told them they could expect to be attacked at any time and that if they were going to be sunk, they were going to go down fighting, "throwing spuds at them if nothing else was available."[13] If they were desperate and it was possible, the captain told Alford, Buaas, and the men, then they would ram whatever Japanese ships attacked them. They were told to put their life jackets on and keep them on, and to collect all their valuables and protect them as best they could.

"God bless you all, and good luck."[14]

As Alford described it,

> There followed the most awful, terror-filled hours of my whole life before or since. . . . The doom we felt. . . . *Isabel* had no effective means of defense. . . . The tension that afternoon . . . was close to unbearable. Anyone who shouted, talked loud, or attempted a bit of humor was immediately glared at and cursed out the side of mouths drawn with anxiety. A slammed door was like a cannon shot signaling the start of death throes of *Isabel* and our last minutes of life on this earth. . . . I think I know now how a prisoner under death sentence feels as he sits in his cell waiting for guards to come and escort him to the electric chair. Darkness came as a reprieve.[15]

The *Isabel* made for the Indian Ocean. Perhaps because she was so small, the yacht was overlooked until 0900 on the morning of March 3, when a cruiser appeared in the distance on a course designed to intercept. Alford was officer of the deck at the time, and he climbed up into a high search platform on the foremast to get a better view. The ship looked Japanese, perhaps a cruiser of the *Mogami* class, and his heart stopped beating. Surely it was all over. But as Alford continued to look, he noticed something familiar on the cruiser—an airplane crane. That detail quickly reminded him of the American cruisers he had served on, and when the ship challenged them with a signal light, Alford responded with, "Don't shoot!" Across the water was the USS *Phoenix*, Alford's old home and a ship he had no idea was within ten thousand miles of the area.

"What a break! Oh, my Guardian Angel!" Alford remembered.[16]

The *Isabel* reached Fremantle on March 6. They had made it through the gauntlet of almost an entire Japanese fleet, with enough fuel left for one more hour of steaming. The mood of the crew improved even more when the *Parrott* steamed into the harbor later that day, carrying roughly one-third of Alford's shipmates from the *Stewart*, but they all waited in vain for the *Pillsbury*, which had disappeared. Later it was learned that the *Pillsbury* had been sunk on March 2 by two heavy Japanese cruisers due south of Bali Strait. She had been run down and smothered by the cruisers' concentrated 8-inch gunfire. Along with the thirty or so former members of the *Stewart* on board when she went down were two of Alford's classmates: Edmundo Gandia from Puerto Rico and Howard P. Fischer, who had been Alford's roommate during that long sail from San Francisco to Manila the previous autumn. Both men were killed. For Alford, learning of their deaths "was one of the most painful experiences of the war."[17]

1938
US NA

JAMES ALEXANDER MARKS

Washington, DC

Valedictorian of his class in high school and captain of Cadets, Jim entered the Academy with a high set of standards to which he has never been false. His wide range of talents and his infectious enthusiasm have made him a mainstay of the NA-10 as well as a savior of no mean order. In athletics his success has been only moderate—a shortcoming explained perhaps by his frequent attendance at hops. However, it is for his ability to bring a smile to even the most bewildered face at the end of a long steam drill and his unfailing willingness to let others benefit from his prowess at academics—especially Dago—that Jim is most valued as a classmate and a friend. With his willingness to work, his much appreciated ability to get the word, and his warm sense of humor, Jim is certain to meet with success in the fleet.

The Lucky Bag, 1938

Chapter Ten

IN IRONS

The Pacific Ocean is a massively tempestuous body of water, complex in its patterns, currents, and weather systems; staggering in its scale, depths, and dimensions; and terrifying in its power, energy, and capacity for violence. Storms there become enormous events that reduce even the most awesome fleets to messy, discombobulated things. Synchronization, formation, and order are lost, replaced by whatever the sea demands; and each vessel in a fleet, formerly part of something large and expansive, can be left to its own individual and terrifying struggle.

By October 1944, after the initial Japanese onslaughts of the war had been checked and the American air, land, and sea forces had begun their inexorable push toward Japan, General Douglas MacArthur's Sixth Army, with the Seventh Fleet under Vice Admiral Thomas C. Kinkaid supporting, prepared the next phase of its "island-hopping" campaign, this time from New Guinea to the centrally located Philippine island of Leyte, between Luzon to the north and Mindanao to the south. In response, the Japanese Imperial Army and Navy made their own preparations for one final attempt to destroy the American ships and push back MacArthur's invasion forces, and they eyed Leyte Gulf as their chosen battleground. At the same time, Admiral William F. Halsey, then in command of Third Fleet, was instructed to take his Task Force 38 (TF 38) west from the recently captured Ulithi Atoll and protect MacArthur's northern flank against any Japanese encroachments. In the same set of instructions, he was also told to destroy any enemy fleet in the area if such an opportunity presented itself—a somewhat ambiguous and conflicting set of orders, especially for Halsey, who chafed at having to "babysit" any movements by MacArthur.[1] He took his task force with its three aircraft carriers into the Philippine Sea near the San Bernardino Strait and watched for any approaching Japanese ships as MacArthur's men went ashore at Leyte Gulf on October 20. After ravaging an approaching group of Japanese battleships, cruisers, and destroyers on the 24th, Halsey waited for the Japanese carriers he felt must be behind them. Before long, his reconnaissance pilots spotted the prey, the Imperial Japanese Navy's last four attack aircraft carriers with their supporting vessels, sailing one hundred miles to the north on the Sibuyan Sea. It was just what Halsey was hunting for, a target he could not resist, and it was a glorious decoy. The Japanese carriers under the command of Admiral Jisaburo Ozawa had sailed into the area on a suicide mission to lure the Americans away. Halsey's eagerness to attack got the better of him and he quickly directed all of Third Fleet to give chase. Once his scout planes confirmed the Americans were pursuing, Ozawa reversed course, but Halsey continued his chase, letting himself be pulled hundreds of miles from his assigned position, through which an unseen Japanese force was even then charging to attack MacArthur's now wide-open northern flank. Only three small backup task groups left behind by Kinkaid stood between the onrushing Japanese ships and MacArthur's "certain destruction."[2]

It would be one of the most famous American actions of the war. Outgunned and outnumbered, these few American ships resisted with everything they had. All took hits and four were sunk, including an escort carrier, and over one thousand American sailors died, but their heroism was sufficient to beat back the Japanese fleet a mere forty miles from MacArthur's invasion force, and save his army. Halsey missed it all, having allowed himself to be duped.

A few weeks later, MacArthur prepared for the next phase of his operations, taking his army 250 miles north of Leyte to the small island of Mindoro, where he wished to construct an air base that could support his later landings on Luzon and where 250,000 seasoned Japanese troops bent on a last stand waited for him. MacArthur planned his invasion for December 15. Halsey once again was handed the responsibility of protecting MacArthur's invasion force, this time by staying close to the Philippine coast and striking targets in Manila, suppressing any land-based Japanese airpower in the Luzon area, and keeping the new "kamikazes" away from the Army's convoys and landing ships. He set out for this area of operations in early December, planning to refuel on December 17 and begin his air strikes two days later.

Sailing with Halsey's task force as it set out from Ulithi Lagoon on December 10 was the USS *Hull*, a *Farragut*-class double-stacked destroyer launched on January 31, 1934. She displaced 1,365 tons, was 341 feet long, and could be powered through the water by her twin screws at a springy thirty-six knots. Captain of her 160-man crew was Lieutenant Commander James Marks, USNA '38. It was his first combat command.

The *Farragut*-class destroyers were some of the smallest in the U.S. fleet and were therefore skippered by the most junior destroyer captains in the Navy. Aside from Marks, also taking *Farragut*-class destroyers out to sea with Halsey's task force were his Academy classmates Raymond Calhoun aboard the *Dewey*, Bill Rogers aboard the *Aylwin*, and Bruce Garrett aboard the *Monaghan*.

By that late stage of the war, the *Farragut*s were outdated warships, unable to match the firepower of the newer and more sophisticated destroyers being produced. The Navy had taken steps to modernize the *Farragut* class of ships by adding additional guns and torpedo tubes and, in the process, five hundred tons more deck weight than she had been designed for, and it was weight that was poorly distributed to boot. As such, the ships' abilities to remain on an even keel had been hampered, and her officers and crews knew it. "It was no secret among seamen . . . that certain classes of DDs, in particular the *Farragut*s, were prone to hazardous rolls."[3] Jim Marks, for instance, had had firsthand experience with these deficiencies when, during a test power run aboard the *Hull* in the calm waters of the Strait of Juan de Fuca near Washington State's Bremerton Navy Yard a few months prior, he had called for left full rudder at twenty-eight knots and 50,000 horsepower. The destroyer laid over dangerously and had to be slowly returned to an even keel with an immediate countermanding right full rudder.[4] Tests had also been conducted on both the *Dewey* and *Aylwin*, and their stability too had been found to be substantially reduced by the refits. The Navy's Bureau of Ships was informed of the tests but took no action to remedy the situation, nor did they express any serious concerns. All available destroyers were needed in the far reaches of the Western Pacific, thus the captains and crews of the *Farragut*s would just have to accept less than optimum stability and get on with it.

Since Jim Marks had taken command of the *Hull* three months earlier, morale on the ship had declined. Short and slight, handsome, with dark eyes and an olive complexion, the Washington, DC, native had spent most of the war ferrying convoys across the North Atlantic. Known as a very serious and strict interpreter of the rulebook, he possessed the qualifications to effectively skipper the *Hull*, but as historians Bob Drury and Tom Clavin wrote, "there lingered about Marks the scent of the pretender who had alienated the crew from the moment he'd toted his seabag up the gangway [back at Bremerton]."[5] He seemed to lack the more intangible characteristics of successful ship captains during the war. Marks forbade fraternization, even social conversation, between officers and enlisted men. He liberally canceled shore leaves for seemingly minor infractions and insisted on rigorously enforcing even the most mundane of regulations. He was quickly regarded as someone who was "not a sailor"—a serious insult.[6] Even before the vessel sailed, there were problems. More than a dozen crewmen jumped ship before the *Hull* left the Bremerton docks, tipped off by a Seattle fortune teller who predicted tragedy in the offing. Several more old-timers, recognizing the situation for what it was, picked fights and successfully got themselves tossed into the Pearl Harbor brig. They shed no tears when the destroyer pulled away from its pier and left them behind.

The nearby *Aylwin* had survived each of her previous engagements during the war without suffering a scratch. In her captain's chair was the Class of '38's Bill Rogers, from Haddonfield, New Jersey. Of medium build, with thinning hair and a sharp nose, Rogers was, like Marks, of a more formal and serious temperament, but whereas Marks seemed callow, Rogers had a reputation for being deliberate and prudent. He was regarded as a "man's man and a man's friend" by his roommates at the Academy and a good seaman and ship handler by his peers in the fleet.[7] Tough as a "sandbag" and smart, Rogers knew the *Farragut*s almost instinctively, having been aboard the USS *O'Brien* when she sank earlier in the war. The *Aylwin* was Rogers' first command.[8]

The role of the *Farragut*-class destroyers during Halsey's cruise would be to escort Captain Jasper Acuff's oiler task force and screen for enemy submarines by maintaining a circular net of overlapping sonar arcs that enveloped and protected the American oilers and tankers. It was difficult, unpleasant duty, requiring constant positioning that forced the small destroyers to make incessant high-speed runs, often against the wind, to keep pace with the larger ships. Remaining always on station was of the utmost importance if enemy submarines were to be detected and kept clear. But sailing in rough seas was much more comfortable aboard a large flattop or battleship. When the ocean kicked up and the carriers were moving fast and the small, low-to-the-water *Farragut*s were doing all they could to maintain their positions in the formation, they were forced to plow through waves and smash through troughs without slowing down, thrashing about like corks, bouncing over the crests with thunderous *bang*s that reverberated throughout the ships like hammer blows.

The destroyers left Ulithi and joined Acuff's Task Group (given the designation 30.8), consisting of about fifty tankers, hospital ships, ammunition haulers, fleet tugs, and jeep carriers. Acuff chose Rogers' *Aylwin* as his flagship, and the task group proceeded to a refueling rendezvous eight hundred miles to the northwest, where they would meet up with Halsey's much larger TF 38, numbering ninety-seven ships. These replenishment operations were critical to the success of Halsey's operations, as they enabled the carriers and their escorts to remain on station and conduct their air strikes for weeks at a time. Without Acuff's fuel and oil, everything would grind to a halt.

Despite its obvious importance, meteorology was not high on the U.S. Navy's list of priorities during World War II. In the early 1940s, weather-forecasting radar on American warships was rudimentary at best and not intended to allow for any sort of future projections; rather, it was used primarily to report current weather conditions only. What is more, reconnaissance planes that could be used for weather reporting and forecasting were always in short supply and needed for more immediate purposes, such as determining when and where enemy fleets were located. There were also natural features of Pacific storms that rendered even the most advanced radar and the most numerous reconnaissance patrols practically useless: typhoons did not follow directional patterns.[9] Therefore, even when storms were detected and even when wartime commodores and admirals were aware of their positions, understanding where they were headed in the next six hours, or the following day, or the subsequent week was exceedingly difficult, dangerous even, since "weather broadcasts in some cases may have been worse than no broadcasts at all."[10] Though the Navy's Fleet Weather Station at Pearl Harbor began receiving and collating hints of a potentially troublesome weather system developing in the far Pacific starting on December 11, no one was in much of a position to begin making serious recommendations about where it was headed that early. Combat operations in the Philippines continued apace.

By dawn on December 14, 1944, the escorting destroyers of Task Group 30.8, including the *Hull*, *Aylwin*, *Monaghan*, and *Dewey*, began refueling at sea from nearby oilers. At the same time, Halsey's TF 38, away to the west and about two hundred miles northeast of Manila, readied a series of heavy air-strike operations by its Hellcat dive-bombers and Avenger torpedo planes against Japanese targets on Luzon. MacArthur's invasion of Mindoro by Sixth Army went off as scheduled the next day. On the 16th, a Saturday, Halsey opted to withdraw his entire carrier strike force eastward to join Task Group 30.8 at their prearranged coordinates and refuel. Halsey wanted to renew his air strikes as quickly as possible; however, many of the destroyers that had sailed with him the last few days, offering constant protection for his flanks, were already critically low on fuel and riding high in the water, so he pulled away four hundred miles to the east into the Philippine Sea (well away from any kamikazes) to meet up with Acuff's oilers. Halsey would begin refueling operations the next day, and he radioed MacArthur that he would return as soon as possible for another three days of strikes on Luzon.

As his ships raced to refuel and he focused on finalizing plans for his follow-up attacks, Halsey's fleet meteorologist entered flag plot with information about a tropical disturbance developing to the east and moving north-northwest at roughly nine knots. The man was quick to tell Halsey that what he was tracking was "not necessarily a typhoon," but he did say that it was an "evil thing dedicated to death and destruction."[11] He was confident, however, that the storm would bounce away to the northeast. Satisfied, Halsey turned his attention back to what he considered the more pressing issues in front of him.

The meteorologist's name was Commander George Kosco. He was chief aerologist of Halsey's Third Fleet, and what he had been tracking had already been dubbed "Cobra." This particular storm had originated well to the east and subsequently slid through the doldrums, almost taking its time, before gliding across bathwater-warm seas and sucking up enough energy to sustain it. The barometric pressure dropped before it and nearby clouds moved into its center, slowly at first, then more rapidly, sending lightning arcing across the sky. The storm's cloud towers climbed higher and higher, and Cobra quickly grew beyond a mere tropical depression as it continued to increase in size and head toward Ulithi. Somewhere over the sea, Cobra stopped and loitered for a bit. It grew stronger, its circumference elongating, its winds picking up to between thirty and forty knots. Some gusts reached sixty-four knots. By December 16, the storm had morphed into a massive maelstrom, covering several hundred square miles and rising thousands of feet into the sky as it moved inexorably westward.

The U.S. Navy's guidelines for avoiding such storms when they were discovered were simple. Vessels to the right of a typhoon's track and heading in the same direction were said to be in the storm's dangerous semicircle and should put the wind on the starboard bow and try like hell to run out of it. Ships directly in the typhoon's path or to the left of its track, in what was called the "navigable" semicircle, should put the wind in the starboard quarter and run.[12] Admiral Halsey had other things on his mind, however. He had learned from the mistakes of two months earlier when he had left MacArthur's side and chased what he thought was bigger game. He had blundered, been made to look a fool, and he would not do so again. He had resolved that he would not leave the area, regardless of the circumstances. Halsey was also anxious to get his planes back in the air and resume the strikes that were proving so deadly to Japanese forces in the Philippines. Perhaps it would have been too much to ask Halsey or any other commander to exercise an abundance of caution with such scant information and turn away from combat operations currently ongoing so close by, particularly when his own meteorologist suggested the storm would veer away from them. Regardless, instead of steaming away from the approaching storm on December 16, Halsey sailed his ships eastward to meet his oilers, and headed directly toward it.

At 0100 on December 17, the deck log of Halsey's flagship, the battleship *New Jersey*, recorded a barometer reading of 29.88 with winds at twenty-three knots out of the northeast and a temperature of 81 degrees. Normal barometric pressure at sea level is 29.92, so such a reading, only slightly below average, aroused no suspicion. Yet at that same time, heading on a course of 180 degrees at twelve knots and two hundred miles east-southeast of Halsey, the entry log of the USS *Dewey*, Ray Calhoun's ship, recorded 29.72. An experienced destroyer captain, Calhoun sailed directly in front of the precious oilers, and he was already running into the outer fringes of Cobra. But he was not yet overly concerned either, reasoning that as long as they sailed in the company of the fleet, he could trust Halsey and Acuff to make decisions regarding the weather and their course. Only when they operated independently did Calhoun customarily concern himself with identifying and avoiding storms. Even so, some individual ship commanders in Acuff's Task Group were by then diagnosing the approach of something big, using only the tools they had at hand. By 0400, as Halsey's force drew closer to them, Task Group 30.8 was subdivided into three units and told to proceed independently to assume preset stations for refueling operations.

Over the next several hours, conditions deteriorated rapidly. By 0500 the crew of a seaplane out of Ulithi spotted the "zero-zero visibility" of a tropical disturbance 225 miles southeast of the position where Halsey's Third Fleet would rendezvous with Acuff's oilers.[13] The storm was much closer than Kosco had said it would be. According to the pilot what they were seeing was most definitely a typhoon that was now curving to the north, directly toward Halsey's ships. The seaplane pilots, forcefully one presumes, radioed their report to Saipan and Pearl Harbor, but the alerts would not reach Halsey for another nine hours. Once they did, they would be buried under a stack of higher-priority messages from MacArthur and Nimitz, and Kosco would not see them until thirty-six hours later. Halsey's escort carriers started bobbing and heaving in seas that had become tempestuous. He was forced to cancel flight recovery operations (forcing two planes aloft to ditch) and ground all aircraft. By daylight, in a dirty haze, Third Fleet rendezvoused with Task Group 30.8 roughly five hundred miles east of Luzon.

By this point the admiral's small destroyers were dangerously low on fuel, so they were his first order of business. But refueling at sea was difficult and dangerous, and as the winds blew at near gale force, and the seas grew rougher with a cross-swell of watery hills, and the black rain bands thickened on the southeastern horizon, the ships rolled and tossed and the operations broke down. Fuel hoses and mooring lines snapped. Ships could not maintain station alongside the tankers, almost colliding with one another. Bill Rogers on the *Aylwin* confessed to his executive officer that he had a "bad feeling" about the approaching storm and its low-scudding rain clouds and lightning bolts.[14] He knew how *Farragut*-class destroyers handled high seas and heavy winds, and of their propensity to push over in such conditions, and he was well aware of the extra radar antennas and the additional armament that had earlier been bolted to his deck, making the ship even more top-heavy. He gave the order for his deck crew to clear every object that could be blown overboard and double lash all essential topside gear. He formed damage control parties to fight any electrical fires that might spark and ordered the oil gang to pump seawater into the ship's empty holds as ballast.

By 1000 the fleet was measuring sustained wind speeds of twenty knots, gusts at thirty-five, and a barometer reading of 29.70. Reports of the difficulties in transferring fuel flooded Admiral Halsey's flag plot all morning, and he realized that his small boys were desperate. Halsey experienced the storm differently on the big battleship *New Jersey* than Calhoun, Rogers, Marks, and Garrett did aboard the small, low-to-the-water destroyers. On a battleship or carrier, rough seas were an inconvenience; massive waves resulted in minor rolls or dips that were, at worst, vaguely noticeable. On destroyers and destroyer escorts, particularly the top-heavy ones, such conditions took on a "more personal dimension": heavy lists and severe slams up and over waves and down into troughs.[15] By 1100 the destroyers were pitching violently and getting knocked about like "matchsticks" on the sea.[16] Clouds in the eastern sky looked swirling and multicolored, and the ocean's surface, a drab olive green, resembled "water coming to a boil."[17] The sea's currents grew messy and ambiguous, and the men trying to interpret them were confused at their lack of patterns or predictability. Kosco, by this point frustrated and unaware of any recent weather reports that may have arrived from Pearl Harbor, complained to Halsey that no fleet weather stations had disclosed anything about serious weather in the area, certainly not a typhoon. Halsey betrayed no apprehension, perhaps relying too much on his aerologist. Likely he was also preoccupied by his fleet's upcoming combat operations. It was his general belief that "in time of war, when combat objectives rise above all other priorities, it is not the rule to bestow grave concern on incidental dangers. Planes do not stay grounded and fleets do not run scared because of ugly weather."[18]

As the morning of December 17 passed, marred by increasingly heavy seas and rain squalls, Halsey's smaller ships flashed up and over the waves with their rivets straining. Bells tolled in the howling winds, clappers swinging back and forth on ships bouncing on the green sea. Aboard the *Dewey*, Calhoun watched with increasing concern as his barometer dropped even farther, 0.12 inches in the last three hours.

With noon approaching Halsey's concerns over his fleet's inability to refuel rose. He knew several of his ships were then at less than 70 percent fuel capacity, which was extremely dangerous in high seas, particularly for the smaller destroyers, for it was the weight of the fuel that figured prominently in determining how far they would roll in the waves. Halsey paced the flag bridge on the *New Jersey*, chain-smoking cigarettes. The thirstiest of his destroyers were unable to hold station alongside the tankers in the waves and wind. Before long, with no other choice, he ordered refueling operations suspended, though Acuff's task unit commanders would keep at it for a few hours more with no success. By 1400, as wind gusts on the *Aylwin* reached force 4, Kosco completed a new set of calculations and brought them up to *Halsey*. He placed the center of what he still regarded as a "tropical disturbance" a good four hundred miles southeast of the fleet. In reality, the typhoon spun angrily just 120 miles distant, but Halsey, still trusting his aerologist's reasoning and believing he was angling away from the storm, plotted a new rendezvous with his oilers to the northwest, 160 miles farther on, for daybreak the next morning. He did not know it, but his course paralleled the storm, ensuring that the fleet remained firmly within the typhoon's great sweep as it churned over the water. About ninety minutes later, after Kosco received new positioning reports from Pearl Harbor indicating that the storm, whatever it was, had changed direction, Halsey revised the rendezvous again, altering its location to a point 180 miles south of what he had sent to his ships just a short time earlier. This new meeting site would prove to be only fifty-five miles south of the typhoon's ultimate track.

By then Ray Calhoun, for one, believed that what the fleet was sailing through was a massive typhoon somewhere to the south-southeast. He had studied the tracks of earlier storms in the area and had a decent idea of where the storm would head, and the course ordered by Halsey made him nervous. At 1600 Calhoun's destroyer, the *Dewey*, received a call from Captain Acuff asking his thoughts on whether or not they should continue their efforts to fuel those destroyers critically low: the *Spence*, *Hickox*, and *Maddox*, among others. Calhoun's ship sailed with

78 percent fuel capacity and was therefore well ballasted, so he brought his destroyer alongside the oilers to judge firsthand how difficult the conditions were. Though Calhoun was able to maintain station, the winds and the waves and the yawing they produced made it impossible to hold a steady course. Each swell pushed the small destroyer over 20 degrees, and one swell brought the *Dewey* as close as five yards to one of the oilers, nearly ramming her bow. Only "a superb performance by our helmsman [and] a large measure of good luck, bolstered by many silent prayers" kept the two ships from colliding.[19] Calhoun subsequently advised Acuff that he believed fueling would be impossible under such conditions and that it was useless to continue those operations. Acuff concurred and shut them down. The ships of Task Group 30.8 (TG 30.8) continued to sail independently toward Halsey's rendezvous point through driving rain, under an afternoon sky the color of brass, on a sea now black as coal.[20]

The USS *Hull* underway, October 10, 1944

Jim Marks, aboard the *Hull*, was screening the northernmost of the oiler group's three units. That afternoon he had attempted to transfer forty sacks of mail intended for Third Fleet's sailors to the battleship *South Dakota* for safekeeping, but the high seas, the water that crashed over the ship's decks, and the salt spray that blacked out the ship's radar equipment ruined the transfer: several precious sacks dropped into the water. According to some of his officers and crew, Marks was by this time struggling to maintain his composure. When the ship's radar blinked out, he loudly berated his radarmen and insisted they fix the problem. He stuck his head out of a window and "nearly had it ripped off by the wind, scud, and rain."[21] His men grumbled among themselves that he lacked the seamanship to handle the conditions effectively. At times he seemed indecisive, even visibly frightened and overwhelmed, wedging himself into a corner of the bridge as the ship rocked and rose and fell. As visibility declined, the *Hull* lost visual contact with the rest of the fleet, increasing the crew's and Marks' anxiety.[22] The ship's chief boatswain mate approached Marks and asked for permission to order all hands to don life jackets. Marks declined the request. "What do you want to do?" he asked. "Frighten the crew?"[23]

Outside the *Dewey* the sea was a mass of chop and long diagonal cross swells driven by a powerful backing wind. The officers on the bridge and the men below were becoming physically exhausted from the poundings. To Calhoun the conditions were "eerie and ominous."[24] He had lifelines rigged around the weather deck and all loose gear stowed and had transferred the ship's fresh water to the high and low tanks. His ships' bells continued to toll on the waves, and the wind moaned as it blew at thirty-six knots through the guy wires. It was proving extremely difficult for Calhoun to keep the *Dewey* on station, but he maintained his course through the evening, still trusting Halsey's orders.

By 0200 on December 18, the admiral Calhoun so fervently trusted was readying himself for bed aboard the *New Jersey*. Dressed in his pajamas, Halsey listened as Kosco updated him on the latest storm information. The weatherman still could not determine where the center of the "tropical depression" was (Kosco remained unprepared to classify it a typhoon), or where it was headed, but he continued to believe that turning the fleet to the south had been the correct decision. He also informed Halsey that his screening ships were increasingly unable to maintain their stations in the weather and that Acuff's destroyers and destroyer escorts were in some distress. Kosco recommended that they hold their course. Halsey agreed, then went to bed.

Aboard the *Aylwin* Bill Rogers' anemometer measured wind speeds at force 5. The waves were now "towering masses of dull gray water."[25] The small vessel yawed as each wave slapped her beam and crashed over her deck. As the *Aylwin* rode the waves' crests, her screws spun free of the sea. The wind howled and shrieked through the rigging, and Rogers had to scream to be heard by his officers on the bridge. All hands by now wore their kapoks. Through the long night, sleep was impossible belowdecks as the ship rolled and pitched violently. Shortly after 0300 Typhoon Cobra's eye was swirling a mere ninety miles to the east-southeast.

At 0349 Rogers' officer of the deck broadcast a distress call to the Task Group: "*Aylwin* to TG-30.8. We are broken down. Have lost all power. On generators. Am trying to come to base course." Rogers had taken every precaution, yet it had not been enough. A hatch had sprung on the weather deck, and water was now pouring into his ship. Soon after, each of the ship's generators shorted and her belowdecks were cast into darkness. She went dead in the water. Rogers raced to his quarters, threw on his foul-weather gear, and rushed back to the bridge. Quickly he ordered his chief quartermaster to head across the deck through the rain and wind and the waves to the aft fantail, where the hand-steering mechanism was located, while Rogers took the conn. Without steering, the seas beat the destroyer mercilessly and twisted her to the north for a bit before the quartermaster and the hand-steering crew managed to get her back on the proper course. Not long after, her lights and electronic steering were brought back on line. By that time, however, she was lagging well behind the rest of the task group, alone in the storm.

Halsey did not sleep long on his big battleship. He was up before 0500 and instantly received new weather reports. The gale was now running hard out of the north and had shown no signs of abating. He canceled the previously arranged rendezvous, set a course of 180 degrees, and ordered all his task groups to begin refueling as soon as practical after daylight. The course change in such weather was an ill-advised order, as it required every ship of the screen to reorient themselves to the same relative bearing, in effect turning like a marching column. In order to do that, the escorts had to increase speed above what the rest of the formation was doing to regain their stations, and they were already struggling to keep up with the larger ships. Halsey's order to refuel was likewise impractical. With the wind and the waves beating at them from the north, refueling on a southerly course would simply not be possible.

A huge wave hit the *Dewey* at about that time, and the ship rolled violently to starboard. Calhoun was tossed from his bunk, landing under a pile of books flung from his shelf. After muttering a few expletives, he decided Fate was telling him to get up and look at the weather. It was then that a messenger brought him news of the course change. Turning the ship would mean putting her at almost right angles to the waves. The cross swells would be smashing into them from just a point or two forward of their port beam. The ship heaved and pitched and rolled as it made the turn. She creaked and groaned. To Calhoun, the ship "sounded as though she were in pain."[26] He stepped onto his weather bridge where he was greeted by Bill Buzick, the officer of the watch. Always humorous, always smiling, Buzick leaned over and told Calhoun that weather such as this was great for building character. Calhoun chuckled, replying if such a thing were true, they were all going to be building a lot of character in the next few hours. The wind, from out of the east-northeast, howled at between twenty-eight and thirty-three knots. Just a pair of other ships in the task group were visible through the rain and the now slate-gray waves and the dark sky. The ship wallowed in the monstrously high seas. Calhoun estimated the waves to be sixty feet tall, above his eye level on the bridge. He was certain that a typhoon was upon them.

In Bowditch's *American Practical Navigator*, it very clearly states that "if the wind remains in direction and increases in force in heavy squalls while the barometer falls rapidly, say, at a greater rate than .03 of an inch per hour, the vessel is probably on or near the track of the storm and in advance of the center."[27] Its recommendation is to put "as much distance as possible between the ship and the storm center." At 0616 Vice Admiral John S. McCain Sr. ordered a fleet-wide 120-degree course change, turning from due south to the northeast, and instructed his ships to commence fueling. Halsey, aware of the order, did nothing to countermand it. McCain later stated that he did not fully appreciate how fast the storm was overtaking the fleet and was focused on Third Fleet's commitment to striking Luzon, a wildly misplaced priority when ships in the screen were fighting for their very lives. Regardless, as the fleet worked in the brutal conditions and now gale-strength winds to follow his directive, they were steaming directly toward the typhoon's eye. Calhoun's deck log summarized the plight of all but the largest ships in the task force: "Found it impossible to countermarch to new station because of unfavorable conditions of wind and sea."[28]

Kosco's proclamations notwithstanding, by 0800 on December 18 virtually every ship's commander in Third Fleet, regardless of where they were in the formation and in what direction they were headed, had concluded the fleet was in the middle of a massive typhoon. On the *Dewey* the barometer dropped to 29.49. With the savagery of the storm and the direction of the winds and the waves apparent to everyone, Halsey canceled the refueling order and McCain instructed Acuff's oilers and destroyers to run to the lee of the storm, wherever they could find it. The fleet was by now thoroughly scattered and dysfunctional. Halsey took a moment to send a message to MacArthur that his planned return the next morning was out of the question. As Ray Calhoun wrote in his memoir of the storm, Cobra "had reduced the business of war to an insignificant consideration."[29] But Halsey's actions to keep his fleet safe were, by this point, ineffectual. In his zeal to remain within striking distance of Luzon and with his focus on nothing but supporting MacArthur, he had sailed his fleet into the very center of a typhoon and kept it there, issuing orders that were impractical, unhelpful, ill informed, and, as it turned out, deadly. Even Kosco, no doubt bearing some of the blame for Halsey's decision-making, recognized this later, noting that Third Fleet's "primary mission should have been to get

. . . away from there fast. The enemy could wait. The storm did not."[30] Third Fleet's destroyers, on the edges of the formation and low to the water, were careening blindly over the sea in various stages of disrepair on the morning of the 18th. Radar was too cluttered, unable to distinguish between real ships and mountainous waves, but the lookouts on the destroyers and destroyer escorts had been pulled in due to the conditions. As such, collisions were a constant worry for the ships' captains and crews.

During the night, Jim Marks' executive officer on board the *Hull*, Lieutenant Greil Gerstley, had asked Marks if he could have a crew strike all superfluous topside weight, the ammunition lockers in particular, and move it belowdecks, as the ship needed ballast, but Marks rejected the request, reminding Gerstley they were in the middle of a war zone. At one point that morning, the *Hull* lay over on her side in the water, her starboard beam submerged. Visibility was so poor that the men on the bridge could not even make out the bow through the spendthrift and torrential rain. Relentless winds and waves continued to roll the ship from port to starboard and spin the destroyer like a toy. Marks appeared to shut down. He remained silent, issuing no orders, providing no encouragement, asking no questions.

On the *Dewey* the seas were now higher than sixty feet, higher than the destroyer itself, and when they wallowed in a trough, the men could not see over the tops of the waves. Calhoun heard radio transmissions squawking out incessantly with reports of ships floundering in the sea and running low on fuel. Several captains reported men overboard. Calhoun ordered all gun and topside watches to secure from their stations and seek shelter inside the ship. He set Condition Affirm and sealed all watertight doors and hatches. As Calhoun described it, "On the bridge we were engaged in hand-to-hand combat with the storm. We had to struggle constantly to remain upright. The helmsman had to fight the ships' wheel to stay on course . . . because his footing was so unsteady he often found himself unable to exert any leverage . . . an exhausting task. It was so difficult to stand that I looked for some part of the ship's structure against which I could brace myself."[31] He would summarize the situation thus: "We just continued to wallow in this mess with everything going to hell in a handbasket."[32]

Either still failing to grasp what he was facing or refusing to admit it, Halsey at 0915 sent a communiqué to Admiral Chester Nimitz in which he referred to the storm his fleet was battling as still a mere "tropical disturbance." Regardless of what words he chose to use, he was receiving messages all morning from the fleet surrounding him that were alarming and extreme. Even the light and escort carriers were reporting horrific conditions, rolling heavily and suffering extensive damage. But Halsey's fleet staff had lost control of the picture, if they ever had it to begin with. They had no idea where individual task groups and ships were out there, or what condition most were in, so any orders they issued only confused things.

On the *Hull* the biggest wave yet, one streaked with blue shadows, slammed into the destroyer's starboard quarter. The *Hull* heeled to port and stayed there, refusing to respond to any of Marks' rudder or engine commands. He continued to stare straight ahead, still wedged into the rear port corner of the pilothouse. The weather was seizing control of the ship from him. A series of electrical failures cropped up, affecting the radio, radar, and steering motor, yet Marks insisted they stay in formation, straining the engine at twenty-two knots and relying on the screen commander on the nearby *Laws* to advise him of the proper courses to maintain, as he could see nothing through his shattered wheelhouse windows. Though he had experienced very heavy weather before, Marks was reading his ship's handling wrong, failing to appreciate that the *Hull* was not as stable in bad weather as the previous destroyers he had served on. The ship's funnel belched black fumes. Her depth charges were ripped loose from their K-guns and thrown overboard. The roar of the storm drowned out all sound around Marks. No one could hear anything. Marks found himself wondering if the ship's bridge structure was going to disintegrate.

Across the sea Bill Rogers' *Aylwin* reported narrowly avoiding a collision with another of the task group's screening vessels. His ship too was by now rolling violently, but he tried to execute a turn to clear the screen that the wind and waves had pushed him into.

On board Halsey's flagship the *New Jersey*, Kosco stepped outside flag chart to observe the angry green water firsthand and to feel the winds and the salt spray. Though conditions were much milder where the *New Jersey* was located in the storm, he was receiving reports that waves in the area were as tall as one hundred feet and that the winds, gale force now, were blowing steadily at 125 knots and backing counterclockwise. He could no longer call the storm anything but what it was. When the carrier *Wasp*, steaming well to the east, sent along a report picking up the eye of the storm on her short-range radar, Kosco officially, and belatedly, designated it a "typhoon."

At 1100 another massive wall of water slammed into the *Hull* and sent the ship rolling 75 degrees to port. The wave practically stripped clean the destroyer's decks, and it sheared off the forward davit securing the whaleboat, which swung around and smashed into the deck housing. Marks' chief boatswain mate screamed for the dory to be jettisoned, but Marks would not allow it. Instead, he ordered the man to form a crew, go out there, and secure the swinging boat. Moments later, as the men worked their way toward it, the whaleboat broke free, slid across the deck, and swept several crewmen over the side. They could not be saved. Men alongside Marks grew silent and surly. Crewmen began acting insubordinate in his presence. They reportedly asked the ship's executive officer, out of Marks' earshot, if he would assume command. He refused their entreaty to mutiny. With each roll the deckhouse filled with water, and though his officers and crew shouted for him to reverse the rudders, Marks refused to break station. He complied with every course change he received, even as his ship lay rolling in the wave troughs. In ordinary circumstances such insistence on maintaining his course would have been admirable. In the midst of Typhoon Cobra's wind blasts and walls of water, his intransigence was accomplishing nothing but the destruction of his ship. The *Hull* was still well ballasted, and he may have thought her ultimate stability therefore secured, the repeated rolls notwithstanding. But had he been more experienced he would have known that the ship was almost in extremis and would have focused on its survival, not its place in the fleet's formation.

On the *Dewey*, after corkscrewing around other ships in the formation, Calhoun noted a barometer reading of 28.84. It had dropped half an inch in one hour. The wind was a "wild howl."[33] To be heard, Calhoun and his bridge crew were forced to yell at the top of their lungs. They had earlier lost communication with the rest of the ship, and their isolation brought with it a sense of hopelessness and despair. Calhoun wracked his mind for something, some new idea that might improve their situation, but could think of nothing they had not already tried. He refused to imagine what a rollover would be like, believing that imagining such a thing would only make it happen. He clung to the idea that they would somehow get through the storm. Eight inches of water had by then accumulated in all living spaces, so Calhoun sent bucket brigades into the mess hall and living compartments, the men bailing in the dim glow of battle lanterns. The waves and the rolls of the ship continued unabated. With each roll Calhoun hung from the support of his bridge chair. During the worst of the rolls, in the seconds before the ship righted itself, he was able look down past his feet through the bridge window into the sea. Had Calhoun let go, he would have fallen right into the ocean. He prayed silently each time the inclinometer climbed to and then exceeded 70 degrees, eventually approaching the limit of its scale, 73 degrees. His barometer continued to plummet, reaching 28.10 at noon.

On his classmate Bill Rogers' *Aylwin*, the ship was also enduring 70-degree rolls. At one point she lay over in a cant on her beam for twenty minutes, completely out of control, before ever so slowly returning to an even keel. Rogers, still on the bridge, watched the green seawater crash into his depth-charge racks. His engines had failed, and he had ordered as many men as possible into the ship's starboard living quarters in an effort to counteract the giant rolls to port. Electrical fires broke out, one even burning on the bridge in front of him, though they were all quickly brought under control. He eventually stopped trying to steer the ship, ceded control to the sea, and settled into irons like so many of the others, heading downwind, wallowing in the troughs, massive quantities of seawater flooding her engine-blower intakes. One of the generators died. Five feet of water lay sloshing in the engine room bilges. The steel of the bulkheads belowdecks grew superheated as steam filled the engineering spaces. Rogers' chief engineer and one of his machinist's mates were blown overboard. Though the crew tried, neither could be recovered, and Rogers wondered if he and the rest of the crew would soon join them. Eventually, by putting his rudder into the wind and backing, Rogers was able to twist his ship back to the south, but he then lost steering control once again. He shut the engines down, and another wave slammed into them, rolling the ship 70 degrees, where it stayed for fifteen interminable seconds before righting itself to 60 degrees. Four more rolls occurred over the next twenty minutes. Captain Acuff, also on board the *Aylwin*, moved his command post to the ship's chart room, where the shriek of the wind was quieter and where he was able to get off a message over the VHF to Vice Admiral McCain on the *Wasp*: "[I have] lost control. Commander Task Group 30.8 unable to control his group."[34]

On the *Dewey*, a quartermaster who acted as the ship's lay leader led some of the men on the bridge in prayer. They said the words to the Navy Hymn, too: "Eternal Father, strong to save, whose arm does battle with the rest of this wave. Oh, hear us when we cry to Thee for those in peril on the sea." The rolls were coming more frequently, the waves outside towering, the wind velocity at a sustained one hundred knots, its bellowing incessant. During one roll, Calhoun found himself face to face, hanging from supports, with one of the other officers aboard, Captain Preston Mercer, commodore of the destroyer squadron, who asked him, "If we go over and you end up in the sea, do you think [you] can make it?" Calhoun thought of his wife, Ginny, and their baby son. He answered, "Yes, I think I can." Mercer said he doubted he could—he was not a strong swimmer. "I don't feel too badly about it. I've had a good life, and my insurance is all paid up, but I feel sorry for all of these youngsters, many of them married and with families. Their lives have hardly begun and a lot of them wouldn't make it."[35]

At 1149 that morning, Halsey finally issued the order releasing all vessels from their fleet-wide formations and directing them to take the most comfortable course with the wind on the port quarter. In the present conditions it was of no help, certainly not to the destroyers. And it was not just the top-heavy *Farragut*s that were rolling dangerously in the seas now, threatening at any moment to wallow and sink. Even the more stable destroyers of the *Fletcher* class were fighting for their lives. The USS *Hickox* was rolling 70 degrees and higher, like the *Hull*, the *Dewey*, the *Aylwin*, and Bruce Garrett's *Monaghan*. Soon the USS *Spence*, which had been unable to fuel earlier in the day and thus had almost no ballast, rolled over, stayed there, and sank in the seas.

She would not be the only one. Shortly before noon the *Hull* took several rolls caused by "high velocity gusts" during which the ship's junior officer was thrown from the port side of the pilothouse, through the air, to the upper portion of the starboard side.[36] Marks believed that no wind could be worse than what he had just witnessed. He estimated the gusts at 110 knots, and they lay the ship on her starboard side at an 80-degree angle and held her down until the ocean water flowed into the pilothouse itself and flooded her upper structures. The ship had been dealt a knock-out blow, pushed over onto her side at such an angle that there was no righting herself. Marks, from his position on the port wing of the bridge, waited until the water reached him, then stepped into the sea's froth, and he felt the suction as his ship went down and then a concussion as the boilers exploded under the sea. He could only see a few feet in the water but around him roughly 160 men thrashed. The rest had been trapped belowdecks when the *Hull* rolled for the last time. A few of the survivors managed to cling to three life rafts that bobbed to the surface, but the rest floated in the roiling waves, only their life jackets keeping their heads above the water. When the waves crashed over them or they were swept up onto the breaking crests, they tumbled and flipped and tried to stay afloat.

On the *Dewey* Calhoun's bulkheads had been crushed inward in places, and the rest of the frame was creaking and leaking badly. Desperate, he sent three volunteers out into the typhoon to try to cut the mast with acetylene torches. One of Calhoun's boatswains stumbled over to him and asked, "Captain, are we going to abandon ship?"

"Not if I can help it, Boats. So long as the *Dewey* doesn't abandon us, we're not going to abandon her."[37]

The man seemed reassured by Calhoun's confidence, but soon another wave slammed into them, and they rolled again more than 70 degrees to port. Seawater rushed into the bridge through the broken windows. Calhoun was thrown against the bulkhead and landed in a pile of arms and legs with one of his officers. He got to his feet and watched incredulously as the ship's inclinometer swung past 80 degrees, stopping at 84.

"She's going!" his helmsman hollered.[38]

Calhoun then heard a sound like a cannon firing: the guy wire, half an inch thick, that ran from the deck to support the main forward stack had snapped. The funnel popped off at its base and collapsed onto the deck in front of him, knocking a gun turret into the stormy sea along with a pair of ammunition lockers and the ship's whaleboat. From the gaping hole now in her deck belched black smoke and hot steam that was venting at four hundred pounds of boiler pressure, yet with the reduction in sail caused by the funnel's collapse, the *Dewey* began to stabilize. In the words of military editor and historian Hanson W. Baldwin, Calhoun's ship had just become "the first vessel in the history of the sea to survive such a roll."[39] Waves continued to pummel her, but she never rolled so far again, or remained on her side as long.

The barometer on the *Dewey*, stackless now but still afloat, reached its lowest point around 1300, estimated to be at 27.30, completely off the scale. One officer believed it sank to as low as 26.30 around that time, which would have made it the lowest barometer reading ever recorded by the U.S. Navy. The wind came from the north, force 17, sea condition 9. Calhoun estimated the gusts at 125 knots, though "it could have been more."[40] The ship was sailing through the eye of the typhoon, exiting the vortex to emerge under a white sun in the sky. Said Calhoun, "One minute we were in a thick soup of violent wind and spray, and the next we were out in the clear."[41]

The *New Jersey*, on which Halsey was recording the wind velocities in his diary, finally started getting a taste of what TG 30.8 was going through as wind gusts of ninety-three knots swept through and around her superstructure and the barometer fell to 29.23, dropping .07 inches in ten minutes. At 1345 he sent a message to Nimitz in which he reported confused seas, a ragged ceiling, heavy rains, winds west-northwest at seventy knots, and finally acknowledged that his fleet had sailed into and been swamped by a massive typhoon. It was the first message Nimitz received from any source that indicated a typhoon was in his fleet's area of operations. Halsey issued an order for all ships to steam southeast toward the more navigable part of the typhoon and set a rendezvous site for 0700 the next morning seventy miles away.

Now in the water, Marks and his surviving crew struggled to stay afloat. The typhoon's winds were deafening, and they could not hear one another shout. The men were forced to cup their hands around their noses just to breathe. The driving rain flayed away the skin from their noses and necks and ears. It also whipped the ocean water and the salt spray and the oil on the surface into a dense froth that reduced visibility to just a few yards. Marks grew so sick from swallowing seawater while bouncing over the whitecaps that he retched over and over. Hours later, ravenous, Marks began chewing on his life jacket's whistle and then on a strip of shoe leather. Sharks and barracudas were in the area, so Marks grabbed a hatchet he had carried with him and gripped it tightly. Over time, as the hours passed, his eyes grew swollen and red-colored from battling the surf. He developed hypothermia, his skin turned pale and rubbery, and his muscles stiffened as he floated, the storm's last bands unfurling in the sky.

Finally, at 1400, the air pressure around the *Dewey* began to rise again. When the higher readings were reported to Calhoun, he hollered, "Thank God! We're going to make it."[42] They had hours still to go before they were clear, and the ship continued to roll in the "berserk" seas and the hurricane-force winds, but they began riding the waves just a bit better as each hour passed, and they could make turns at three knots and begin to inspect their damage.[43]

As evening settled slowly Marks continued to bob in the violent water, riding the high waves and skimming down their far sides, the wind and spray in his face. At one point, as he settled into a trough, he came across one of his officers, Archie DeRyckere. As DeRyckere told it, Marks said to him, "Hey, DeRyckere, like to know what time it is?" DeRyckere, thoroughly confused, replied, "Yes, sir, Captain. I would." Marks' watch was waterproof and still working perfectly. "A little past 6:00 p.m."[44] Then the two men were separated again. DeRyckere was critical of Marks' leadership, during the storm and after. As he described it years later, Marks disappeared without "a word about attaching lines and staying together. Not a thought for his crew. Just gone."[45]

At 1745, believing all of his ships and task groups were heading for the new rendezvous point, Halsey sent a message across Third Fleet requesting prompt reports of any storm damage and deficiencies. It was then that Halsey learned that he had destroyers unaccounted for—the *Hull*, *Monaghan*, and *Spence*. He sent an alert to McCain over TVS and told him to have his ships post lookouts for survivors and conduct a thorough search of the area. Then the admiral directed the most battered vessels to form up on the light carrier *Monterey*, herself wounded, where they could be refueled before heading off together for Ulithi.

Among those ships ordered to the *Monterey* was the battered *Aylwin*. She had leaks in her engine room and water one foot above the floor plates, but repair parties were shoring up the bulkheads, and the pumps were all in operation. Her communications were out, but she indicated her position on the sea by shining what still-functioning searchlights she had vertically. As the winds continued to subside, Bill Rogers felt as if he and his crew had been granted a last-minute reprieve from a death sentence. "That she did not capsize was miraculous," he wrote.[46] As soon as the flooding was brought under control, Rogers put both engines in motion and pointed the ship through the choppy seas toward Halsey's rendezvous.

As Preston Mercer left the bridge of the *Dewey* at 2100, he turned to Calhoun and said, "Well, Skipper, we've weathered an experience which will become famous in history. Everyone will want to hear about it. Tell them as well as you can what it was like, but don't expect them to believe you, for no one who has had no similar experience can conceive of anything like these past twelve hours [*sic*]."[47]

Later, near midnight, Calhoun's lookouts spotted a searchlight sweeping back and forth across the horizon on their port beam. Still on the bridge, Calhoun thought it might be the *Tabberer* searching for someone in the water, so he turned his stackless ship to assist. Over the TBS he heard snatches of conversation between the *Tabberer* and some other unknown ship, and he heard the word "survivors." *Had some ship gone down in the storm?* He tried to raise the *Tabberer* on the TBS to ascertain what was happening, but he could not reach her. Calhoun steered toward the distant light, but water poured into the hole left by the shorn stack and he nearly scuttled his vessel. The *Dewey* was in rotten shape, her deck a tangled mass of ropes and lines and guy wires and loose wreckage and twisted steel. Eventually she and the *Tabberer* made visual contact, but Calhoun was forced to flash a message: "We are leaving the area."[48] His lurching, beaten ship could not support any rescue operations. By then Halsey had learned of the *Dewey*'s condition and given Calhoun permission to leave the scene immediately and head straight for Ulithi.

Early the next morning, as the battered *Dewey* made her way to the Ulithi anchorage, Calhoun and his officers finally had a moment to start rummaging through the dispatches that had arrived from the fleet in the last few hours. One of them was from the *Tabberer*. It read, "*Hull* capsized with little warning. Only two life rafts launched and neither yet sighted by us. Have 10 enlisted survivors and will remain in area searching."[49] Calhoun knew the *Hull* was Jim Marks' ship, and his heart sank.

By 0922 Third Fleet's scattered vessels were slowly starting to coalesce around Halsey and the *New Jersey*. In the preceding hours Typhoon Cobra had moved on, curving sharply to the northwest, still swirling and angry but away from them now. Halsey continued to update Nimitz on what had happened and his fleet's condition: "Typhoon center passed thirty miles north of fleet guide mid-day 18th. Tracked by surface radar. Gusts to 93 knots. Fleet took beating. *Tabberer* reports *Hull* capsized with little warning. . . . Only 10 enlisted survivors at time of report. Several other stragglers still unreported."[50] Halsey then set to work that morning planning the rescue mission that had now become his priority. He set his navigators and his aerologists to the task, instructing them to plot the currents and the trade winds and prepare recommendations for where the ships should search for any sailors in the water. As soon as his larger ships were refueled, Halsey sent them off with extra lookouts posted. Hundreds of airmen were ordered aloft too.

James Marks was picked up by the *Tabberer* that morning. Four other officers and fifty-seven of the *Hull*'s seamen were also rescued. Only seven men from the *Monaghan* were found.

In all nearly eight hundred American sailors died during the storm, and over eighty were injured. It was an enormous loss of life, with more men killed by Cobra than had been lost during the Battle of Midway. In addition to the three destroyers that capsized and sank, another twelve ships were damaged so severely as to become inoperable. Almost 150 aircraft were lost or damaged. For the men of the Big Blue Fleet who had endured the storm, it had been a "traumatic, soul-searing, and humbling experience" that had "left its indelible imprint on each of them."[51]

The *Dewey* arrived in Ulithi shortly after 1100 on December 20. Calhoun met up with Rogers after he brought the *Aylwin* limping into the harbor, and the two classmates swapped stories. Though nothing had been made official yet, they both felt the *Hull* and *Monaghan* must have capsized. They knew how unstable their own ships had been and how close they themselves had come to going under. Jim Marks appeared in Ulithi on December 22 and came aboard the *Dewey* to talk things over with Captain Mercer. Marks stopped by Calhoun's cabin before leaving and the two classmates talked briefly about Marks' time in the water. Marks told Calhoun of the huge waves he had faced and how, after a time, he had accepted the fact that he was going to die. His classmate's face "was a mass of saltwater sores," Calhoun wrote. "His eyes were blackened. He clearly showed the strain of his ordeal. I could not even begin to appreciate the sadness and despair that I knew he must feel, and I sympathized with him. Unfortunately, such things are difficult to verbalize, and I could find no way to express adequately what I felt. I was deeply thankful that he had survived."[52]

For Marks, the ordeal of the typhoon did not officially end with the storm's passing. He was the only captain of a lost ship to survive and, the day after Christmas 1944, was named a "defendant" by an official court of inquiry investigating the matter. Marks was the only man so designated. He was assigned a lawyer and gave his testimony aboard the USS *Cascade* in Ulithi, his face still pockmarked by sores and his eyes still blackened. Marks defended his command decisions during the storm by stating that he had been ordered to maintain station and had tried to do so to the best of his ability. He testified that if he had been released from his position in the screen earlier in the storm, he might have been able to outrun the typhoon to the south. As it was, he said, he was simply following orders to remain in formation.

Marks' description of his ship's final hours before her sinking was read aloud to the court and to the trio of admirals who officiated over it. It was sanitized and straightforward, clipped and unemotional. At the conclusion of his testimony, Marks was asked if he wished to register an official complaint against any of his surviving officers or crew. He declined to do so, as did all other surviving officers and crew of the *Hull* when they were given the same chance, most likely because they were young, with long careers ahead of them, and they understood that registering such complaints about a superior in public would do them no good.

Calhoun was called to participate in the inquiry as well and took a whaleboat over to the *Cascade* on the afternoon of December 28. His classmate Bill Rogers was already there, waiting outside the ship's pilothouse. When Calhoun was called in by a Marine orderly, he entered the wardroom and saw a dozen men dressed in freshly laundered khakis seated at a long table. Captain Mercer was in the room, as was Jim Marks. The mood was somber, but he was questioned in a polite, friendly way by the admirals who asked Calhoun to explain, among other things, the cause of the *Dewey's* electrical difficulties and how far his ship had rolled. Calhoun reported that he had personally seen his inclinometer indicate 73 degrees.

Later, when Halsey was interviewed, he reported to the court that he had received no advance warning of the storm's approach, and though local conditions indicated a storm was coming, he had no way of knowing if it was severe or a mere tropical disturbance. He thought the storm would curve away northward and eastward, and the fleet movements he directed were intended to guide them away from it, not deeper into it. As if to explain why his thoughts in the days preceding the storm were distracted, he also made sure to mention that "the thought of striking Luzon [and supporting MacArthur's advances] was uppermost in our heads right up to the last minute."[53]

Marks prudently declined to question Halsey himself, but he did take advantage of the opportunity to request explanations from Commander George Kosco. Earlier, Halsey's chief aerologist had testified that he had based his forecast data and his determination that the fleet was facing a tropical storm, not a typhoon, on radio weather reports, and he admitted that on December 17 he had erroneously estimated the storm's location. These reports, as well as concerns over the fleet's proximity to Japanese air bases in the Philippines, had ultimately determined the course Halsey ordered. Marks' initial questions for Kosco were straightforward. He asked the aerologist to state once again the source of his weather reports, whether or not he received them at the times expected, and whether or not he believed them to be adequate. The court then interjected and asked Kosco when he could plot the storm with accuracy ("the morning of the 18th") and when he determined it was a typhoon ("0800, again on the 18th"). Neither Marks nor the board followed up with the fairly obvious question of why, if Kosco knew the storm was a typhoon early on the 18th, Halsey's message at 0915 that morning made no mention of it. Kosco was then asked to comment on something Halsey had said, that warnings about the weather were, in his words, "nonexistent."[54] Kosco replied rather disingenuously that Typhoon Cobra had formed on top of the fleet and, because of that, there had been no clear advance warnings.

No representatives of the Bureau of Ships were ever called to speak about the stability, or lack thereof, of the *Farragut*-class destroyers. In Calhoun's mind, as he would say later, the Bureau of Ships was "criminally negligent" for not retrofitting the *Farragut*s properly to ensure their stability in high seas.[55]

At the end of its investigation, the court of inquiry released eighty-four findings and sixty-three opinions, among other things determining that Marks, as well as Garrett on the *Monaghan* and the captain of the third ship to sink, the *Spence*, "maneuvered too long in an endeavor to keep station, which prevented them from concentrating early enough on saving their ships."[56] It was also declared that Marks and Garrett had not been experienced enough to decide on their own that the weather conditions were so extreme that they should break station and tend to their ships' safety. The court admitted, however, that such judgments required more experience than these new, young officers could be expected to possess. The court also found that the sinkings of the *Hull* and *Monaghan* were due primarily to the inherent instability of the top-heavy *Farragut*-class destroyers. Ultimately, the losses of the ships were attributed directly to the typhoon and "no blame for those damages [were] attached to any officer or man serving in those ships."[57] But Halsey did not escape judgment entirely. The court did declare that the responsibility for the damage and the loss of life and ships caused by the typhoon belonged with him. Specifically, he had failed to send up special weather flights to determine definitively where the storm was while he still had time to evade it, had put too much stock in weather reports and analysis emanating from Pearl Harbor, and had failed to issue a fleet-wide typhoon warning early enough. The damage to his fleet and losses sustained had been aggravated by the courses, speeds, and formations he had ordered up to and during the storm's worst hours. Critically, however, his mistakes were judged "errors in judgment under stress of war operations" rather than offenses caused by negligence.[58] The catastrophe was an "act of God" and therefore the extent of the blame assigned to Halsey was labeled "impractical to assess."[59] Given the death toll, the court's proclamations were decidedly lenient.

The court of inquiry was focused on moving forward and putting the matter to rest. It was clearly not interested in ruining careers, weakening the war effort, or delivering any semblance of justice. It had compelling reasons for avoiding such steps: MacArthur's invasion of Luzon was scheduled to begin in just a few short weeks, and TF 38 was once again needed to provide air cover for that invasion. Like a gristmill, the war rolled on, pausing for no one.

Part Three

ABOVE THE WAVES

NORMAN JACK KLEISS

Coffeyville, Kansas

Jack's a true savior from out Kansas way. With a minimum devoted to academics, Jack spent his time between his two true loves, wrestling and letter-writing. Keeping his batting average perfect in all departments of Naval Academy life, wifey scored heavily as a snake. A hop was sure to find him dragging. No biography would be complete without telling of Jack's passion for guns. During his years here he built everything from a pocket pistol to a machine gun. When he really gets out working for Uncle Sam, he will probably make the Germans and their Big Berthas look like pikers. Although Jack hasn't had much practice as an admiral out on the sand-blown plains of Kansas, he is going to be a fine naval officer.

The Lucky Bag, 1938

Chapter Eleven

DUSTY

Naval aviators in World War II were unique members of the branch, regarded, not always kindly, as a "separate breed" by the seamen, officers, and captains who shared the aircraft carriers with them.[1] They were the peculiar and distant "flyboys," members of the "brown shoe navy" (rather than the "black"), the ones with separate missions and routines, separate skills and traditions, and, as such, they sat apart, hunkering by themselves in the squadron ready rooms on board the carriers, talking tactics, studying navigational charts, drawing maps, drinking coffee by the urn, and waiting for orders to take flight into the far distance in their tight packs.[2] Surface officers considered airpower unnecessary, a "short-lived fad" inferior to the battleships and cruisers that were and always would be, in their eyes, the real backbone of the U.S. Navy.[3]

Aviators certainly looked different. Ashore officers of the surface fleet wore the traditional double-breasted blue uniforms with gold stripes, while pilots wore forest green uniforms with black stripes when on base. And pilots faced different lengths of time at sea than their regular Navy colleagues. While the carrier crews and men in the cruisers and destroyers arrayed around the flattops often remained at sea for years on end, the aviators of the air groups were only passing visitors on board the *Lexington*, or the *Yorktown*, or the *Saratoga*, *Hornet*, *Enterprise*, or *Wasp*. If they were not killed or hurt, they were rotated ashore after six months. The general thinking among Navy officials was that after two combat tours pilots grew resentful, then lost their daring and effectiveness. Those still alive felt they had "done their parts and other pilots who [had] not fought should take over the burden."[4] Their resentment was perhaps understandable. Planners anticipated that 10 percent of all carrier aircraft would be lost each month, either in combat, from getting lost over the trackless sea (what Dusty Kleiss called the "blank canvas" of the Pacific Ocean), or from the innumerable accidents and mechanical mishaps that so regularly occurred in their profession, and not until the last stages of the war did those statistics improve.[5]

But flying a plane off an aircraft carrier was a new, invigorating, and decidedly raucous endeavor for the Navy's pilots during World War II. Most were learning on the job. Even in ideal weather, accidents were common. But the men were addicted to it. They had volunteered. It was in their blood.

Those aviators assigned to fighter squadrons in the first year and a half of the war primarily flew the tough, fast Grumman F4F Wildcats. Squat, hearty, and big-bellied, with narrow landing gear and sharp angles, the single-seat fighters boasted Pratt & Whitney engines that could zip them through the air at 325 miles per hour. Pilots appreciated the plane's handling: it could absorb a great deal of punishment, much more than the Japanese fighters it often faced could, yet the plane retained enough agility with its large square-cut wings to out-turn and outmaneuver enemy Zeros.

Pilots assigned to torpedo squadrons flew Douglas TBD Devastators, carrier-based two-man bombers with a maximum speed of 206 miles per hour and a flight ceiling of 19,700 feet (low compared to the Wildcat's 35,000). With a heavy torpedo slung underneath, a Devastator had a range of 435 miles. By 1942, when it was a key part of air operations against the Japanese carrier fleets marauding through the Pacific, it was already obsolescent, and no match for Japanese fighters, yet the plane's inherent faults and disadvantages were understood too slowly by the Navy's planners and strategists, and they would be slaughtered a squadron at a time in the year's key battles.

The plane that would achieve lasting renown early in the war for sinking Japanese carriers, while there were still carriers to sink, was the Douglas Dauntless SBD dive-bomber, a two-seat plane with a maximum speed of 252 miles per hour, a service ceiling of 24,300 feet, and a range of 456 miles. Dauntlesses sported very broad wings (41′6″) with horizontal center sections, tapered outer panels, and perforated split flaps that, when opened fully, served as air breaks in steep dive-bombing attacks. Each carried a large bomb slung underneath the fuselage (either a 500- or 1,000-pounder), smaller bombs underneath the wings, and four .50-caliber machine guns.

Norman "Jack" Kleiss, USNA '38, was a twenty-four-year-old lieutenant (jg) in 1942. Born on March 7, 1916, in Coffeyville, Kansas, he had endured a hardscrabble and difficult childhood in the Dust Bowl of the Depression, made so not just by the area's ruined cornfields and empty bank accounts but also by his mother's death from stomach cancer in 1930. He had wanted to fly since he was fifteen, when, while serving as a cavalryman in the Kansas National Guard during a mock battle out in the dust fields, he had seen the fast and looping biplanes of the Army Air Corps for the first time. Kleiss stared at them in awe and decided right then that he would someday fight above the ground, not on it. Whatever the cost, he would soar with those men in their machines. He liked horses well enough but understood, even as a youngster, that the airplane was the future. That was where the glory and the fun lay. As Kleiss put it with a flourish in his memoirs, "I wanted to become a cavalryman mounted on wings, a knight of the airborne battlefield."[6] After mustering out of the National Guard, Kleiss passed on a prestigious scholarship to the University of Kansas and instead accepted an appointment to the Naval Academy because he believed the Navy's aviation program was expanding more rapidly than the Army's.

He spent his two required years of surface duty after graduation as a junior gunnery officer on board the heavy cruiser *Vincennes*, sailing out of Long Beach, California. One day while in Long Beach, Kleiss ran into a friend from back home who subsequently told a young woman he knew, a Ms. Jean Mochon, about the "lonely sailor who needed some attention."[7] Jean, then working as a stenotypist in Los Angeles, agreed to meet the young officer, and Kleiss was immediately smitten with the tall brunette and her warm and vivacious personality. "The first time I saw her, I said, 'she's the one for me.'"[8] Very quickly, Jean was equally interested in him despite her many suitors, his cause aided by her French Canadian father, who was impressed that Kleiss knew some French, which he had fortuitously opted to study at Annapolis.

Over the next several months, Kleiss visited Jean at her parents' home and listened to her play the family's grand piano, played bridge with her family, and drank wine in the evenings with her father. He watched Jean act in local plays and was racked with self-doubt when she passionately kissed other actors on stage. Jean's cool and cautious approach to their relationship did not help matters. Though they both cared for each other, the burgeoning relationship was quickly tested when Cruiser Division Seven and the *Vincennes* were transferred from Long Beach and the Pacific Fleet to Norfolk, Virginia. The day the ships left port, Jean called Kleiss on the phone and told him that she loved him. The two wrote to each other every week for the next two years, but being so far apart was difficult on them both. As Jean wrote after his departure, "I can't help but feel a little on the low side. For the first time in my life, I'm sure of my feelings and then something like this has to happen."[9]

At midnight on September 6, 1939, Kleiss was telephoned and told that he was being reassigned to another destroyer nearby, the USS *Goff*, because one of his Academy classmates, Ensign Jamie Adair, had fallen off a gangway and broken his ankle. Kleiss had mixed feelings about the transfer. The Atlantic Fleet was conducting neutrality patrols at the time, and the *Goff* was smaller and less suited for the Atlantic's swells than the *Vincennes*, but her officer corps was tight-knit and included another of his classmates with whom he was close: Ensign Elton Knapp, serving as the ship's communications officer. The environment was more carefree, and female visitors were allowed on board late into the evening. Kleiss, the only officer without a wedding band, spent nights in port dodging clusters of "New England beauties" looking for romance.[10] Just after Christmas, he was transferred again.

His new ship, the USS *Yarnall*, was a significant downgrade. Launched during World War I, the ship had been brought out of retirement and still looked and handled like an "ancient relic, utterly incapable of deep water transit."[11] One afternoon while on board the destroyer Kleiss was staring at a photo of Jean when his commanding officer happened by. "Boy, she's pretty," he said. "Marry her before she gets away."[12] While Kleiss harbored similar thoughts, Navy regulations prohibited Academy graduates from marrying within two years of their graduation. For the time being, he would have to wait.

Though Kleiss was busy, his affection and longing for Jean never slackened during his time away. Writing from Norfolk in April 1940, he was honest about his feelings and clearly overcome by them: "Subject: It must be love. Love is something where when you got so much you can't hold any more you feel like you almost hardly ain't got any. . . . You ought to be told how nice you are, 'cause it's nice to tell you. The idea is I think you're pretty swell."[13]

Throughout his time in the surface fleet, Jack Kleiss never lost his fervent desire to become an airman. He left the *Yarnall* that April and began his flight training at Pensacola NAS the following month. Jean was unsure of his plans. She found the prospect of dating such a daredevil appealing, but worried about the dangers involved and ultimately asked him to forgo the air service.[14] Kleiss refused. For eleven months, with a few of his Academy classmates alongside him, including best friend Tom Eversole, he progressed through the various levels of instruction while 40 percent of his fellow trainees were either washed out or killed in accidents. He learned to fly the N3N "Yellow Peril" 300-horsepower biplane, then the 600-horsepower North American SNJ Texan single-wing trainer, in the process becoming proficient in instrument flying, aerial gunnery, and formation flying. Throughout the training Kleiss never lost his focus or his drive. As historian Stephen Moore wrote, "[Kleiss] knew that he would leave the Florida flight training program in only one of three ways: with the coveted gold aviator wings on his uniform, washed out and disgraced because he did not possess 'the stuff' to advance; or in a pine box shipped home to his family."[15] After flight instruction Kleiss wanted to serve on board a carrier, so he was sent to Opa-Locka, Florida, for specialized combat instruction involving naval landings and takeoffs, dive-bombing tactics, and dogfighting. In the spring of 1941 he successfully graduated, earning an assignment to the carrier USS *Enterprise*. One of the U.S. Navy's largest ships, the Big E was based, providentially, in San Diego, California. "Have I got wings!" he wrote to Jean. "Am I good!"[16]

Once more on the same coast, Kleiss and Jean reignited their courtship. When the *Enterprise* was at sea, he and the other members of VS-6 spent their downtime telling one another about their significant others, and Kleiss and Jean continued their tradition of sending each other weekly notes. Life as a pilot on an aircraft carrier at sea was grueling and dangerous, and Kleiss was kept busy. His squadron's third-in-command, Lieutenant Earl Gallaher, drove his men hard, even demanding they partake in additional training flights instead of liberty weekends. Over and over, again and again, he put his men through gunnery practices, night flying exercises, formation training, and anything else he felt the men needed. Through it all, Jean was a welcome presence, someone he could share his thoughts and concerns with. In a letter to her in the summer of 1941, Kleiss wrote that he and his squadron mates flew so frequently, "we've been considering putting coffeepots in the planes and bunks in the ready room."[17]

It was during the summer while training in Hawaii that Kleiss earned the sobriquet by which he would be known for the rest of his life. He and his gunner, John Snowden, approached the airstrip at Ewa Field in their Dauntless dive-bomber ahead of a line of Marine fighter pilots lining up for landings of their own. After touching down, Kleiss quickly taxied off the airstrip to make room for the fighters, steering out onto a dirt field of hard-packed red clay. The plane bounced over the rough ground, and very quickly his prop blast blew a huge cloud of bright dust into the air, covering the airstrip and sending such a plume of dirt skyward that it prevented the Marines behind him from landing. They were waved off as the dust rose almost a mile high. The Ewa Field tower controller hollered over the radio, "Unknown dust cloud, who the hell are you?"[18] The Marine pilots turning away added their curses to the radio net. Not a little embarrassed, Kleiss returned to the airstrip, but his "dusting" of Ewa Field would not be quickly forgotten. His fellow Scouting Six aviator Cleo Dobson, who had seen everything from his own plane, greeted him afterward with a "Hello, Dusty," and the name was born.

Kleiss was on board the nearby *Enterprise* when the Japanese attacked Pearl Harbor. He sailed with her in the early days of the war conducting long patrols in the central Pacific and hunting for enemy surface ships and submarines, anxious to inflict some kind of damage on the Japanese navy. In early January 1942, the *Enterprise* was given a real opportunity to do just that. Admiral Chester Nimitz, the commander in chief of the U.S. Pacific Fleet, with some prodding by his boss, Admiral Ernest J. King, believed the time was right for a hit-and-run raid on one of Japan's "fixed aircraft carriers," her Pacific island bases.[19] Though the raid would involve very real threats to his irreplaceable flattops, King more than anything wanted to launch some sort of aggressive action against the Japanese, if for no other reason than to boost general morale among his seamen, and among the Americans at home.

Nimitz was always ready for a fight, and he decided the first target for his carrier-based air crews would be Japanese bases in the southern Marshall Island chain. The carriers chosen for the mission were Admiral Halsey's *Enterprise* and the *Saratoga*, but the "Sister Sara" was promptly hit by a Japanese torpedo on January 11 about five hundred miles south of Oahu and forced to return to the mainland for significant and time-consuming repairs. It was then decided that Halsey would meet up instead with Task Force 17 and the USS *Yorktown*, recently arrived from the Atlantic and under the command of the well-regarded Admiral Frank Jack Fletcher. Together they would sail across the international date line and then separate: while Kleiss and the *Enterprise* sailed to their targets, Kwajalein, Maloelap, and Wotje in the Marshalls, the *Yorktown* would strike the islands of Makin, Mili, and Jaluit. Halsey informed Kleiss and his air crews where they were going on January 11, once the *Enterprise* was far out to sea. The lift in the morale of the men was palpable. They would finally be punching back.

As the task force headed south, Kleiss occupied his days flying combat air patrol over the carrier, the ships splayed out in miniature across the blue sea beneath him. He flew with the canopy open to cool himself, but "even the wind was sultry and oppressive."[20] The pilots looked for rain squalls in the distance, which they could pop into to cool off. At this point in the war, good, experienced aviators were in short supply. Greenhorn pilots made their first carrier landings while the ships headed for their air strikes. Everything was being learned, practiced, and refined on the fly, so to speak, and while performances improved with repetition, there were still too many mistakes being committed by the young airmen.

The two carriers rendezvoused on January 23 and sailed toward the Marshall Islands together, zigzagging as they went, the *Yorktown* about 150 miles astern of Halsey and the *Enterprise*. They parted ways again on January 31, the *Enterprise* speeding northward at thirty knots. Her engines droned loudly belowdecks, and her hull thrummed. In a risky move, Halsey decided to bring the carrier close in to Kwajalein, within twenty or thirty miles of the large Japanese base there. That suited Kleiss and his fellow aviators just fine, as it meant they would use little fuel in getting over the target and thus would be able to spend more time bombing and strafing the bases. But it left the *Enterprise* dangerously exposed and with little room to maneuver if it was spotted by Japanese scout planes.

The night before the attacks, the men on board the *Enterprise* slept fitfully, the hours long and uncomfortable. The heat belowdecks was stifling and all of the seamen sweated through their sheets.[21] Kleiss' ability to sleep through anything was sorely tested, and not just because of the dank humidity. Their operational plan was still too light in certain areas for the aviators' total comfort. For one thing, the American fleet possessed no accurate maps of the island chain and the target area. Additionally, the dive-bomber crews, including Kleiss, had just been informed that there would be no fighter protection available to them during the raid, as the Wildcats were needed for combat air patrol over the carriers. Bomber pilots needed fighter escorts to keep Japanese Zeros from tearing them apart, but there were simply too few available, so Kleiss and the other Dauntlesses would go in alone.

Reveille on February 1, 1942, came at three in the morning, the sea a black and heaving thing, the sky lightless, the carrier's engines throbbing from deep below. Most of the aviators had slept little. Once up, Kleiss and the others made their way down long, dark, quiet, blue-lit passageways to a big wardroom for breakfast: eggs, bacon, coffee, and juice eaten shoulder to shoulder at long tables, the men chatting about the day ahead. Then they retreated by squadrons to their respective ready rooms, where they were briefed and listened for any updates. The operational details were passed down from Commander Thomas P. Jeter, the *Enterprise*'s executive officer. Included in his orders were words of encouragement: "We can take pride in being privileged to participate in the first offensive engagement of the Pacific Fleet, and in the first naval action in which an American aircraft carrier has taken part. Remember Pearl Harbor."[22] The men were alert now, running on adrenaline, nerves, and coffee. They chain-smoked cigarettes. They made notes of all prestrike intelligence and memorized Point Option—the location on the sea where the *Enterprise* was expected to be upon their return from the raid. They did not know anything about the targets, what defenses were there, or what ships they would find. None of that information was available, for no preraid aerial reconnaissance had been conducted.

Kleiss felt no fear that morning.[23] Not sure why, he thought it had something to do with his childhood on the prairie, where the presence of death always hunkered nearby. If anything, he was eager, jittery, ready to get the whole thing going. He thought of Jean and his wish to marry her, and stories from his childhood, "Popeye" and "Jack and the Beanstalk," and of all the possible contingencies of the coming raid.

Flight quarters sounded at 0345, and a yeoman in each ready room passed along word for the pilots to man their planes. In their khaki uniforms, with flight goggles on their foreheads and parachutes on their backs, Kleiss and the others climbed to the deck and were led by ground crew through the mass of parked planes to the specific aircraft each had been assigned. The process was efficient and business like. The morning air was mild, and a full moon on the western horizon was veiled behind low clouds. The seas were calming. From a loudspeaker bellowed the order "Start engines!," and as one the propellers all sputtered and caught, the noise deafening, smoke belching from each plane's exhaust. The first aircraft rolled into their takeoffs at 0443: fighters assigned to the combat air patrol that morning, dive-bombers from Bombing Six and Scouting Six, and then, following every fifteen seconds, Devastators from Torpedo Six.

Two air strikes consisting of thirty-seven Dauntlesses and nine torpedo bombers formed in the dark sky and headed west in a series of V-formations for the Kwajalein atoll, with its twin islands of Roi and Namur lying flat in the dark sea. Flying in formation at night was dangerous business, but the planes managed to get over the target without any collisions, the full moon providing helpful light. They arrived over Roi and its island air base a few minutes earlier than expected, while the sun was just rising in the east, but dense fog obscured the island, and the dive-bomber pilots could see little of the coral airstrip. They circled, hoping the mist would lift, and the drone of their engines alerted the Japanese antiaircraft gunners, who rushed to their stations. After a few minutes the American aviators of Scouting Six could begin to make things out in the gloom, and they tipped over into their glide-bombing attacks, flying quickly through the antiaircraft fire, and released their bombs, the first American ordnance of the war to be dropped on Japanese territory.[24] The bombs destroyed several hangars and a few parked bombers and left the airstrip pockmarked. A fuel tank was hit, and with a clap a huge ball of fire bloomed hundreds of feet into the air. Then the planes turned back around to conduct strafing runs though the flak blossomed on either side of their wingtips, and Japanese fighters, older and slower Type 96s that had scrambled as the Americans approached, caused some trouble. Four American dive-bombers were lost, their pilots and rear gunners killed.

Over Roi, Kleiss prepped his SBD for a diving attack, first alerting his gunner over the interphone, then taking a dose of ephedrine to prevent burst eardrums. Kleiss then reached under his seat to pull his bombs' arming pins and switched his plane to low blower and low prop pitch. He engaged the split flaps, opened the cockpit hatch, and "pushed over" by ramming the stick forward and pulling the nose of the plane downward. The plane descended from 14,000 feet to 2,000 feet in approximately thirty seconds, and Kleiss stared through his Mark-3 bomb scope, dropping his small 100-pound wing bombs into a parked plane. He then switched to his machine guns and, fighting 9 g's and tunnel vision, strafed the island. After pulling out he attempted to rejoin his section, but in his peripheral vision he saw a Japanese fighter zip by and shoot down one of his squadron mates, Earl Donnell. John Snowden (according to Kleiss, the "best gunner in the whole business") fired on the plane with his .30-caliber gun.[25] Handpicked by Kleiss for his marksmanship, Snowden sent a line of bullets into the Japanese fighter, which then exploded and spun one thousand feet down into the water. Kleiss then joined formation with two other planes, and together they circled around to make another attack, this time on nearby Kwajalein, but were immediately set upon by three more Japanese fighters. Curiously, though, the fighters did not press their attacks, so a relieved Kleiss focused on what he believed was a large cruiser in Kwajalein's harbor, and he flipped into a 70-degree dive from a mile and a half above the water, using his dive breaks to check his speed as he plummeted. Dive-bombing required delicate judgment: the longer a pilot waited, the better odds he had of scoring a hit, but if he stayed too long in a dive, the plane could not recover in time before it smacked into the water. There was a perfect midpoint somewhere between personal safety and an effective bomb run, but finding it was up to the pilot's guts, skill, and, each and every time, his luck. The fact that the SBDs' altimeters often gauged the altitude incorrectly did not help matters. During the twenty-second dive Kleiss squinted through the telescope mounted above his instrument panel. While staring ahead he struggled to keep the plane from skidding laterally. He held the dive until he passed below two thousand feet, then he pulled the release to his 500-pound bomb, closed his dive breaks, and began his desperate pullout. He and Snowden again felt the pressure in their heads and torsos, but neither blacked out. As the plane leveled out just above the waves, Snowden opened up with his machine gun again, stitching bullets into the cruiser. Their bomb landed dead center on the Japanese vessel.

When Kleiss and the other pilots from his squadron who survived the raids landed back on deck, they parked their planes, climbed from the cockpits, removed their helmets and goggles, and, their hair matted, descended to their ready rooms for sandwiches, juice, and a debriefing. They looked around to see who was still there and who was missing. Kleiss, for one, thought the personnel losses they had suffered were too severe.

"It was not a real successful attack," he thought. "We lost as much as we gained."[26] The men remained in their flight uniforms and waited while their planes were rearmed and refueled on deck.

Kleiss was sent off once more at 1015 for his second raid of the day, joining a nine-plane group that was again without any fighter protection. They all supposed that Japanese fighters were in the air by now, surely alert and swarming. The group climbed steadily while turning east toward Maloelap, their leader Dick Best bringing them down to windward so they could attack from out of the sun.[27] Over Maloelap they saw four Japanese fighters on patrol, similar old Type 96 "Claudes" from the Chitose Air Group that had bedeviled them earlier, so the dive-bombers leveled off to gain speed as the enemy fighters turned toward them to engage. Kleiss and the other American pilots flew in column in two-hundred-knot power glides as the Claudes closed and ground gunners on Maloelap opened up. Kleiss had three Japanese fighters behind him during the ten-mile glide, but he eluded them by splitting his flaps and chopping his throttle. The fighters flew past him, Kleiss spotting an enemy pilot's goggled face staring at him as he sped by, and he dropped his big 500-pound bomb on a large hangar. He then picked his way through antiaircraft fire and headed for the safety of nearby cloud formations, but three more Japanese fighters again turned to follow. Johnny Snowden on the machine gun behind Kleiss was busy reloading, so the closest fighter got off a burst from his wing guns that punctured Kleiss' two right-side fuel tanks and grazed Snowden's right leg. Another bullet glanced off the antenna post above Kleiss' headrest. "Had I been taller," he recalled, "I would have been killed."[28] Kleiss yanked into a tight wingover and traded close-in, head-on shots, sending the three fighters scurrying away. His SBD a mess and his ammunition belts down to a mere fifty rounds, Kleiss decided to leave well enough alone and turned away to begin the flight back home. He noticed gasoline streaming from his starboard fuel tank, which was soon bone dry, but the bigger worry was the oil leaking from his engine cylinder and splashing onto his windshield. It forced Kleiss to stand periodically in the cockpit to wipe down the Plexiglas. Despite all this, he managed to find the carrier and land safely at 1315.

After the morning's action, Halsey was left unsatisfied. He sent yet another strike of Dauntlesses back to Kwajalein and a fourth strike of dive-bombers and torpedo planes back to attack Wotje. Originally conceived as a mere hit-and-run attack, the day's operations evolved into a "9-hour shuttle bombing operation in which returning planes landed, refueled, rearmed, and then headed back into the sky to revisit the enemy bases."[29] By day's end enemy bombers, as well as multiple fuel tanks, hangars, radio stations, ships in the harbor, and the airstrips themselves, were all left severely damaged or destroyed. At around 1322 the last of Halsey's planes was brought aboard the carrier, and the entire task force turned northeast and sped out of the area.

During the afternoon, Dusty Kleiss and other airmen visited their wounded squadron mates in sick bay, handing out "medicinal" bourbon to those aviators in need of something to calm their nerves or help them sleep. Then he returned to his stateroom and wrote Jean a new letter: "I wish I could tell you some of the places I've been and what we've been doing. But just now all I can say is that our men have got more guts and our gunners have a better eye than those of any other country."[30]

Weeks later, lookouts on board the *Enterprise* spotted the hazy green mountains of Oahu in the distance. Halsey ordered all hands to dress in their whites and man their battle stations for the arrival. Huge battle flags were draped from the carrier, and as the ship slid into its pier, other vessels docked nearby greeted her with a cacophony of blasts from their big whistles and sirens. Sailors and workmen lined the decks and waved to the Big E, hollering three cheers, all aware that the carrier had done something quite special indeed: conducted the first American carrier offensive of the Pacific War. The raids would be widely and ecstatically reported in the American newspapers. Though the tactical results had been small, and the strategic implications even more slight, the news provided a badly needed respite to the string of setbacks, defeats, and poor performances emanating from the Pacific area of operations. It was an important and much-needed boost to morale, both among the fleet and back home.

The *Enterprise*'s Air Group had left the carrier and flown into NAS Pearl Harbor earlier that day, landing in a heavy rain. They waited for the *Enterprise* to dock, cheered her arrival, had lunch, and then headed away en masse to the Royal Hawaiian Hotel on Waikiki Beach for three days of rest.

Kleiss avoided getting into too much trouble during his brief time off, content to merely relax for the first time since the war had started two months prior. He smoked cigarettes, sipped a cocktail or two, and "stare[d] out past the palm trees at the calm Pacific surf off Waikiki."[31] He wrote, "When you have a chance to relax, you must do it. . . . The return to combat would come quickly enough."[33] Even then his squadron mates who had been lost during the strike on the Marshalls were being replaced. The American war machine continued to gather steam, ramping up for the long haul.

On Valentine's Day, the *Enterprise* again set sail, this time as the centerpiece of Task Force 16, Admiral Halsey in overall command once more. Their orders were to proceed with strikes against Wake Island, almost due west of Pearl Harbor, over two thousand miles away. But just days out, on February 18, Kleiss' Academy classmate, fellow aviator, and best friend Lieutenant (jg) Thomas Eversole, USNA '38, from Pocatello, Idaho, a member of 12th Company at Annapolis alongside Leon Rogers, Ben Pickett, Marion Buaas, and Eric Allen, became disoriented while on a patrol flight during a storm and was forced to ditch his TBD Devastator out in the open ocean some sixty miles from the carrier. Halsey would have been forgiven had he refused to slow down or deviate from his course, but he halted the entire task force to search the sea for Eversole and his gunner. The next morning Eversole's life raft was spotted on the water, and Halsey detailed the destroyer *Dunlap* to fetch them. Kleiss flew out to help lead the destroyer to the men, dropping smoke bombs next to Eversole and his gunner for the ship to follow. What Halsey did had ramifications far larger than merely saving the lives of two airmen. His evident compassion and his willingness to delay the force and send all available personnel to hunt the men down on the open sea demonstrated to Kleiss and the other pilots on board (who every day faced the very real possibility of becoming lost and ditching themselves) that their admiral would do whatever he could to find them. It was tremendously uplifting to them all.

The *Enterprise*'s air crews attacked Wake Island, which had been invaded and seized by Japan earlier in December, on February 24. Kleiss and Snowden took off in a misty rain before dawn that morning alongside seventeen other SBDs with 500-pound bombs latched to their fuselages. He flew as part of Second Division, in plane 6-S-11. His classmate Edward Lee Anderson took off with him, in plane 6-B-11. In all, a mixture of fifty-one dive-bombers, torpedo planes, and fighters droned southward toward Wake Island that morning. It took an hour for the massive air group to reach Wake and its two smaller islands, and flak started popping up over the coral atoll while they were still twenty miles out. Anderson was with the first group of planes to dive in, and he and his squadron mates put holes in the island's runway and destroyed a seaplane and a barge. Kleiss, diving in after Anderson, dropped his bomb squarely on an ammunition magazine and then strafed Japanese gun positions along the island's eastern shore. On the way back, Kleiss and other aviators spotted a 120-foot patrol vessel out in the open water and hit it with everything they had left. Kleiss dropped his two wing bombs on the enemy craft but rushed his shot and missed as the small boat made violent turns beneath him. A group of pilots swung back around to rake the craft with their .50-caliber machine guns. "The wonder is we didn't shoot each other," Kleiss said.[33] When the planes departed the area, the vessel was spewing oil and turning in circles. The strike force returned to the *Enterprise* at 0945, losing two SBDs in the attack. Cleo Dobson, for one, was growing increasingly frustrated by the incessant losses his squadron was taking. "All told we have lost nine pilots and eleven rear seat gunners since December 7th. From that figure, we can expect only about two and a half months left and by God I don't like it. I am ready to turn in my suit."[34]

Halsey withdrew to the northwest but received an urgent message from Nimitz a few days later, urging him to press on and attack Marcus Island to the south, only one thousand miles from Tokyo. Kleiss, Dobson, and the rest of Bombing Six grumbled among themselves, wondering why it seemed as if the *Enterprise* was the only ship fighting this war. On the way to the island Kleiss wrote to Jean, "If anything should ever happen to me, my biggest regret would be not getting to see you again. Maybe you could swoop down from heaven much later—I wouldn't mind waiting—

and I could tip toe my way up through Hell—'cause that's where I'm sure to go—and then I could see you again. . . . Night and happy dreams, Jean, and always my last thoughts and words will be to you."[35]

They scrambled yet again at 0435 on the morning of March 4, heavy moonlight washing over the waves and the carrier's deck. It cheered Kleiss: he thought the moonlight heaven-sent, and it helped the aviators get their planes aloft more safely and efficiently. After forming up, the packs of planes flew the 128 miles to Marcus Island, the sky growing increasingly overcast. The various units of the strike force became separated, pilots losing sight of their squadron mates' position lights in front of them, a tailwind boosting their speed and adding to the difficulty of keeping formation. Still, the *Enterprise* was able to use its new radar technology to guide the bulk of the strike force to the island despite the weather, and the target, with its three white runways, was first spotted through a break in the clouds at 0630. In the predawn darkness Kleiss and his fellow pilots used parachute flares to help illuminate the island, but the blackness and the persistent cloud cover made accurate bombing difficult, as did the stout and well-aimed antiaircraft fire the Japanese defenders hurled up. Kleiss and Snowden were rocked by eight near misses. On his attack run, Kleiss skimmed through the fringe of a hole in the clouds at five thousand feet and "laid [his] eggs" in the middle of a group of barracks buildings alongside one of the runways, starting fires that burned in the early morning.[36] His 500-pound bomb got snagged in its rack, however, and Kleiss was forced to shake the plane until it dropped off over the ocean on his return flight to the *Enterprise*.

As the spring of 1942 passed, the Navy's aviators continued to feel the brunt of the war's demands. Kleiss lost two good friends that spring to accidents. He wrote of the losses in his diary: "This makes the trip a most unhappy one. Two of my best friends."[37] He struggled with the finality of it all; the men were gone so suddenly. But for Kleiss and his fellow aviators, heading back to Hawaii and some rest and already feeling saddened and tired and over it all, things were just getting started.

1938
USNA

MARION WILLIAM DUFILHO

Opelousas, Louisiana

From way down South, Bill brought his sunny smile to brighten our four years here. Although having a strong tendency to quietness, this modest young man possesses such a number of deep, hidden qualities that all those who know him swear by him. A true friend, who has often endangered his own welfare in the interests of a kindred spirit, a living example of Marcus Aurelius' belief that "Manners are the better part of morals," and a healthy lad who seasons strenuous workouts on the mat with equally sonorous fade-outs on the bunk. Others may spend more time in this last-named sport, but no one derives more pleasure from it than our Jughaid. A good wife who hardly murmurs over parting with his last stamp even when soft, dreamy music sets him thinking of the girl(s) at home.

The Lucky Bag, 1938

Chapter Twelve

THE WINGMAN

Despite the early American raids by the *Enterprise* and her aviators, it did not take long for Japan to complete the establishment of what it called its "Greater East Asia Empire," encompassing by the spring of 1942 several strategic airstrips and ports, numerous mineral-rich islands, and a newfound industrial capacity that would satisfy the emperor's war-making needs for the foreseeable future, all enclosed within a strong perimeter that could be defended and with supply lines in the process of being secured. The Japanese military had handled itself superbly during its offensive operations and forged an undeniable new reputation among its adversaries. Her troops and sailors were now regarded by the Allies as fearsome warriors with tactically sound, if not brilliant, leaders who had at their disposal some of the best equipment in the world, from torpedoes to fighter planes. They had reduced prewar stereotypes held by Pacific-based Dutchmen, Americans, and Britons alike to foolish prattle. Allied soldiers and sailors were now very much afraid of them and wondering if, just perhaps, the Japanese were unbeatable.

But not every Japanese admiral or commander was fully satisfied with what the emperor's military forces had accomplished thus far. Isoroku Yamamoto, for one, Marshal Admiral of the Imperial Japanese Navy, still complained, for he was well aware that the decisive battle with the American Navy had not yet taken place, and he knew that in America industrial plants were even then switching over their production lines and ramping up their workforces and, given time, would quickly produce a navy far better and more heavily supplied than anything his country could hope to possess. What Japan needed, and what Yamamoto was desperately anxious to deliver, was an operation that would precipitate a colossal set piece with the whole of the U.S. Navy's Pacific Fleet, a battle that would be fought on Japan's terms and, once won, would force the Americans to sue for peace, end the war, and preserve all the empire's glorious gains.

Yamamoto quickly cast his eyes on Midway, a speck of coral thrusting haphazardly out of the vast expanses of the Middle Pacific and an island whose potential capture, he believed, would be most likely to compel the American fleet to sail out and do battle. But, frustratingly for Yamamoto, other matters needed to be attended to first. The Japanese army was growing wary of what was becoming an increasingly nettlesome Allied threat from Australia and needed time to strengthen its southern perimeter, so before operations against Midway Island could begin, it was necessary for IJN forces to sail southward to support the Japanese army's operations in the Southwest Pacific. This operation, this distraction, annoyed Yamamoto. He knew nothing that took place in the waters around Australia would help him accomplish his ultimate objective, yet he also believed the mission would be simple and quick, a minor delay and nothing more, so he allowed his forces to be diminished in the near term and a task force to be sent steaming down to the Coral Sea to support the capture of Port Moresby on Papua New Guinea's southern coast.

Thanks to his cryptographers, Admiral Nimitz already knew Yamamoto was preparing something for the Central Pacific, but separate intelligence reports describing the movements of the Japanese navy in the direction of the Coral Sea were of more immediate concern to him. He could ignore no threats to Australia; they had to be addressed.

The flight of Lieutenant Edward Henry "Butch" O'Hare (for which he received the Medal of Honor) has gone down in the annals of the U.S. Navy as one of its most legendary and celebrated individual actions, perhaps the most famous dogfight in American history, and rightly so, for it is a story of the utmost courage and selflessness, as well as exquisite dogfighting and near-impossible aerial marksmanship. O'Hare's exploits on the afternoon of February 20, 1942, have been lauded for upholding the highest ideals of the Navy and would bring him lasting glory.[1] Butch O'Hare was not a member of the

Naval Academy's Class of 1938—he graduated one year earlier—but his wingman that fateful day, Lieutenant (jg) Marion W. "Duff" Dufilho, was.

Dufilho had won an appointment to the Academy from Louisiana's Seventh District. While at Annapolis he had served on the staff of the yearbook, wrestled for his company, and achieved the rank of battalion chief petty officer. He then served on board the battleship *Mississippi* before opting to become an aviator and graduating from flight training in February 1941.

By the early months of 1942, Dufilho was serving in a fighter squadron on board the *Lexington* and longing for the simple farm life he had left behind in Louisiana so many years before, and for his wife Betty, waiting for him in California. He was already weary of being away, of "roaming around" with the sea constantly under his feet, yet Dufilho knew even then that the war would not be a short one.[2] There was still so much more to do. As he colorfully put it in a letter back to his parents, "We know that we have made only a beginning. Before long we must really start to battle in earnest and run the snakes back to its [*sic*] hole—then pour hot water down it."[3] Still, as the *Lexington* churned through the deep waters of the distant Pacific, far from home and heading ever southward, Dufilho wished for duty that would let him see land again, even if only for a bit.

Throughout early February, while the Asiatic Fleet tried its best to halt the advances of the Japanese navy in the Dutch East Indies and watched its big ships trapped in the Java Sea for their efforts, the *Lexington*, old, large, and 888 feet long (about 70 feet longer than her newer sisters in the Pacific, the *Enterprise*, *Yorktown*, and *Hornet*), with its deck bolted atop the converted hull of an old battle cruiser, sailed southward to penetrate Japanese-held waters north of New Ireland and to attack Rabaul, a key Japanese air base on the tip of New Britain. The mission was intended to try to slow the speed with which the Japanese were conquering the Southwest Pacific and was good for the ship's morale because, up to that point, the *Lexington* had been merely "flailing about—and none too successfully."[4] The carrier, the flagship of Vice Admiral Wilson Brown (who had served as superintendent of the Naval Academy when the Class of '38 was on the Yard), entered the waters of the Coral Sea with Task Force 11 (TF 11) in mid-February. Their strike on Rabaul was scheduled for February 21.

But the task force was spotted on the morning of February 20 by a Japanese flying boat while still some 453 nautical miles northeast of the target, about twenty hours of sailing time, so the *Lexington* quickly launched a six-plane combat air patrol and sent two planes, including one piloted by Lieutenant Commander Jimmy Thach, the superb commanding officer of Fighter Squadron Three (VF-3), after the Japanese scout. Thach and his wingman caught the Mavis and shot it down, but it took some time, as the Japanese pilot used banks of cumulous clouds heavy with rain as hiding places, buying precious minutes with which to report the *Lexington*'s position.

The attack on Rabaul depended on the element of surprise, which TF 11 had just lost, so Admiral Brown canceled the operation around noon. But Captain Frederick C. "Ted" Sherman, the *Lexington*'s commanding officer, forcefully advocated for staying in the area and stirring up another fight, and after heated arguments with his staff, Brown agreed to a feint that would at least distract the Japanese and perhaps divert some of their forces away from the East Indies. Ultimately, the plan was to continue directly to the target area for the next few hours in an effort to coax the Japanese on Rabaul and the nearby airfield of Truk to come out and meet them. It was a gambler's move and one that put the burden of defending the task force from the expected aerial attacks squarely on the shoulders of Dufilho, O'Hare, and Fighting Three.

It did not take long for the feint to produce results. That afternoon, at 1611, radar on the *Lexington* picked up nine twin-engine Japanese heavy bombers inbound, bearing 255 degrees, seventy-five miles out, speed about 170 knots, and section leader Noel A. M. Gayler was sent airborne into the light cloud cover with five other Wildcats to intercept them while the carrier gunned her engines to flank speed. Among these fighter pilots was Lieutenant (jg) Howard F. "Spud" Clark, yet another member of the Naval Academy's Class of 1938. VF-3's sortie was a success, despite blistering machine-gun fire from the mottled brown and green Japanese bombers: each of the Wildcats scored a kill, including Clark, two more of the enemy bombers were damaged and flew away fast, and the task force's antiaircraft guns finished off the last plane before it could get close enough to release its bomb on the *Lexington*.

But the carrier had kicked an anthill, and not thirty minutes later the *Lexington*'s radar again picked up incoming enemy planes, this time a formation of eight bombers only twelve miles out, dangerously close to the task force. A second formation of six more Wildcats from VF-3, Felix the Cat insignia painted on their fuselages, was again launched from the *Lexington*'s deck, among them the planes of Butch O'Hare, a modest and highly respected section leader, and Dufilho, his wingman. Four of the planes were sent after the inbound formation, leaving only O'Hare and Dufilho above the carrier as protection, both men disgusted with being left behind and "stewing on the sidelines like third stringers."[5]

It was at that exact moment, however, after the bulk of the American fighters had left the area, that still another group of Japanese bombers unexpectedly arrived north of the *Lexington*, only ten miles distant, frighteningly close. The carrier's radar was already filled with contacts and had numerous gaps besides, and the new flight of bombers had not been seen until they were within eyesight. The first to spot them, at 1656, were lookouts on board the destroyer USS *Patterson* out in the *Lexington*'s screen, and she frantically flashed a warning signal to the carrier ahead of her. With no other fighters nearby save O'Hare and Dufilho, the *Lexington*'s flight direction officer ordered them to intercept the enemy planes while he called back some fighters to help. The carrier's crew scrambled to their defense stations. Surprised to learn they were all that was left to cover the carrier, O'Hare and Dufilho instantly clawed for altitude in their heavy Grummans and turned eastward to do what they could.

At 1705 the two men spied the nine Japanese Bettys, 1,500 feet below them in a large and tight V-shaped formation, now nine miles out from the carrier's stern. The enemy planes were heavily laden and already in shallow dives, gaining speed, and lining up for their bomb runs. O'Hare and Dufilho cut inside the bombers' turns to get between them and the task force. At 12,000 feet and with the altitude in their favor, they then rolled over to attack from above in shallow dives of their own, aiming for the right side of the Japanese formation.

Following procedure, the two pilots charged their guns, turned on the light bulbs in their illuminated gun sights, and fired brief test bursts. Immediately, Dufilho discovered that all four of his .50-caliber M2 Brownings were jammed and would not shoot—shifting ammunition belts had fouled them. O'Hare, aware of what was happening, gestured through the canopy of his cockpit for Dufilho to return to the *Lex*, but Dufilho would not leave, even after O'Hare shook his fist at him. With no other options, Dufilho decided he would try to draw the bombers' fire away from O'Hare as best he could by making several feints at the Japanese formation, which he did before, to his "intense chagrin," disengaging to give O'Hare a clear shot at the bombers while he tried to free his fouled Brownings.[6] As historian John Lundstrom wrote, "Events rapidly left [Dufilho] behind," and he became, through no fault of his own, a footnote to the day's glories.[7]

It was undeniably heroic for O'Hare to continue without a partner covering his wing, but, once he realized Dufilho was having problems, he did not hesitate to press forward, not with the *Lexington* under such terrible threat. Four times he swept in on the enemy bombers: his first run, at full throttle, was a high-side diving attack during which he was able to shoot down one of the Bettys, sending .50-caliber slugs into its starboard engine nacelle and wing root and leaving the plane smoking, spurting streams of oil, and spinning crazily for the water. Then, still in his initial firing run, O'Hare quickly turned, aimed again, and damaged another of the bombers with a short burst, sending it downward with a thin white contrail spewing from its ruptured wing tank. O'Hare had destroyed two planes on his first pass.

He then maneuvered around the formation and attacked again from the left side, sending the rearmost bomber downward in flames, followed by another that he shot with a long burst through the left wing and the pilot cockpit. Soon every gun within the Japanese formation, as many as two dozen, was aimed at O'Hare, bullets zipping outward from their "dorsal blisters, beam hatches, and tail stingers," gunfire Jimmy Thach would call the "red rain of battle," but O'Hare was oblivious to the streams of tracer fire, and he continued to wreak havoc with his high-deflection firing runs and his opportunistic and superbly well-placed shots.[8]

As he flew down on his third and fourth dives, the Bettys by this time were within range of the 5-inch antiaircraft guns of TF 11 below, and they opened fire too. Though their bursts were low, they were still dangerous.

O'Hare ignored these explosions, so focused was he on his task. He dispatched the new trailing plane on the formation's left side, then shot at the lead Japanese bomber, hoping to eliminate the master bombardier of the formation or, at the least, distract him from his sites. Approaching to within point-blank range of the enemy plane, he fired another burst of .50-caliber slugs that tore into the bomber's nacelle, shearing the portside engine from its wing mount and causing the plane to explode. Ultimately, only four of the Bettys managed to drop their bombs. Captain Sherman, a cool-headed and pugnacious commanding officer, twisted his carrier wildly on the sea to avoid them. The bombs all missed, though the nearest landed a mere one hundred feet from the *Lex*'s fantail.

In four minutes, O'Hare had single-handedly, and famously, destroyed or severely damaged five of the bombers and rendered what could have been a devastating Japanese attack completely ineffective. Perhaps the most amazing detail about O'Hare's flight is that his ammunition was limited; it is estimated he had only sixty rounds for each of the bombers, but he was a supremely skilled marksman with the stick of a Wildcat and, despite the limitations of his ammunition, proved lethally effective that afternoon.

By the time Thach reached him with other Wildcats to assist, O'Hare had both run out of ammunition and become the U.S. Navy's first flying ace of World War II. He finally gave in to the tension: "Time seems to stand still while you're at it," he said later. "Your mouth and throat get so dry it's hard to talk. Mine was so dry I thought I'd lost my voice."[9] When he landed back on the *Lexington*'s deck, O'Hare was mobbed by the yellow-jerseyed plane handlers and deck hands, but all he wanted were more bullets, a cup of water, and clearance to get back up in the air.[10] Instead he was brought up to shake hands with Captain Sherman and Admiral Brown. As the ship turned and sailed southeast in the dusk at twenty-two knots, both senior officers believed that what O'Hare had done had most certainly saved the carrier. He would be promoted to the rank of lieutenant commander and, the following April in Washington, DC, received the Congressional Medal of Honor from President Roosevelt personally. His wife Rita was there to place the medal around his neck.

WILLIAM NICHOLAS LEONARD

St. Petersburg, Florida

SPLASH—and away goes Bill on another fast fifty! Almost any afternoon will find him in the pool working at his favorite sport. His other activities include building model airplanes and boats, seeking chow, and keeping just one jump ahead of the Academic Departments. His saying, "The book is wrong," has almost landed him in trouble on several occasions, but a little boning has always pulled him out of any difficulties. Only one thing keeps Bill from being a perfect roommate—he has always refused to drag blind, remaining adamant on his Red Miking policy. Whenever any other Army brats like Bill decide to go to sea, we will always welcome them, for we know they will make the best of pals and shipmates.

The Lucky Bag, 1938

Chapter Thirteen

FIRST SKIRMISHES

On February 28 the *Lexington* and TF 11 nestled around her turned south in the general direction of Australia. They sailed within 250 miles of mountainous, cloud-capped Rossel Island before, on March 1, swinging northeastward toward the New Hebrides, where they would join forces with the USS *Yorktown*'s TF 17 and an ANZAC squadron, bringing the combined Allied force in the seas to a very respectable complement of two aircraft carriers, eight heavy cruisers, and more than a dozen destroyers.

Off the villages of Lae and Salamua, on Papua New Guinea's eastern coast, the Imperial Japanese Navy had assembled a large fleet of ships and ordered them to linger there in the Solomon Sea while transports offloaded troops and supplies to the island's beaches. Unable to leave the area, the force represented a tantalizing target to Vice Admiral Wilson Brown, and he opted to send his air groups in to attack from a launch point in the Gulf of Papua. This approach from the south would leave the American task force far less exposed to Japanese search planes out of Rabaul and would probably catch the Japanese ships by surprise, but it would also necessitate a much tougher flight for Brown's air crews, one that would involve cutting across the trackless jungles and sharp peaks of the Owen Stanley Mountains, which formed the spine of Papua New Guinea and were notorious for their towering cloud formations, often horrendous weather, and usually limited visibility.[1] The mountains were also high, 14,000 feet, and would be very difficult for the dive-bombers and torpedo planes to surmount, weighted as they were by their heavy loads. Adding to the operation's dangers was that in order to get the planes on target with sufficient fuel, the American fleet would have to sail in close to the Papua New Guinean shoreline, and a scant 125 miles from Lae, Salamaua, and the enemy fleet anchored just offshore. Despite the challenges, the mission was approved, and 108 planes were assigned to the raid, scheduled for March 10. Captain Sherman set the launch time for 0800, hoping that a well-known pass through the mountains would be clear enough for his planes to slip through—it often was in the mornings, and at 7,500 feet it was a much easier route for his airmen.

March 10 dawned clear. Leading the assault, and first off the *Lexington*'s deck, were eight fighters commanded by Jimmy Thach, including Marion Dufilho's. In short order the eighteen Dauntless dive-bombers of Scouting Two followed them up, then twelve dive-bombers from VB-2, and thirteen lumbering Devastators from Torpedo Two. The plan was for the *Lexington*'s planes to bomb Lae and the ships anchored there and then, twenty minutes later, conduct a coordinated attack on Salamaua harbor. The planes of the *Yorktown* would then repeat the process when they arrived a few minutes later. The *Lexington*'s bombers and fighters were in the air by 0834; the *Yorktown*'s contingent was airborne twenty-one minutes behind them.

As the planes approached the mountain range, the real concern was how the slow torpedo planes would fare on the climb. The pass was much lower than the peaks, but even asking the Devastators to climb to 7,500 feet with long, heavy torpedoes slung under their bellies was a stretch, and for a time the pilots noticed apprehensively that they could not climb as fast as they needed to—the green flanks of the mountain chain were rearing up before them, quickly filling their canopies, and they feared they would have to abort the mission. In time, however, the pilots spotted the flat green expanse in the saddle of the pass and found a thermal updraft that flowed through it, and they felt its pull wash them gently up and over the top and down the other side, and the attack was on. The fighters swept by, graceful and quick, and took over the lead as the planes descended, and the advanced elements of the formations were over the target area by 0920.

The sky above the Japanese ships in Huon Gulf was bright blue and dotted with tufts of white cumulus clouds, and when the American strike planes glided down the far side of the mountains' green slopes, across the airfield, and out over the enemy fleet, they looked like "silver streaks," and thoroughly surprised the Japanese lookouts and ship captains.[2] Thach, Dufilho, and the other aviators of their fighter section scanned the skies for enemy Zeros, but they were clear. The attack was a thunderbolt for which the Japanese were thoroughly unprepared, and quickly the dive-bombers of Scouting Two arrived behind the fighters and turned over into their runs, aiming for the fat transports in the shallow water just off the beach. They dropped their 500-pounders on the ships, saving their 100-pounders for Lae's buildings. Thach, Dufilho, and Butch O'Hare stayed to look for targets on Lae while the rest of the *Lexington*'s planes flew south as planned to attack Salamaua. Dufilho strafed Japanese troops, sending them scrambling for cover, and then fired at gun positions dug into the sand and made dummy runs to draw the ineffective antiaircraft fire that had belatedly popped up away from the slow torpedo planes.

Not long after the *Lexington*'s strike force cleared the area, the second attack by the *Yorktown*'s formations arrived out of the sun. They too had had no trouble navigating over the Owen Stanley range and reached the gulf and its smoking ships and beaches fifteen minutes later. Among the escort fighters who arrived first were two men from the Class of '38: William N. Leonard from St. Petersburg, Florida, and Richard G. Cromelin, known everywhere as "Dick." Like Thach, Dufilho, and O'Hare before them, the fighter pilots found little to do, so they patrolled offshore and scanned the sky for any Japanese fighters that might be approaching, while the seventeen SBDs of Bombing Five set to work attacking the light cruiser *Yubari*. Meanwhile, the dive-bombers of Scouting Five lined up for their own attacks on transports moored close inshore to Lae, then the torpedo planes arrived and dropped down at 1020 for runs on the beleaguered Japanese ships and sailors off Salamaua.

The combined attacks by the American pilots sank three transports and a converted minesweeper. A light cruiser, a merchant vessel, three destroyers, and a seaplane tender also lay burning and damaged. They were the IJN's heaviest losses since the war had started that December morning three months earlier.[3] The losses suffered by the enemy were not on par with the *Arizona* or *Tennessee* or *Oklahoma*, but it was Japanese steel nonetheless. Jimmy Thach would later write, "This whole flight was a sort of picnic because we had no air opposition to speak of. We destroyed everything worthwhile in the vicinity."[4] Only one American plane was lost.[5]

Once their aviators returned, the *Lexington* and *Yorktown* steamed quickly to the southeast and safer waters. The *Lexington* would return to Pearl Harbor. Though the strike's tally was modest, it came in the middle of a string of Japanese victories in the Southwest Pacific and caused a great boost in morale among the Allies. Just as importantly, it caused the Japanese, amid rising anxiety, to postpone their planned invasions of Port Moresby and Tulagi for one month, invasions Admiral Yamamoto had wanted done and over with so he could turn his attention to Midway and his grand and final battle with the U.S. Navy. Now that would have to wait.

When news of the successful attack reached President Roosevelt in Washington, DC, he was so pleased that he sent a message to Churchill: "It was by all means the best day's work we have had."[6]

A few weeks later, plans for the Japanese invasion of Port Moresby were restarted, and the threat of enemy control of Eastern New Guinea and, by extension, northern Australia once again became all too real for Allied leadership. Intelligence reports indicated the Japanese were beginning to build up their strength in the region anew, through a complex plan that involved flooding the area with land-based air units, submarines, lumbering troopships packed with ten thousand soldiers, and swarms of supply freighters, minelayers, gunboats, tenders, and aircraft carriers that would take Tulagi (in the Solomon Islands) on May 3 and Port Moresby one week later. If true, this so-called Operation MO demanded another response from the Allies.

Admiral Nimitz rapidly put a strategy together to counter this renewed threat and shared what he wanted to do with his boss, Admiral Ernest King. As its main component, Nimitz's proposal involved a confrontation with the Japanese in the Coral Sea area, southeast of Port Moresby and northeast of Australia's Great Barrier Reef. He opted to send a carrier task force back in the direction of the Coral Sea and Australia to meet up with the *Yorktown* (TF 17), which had stayed in the area after the Lae and Salamaua raids to fix a nagging fuel tank problem. In truth, the only carrier he could have sent in was the *Lexington* again, now commanded by Rear Admiral Aubrey "Jack" Fitch and just returned to Pearl Harbor to refuel and rearm. Once the *Lex* and TF 11 had sailed back into the South Pacific, the two task forces would find and attack the oncoming Japanese invasion fleet and subsequently check the enemy's advance into the New Guinea–Solomons theater.

Task Force 11, with the heavy cruisers *Minneapolis* and *New Orleans* and seven destroyers accompanying the Lady Lex, steamed out of Pearl Harbor on April 14, zigzagging on a southerly course toward distant Palmyra Island. Included in the *Lexington*'s Air Group were Class of '38 schoolmates Brink Bass in an SBD dive-bomber; Leonard Thornhill flying a torpedo plane; Roy Hale, assigned to VS-2; and, in Fighter Squadron Two, Robert Morgan, Marion Dufilho, and Howard Clark. A redhead from Salisbury, Maryland, across the Chesapeake Bay from Annapolis, "Red" Clark had been a member of 2nd Company at the Academy alongside Bruce Garrett and Frank Lynch and had wanted to be an aviator since his early days on the Yard. A runner and dancer, he was a practical man and a clear-headed pilot, pragmatic and reserved. By the spring of 1942, he had already seen battle, as had most of the *Lexington*'s air crew.

On April 27, once repairs had been completed, the *Yorktown* steamed into the inaccessible middle Pacific, where the ocean is dark blue and incomprehensibly deep. Among her complement of aviators were 1938 First Classmen Bill Leonard and Dick Crommelin, both still flying fighters with VF-42.

The two American carriers sighted each other just after sunrise on May 1 and Admiral Frank Jack Fletcher, USNA '06, a stern Iowan, assumed command of the combined force. All crews were placed on a twenty-four-hour alert and strict radio silence was established. The *Lexington* group, after its long sail, set about the arduous task of refueling at sea. By this point, Fletcher knew from fresh intelligence breaks that a Japanese invasion force was even then moving down from the Bismarcks into the Eastern Solomons.[7] He opted to hang back out of range of the enemy fleet's patrol flights and try to time his attack for when the force was on the beaches and most vulnerable.

Throughout the afternoon of May 3, Fletcher monitored the contact reports of his scout planes scanning the Bismarcks and Solomons for signs of the enemy. That evening, at 1900, he received word from Australia-based army air patrols that enemy ships had been spotted off Santa Isabell Island in the Solomons, closing in on the Australian base at Tulagi. It was an excellent opportunity for the Americans and "the kind of report we had been waiting two months to receive," Fletcher wrote.[8] Excitedly, he opted to split his forces and take the *Yorktown* and his other ships that were fully fueled away to the northwest, while Fitch stayed off New Caledonia to continue to fill the *Lexington*'s fuel tanks. The two carriers would rendezvous again in two days at a point farther north in the direction of the Luisiades, between Port Moresby and Tulagi. Fletcher turned the *Yorktown* in the darkness, upped her speed to twenty-seven knots (near peak), and scanned his maps for a suitable launch site near the island of Guadalcanal. His pilots gathered in their ready rooms and studied whatever charts they could find of the target area, small specks of green amid great swaths of blue.

May 4 dawned cold and gray, with sporadic rain and heavy wind gusts, and Fletcher, having slipped his TF 17 in undetected during the night, to a spot one hundred miles southwest of Guadalcanal's southern beaches, launched three air strikes on the minesweepers, transports, and destroyers of the Japanese invasion force, which by then crowded Tulagi's small harbor after discharging its ground soldiers.[9] The American planes, twenty-eight dive-bombers and twelve torpedo bombers, lifted off from the carrier beginning at 0701. No fighters were sent along, as the bombers were not expected to meet any opposition, so the VF-42 pilots, including Leonard and Crommelin, initially stayed behind to fly combat air patrols over the carrier. The strike force flew through the hazy weather directly over the seventy-mile-long axis of Guadalcanal, over the dense jungle ridges and sharply peaked mountaintops at its spine, and back down the northern slopes before completely surprising the Japanese in Gavutu harbor, where the weather was fine and clear, the air warm and humid, and where the Americans screamed in just above the island's treetops a little after 0800. Two additional strikes were launched at 1210 and 1500, and despite a massive volume of bombs and torpedoes expended throughout the day, the American fliers managed to sink only one Japanese destroyer, one transport, and a pair of small patrol boats (though at the time the pilots believed they had caused much greater damage). It was a small bounty indeed, but the attack was sufficient to send the Japanese invasion force scurrying back through Sealark Channel to open sea and Rabaul. It also revealed to the Japanese that there was at least one American carrier in the area.

At 1303 that afternoon, the *Yorktown*'s commanding officer, Captain Elliott Buckmaster, heard through the radio traffic emanating from his torpedo bomber squadron over the target area that enemy fighters had been spotted nearby. Immediately he ordered four of his fighters to head over and assist them. In the carrier's ready room, Bill Leonard heard the order to man aircraft over the sound-powered phone and raced out on deck with the rest of his squadron toward his plane; the engines had already been started by the flight deck personnel. Once he was strapped in, airdales coaxed four of the planes into launch positions; none of the pilots knew which four would be chosen, but Leonard was pulled forward, and a deck officer held aloft a chalkboard with his orders: "Proceed to Tulagi" and, scrawled underneath, the island's course and distance. The launching officer waved his flag at each of the four planes in turn and, one by one, beginning at 1311, Leonard and the other fighters bellowed down the carrier and into the air.

Bill Leonard was in command of the four-plane section and pushed them forward at a quick pace, knowing that if they were to do any good, they must get over Tulagi promptly.[10] The fighters winged through a narrow band of bad weather before emerging into the bright sunlight off Guadalcanal's southern coast, flying over the island's mountains, then turning northwest over Sealark Channel and descending to four thousand feet, eyes scanning the skies. The *Yorktown*'s planes they had been sent to protect had already turned back to the carrier and the skies were empty, so Leonard led the three planes in formation around him northwestward again along the coast of Florida Island to see what he could find.

At 1350 a trio of Japanese seaplanes appeared below them, big Mitsubishi F1M2 Type 0 observation floatplanes sent to aid in Tulagi's defense. Leonard tipped over into a dive on the planes, which were flying in the opposite direction. He and his wingman made high-side runs on the Japanese formation. Leonard aimed for the second floatplane in line, but the Japanese pilot pulled into a tight turn. Leonard's four .50-caliber machine guns were aimed well, though, and the floatplane belched flame and smoke and fluttered toward the wave tops. Recovering from his dive, Leonard looked back to see the leader of the Japanese floatplanes turn tightly and take position on his tail, an aggressive move for such a bulky plane. Leonard tightened his own turn, the floatplane fired and missed, and Leonard was able to speed away and regain altitude over the Japanese formation once again. He flipped into a second steep dive and shot up another of the floatplanes. His wingman, Edgar Bassett, dropped a third as it tried to flee toward Tulagi.

There was more to do. Leonard next led his fighters over a Japanese minesweeper that was sailing away from the island, and the four planes took turns making low, coordinated strafing runs, flying just over the ship's masthead before pulling back up. Leonard concentrated his fire on the minesweeper's bridge, machinery spaces, and torpedo mounts, and between them the four Americans riddled the vessel with their slugs, igniting fires and blowing holes in her oil bunkers. They broke off at 1410, the ship beneath them trailing oil and aflame, and set a southeasterly course toward home, cutting across the western tip of Guadalcanal before heading back out into the Coral Sea.

After these skirmishes the *Yorktown* rejoined Fitch and the *Lexington* 320 miles south of Guadalcanal at 0800 the next morning, then they turned together back to the northwest to again try to intercept the Port Moresby invasion force. Fletcher believed the enemy would come through the reeds, shallows, and straits of the Jomard Passage, a narrow seaway into the Coral Sea past New Guinea's eastern tip.[11] He was expecting them around

May 7 and assumed the flanks of the invasion force would be covered by the Japanese carriers—he had no idea that the two big flattops of the Japanese fleet, the *Zuikaku* and the *Shokaku*, both of which had taken part in the Pearl Harbor raid, were in fact detached from the invasion convoy.

Sailing together, the task forces of the *Yorktown* and *Lexington* arrayed themselves in a wide circular formation on the sea, with the two carriers in the center and the cruisers and destroyers in protective rings around them. While Fletcher commanded the combined task force (TF 17), he turned over tactical control of the two carriers' air operations to Fitch on board the *Lexington*, who was an aviator and a veteran carrier officer. Fletcher's orders to the combined fleet were to continue to "destroy enemy ships, shipping, and aircraft at favorable opportunities in order to assist in checking further advances by the enemy in the New Guinea–Solomon area."[12]

Though the damage to Tulagi had been slight, the Japanese had been shocked by the sudden and unexpected appearance of U.S. carrier planes in the area, particularly Rear Admiral Chuichi "King Kong" Hara and the rest of the officers of the IJN's 5th Carrier Division on board the *Zuikaku* and *Shokaku*. In their minds things had suddenly become much more serious, the stakes much deadlier. The big Japanese carriers had been refueling 350 miles to the north when they received the news of the raid, and they quickly disconnected the fuel hoses, threw them over the sides, raised steam, and raced south toward the eastern Solomons. Admiral Aritomo Goto, leading the empire's Port Moresby invasion force, also dispatched his 12,000-ton escort carrier *Shoho* to hunt the enemy in the fading light. He was taking no chances.

The chessboard for the battle was thus set. It would be carrier-against-carrier, that much was certain, but neither side had any real idea of the best tactics and strategies to use in such a fight. The carrier captains intuitively understood that victory would depend on striking first, but the problem for both sides, one that would often bedevil carrier battles in the months to come, was that neither the Americans nor the Japanese knew where the other side was. For the next few hours, both carrier groups "groped" for each other across the sea, through the low cloud banks and around the area's islands and passageways.[13] Mystifying intelligence was received in both flag plots, contradictory and erroneous scouting reports were pursued, and poorly planned and ineffective attacks were launched, all to no avail. All the while, the Japanese and American carrier groups drew closer and closer, unseen but wary, waiting for that one report from their airborne scouts flying in wedge-shaped search sectors two hundred miles long that would signal the enemy had been found.

Carriers were vulnerable. Though fast and surprisingly nimble and surrounded by entire task forces of cruisers, destroyers, and submarines whose sole job was to protect them, they were also big, easy to spot, usually crowded with highly flammable airplanes and ordnance, and relatively simple to bomb: best suited for hit-and-run warfare, not careful patrolling or probing or hiding. The carriers were excellent at inflicting heavy punishment, but to be successful it was critical they learned where the enemy was before he found them. While the carriers' air crews flew their around-the-clock patrol patterns, Sherman and Buckmaster, the two American carrier captains, did their best to hide their big ships in whatever weather fronts they could find and continued to wait tensely for their scouts' reports.

In the carriers' ready rooms, Leonard, Crommelin, Bass, Clark, and their squadron mates were nervous, to be sure, but also surprisingly upbeat as they whiled away the hours between their patrol duties familiarizing themselves with the islands and passages and straits and towns around them with such curious names: Trobriand, Misima, and Samairai; Kulumadau, Choiseul, and Malaita. Intelligence reports continued to flood into Fletcher from the Navy's codebreakers in a Pearl Harbor basement, but the messages were light on specifics. They included little concrete information about the direction and position of the Japanese fleet, so little in fact as to be almost worthless. The only thing the Allies knew in those long, tense days in early May was that Port Moresby was the enemy's target, and they had to make use of that information as best they could. The Japanese fleet was out there somewhere. To Fletcher, the only good thing about the situation on May 4 was that no Japanese scout planes had found him yet either, hidden as he was out in the empty wastes of the northern Coral Sea, southwest of Rennell Island, flitting in between rainstorms.

By the morning of May 5, the Japanese had consolidated their forces sufficiently to begin attacks on Port Moresby, but American intelligence had, just a few hours earlier, come through mightily for Fletcher. They supplied him with intercepted orders which finally revealed the Japanese fleet's position and plans with certainty. It was now clear that the Japanese invasion force would advance on Port Moresby by sailing around the eastern edge of New Guinea through the Jomard Passage, as Fletcher had long believed, before making its invasion run on either May 7 or 8. With this information, specific and detailed, Fletcher was able to take his two carriers well to the south, out of the way of the search patterns of Vice Admiral Takeo Takagi's planes on the *Shokaku* and *Zuikaku*, and pause to decide when the most advantageous time to come storming northward for his attack would be. He started his turn to the northwest late in the day on May 6, his carriers "cocked," ready to launch an all-out air strike the minute a contact report was received.[14]

When Fletcher made his turn, he assumed the Japanese carriers were hundreds of miles to the north and squatting protectively alongside the transports and convoys of the Occupation Force. But they were not. The carriers were just to his east, off his starboard rails, well into the Coral Sea, and much, much closer than he knew. Ignorance was true bliss, for had he known, it would surely have provoked a panic in flag plot. Takagi had received a contact report earlier that morning alerting him to the presence of the American carriers, and he had ordered his own carrier task force under Rear Admiral Hara on board the *Zuikaku* to make an end run around the southern Solomon Islands, then find and destroy the *Yorktown* and the *Lexington*. According to Ian Toll, "At that moment, Task Force 17 was totally exposed and in mortal peril."[15] The Japanese had found them, and found them first, and Fletcher was still unaware of it. "If the Japanese had been luckier, they could have won the battle outright," attacking and sinking the American carriers as they refueled, exposed and unprepared, for their northward turn that evening.[16] Such a catastrophic blow could very well have changed the course of the entire war. But the Japanese scout's contact report back to Takagi was dead wrong. It reported the American carriers on a bearing of 190 degrees, almost due south, deep in the Coral Sea, and nowhere near his invasion force's route of advance. That misleading information saved the American fleet and led to one of the more farcical episodes of the entire war: two carrier fleets, massive, spread out over the seas, and primed for combat, ignorantly passing each other only seventy miles apart. Had either discovered the other, it would have taken their dive-bombers no more than twenty minutes of flight time to get over the enemy carriers and begin their attacking dives. As it was, the two opposing fleets slipped by, heading in opposite directions, both admirals unaware, ships truly passing in the darkness.

By dawn on May 7, TF 17 was nearing the end of its overnight run to the northwest and was approaching the cluttered Louisiades, a string of ten volcanic islands fringed by coral reefs southeast of New Guinea. American search planes and combat air patrols were thick in the air, droning about in a leaden sky with cumulus clouds; cool, gusty winds; and intermittent rain squalls that limited visibility to fifteen miles. Fletcher's plan that morning was to launch a search mission to the north, above the island of Tagula, where the Japanese invasion convoy and its accompanying flattops were thought to be, so that he would know exactly where to send his air strikes. Ranged across the decks of his two carriers, rising and falling in the choppy seas, were 36 fighters, 70 dive-bombers, and 22 torpedo planes—128 aircraft in all.

A first contact report came back at 0815 describing two enemy carriers and two heavy cruisers northeast of Misima Island, about 175 miles to the west-northwest, exactly where they were supposed to be and within range of the American strike aircraft. Fletcher did not hesitate. Assuming that what his scout had found was the main Japanese mobile carrier force, with the *Shokaku* and *Zuikaku*, he ordered up everything he had, and a full strike package soon launched simultaneously from both carriers, comprising 16 fighters, 36 dive-bombers, and all 22 of his torpedo planes.

At about that time, the *Lexington*'s radar detected a single blip in the sky twenty-five miles distant. Whatever it was, it was circling. Lieutenant (jg) Red Clark, USNA '38, was sent in his fighter to investigate, but he could not catch the plane before it ducked away into the heavy, dark clouds of a weather frontal zone to the north. The plane disappeared from the *Lexington*'s scopes and did not reappear. Most believed the plane they had seen was a Japanese "snooper," which meant, disturbingly, that TF 17 had most likely been discovered.[17]

The task force was spotted again at 1015. Radar operators on the *Yorktown* detected a bogey lurking once more on the edge of the nearby cold front, and two fighters were scrambled. There was a bit of a mix-up; normally two section leaders were not sent aloft together, but at that moment Bill Leonard ended up climbing into the sky alongside his roommate on board the carrier, and his classmate on the Yard, Dick Crommelin. The two friends hunted through the heavy overcast north of the task force, diligently scanning for the snooper, exploring every altitude from 1,000 feet up to 27,000, but they were unable to find the plane. Fletcher now knew without question that he had been spotted.

LEONARD WILSON THORNHILL

Selma, Alabama

When he left the Alabama cotton fields, Toots brought his southern sunshine with him into these grey walls. But although his cheerful disposition makes him the friend of all, he will never forget the pleasant memories of home. Wilson's idea of the Navy may have changed a bit with Academy life, but homesick, lovesick, or seasick, he will do well wherever he goes. Serious, earnest, and conscientious, he has held to his work believing that he does well only when he does his best. Toots has a Southern gentleman's liking for good food and beautiful ladies. Ever see him chow up? Ever see him at a hop? Does a duck swim? On ship or on shore, "The man from Alabama" needs no introduction.

The Lucky Bag, 1938

Chapter Fourteen

TOOTS FROM ALABAMA

As he sailed southward deeper into the Coral Sea on the morning of May 7, 1942, Rear Admiral Chuichi Hara, commander of the Japanese Striking Force's two big aircraft carriers, was eager for battle, confident he would soon destroy a large American naval group.

He launched his own scout missions to search the ocean farther ahead of him, believing the Americans were in that direction when, in reality, Fletcher and TF 17 were now well behind, to the northwest, and almost three hundred miles away. At 0722, one of Hara's floatplanes spotted a single "carrier" with an escorting cruiser 163 miles due south, and the sighting was confirmed by a second scout plane twenty minutes later. Hara assumed that what he had found was the USS *Saratoga*, believed by the Japanese to be the only American flattop in the area, and therefore an appealing target. A massive air attack was ordered: seventy-eight aircraft in total.

But again the crews of the Japanese scout planes had blundered. What they had seen on the surface of the ocean beneath them was not an American carrier task force; what they took to be the *Saratoga* was the American tanker *Neosho*. The "cruiser" they had reported was the destroyer USS *Sims*, there to protect the tanker. Fletcher had sent them south the day before in what he thought was a safe direction, and the enormous attack Hara had ordered was being wasted on a single oiler and its unfortunate escort.

Soon after his air strike had disappeared to the south, Hara received another contact report on the bridge, informing him at about 0810 of the presence of a huge American force, including at least one possible carrier,

288 miles away to the northwest. This was the report from the plane Red Clark had been sent after, and Hara was stunned, then flustered. His planes were attacking the wrong target! To avoid any further confusion, Hara allowed the massive formations to continue on as planned but turned his carriers to the northwest, hoping that when he recovered his planes after their attack, refueled them, and sent them after this new threat, they would be close enough to catch the Americans by surprise later in the day.

Alone on the open sea, both the *Sims* and the *Neosho* would suffer grievously from the onrushing Japanese attacks. The *Sims* was hit by three bombs, broke in half, and sank in minutes; only 14 members of her 192-man crew survived. The tanker *Neosho* was pummeled by seven bomb hits but proved remarkably durable, only sinking four days later when the American destroyer *Henley*, on scene to pick up survivors, sent the hopelessly damaged ship to the bottom with a pair of torpedoes.

The American strike force that had launched from both the *Lexington* and the *Yorktown* after the 0815 contact report that morning flew through clear, sunny skies toward the Japanese force, but it was not the *Shokaku* or the *Zuikaku* they approached as Fletcher and Admiral Aubrey Fitch had been led to believe. In fact, after the large strike formation had flown away, Fletcher then learned, in a situation oddly similar to his counterpart Hara's, that his planes were also attacking the wrong target, the result of an errant contact report.

Fletcher briefly considered recalling the strike group but, again like Hara, he did not. He thought they might still attack and score some hits on the Japanese invasion force itself, believed also to be nearby. Fortunately, Fletcher was then handed another report, this one from an Army B-17 in the area. Its pilots reported sighting one carrier, ten transports, and sixteen other warships only thirty-five miles southeast of the location of the previous, erroneous report. Quickly, the *Yorktown* radioed her strike group and redirected them to the location of the Army scout's sighting. It was an aggressive, and ultimately fortuitous, decision.

The *Shoho* under attack, May 7, 1942

About forty minutes after departing TF 17, the strike planes of the *Lexington*'s air group crossed the northwestern tip of Tagula Island and spotted their target. It was a marvelous sight to the American pilots: an enemy carrier, 15,000 feet below them in the sun, with her planes unlaunched and spread out on her deck, steaming slowly through the Louisiade Archipelago, with its small tropical islets and submerged reefs, all splayed out across an ocean of clear water through which the shallow, sandy bottom was visible. The Japanese flattop was the *Shoho*, a 12,000-ton escort carrier, in the vanguard of the Port Moresby Invasion Force.

The American planes approached the *Shoho*'s starboard bow around 1107, managing to catch the Japanese carrier with only three fighters aloft to defend her. The Americans planned a coordinated attack, and it would be historic: the first by American carrier-based aircraft against a Japanese capital ship. A group of three Dauntless dive-bombers were the first planes to roll over into their attacks, but their 500-pound bombs narrowly missed when the Japanese carrier's captain executed a well-timed port turn. Still, the bomb blasts were sufficiently close to bathe the carrier in seawater and blow overboard a few fighter planes arrayed on her deck. A much larger group of ten SBDs then quickly followed from 12,500 feet, but these pilots also missed, their shots distracted by the continuing hard turn of the carrier and by the three Japanese planes defending her, which strafed the American bombers as they dove. Then fifteen more dive-bombers from Bombing Two, each armed with heavy 1,000-pound bombs, pitched over and attacked from downwind at 1118. The *Shoho*, which had up to then avoided thirteen bombs, saw her good luck run out as this third group of planes swept in just as she came out of her turn. One of the American pilots put his bomb squarely in the middle of the *Shoho*'s flight deck, just abaft amidships, and a huge explosion set the carrier ablaze and belching black smoke. A second bomb quickly struck her centerline-aft, near the ship's elevator. The small carrier was reduced in moments to flaming steel and wood.[1]

The twelve slow Devastator torpedo bombers of Lieutenant Commander James Brett's Torpedo Squadron Two then approached the target area from the southwest, the last to arrive as they often were, the planes lumbering and low to the water. In the formation was Lieutenant (jg) Leonard W. Thornhill, USNA '38, from Selma, Alabama. "Toots" had earned his wings in January 1941 and been a member of VT-2 aboard the *Lexington* since the previous August.

Thornhill, in plane 2-T-10, and his squadron mates picked their way through the fierce antiaircraft fire thrown up by the surely frustrated gunners of the *Shoho*'s screen, and then Brett spread them out to attack the burning ship from both sides at once, an approach that, if executed properly, would box the carrier in. Somehow the antiaircraft fire missed them all. The torpedo planes made excellent drops one hundred feet above the water, the torpedoes throwing up huge splashes as they nosed in. The fish fired by Leonard Thornhill was the first to hit home, and the first strike in history for an American torpedo squadron against an enemy carrier.[2] His torpedo struck the burning escort carrier's starboard quarter in a powerful blast. Four more torpedoes from VT-2 followed, exploding into the *Shoho* in quick succession, tearing holes in her hull, flooding her lower spaces, knocking out power, and causing a list. The Devastators all escaped cleanly.

By now a pyre of flame, the Japanese carrier sank around 1135, taking her entire complement of planes and 1,800 men with her. Though she was merely a baby flattop, and much less dangerous than the *Zuikaku* and the *Shokaku* still afloat and somewhere on the sea, the loss was momentous nonetheless, for it was the first major Japanese ship destroyed in the war.

The sinking of the carrier resulted in more than the loss of one ship; it spooked the commander of the Port Moresby invasion convoy following behind.[3] Unwilling to risk the safety of his troops, Vice Admiral Shigeyoshi Inoue ordered the flotilla to reverse its course and beat a hasty retreat northward, thereby abandoning, at least temporarily, the entire Port Moresby operation and placing Australia beyond the threat of invasion.

Thornhill and the American air group flew back to their carriers through the thick clouds, thirty-knot wind gusts, and intermittent rain squalls of a warm frontal zone that had settled over the area. The two American carriers recovered the returning planes safely in the early afternoon. Total American losses from the raid amounted to three dive-bombers.

ROY ORESTUS HALE JR.

Monroe, Louisiana

Blessed with a rare terpsichorean skill and a mellow voice, Roy has long been the answer to a maiden's prayer. But answering prayers has sometimes proved dull. Then he has sought diversion elsewhere. Choosing his athletics mainly for genuine enjoyment, Roy has been a steady customer of the tennis court and the big pool. Never too busy for a bull session or a bridge game, he has turned in some remarkable performances. Good music, a good book, a good snooze—he enjoys nothing better. A delightful whimsicality and an uncanny intuition for the unusual have added flavor to even his commonplace doings. Generous and dependable, Roy has never forgotten the Golden Rule. To meet again someday somewhere will be a privilege.

The Lucky Bag, 1938

Chapter Fifteen

JUST GONE

The Americans of Task Force 17 waited on the open water for the Japanese counterattack they assumed must be coming. Admiral Jack Fletcher kept his combat air patrols rotating overhead, and among the fighter pilots sent aloft was Bill Leonard, USNA '38, who circled the force protectively and scanned the skies for signs of approaching Japanese planes, black specks in the distant blue.

Dick Crommelin, USNA '38, had seen some spirited action earlier that morning while also flying combat air patrol above the vast formation. At 1041, a mere twenty-six minutes after he and his classmate Bill Leonard had flown out together, the *Lexington*'s radar spotted another blip forty-one miles out from the fleet on a bearing of 45 degrees. Crommelin and his new wingman, Ensign Richard Wright, were vectored to intercept, but in that direction were thick cloud banks that limited visibility so severely the two men flew using only their instruments. In that soup, overhauling and spotting, much less shooting down, an enemy snooper would require the purest of luck—but the two men had it in spades that morning. About eight miles out they quite surprisingly broke into sunny sky and spotted their target, a Kawanishi Type 97 flying boat cruising at fifteen hundred feet and as yet unaware of their presence. Crommelin and Wright pushed their throttles forward and screamed in, hoping to pounce on the plane before the pilot could escape back into the thick wall of clouds nearby. The Japanese pilot saw them and banked away, but the two Americans managed one high side pass before he disappeared. Crommelin and Wright then split up to chase the plane into the dense whiteness. What

Richard Gunter Crommelin

resulted was a frenzied game of hide-and-seek. Every few minutes Crommelin caught bursts of the big flying boat in the clouds, requiring, as Crommelin described it in his debrief, "dog-fighting tactics as maneuvers were of a necessity very radical."[1] Eventually, the Japanese flying boat ran out of clouds one thousand feet above the water. Both Crommelin and Wright spotted him at the same time, and they banked together to pursue. Crommelin rolled into a high-side run from the port side and, with a clear shot, sent .50-caliber slugs tearing into the Japanese plane's engine and fuel tanks. Suddenly in flames, the plane tipped over and crashed into the sea.

When Admiral Fletcher received an urgent distress signal from the tanker *Neosho* later that morning reporting the attack by Japanese carrier-based aircraft, he was stunned. The report could only mean that the Japanese carriers were somehow behind him, well to his south, and that they had for some unknown reason launched their planes for a full strike on two rather minor targets. If that were true, they would not be in a position to attack TF 17 until later that day. His fears of an imminent attack could be put aside for the moment.

By early afternoon, whatever remaining doubts Fletcher and his lieutenants had that the enemy knew where they were located were quickly put to rest. Despite the best efforts of Crommelin, Leonard, and Clark that morning, there was ample evidence that enemy scout planes were again shadowing the task force and radio messages reporting the fleet's approximate position were being intercepted. The overcast and squally weather could not hide a fleet their size forever. TF 17's air groups were quickly rearmed and refueled after their morning raid on the *Shoho*, but Fletcher, ever cautious, opted not to send them back out for a second raid on the Port Moresby

Invasion Force, choosing instead to keep the planes ready but quiet on his carrier decks for the rest of the afternoon. He did not know exactly where the Japanese flattops were, he thought there might be still yet another carrier to the north bracketing them, and he did not want to be caught without any planes when the Japanese air attacks did arrive, for they surely would. Ultimately, he believed that another attack simply carried too many risks, so Fletcher turned the task force southwest and spent the rest of May 7 sailing within the protective cloud cover of the weather front.

For the Japanese, nothing had gone right that day, and the Imperial Japanese Navy's admirals and ship captains spread across the Coral and Solomon Seas were both dejected and ashamed.[2] Their mighty strike force had turned around and fled, the invasion of Port Moresby had been indefinitely postponed, and all they had managed to sink were an American tanker and destroyer, prizes hardly worth mentioning in their reports of the day's action.

At 1615 that afternoon, with a new sighting report in hand, Rear Admiral Chuichi Hara decided to roll the dice on a late-day strike that missed spotting the American task force only 170 miles away and whose pilots jettisoned their bombs when they found nothing. On their return flight, the experienced airmen happened upon the American carriers, mistook them for their own, and lined up for landings with their lights burning before realizing their mistake and quickly fleeing the area. They were observed by the American radar operators landing a mere thirty miles distant on what must be the *Zuikaku* and the *Shokaku*. Fletcher could not believe the Japanese had managed to sail so close without being seen. He decided he must attack the enemy carriers first thing in the morning.

For both sides, surprise had been lost. The men waited only for daylight.

As night deepened the Japanese headed northward, the Americans southwestward. Leonard, Crommelin, and the other aviators in the squadrons on board the *Lexington* and *Yorktown* ate early dinners, debriefed in their ready rooms, and then tried to sleep. In his official Armed Forces history of World War II, Francis Miller wrote, "During the night everything was made ready for what all knew would be a terrific day."[3]

The pilots on board the two carriers were shaken awake at 0540. Mimeographed copies of the day's operations plan had by then been tacked up in the ready rooms. After breakfast, Roy Hale, USNA '38, and the rest of the aviators on board the *Lexington* walked up to the flight deck, goggles on their foreheads, stepped around and past the parked planes, climbed into their assigned cockpits, and warmed their engines. In the predawn darkness, a half-moon shined in the west as the fighters, dive-bombers, and torpedo planes all shook to life, harshly shattering the morning's placidity. The sky was clear, the visibility unlimited. The task force had sailed out of the frontal zone that had so ably hidden it the previous day; even the fog had lifted. They were now fully exposed on the open sea. The phosphorescence from the ships' screws marked the water's surface as though a great hand scratched a path through the ocean directly behind them. Belowdecks, the sailors on both carriers went to General Quarters: they donned life jackets and helmets, shut all interior doors and hatches, stowed extra gear, cut off the air ventilation, drained the fuel hoses, primed the antiaircraft guns, and prepared the firefighting equipment.[4]

Admiral Fletcher ordered a 360-degree search for the Japanese carriers at dawn. He knew they were close by, but he was not exactly sure where they had sailed during the night. The sun rose beautifully at 0600, and eighteen scout planes winged aloft from his two carriers to begin their search patterns while fighters took their covering positions above the task force. The Americans waited nervously for either a sighting report from the scouts or for bomb-laden Japanese planes to appear. It was the sighting report that arrived first, at 0820, telling of a Japanese formation of two aircraft carriers, four cruisers, and three destroyers, course 120, speed fifteen knots. Whereas the American ships were in the sunlight, the Japanese had sailed into the frontal zone the Americans had used the day before. They now owned the advantage of its gloom, rain, and heavy cloud belts. The Japanese carriers were pointed into the wind, their planes already on deck and preparing to launch.

At about the same time the American report came in, a Japanese scout spied TF 17 and sent his own message back to his admirals with details that were clear and precise.

Rear Admiral Aubrey Fitch, in charge of flight operations for the Americans, knew it was critical to get his planes aloft before the Japanese attacked. The U.S. carriers turned into the wind, and a strike package consisting of seventy-five dive-bombers, fighters, and torpedo planes was ordered up at 0838. The first plane took off at 0900.

The *Yorktown* launched her planes first, and once aloft in his fighter Bill Leonard, USNA '38, winged northward toward the Japanese as part of a four-plane section flying escort to a formation of slow Devastators. The torpedo planes cruised at 105 knots, the fighters 130, so Leonard and the other fighter pilots flew gentle S-turns over the wave tops to maintain their relative positions near the TBDs. His classmate Red Clark flew nearby, also escorting a formation of vulnerable torpedo planes. The seventy-five-plane armada was not in good order.[5] The various sections and formations inevitably drifted from each other as they flew toward the storm front at various speeds and altitudes, losing any cohesion and the ability to launch one coordinated strike. Flying low, the fighters were vulnerable if Zeros found them, but the torpedo planes could not burn the fuel it would take to climb higher, so the fighters stayed with them just above the water. Visibility soon worsened as the planes staggered into the frontal zone. Aviators scanned what areas of the ocean they could, but many soon lost sight of everything in the clouds and the rain squalls, including their wingmen.

The Japanese strike force had launched just a few minutes after the Americans' at 0907. The crewmen on board the *Shokaku* and *Zuikaku* lined the decks and cheered each of the sixty-nine planes as they roared down the runway, just as they had done before the Pearl Harbor raid five months prior. The two nations' planes passed each other in the clouds. Some of the SBD pilots spotted the Japanese aircraft but had neither the orders nor the fuel to do anything about it. They "hoped fondly that there would be friendly decks still in service after the Japanese had done their worst."[6]

Dive-bombers of Scouting Five off the *Yorktown* were the first to spot the Japanese fleet at 1032, after a short flight of only an hour and fifteen minutes, and by that time the *Shokaku* and *Zuikaku* had drifted about five miles apart. Lieutenant Commander William Burch Jr. kept his dive-bombers in the cloud cover to conceal their approach and skirted around

Bombs explode near the *Shokaku*, May 8, 1942

the Japanese to take positions upwind. Though they had excellent attack angles, they were forced to wait for the lumbering Devastators still some distance away. For twenty minutes, Burch and his bomber pilots watched nervously as the *Zuikaku* up ahead approached the black clouds of a heavy rainstorm. Both carriers on the water were still unaware of their presence, and the Americans continued to circle until, inevitably, they were seen by lookouts below. The two Japanese carriers instantly heeled sharply to port, into the wind, to launch fighters.

The *Yorktown*'s torpedo planes finally arrived on the scene at 1057 and started their runs, fanning out at just two hundred feet above the water to make an anvil approach on the *Shokaku*. Above, Burch immediately led his seven SBDs into their 70-degree dives. As often happened, as soon as the SBDs dropped below eight thousand feet, they encountered air that was both warm and wet, which fogged their sights and blurred their windscreens. The bomber pilots were then forced to "bomb from memory."[7] Seven bombs were dropped, but the *Shokaku* was twisting and turning wildly and tearing through the water at thirty-four knots, and each bomb missed, splashing the deck with seawater but causing the carrier no real harm. Seventeen more SBDs of Lieutenant Wally Short's Bombing Five then followed, also suffering from fogged sights and windshields, but with the added distraction of Japanese Zeros that strafed them as they dove. They did manage, however, to plant two 1,000-pound bombs on the *Shokaku*'s flight deck. The blasts tore huge holes in the carrier, disabled the forward elevator, and sparked furious fires belowdecks. The SBDs, minus one that crashed before it could pull out, withdrew at low altitude toward the northwest and the cloud cover there, dodging Japanese fighters as they made their escape.

At the same time, the Devastators of Torpedo Five attacked from the southeast. Maintaining his position as escort while the torpedo planes flew in, Bill Leonard scanned the skies for Japanese fighters, his fuel mixture set to rich, and his guns charged. He was surprised, however, that no Zeros presented themselves. With nothing to do, he momentarily contemplated making a strafing run on a nearby screening ship, but before he could, black flak bursts exploded ahead and beneath him.[8] Leonard's wingman that day was Scott McCuskey, flying loosely behind and above him. As the flak opened up, three Japanese fighters spotted the Americans and dove down, aiming for McCuskey. He saw them but did not have the time to warn Leonard. He yanked left and climbed, "bitching" the Zero lining up for a shot, and Leonard glanced over just in time to see the Zeros now charging toward him, the closest moving up on his tail.[9] It was an easy stern shot for the Japanese pilot, but he hesitated, giving Leonard just enough time to swing into a tight turn. The Zero twisted to stay with him but lost his shot, and Leonard was able to stay clear of the Japanese pilot's gun sight through two more turns before he disappeared into a cloud bank. McCuskey, after whipping away from the Zeros, circled back and shot down two enemy planes. He and Leonard had done their jobs, successfully keeping the fighters away from the slower TBDs.

Once near the target the Devastators formed a single line abreast and dropped their Bliss-Leavitt aerial torpedoes. The *Shokaku* was already on fire, and the torpedo crews hoped to add more carnage to the scene, but their torpedoes all ran erratically and missed. The slow planes used the cloud cover to escape eastward, torpedo straps dangling from their underbellies. Amazingly, none of the Devastators were shot down.

Though the *Shokaku* was burning furiously from the two bomb strikes she had suffered, her injuries were not mortal. Because none of the Devastators' torpedoes had hit, the Japanese carrier suffered no underwater damage and could still make speed, steer, and shoot back. She was spouting orange flames and night black smoke, but at the moment she was alive.

While the *Yorktown*'s planes had managed to find the Japanese carrier force, the air crews of the *Lexington* had not all been so lucky. The low ceiling, overcast skies, and rain clouds thousands of feet tall confused and disoriented the *Lex*'s aviators, and they struggled to maintain cohesion on their way in to the target area. A dozen planes from the *Lexington* failed to find the Japanese and began to turn back singly or in groups. Those that did find the carrier were a mixed bag: four dive-bombers, eleven torpedo planes, and only six fighters. Japanese Zeros were everywhere, harassing them in and out of the cloud banks.

Red Clark, protecting the lumbering Devastators of Torpedo Two in his fighter, was one of those who arrived over the Japanese carrier, and he was set upon almost immediately by enemy fighters who bounced him from out of the nearby clouds. Clark and his wingman, Richard Rowell, were at a severe disadvantage in a dogfight as they flew low and slow to protect the Devastators and were thus momentarily unable to maneuver and given no time to accelerate to combat speed. The Japanese fighter pilots knifed in, shooting up and scattering the formation. "Soon it was every man for himself."[10] Clark and Rowell were witnessed disappearing into a cloud bank with Zeros on their tails. For a moment, Clark was heard over the radio, his voice one of many frantically shouting and calling out planes and positions, but contact was soon lost, and he and Rowell were never seen again, both apparently shot down in the clouds. For his actions that day, Clark would receive a posthumous Distinguished Flying Cross, his second.

The nine torpedo planes Clark and Rowell had been shepherding took a high-level approach toward the wounded *Shokaku* and increased their speed to 180 knots. The group stayed in the cloud cover to conceal themselves on the way in, and when they emerged in the clear they were a few miles off the wounded carrier's port bow. The *Shokaku*'s captain heeled her to starboard and her gun crews opened up. The Devastators fanned out and dropped their torpedoes at will, but the fish were faulty and slow and, once again, completely useless. What's more, the American fliers had all dropped too far away, and the carrier easily outran the torpedoes; none hit. Torpedo Two tried to make its escape, but they were harassed continually by the packs of circling Zeros.

Among the pilots of VT-2 now racing back home was Lieutenant (jg) Leonard "Toots" Thornhill. About fifty miles south of the burning *Shokaku*, his flight of nine Devastators huddled together near the waves was spotted by enemy planes above them, including at least four Zeros, which swept down to attack. The rear gunners of all nine torpedo planes opened up on the fighters that screamed by them in pairs, sending two flaming into the water and thwarting the other two from getting close after three or four initial runs. But the Devastators were low on fuel, and twenty miles short of the carrier, the first of the planes sputtered, lost altitude, and ditched into the sea. It was Thornhill's plane. He and his gunner scurried from the sinking aircraft and managed to inflate their life raft. Fletcher dispatched the destroyer USS *Dewey* to look for the two men, but her lookouts could find no trace of their raft in the area where they had gone down. Thornhill and his gunner were never seen again.

By the late morning TF 17 was spread out on the sea under a cloudless, sunny sky "like a worm writhing on a hook."[11] They had nowhere to hide. The escort ships were arrayed protectively in a circular formation around the carriers, the *Yorktown* north of the *Lexington*. On the bridge of the Lady Lex, Captain Frederick Sherman scanned the skies with his men, dressed in his khakis and a windbreaker, a steel helmet strapped to this head. SBD scout bombers were refueling on the deck, and the engine room was raising steam so the carrier could speed up when she needed to. The men had been waiting all morning for a Japanese attack, and it came at 1055, when their radar screens picked up incoming planes eighty miles away on a bearing of 020. The seventeen fighters flying combat air patrol, eight already low on gas, were recalled to the vicinity of the carriers and kept close by, and some dive-bombers, though unsuited for such a task and severely disadvantaged against Zeros, were controversially added to the mix to try to help fight off the approaching planes.[12]

Lookouts spotted the clusters of black dots on the northeastern horizon at 1113. Unlike the Americans' attack, the huge Japanese formations flew in good order, and their glides in toward the American task force were well choreographed—most of the enemy torpedo planes angled toward the bigger and closer *Lexington*, but a handful separated and went after the *Yorktown*. American fighters turned to thwart them, but they were sent out piecemeal and at various altitudes by the flight director on board the *Lexington*, diminishing their effectiveness. The Japanese torpedo planes fanned out to approach the carrier from two directions, diving shallow from four thousand feet against both the port and starboard beams. The American dive-bombers acting as fighters could not catch them as they glided in at high speed and were subsequently attacked by a large number of Japanese Zeros for their efforts. Four of the dive-bombers were shot down, like "small [boys] sent to do a man's job."[13] Almost simultaneously, the Japanese dive-bombers rolled over into their attacks from up high and Sherman gunned the *Lexington* forward to thirty knots. Flak bursts popped in the sky.

Ultimately, eleven Type 91 800-kilogram aerial torpedoes were launched at the *Lexington* at 1118. The Japanese torpedo planes, once lightened by their loads, seemed to graze the *Lexington*'s flight deck as they flew ahead of their just-released torpedoes. Gunners on the carrier shot one of the planes down at point-blank range as it passed overhead, but most antiaircraft fire that day was ineffective. Sherman, measured and calm but facing enemy planes attacking both of his bows, ordered "hard astarboard," then, after a moment, left full rudder, and then a second turn to starboard, and was able to dodge nine of the torpedoes.[14] At 1120, however, one struck the big ship at the port forward gun gallery. One minute later, a second hit the port side amidships opposite the carrier's island. Muffled explosions rumbled through the ship, knocking men to the deck. The Japanese Type 99 dive-bombers, which had started their runs from out of the sun at 17,000 feet, were swooping in at that exact moment, carrying more destruction.

The USS *Lexington* on fire but still steaming, May 8, 1942

Flying combat air patrol over TF 17 that day was Marion Dufilho, USNA '38, sent aloft ninety minutes earlier in a formation with three other fighters. As the torpedo planes dropped their fish and the Japanese dive-bombers tipped over into their dives, Dufilho flew at eight thousand feet on the *Lexington*'s port side. Flying wingman with his division leader, Dufilho gained altitude to try to meet the dive-bombers as they fell, hoping to scatter them before they dropped their bombs. But the two fighters were met at 12,000 feet by an aggressive flight of six Zeros that forced them to turn away. The dive-bombers were then able to drop past and complete their attacks unmolested, releasing their bombs at 1,500 feet. A 1,000-pound bomb struck the *Lex*'s port forward 5-inch battery. Another hit, and several near misses that seemed to smother the ship with seawater caused more damage and killed and injured men in the stack machine guns and after signal station with shell fragments. Fires were started in the main deck, beneath the incinerator, near the gig boat pocket, and near the forward elevator.[15] The principal water main was ruptured. The boilers had to be shut down. A large oil slick appeared on the sea, trailing behind the carrier ingloriously. Smoke poured from her funnels and she took on a list. The air smelled of the oil in the water, smoke, and gunpowder. The ship's steam siren screamed in one long howl for several minutes, as if raised by the ship herself from the depths of her engineering plants, a shriek of distress caused by her wounds.

As Dufilho was being chased away by Zeros over the *Lexington*, another dogfight was raging northwest of TF 17, this one involving Dick Crommelin, USNA '38. Crommelin flew that morning with three other F4Fs from VF-42, part of Lieutenant Commander James H. Flatley's division. They had scrambled off the *Yorktown* when news of the approaching Japanese planes was received and headed out to meet them, Crommelin on Flatley's wing. Expecting to run across approaching Japanese torpedo planes, low to the water, slow and tempting, the four fighter pilots instead found nothing. At 1115 *Lexington*'s flight direction officer, Lieutenant Frank "Red" Gill, then ordered the four planes to climb to ten thousand feet and take on the dive-bombers also known to be heading for the ship. "Vector 020 degrees, Angels 1, Buster," Gill said through the radio.[16] Confused and more than a little irritated at the inconsistent orders, Flatley led Crommelin and his two other pilots up high, anxiously scanning the skies ahead, and when they broke through messy cloud cover at six thousand feet they "beheld the panorama of a modern sea battle: wildly maneuvering ships, black AA bursts, and burning aircraft."[17] On the ocean's surface below them, the two big carriers, with the *Astoria*, *Portland*, *Chester*, *Chicago*, *Morris*, *Anderson*, *Hammann*, and *Perkins* arrayed around them, turned and twisted and dodged, firing all the while as planes in pockets engaged in dozens of individual and small-group dogfights amid the flak. Flatley demanded through his radio that Gill give them something to do! There was nothing in the air around them, and the ships they were tasked with defending were falling increasingly farther astern. But Gill was overwhelmed by the action, his radar screen a confusing swirl of contacts and blips, his carrier twisting on the sea, and he simply instructed Flatley to hurry back—they were under attack. Gill's voice was tinged with obvious signs of panic.

The four F4Fs banked, turned south, and five miles north of TF 17 quickly spotted six Zeros harassing some of the American SBDs trying to fend off the Japanese torpedo planes. The Japanese fighters were causing grievous losses to the SBD crews. Flatley and Crommelin were above the Japanese fighters, who did not see them, and when Flatley hollered out "Bandits! Enemy fighters down here. Let's go," Crommelin and the other two fighter pilots followed him in a shallow but fast dive.[18] Crommelin stayed with Flatley and together they singled out one of the Zeros shooting up an SBD at six thousand feet. The Zero crossed their paths from right to left, a full deflection shot, and Flatley stitched up the plane with his tracers as it loomed two hundred yards in front of them. Crommelin fired a two-second burst at a separate Zero of his own but missed, and then lost track of Flatley, who was by then below and behind him. Without hesitating, Crommelin turned soloist and dove again on more Zeros lurking below. Corkscrewing to cut speed and line up for a favorable shot, Crommelin fired one quick burst before overshooting the Zeros. He recovered at three thousand feet, pulled back into a climb, and spied another Japanese fighter ahead, flying in the same direction he was. Crommelin added throttle and buzzed the Zero from astern with a long burst of red tracers. The Zero turned and climbed sharply, a move Crommelin matched. He kept firing as they climbed. Soon smoke belched from the Japanese plane's cowling, and it disappeared from Crommelin's sight. He spotted another Zero, rolled out of his climb, spiraled down on its tail, and closed the range quickly before firing more red tracers at the enemy plane. Again, the Japanese pilot, upon seeing tracers zip past his canopy, climbed, but not before Crommelin shot away chunks of the Mitsubishi, which then nosed down and spun away crazily. As Crommelin was shooting, yet another Zero was angling in behind him, and when Crommelin heard the gunfire over his engine, he whipped his head around and spotted the plane. Now the hunted, Crommelin turned the F4F into a steep high-speed dive, standard defensive maneuvering for the Americans, and successfully left the enemy plane behind. But he pulled back up into a zoom climb too soon and once again found himself in the midst of a pack of Zeros. He spent the next few minutes flipping the plane wildly about, trying to stay clear of the Japanese pilots' sights and firing at any planes cutting in front of him. No Zeros could get a clear shot. Somehow Crommelin fought clear and, with one last enemy plane on his tail, fled toward a small cloud that offered some hope of sanctuary. Once hidden, he banked hard left, spiraled, and then emerged from underneath it. The Zero stayed with him, but he was too far back to fire now, and Crommelin dove again, too fast for his pursuer.

As Crommelin climbed once more, free of danger for the moment, he turned his head and spotted oil stains on his left wing—one of the Japanese bullets had either blown through a wingroot oil cooler or cut a fuel line. In trouble, he looked about for a friendly carrier deck to land on and spied the damaged *Lexington* two or three miles in the distance. But his ailing plane would give him no time. His oil pressure quickly failed, and the Pratt & Whitney engine coughed and seized loudly, then shut down. It was 1133. He called in his condition over the radio and steered his gliding plane toward the aircraft carrier, the engine thunderously quiet, only the air speed over the wings keeping him aloft. He guessed the best thing to do was to ditch into the sea just ahead of the formation. Calmly, Crommelin brought his Wildcat into what he called a "fairly smooth water landing" just one hundred yards off the big carrier's starboard bow.[19] The plane remained on the surface long enough for Crommelin to unstrap his belts, retrieve his life raft, and scramble free. On his knees in the rubber dinghy, he shouted and waved, and the USS *Phelps*, a destroyer alongside the *Lexington*, pulled aside and brought Crommelin on board at 1144.

Soon the surviving planes of the Japanese strike force disappeared over the horizon, their bomb racks empty, antiaircraft fire speckling the sky behind them. The attack had lasted twelve minutes. Captain Sherman brought the *Lexington* into the wind, and several damaged planes and others low on fuel landed, including Marion Dufilho's.

On board the *Yorktown*, not far away, Captain Elliott Buckmaster had seen the dive-bombers dropping on the *Lexington* but was soon faced with his own attack: enemy torpedo planes approaching his port bow. He immediately ordered up emergency flank speed, then right rudder, to keep his stern pointed south, crosswind, toward the enemy planes. The *Yorktown* was smaller than the *Lexington* and had a tighter turning radius and fewer attackers, so Buckmaster was able to avoid the torpedoes, their wakes streaking past the carrier to port. At 1124, however, the first dive-bomber, a plane from the *Zuikaku*, peeled off and started its drop above him, followed by the rest of its section, between fifteen and eighteen planes. Their paths were steep and aggressive, and they dropped their bombs low, but Buckmaster's ship handling, the planes' crosswind dives, and American fighters who pushed them off their attack angles combined to limit the number of bombs hitting the *Yorktown*. The one that did, however, punched a hole in the center of her flight deck forward of the middle elevator at 1127. The armor-piercing projectile penetrated down to the fourth deck before detonating, lifting the carrier's screws clear of the water and killing thirty-seven men outright. Near misses also shook the ship and sent massive plumes of seawater into the air. Though heavy smoke billowed into the sky after the blast, the damage was not mortal, and the *Yorktown* moved southward quickly, away from the *Lexington*, and continued her flight operations.

Bill Leonard, USNA '38, was flying back to TF 17's position while escorting a shot-up Dauntless from VB-5 when he passed a Japanese dive-bomber flying in the opposite direction. The enemy plane was beneath him and was returning from its own attack on either the *Yorktown* or the *Lexington*. Wasting no time Leonard dropped out of formation and dove into a firing run on the plane. Oddly, the Japanese pilot made no move to evade or maneuver away from him. He simply maintained his heading, speed, and altitude, offering Leonard the easiest of shots. His Grumman's bullets ripped into the enemy plane's innards, and it belched thick smoke, tipped onto a wing, and plummeted to the water. Leonard quickly rejoined the damaged plane he was escorting, unaware that the aviator he had just killed was the senior Japanese pilot on the mission, a man named Takahashi.

The stories of Leonard and Dufilho and Crommelin that day are known but, also aloft over the task force, doing his best to help ward off the Japanese attackers, was Roy Hale, Class of '38 and a young lieutenant (junior grade) with Scouting Squadron Two.

The specifics of Hale's fate that morning, like those of so many pilots sent to battle in the clouds and out over trackless seas during the war, are a mystery. It is not known where or when or how he died. It is unknown whether he took any Japanese planes with him. He simply did not return when the battle ended. In the chaos and the confusion, amid the twisting and the turning planes, the antiaircraft fire and the machine-gun bullets, and the desperate individual actions in the sun and the cloud banks and just over the wave tops, Hale's plane fought until, at some point, it was gone, one less plane in the sky, shot down but untracked, unseen, and unremembered. The accounts of air battles during the war are replete with short and simple sentences in debriefing reports that describe yet another aviator's unknown fate, a friend and wingman and squadron member, a brother, whose destiny was simply to disappear. All that is known about Roy Hale that day is that the sea claimed him. But even though his actions were unknown, Hale was posthumously awarded the Distinguished Flying Cross for outstanding achievement in aerial combat, his citation mentioning his "courageous determination and aggressiveness . . . attacking enemy aircraft in spite of fierce fighter opposition."[20]

The coda of the *Lexington* unfolded across the rest of the afternoon. After the Japanese planes winged away over the horizon, sailors in the screen of TF 17 undoubtedly took a moment to peek over at her and, from all outward appearances, the stricken carrier looked to be in fine shape. She trailed oil in her wake, but otherwise showed no obvious signs of damage. Once her remaining planes were back on board, the carrier and her screen swung to port and headed away to the northeast. Between 1145 and 1200 the reports reaching Captain Sherman from his damage control teams seemed optimistic. She was listing 7 degrees, and the pair of torpedoes that had struck her below the waterline had caused torrents of seawater to enter her lower spaces, but the flooding had been promptly contained, and the list would soon be corrected. Firefighting crews quickly extinguished all active fires, and steel plates were welded over the holes left by the bomb hits. Both elevators were jammed, but the carrier deck was operable and she was still able to launch and land planes. She could do twenty-five knots and maneuver rapidly if pressed. By 1245 it appeared the *Lexington* was squared away and ready to return to her fight.

The problem, however, was that the torpedo blasts had caused leaks in the port stowage gasoline tanks built against the inner hull. The leaks were not visible, but the odor of gasoline fumes was quickly overpowering in nearby compartments, and it was spreading. Even worse, the men in the damage control party could not pinpoint the leaks and thus could not contain them. At 1247 a spark of unknown origin (possibly from an untended electric motor) ignited the fumes and a heavy explosion shook the *Lexington*, instantly killing twenty-five men and starting a bad "cherry red and white" fire belowdecks that quickly spread aft, cut communication throughout the ship, and set off a series of other, smaller explosions at frequent intervals as the gas continued its seepage across ever larger portions of the carrier.[21] As the *Lexington*'s official Report of Action from the battle stated, "From this time on, the ship was doomed."[22] The crews made little headway against the fires. Soon all power was lost belowdecks. Intense heat on the bulkheads began igniting paint, allowing flames to, in effect, penetrate through steel walls. Sealed watertight doors could not contain the blazes. Dufilho and other aviators congregated on her deck, hoping flight operations could resume, but another explosion at 1442 wracked the ship and the hangar deck became uninhabitable. Flight operations were canceled. There were soon no means left with which to fight the fire, so Sherman signaled the *Yorktown*: "*Lexington* has serious explosion." Minutes later, he signaled again: "This ship needs help."[23] All Dufilho could do was continue to wait on the flight deck and try to assist the crew.

At 1525 a third explosion caused the dying ship to shudder again. It was the big carrier's death knell. Fifteen minutes later, what was left of her firefighting crew reported that the belowdecks inferno was now completely out of control. The ship lost steerage. Sherman ordered all crewmen out onto the flight deck as the *Lexington* blew steam and came to a dead stop, riding the sea's gentle swells. Rescue ships passed over fresh water hoses. The wounded were taken off, then Sherman ordered life rafts made ready. Additional explosions continued to blast through the carrier's bowels. The flames soon reached bomb storage areas on the hangar deck, and Sherman was faced with the very real possibility of the fire setting the bombs off in some massive conflagration that would blow apart the entire carrier and kill everyone on board. At 1630 all remaining crewmen were ordered up to the flight deck, and at 1707 Sherman issued orders to abandon ship. Disembarkation was orderly, without panic; most men, including Dufilho and his classmate Robert Morgan, USNA '38, shimmied down knotted lines thrown over the side.[24] Others simply dove the fifty feet. Captain Sherman, his dog in his arms, and Admiral Fitch were the last to leave as more explosions shook the carrier and the sun set over their shoulders in a blaze of light. Dufilho, with hundreds of his shipmates, would spend two hours in the warm sea before he was picked up. His Academy ring was still on board the *Lexington*, which, in the twilight, burned terribly but beautifully. She soon took on a severe list and rattled and blazed as bombs in the parked planes exploded on her deck, one after another. In spots the carrier glowed a hellish red. At 1830 the bombs that had been cooking for so long in the hangar deck finally blew in a "vast, rippling" explosion that sent debris hurtling into the air and splashing into the sea.[25]

But still the carrier would not die, not until a spread of eight torpedoes fired from the destroyer *Phelps* plowed into her starboard side. Bill Leonard, then flying combat air patrol overhead, watched the blazing carrier's death throes that long evening, the fires and explosions accentuated by the deepening blackness of night. As he described it, "Fires, explosions large and small, debris blowing over the side made her look like hell afloat. It was a sad sight."[26] Just after 1952 the great carrier rolled over to port and disappeared in a cloud of steam. Seconds after she slipped beneath the waves, a tremendous underwater explosion ignited down in the dark blue, the concussion reverberating twenty miles away.

In the aftermath of the *Lexington*'s sinking, Fletcher opted to break off the battle for the day, believing there was at least one and possibly two more undamaged enemy carriers still lurking out there (though his pilots claimed hits, both Japanese carriers were spotted afloat) and keenly aware of the fact that the *Yorktown* was now the only American carrier left on the sea. On May 8, Nimitz in Pearl Harbor ordered him to withdraw TF 17 southward, out of attack range, toward the Tonga Islands for refueling. Though Fletcher did not know it, the Japanese were in equally bad straits, low on planes, with a damaged *Shokaku* in need of repairs, and a deteriorating logistical situation. They too would break off the battle.

The Coral Sea fight has been called "one of the most confused and confusing battles in the history of war at sea, characterized on both sides by an almost incredible series of miscues, miscommunications, misidentification, misinterpretations, and miscalculations."[27] TF 17 had successfully defended Port Moresby, but at grievous cost. On the Japanese side, Admiral Shigeyoshi Inoue quickly realized the enormity of the setbacks his fleet had experienced: major plane losses amounting to twice as many as the Americans, including the deaths of some of his most seasoned pilots and gunners, and a badly damaged carrier of his own. Reluctantly, he was forced to postpone the entire landing operation and send both aircraft carriers back toward Truk, though Captain Sherman and other American leaders believed that Inoue could have taken his objective with little trouble had he pressed on. Yamamoto, for his part, was immensely displeased at his admiral's decision.

The Battle of the Coral Sea, as it would be called, had several clear ramifications. The Japanese had been definitively stopped and Australia saved from the threat of invasion. In that sense, it can legitimately be called the "first turning point in the War in the Pacific."[28] What is more, the Japanese had temporarily lost the services of two big carriers, ships which, with their attack on Midway looming, they could ill afford not to have at their disposal. Additionally, American pilots now knew that they could hold their own against Japanese airmen, whom they had previously viewed as unbeatable. Their F4F Wildcats could survive against the enemy's Zeros if used properly, and their tactics, both in dogfights and dive-bombing runs, were improving greatly. So, while a tactical victory for the IJN, the battle was a strategic victory for the United States. Yet the battle's legacy lay elsewhere: it was the first major engagement in naval history in which the opposing surface ships never saw one another and never exchanged a shot.[29] Purely an air action, a previously unheard-of manner of fighting that both sides chose independently, the battle would establish a template that future admirals in future battles would mimic without hesitation, including, in just a few short weeks' time, at the greatest battle in the history of the United States Navy.

EDWARD LEE ANDERSON

Claremont, Virginia

Boasting a long line of rugged seafaring ancestors plus three years of service in our Fleet, Swede comes to us from the heart of the South where he has acquired his full share of suave manners and patriotic ardor. An apparent radical, Swede is at time soft-spoken and quiet, although he never gives vent to lukewarm opinions nor tolerates half-hearted effort. His conscientiousness in his work approaches a point of passion, but his devil-may-care attitude over the week-ends reflects a varied personality somewhat paradoxical. Along with playing unorganized basketball and eternally reading, Swede enjoys deceiving himself about women—particularly Philadelphia's. A dependable, considerate, and honorable roommate who, no matter where he may be, should always be found on top of the proverbial heap. I remain his most sincere well-wisher.

The Lucky Bag, 1938

Chapter Sixteen

COCKED PISTOLS

The Battle of Midway is commonly regarded as one of the most decisive military engagements in world history. For the United States, it was the turning point in World War II's Pacific theater, the point after which its ultimate victory over the Empire of Japan was assured; for the Japanese, the battle was nothing less than the most profound, indeed cataclysmic, military defeat in the annals of their navy.

Eminent historian Gordon W. Prange called the battle a master class in "uncoordinated coordination."[1] Whereas in the weeks leading up to the attack on Pearl Harbor, the Japanese were meticulous, careful, and precise in their training and planning, in the time leading up to Midway they were slipshod and careless. Their victories across the Pacific in the six months since their Hawaii raid had bred in them a "euphoric self-confidence" and arrogance that slowly twisted and marred all that they had learned about how to wage successful carrier warfare against the United States.[2] The Imperial Japanese Navy's senior staff chose to initiate the Battle of Midway without any firsthand intelligence, without knowing their enemy and the ships at his disposal, without first gaining an understanding of what the Americans were thinking and how they were likely to behave, and without training for the particularities of the coming attack. All of this had been done to perfection in advance of the attack on Pearl Harbor. But "victory disease" was rampant, as was a general lack of respect for the U.S. Navy at the time, and these critical steps were overlooked, considered unnecessary, or ignored.[3] Japanese fliers recollected after the battle, "We never doubted our success for a minute.... Midway [would] be very easy."[4]

These attitudinal differences were a crucial advantage for the Americans; their assessments of the difficulties that lay ahead, wherever the next battle was to occur, were understandably more realistic and thus more helpful.

Midway was intended to be the second phase (Pearl Harbor being the first) of the defeat of the U.S. Navy's Pacific Fleet by the IJN, their isolation of Australia, and their eventual takeover of Hawaii. It was designed to initiate Admiral Isoroku Yamamoto's final battle, the one that would destroy the Pacific Fleet as a fighting force, compel the Americans to seek peace, end the war on Japan's terms, and preserve the future of the empire he had done so much to expand.

By the summer of 1942, after following up the Pearl Harbor raid with a string of victories across the western Pacific (the battle in the Coral Sea notwithstanding), Yamamoto enjoyed an aura of infallibility in his country. As such, he was able to influence the navy's General Staff into issuing orders to, with the cooperation of the army, invade and occupy strategic points in the Western Aleutians and Midway Island. Yamamoto's plan called for the creation of five surface fleets, commanded by twenty-eight admirals and comprising nearly two hundred ships in total. Almost the entire complement of the IJN would take part in what would be the largest naval-amphibious operation ever attempted in history. The plan would unfold thus: On June 3, Admiral Kakuji Kakuta's 2nd Carrier Striking Force would launch air raids on Dutch Harbor, the American air base on Unalaska Island in the far northern Pacific Ocean, and then Vice Admiral Boshiro Hosogaya's Northern Force would invade the cold, desolate beaches of three of the outer Aleutian Islands. At dawn on the 4th, the four carriers of Admiral Chuichi Nagumo's 1st Carrier Striking Force, the *Akagi*, *Kaga*, *Soryu*, and *Hiryu*, having steamed across the Central Pacific, would launch air strikes on Midway Island with the intent of destroying the American aircraft on its runway and clearing the defenses for Admiral Nobutake Kondo's 2nd Fleet and Rear Admiral Raizo Tanaka's Midway Occupation Force, which would sail in from the southwest and invade on the night of June 5. These attacks would compel the American Pacific Fleet, undoubtedly with its carriers, to sally forth from Pearl Harbor to do battle, most likely northward against the forces attacking the Aleutians. Once they did, the numerically inferior Pacific Fleet would be set upon and destroyed, after which the IJN could, on its own schedule, take New Caledonia, the Fiji Islands, Johnston Island, and Hawaii in turn.

Yamamoto's plan was not a sound one. It was rife with uncharacteristic problems, unnecessary risks, and unrealistic expectations. It spread Japanese forces too thin and relied on foolish assumptions about how the U.S. Navy and its leaders would react to the threat to Alaska. It demanded too much from the aviators within the Japanese navy, who had been in combat without a rest since December 7. It was not sufficiently adjusted to account for the temporary loss of two Japanese aircraft carriers, the *Zuikaku* and *Shokaku*, damaged at the Battle of the Coral Sea, and, perhaps most critically, it failed to account for the one key advantage the Americans enjoyed in the Pacific theater by mid-1942: radio intelligence.

In the weeks leading up to the Battle of Midway, Admiral Chester Nimitz and his leadership staff at Pearl Harbor were kept busy listening to the reports of their cryptanalysts and trying to predict the target of the Japanese attack they knew was coming. Leading the codebreaking efforts was Commander Joseph Rochefort, the chief of the Combat Intelligence Office (called Station Hyppo). Station Hyppo had by this point cracked the Japanese navy's operational code, JN25, and though its intelligence men could not read complete messages, they were able to decode enough to know within a couple of hundred miles where most Japanese ships were located and, even more importantly, anticipate where they were going. By the spring of 1942, Rochefort was already predicting that the Japanese fleet would be targeting Midway sometime around the end of May or the first week of June.

Nimitz was sleeping little, his nerves wrecked, and though he believed in Rochefort and his team's abilities, he needed more convincing, as did his superiors in Washington. The decision about where to send the Pacific Fleet to ward off the impending Japanese attack had to be correct. If Nimitz got it wrong and the Navy lost its three aircraft carriers, the well was dry. There was nothing to take their place, nothing with which to protect Hawaii or even the West Coast of the United States, nothing with which to stem the Japanese tide. Therefore, understandably cautious, Nimitz wondered if the Japanese were feeding the Americans false information, if they knew about the compromise of their code and were setting a trap. To be fair, though Rochefort was convinced of the accuracy of his analysis, his predictions about Midway were based not on one single, clear communication—the Japanese were quite discreet with the messages they encoded—but, rather, on a combination of various bits and snippets intercepted and pieced together over the preceding weeks.

But Nimitz's trust was well placed. In a flash of brilliance, Rochefort famously devised a ruse to prove his unit's assessment that Midway was the target. The local American commander on Midway was told to transmit a plain-language report back to Pearl Harbor stating the island's desalination plant had broken down. As expected, the message was picked up by Japanese listeners on Wake Island and relayed back to Tokyo, which in turn alerted the IJN's Combined Fleet, a message picked up by Station Hyppo. The message proved that references to "AF" in Japanese transmissions referred to Midway, as Rochefort and his men had believed.

Nimitz was now certain, or as certain as he could be. On May 16, he recalled Admiral Halsey and his task force to Pearl Harbor and alerted his boss, Admiral Ernest J. King, in Washington that he now believed the Japanese navy was preparing to mount an attack involving a major landing by its main striking force on Midway. Though critical details were missing, including exactly when the attack would occur, King bought Nimitz's reasoning and agreed with his decision. Confirmation seemed to arrive on May 24 when Rochefort and his Hyppo staff cracked an unusually long Japanese message detailing the IJN's order of battle for the Midway operation. The Americans would be outnumbered in every way: aircraft carriers, battleships, both heavy and light cruisers, destroyers, and submarines. But they had a single critical advantage: they would know where the Japanese were headed.

The American fleet began to assemble in Pearl Harbor on the 26th, under a sweltering sun bright with heat, when the *Enterprise* nosed into berth F-2 at Ford Island a few minutes before noon and the carrier *Hornet* moored at Berth F-10-S a short time later. The next day the *Yorktown*, leaking oil and with a hole in her flight deck and gaps in her hull plates (her Coral Sea wounds), sailed in at 1420 to an ovation of steam whistles and sirens, then slipped directly into Drydock No. 1. That afternoon, after one more meeting with Rochefort and his chief of intelligence, Nimitz issued Operational Plan 29-42, in which he stated his belief that the Japanese would attempt to capture Midway and that, in response, a fleet designated TF 16 with the *Enterprise* and *Hornet* would proceed to a point 350 miles northeast of the island, where they would rendezvous at so-called Point Luck with Admiral Frank Jack Fletcher, the quickly repaired *Yorktown*, and TF 17. There they would wait until the approaching Japanese carriers were spotted. They would then launch a surprise attack on the enemy's flanks, a nipping attack designed to avoid a "drag-out slugfest."[5] They were to employ "attrition tactics" and not incur heavy losses in carriers or cruisers, something on which King had insisted.[6] Ultimately, the whole affair depended on timing. As Gordon Prange described it, "[The Americans] must permit the Japanese to come in far enough, but not too far. They must go as close to the enemy as possible, but not too close. . . . [They] must attempt to catch the Japanese with planes on deck, and themselves avoid being caught with their own planes down."[7] The entire war hung in the balance.[8]

Nimitz had expected to name Halsey as the commander of the fleet that would save Midway, but as was readily apparent when the two came face to face after the *Enterprise* docked, Halsey was suffering from a severe case of dermatitis, his skin covered in itchy sores, his appearance haggard and worn, the affliction caused by what his doctors believed was a combination of nervous tension and the tropical sun. Though grievously disappointed he could not take the fleet out himself, Halsey was allowed to pick his replacement for the mission, and without hesitation he chose Rear Admiral Raymond A. Spruance, USNA '06, the commander of his cruiser squadrons. Though not an airman, Spruance was liked and respected by Halsey, with whom he had served since Pearl Harbor. Nimitz accepted the suggestion. Physically short yet energetic, fit, introspective, even brilliant, Spruance was surprised but not overcome by the responsibility when Nimitz presented it to him soon after his consultation with Halsey. Spruance would assume command of TF 16 and sail on board the *Enterprise* with the rest of Halsey's now seasoned staff. Once Fletcher arrived at Point Luck, Spruance would turn over tactical command of the combined task forces to him for the coming battle.

Before she could sail, the *Yorktown* needed an array of repairs made, and fourteen hundred electricians, fitters, machinists, welders, carpenters, and riveters were put to the task. They would work all day and night, for they had three days to complete repairs that would normally take three months. The crew remained on board to help with the rearming and reprovisioning. The pilots were granted a short liberty but were recalled on May 27, providing only the briefest of shore leaves, which was particularly hard on those from the *Yorktown*, many of whom had been away for 101 days. The airmen barely had time for barbecue lunches and swims in the pool at the Royal Hawaiian Hotel.

On board the *Enterprise*, Dusty Kleiss, USNA '38, participated in a brief awards ceremony on the flight deck during which he and his squadron mate Cleo Dobson were presented with Distinguished Flying Crosses, Kleiss for his direct hit on a ship during the attack on the Marshall Islands. Nimitz himself pinned the cross to Kleiss' chest. By that point, Kleiss was already one of the U.S. Navy's more experienced dive-bomber pilots, with 826 hours aloft.

Half a world away, powerful Japanese armadas prepared to slip their moorings and sail out into the open sea, including Vice Admiral Chuichi Nagumo's First Carrier Strike Force, his revitalized Kido Butai. Lacking the *Shokaku* and *Zuikaku*, the force would still be fearsome, built around its four carriers and boasting two battleships, three cruisers, twelve destroyers, and five oilers. The sailors and pilots on board were bent on absolute destruction, confident of total victory, blind to any possibility of defeat.

Task Force 16 sortied from Pearl Harbor late on the morning of May 28, the *Enterprise* and *Hornet* the last to depart the shallow water, following the destroyers, oilers, and cruisers that had slipped out before them. The *Yorktown* remained in her dry dock under repair; she would sail the following day. Once clear of the harbor, the line of ships turned and churned away to the northwest.

It was not until the morning of the task force's departure that the various groups of pilots from the *Yorktown*, *Hornet*, and *Enterprise*, still on the island with their planes, learned fully how their squadrons would be reorganized for the coming mission. Losses would be made up by men from the

Saratoga's air group, many of whom up to now had been idling on Oahu while their torpedoed carrier underwent repairs on the West Coast. The *Yorktown*'s Torpedo Five and Scouting Five squadrons would remain behind, replaced by Lieutenant Commander Max Leslie's Bombing Three (which included among its ranks Osborne Wiseman, USNA '38) and Lieutenant Commander Lem Massey's Torpedo Three, while her Bombing Five was temporarily designated Scouting Five and, despite her casualties, kept on board, which chafed its air crews and led to a sag in squadron morale.[9] The seasoned men looked at the replacements joining the groups and saw rookies barely out of flight training with only a few hours of real time in the planes they would be flying, and many of the combat-hardened fliers experienced "a profound feeling of doom."[10]

Fighting Forty-Two, including Bill Leonard and Dick Crommelin, would be merged with Fighting Three for temporary duty under Jimmy Thach. The men of Fighting Forty-Two were understandably angry at losing their designation; to them the whole thing bore the stink of desperation, and they trudged sullenly down to the seaplane base on Ford Island to await a flying boat for the short ride across the island to Kaneohe, where VF-3 was assembling. Thach and his squadron executive officer, Don Lovelace, were there to meet the VF-42 contingent as they exited the flying boat, and the two respected officers received Leonard, Crommelin, and their squadron mates warmly, which Leonard, for one, appreciated. "After about twenty seconds," he recalled, "we were theirs."[11] Thach did not waste the opportunity, quickly asking the seasoned pilots about their Coral Sea experiences and their impressions of the Japanese Zeros. For the rest of the day, he allowed Leonard, Crommelin, and the men of VF-42 to relax a bit, get to know the officers of the squadron, and familiarize themselves with their new F4F-4 Wildcats, a tad less responsive than the F4F-3s they had been flying. Leonard, after a familiarization hop with the plane, thought it had a "better fit and finish."[12] He thought the quality of the fabrication improved, with better Plexiglas in the canopy and good gun-sight installation, but the plane was heavier than the previous models, with the same engine, which worried him when he remembered his previous experiences with the fast, nimble Zeros and their veteran pilots. Thus, "none of the VF-42 crowd was overly pleased with the F4F-4s."[13]

Rumors circulated among the pilots about what was to come. Whatever it was, they knew it was to be big. They could sense an air of foreboding settling over the fleet, a feeling that only worsened when the news about Halsey's illness reached them. The thought of being without "Wild Bill" on this mission unnerved the fliers, who were particularly wary of Spruance's lack of carrier combat experience.

In Japan that same day, more massive Japanese fleets sortied. In Hashirajima, as the ships sailed toward open water, marching songs blared from loudspeakers. The sea was calm, the sky flecked with white clouds, the sun bright on the water. Sailors of the fleets lined the rails, waved their caps, and yelled as the ships churned out into the North Pacific at fourteen knots.

The pilots of the *Enterprise* and *Hornet* air groups left Pearl Harbor and flew out to their carriers on May 29. Upon landing, Dusty Kleiss, still with Scouting Six, was informed of the mission by his squadron leader Earl Gallaher, who had been briefed earlier by Spruance's staff. Gallaher called his division and section leaders together in their ready room and locked the door behind them, cautioning them, "You must not give what I say to anyone!"[14] Kleiss watched Gallaher diagram the area around Midway, describe the powerful Japanese fleets sailing to take it with four or five carriers, and indicate where the Japanese flattops were expected to approach from, and he soaked it all in. "We were told exactly what was going to happen," he would say later.[15] TFs 16 and 17 would lie in wait north of Midway to launch counterstrikes against the Japanese carriers while their air forces were busy hitting the island. The problem was the extreme ranges that were being predicted, likely to exceed the fuel limitations of both the Wildcat fighters and the Devastator torpedo planes. "We knew that only the SBDs could be used for this plan," Kleiss recalled.[16] Gallaher warned his top pilots again to tell no one else, not even the other men in their squadron.

The pilots of the torpedo units had the most to fear in the upcoming battle. By that point in the war, after the Coral Sea fight and the skirmishes that had preceded it, TBD Devastator pilots were well aware that their plane was flawed and overdue for retirement, and that lumbering into the teeth of a Japanese task force at one hundred knots only a few feet above the surface with heavy torpedoes strapped to their undersides made them easy targets for both enemy fighters and antiaircraft gunners, even with fighter protection, which had been a rare thing indeed in the previous months' battles. Their prospects were worrisome, to say the least.

On Saturday, May 30, the swiftly repaired *Yorktown* and her TF 17 finally steamed out of Pearl Harbor at 0900. Her rebuilt air group, including Fighting Three with Crommelin and Leonard, flew out from Kaneohe to join her later that morning as she sailed off the Oahu coast. Their mission began inauspiciously. Jimmy Thach landed beautifully on the carrier's deck, followed by his executive officer, the experienced Don Lovelace. But the third plane to come in landed badly, dropping its nose too sharply, missing the arresting wires, leaping the barriers, and crashing into Lovelace's Wildcat as he taxied to his parking spot. The propeller of Ensign Robert C. Evans' plane landed directly on Lovelace's cockpit, destroying everything inside. Lovelace was killed. "The freak accident had brutally robbed the squadron of one of its most experienced leaders and warmest individuals. . . . There was a replacement for the airplane, but not for Lovelace himself."[17]

Lovelace's loss was particularly hard on Thach. He had counted on his executive officer's presence to help bring this motley assortment of pilots together. After lunch he assembled the men in their ready room and, with Lovelace's absence felt keenly, explained to Crommelin, Leonard, and the rest of the men that they still had a difficult job to do, and a vital one at that. Lovelace's death could not be helped, Thach said. There was a battle coming and it would be up to them to protect the carrier at all costs. Thach "stressed that the fighters had to stop enemy torpedo planes short of their release points even if this meant ramming them."[18] Then he explained how to do just that: move in from below and pull up to allow the prop to sever the enemy torpedo plane's empennage. The men in their chairs knew that Thach was being serious. Afterward, Thach reorganized the squadron, necessary due to Lovelace's death. He appointed Bill Leonard, now the senior VF-42 pilot present, as his new executive officer. Leonard would lead the squadron's 3rd Division in the coming battle, Crommelin the 2nd.

As June approached and the Japanese and American fleets churned toward one another, the weather turned cold and wet, the skies cloudy, the seas marred by rough chop, rain showers, and a thick shroud of fog that hampered the journey for both sides. In each of the fleets, extra lookouts were posted to keep ships from colliding in the gloom. Nagumo allowed searchlights to probe the murk ahead. Despite the atrocious weather, the Americans at least knew generally where the Japanese were, and where they were headed, and where to position themselves to hit their enemy's flanks. From on board his flagship, the carrier *Akagi*, Nagumo could only pose to his senior staff the critical question "Where is the enemy fleet?" He got no answers.[19]

While overconfidence bedeviled large portions of the Japanese navy prior to the battle of Midway, infecting its enlisted men, junior officers, and senior staff alike, the gold-braided Admiral Chuichi Nagumo was, in some respects, immune. From the beginning he had harbored doubts about the men under his command and their level of both preparedness and expertise, among other things. He felt too many were untested, untried, and unready. But he would have to make do. Yamamoto's timetable could not be curtailed, and his concerns were alleviated somewhat by the commanders at the core of his fleet, all seasoned, and by the elite and veteran fliers who led his air-strike forces. The fliers he had at his disposal, and the captains he had around him, could overcome much.

By June 2, 1941, Spruance and TF 16 had reached Point Luck roughly 350 miles northeast of Midway and were awaiting the arrival of Fletcher's forces. The weather in the central Pacific had not improved. A stalled cold front with heavy cloud cover hid the American fleet but had also slowed them down and made the passage unpleasant. Station Hyppo back on Oahu, based on their continued analysis of intercepted transmissions, predicted that the Japanese would strike the Aleutians the next day, thereby opening the offensive. Fletcher's TF 17, built around the *Yorktown*, appeared over the southern horizon at 1600 and sailed into the rendezvous point soon after, the ships arranging themselves on the sea in the waning light, the two fleets separated by about ten miles. Once organized, they represented the greatest American naval force yet assembled in the war. To the west the Japanese Kido Butai, with its four carriers, sailed through its own fogbanks and rain squalls, steaming ever closer to its target. Nagumo believed, reasonably, that the fog and weather were allowing him to approach Midway while maintaining the element of surprise, but it was also preventing his ships from communicating visually. His tension and anxiety seemed to rise with each passing sea mile. Admiral Yamamoto and his senior staff remained well behind Nagumo on board the massive new battleship *Yamato*. Yamamoto had ordered that Nagumo maintain strict radio silence, so the two admirals were not in communication. Nagumo decided to proceed under the assumption that there was no enemy fleet in the area, and he kept to his course.

On the American carriers, flight direction officers exchanged printouts of each fighter and its call sign so as to prevent confusion during the battle. The pilots on board the *Hornet* and *Enterprise* were told they should be prepared to launch as soon as the Japanese carriers were located. Leonard, Crommelin, and the rest of Fighting Three on board the *Yorktown* worked with their mechanics and ordnancemen to ready the brand-new Grummans for the coming fight, as the gun sights had not yet been aligned and many of the Brownings still bore their factory coats of Cosmoline and needed to be boresighted. But they were a bit confused about their tasks. They would be kept behind and used in a search and support role; less glamorous, to be sure, but the memories of the Coral Sea and its nasty surprises were all too clear in Fletcher's mind, and he wanted planes in reserve in case too many search reports again proved erroneous. Either way, on the American ships lying in wait in the gloom, the nerves of the sailors grew frayed, the men grim and quiet. Signs of the collective strain of the officers and men were everywhere, in their looks and behind their eyes, in the galleys and ready rooms, at their battle stations. The ocean beneath them slipped by.

At 0900 on the sunny morning of June 3, a PBY5A flying boat out of Midway Island was cruising at one thousand feet west-southwest of the island when, six hours into its flight and mere seconds from a slow turn onto its homebound line, the pilots spotted specks on the horizon, smudges they at first took to be dirt on the windshield. It was the Midway Invasion Force, twenty-five to thirty miles ahead, bearing 262 degrees in the sun. The Catalina stayed on station and followed the fleet for ninety minutes, flying just above the waves to avoid being seen. Both Nimitz and Fletcher were informed of the scout's report, and though the sighting seemed to indicate the fleet on the sea was the main body, Nimitz doubted that it was, once again buoyed by his intelligence. He immediately radioed Fletcher, "This is not repeat not the enemy striking force—stop—that is the landing force. The striking force will hit from the northwest at daylight tomorrow."[20]

That night, out on the deep, distant Pacific to the east of Midway, there were no religious services on board the ships of the two American task forces, for the officers and men were too busy. They knew a fight was coming in the morning. The air remained cold and wet. The ships zigzagged back and forth in unison to ward off any Japanese submarines potentially lying in wait (they were out there, patrolling areas east of Midway Island, but the American task forces and their precious carriers passed by well away from them). The guns of each aircraft were loaded by their air crews "with loving care," one bullet at a time.[21] Charts and plotting boards were scrubbed clean, empty of numbers for the time being. Though exhausted from the preparations and the tension, few of the pilots on any of the American carriers slept soundly. On board the *Enterprise*, Dusty Kleiss wrote in his logbook, "Tomorrow is likely to be a big day."[22]

Kleiss worried about the upcoming engagement. Though he told himself that if he did his duty and trusted in his training he would make it through to see Jean again, he was also well aware that he had survived three battles already. He wondered if the odds would catch up to him in the morning. What caused him to fret the most was the thought of leaving Jean alone in a "war-torn world."[23] He wrote her a long letter: "I love you, I love you, darling. I only wonder if you will know how much. You mean more to me than anything. . . . I'm living temporarily in another world—

one I hope you know never. It's a cold and ruthless world filled with hate and incalculable cold-bloodedness. But it is necessary for some of us to live there now and then to protect the other world, the one I'm in when I'm with you. . . . Give me courage, Jean, and luck."[24] Then he said a prayer, rolled over, and tried to sleep.

Reveille for the pilots and their air crewmen came early on June 4. At 0200 a messenger tapped Kleiss on the arm: "It's time to wake up."[25]

Kleiss stood, dressed in his flight suit, and headed for the *Enterprise*'s officer's mess, where his fellow aviators were tucking into steak and eggs. When they were finished, each man walked to his ready room, perhaps glanced at the flight rosters grease-penciled on the schedule boards, and then slumped into the soft reclining chairs and started work on his navigational plotting board, every pilot crafting his own solution from the data forwarded down to the room by teletype, which tended to clatter away, violating the stillness. The men constantly checked the course and speed of the fleet and factored in wind corrections and magnetic deviations and the latest sighting reports from Midway's search planes.[26] Hours passed. Each man handled the wait differently. Some were quiet, curt even. Others chattered, needing conversation, something to break the silence. A wondrous few acted as if there was nothing afoot, as if somehow it was just another day on the sea, looking, at least outwardly, calm and collected. They all waited, slept, drank coffee, rechecked their calculations, and waited some more. The ready rooms grew smoke-filled. Kleiss wore Jean's sweater under his flight suit for the extra warmth he would need at high altitudes. In his breast pockets he had stashed pencils for plotting data and a flashlight, Vaseline, and ephedrine. Strapped into his pants were a second flashlight, spare batteries, and wool cloths he would use to wipe his fighter's windshield when it fogged over.[27]

He checked again the plane assignments in Scouting Six's office, then walked through a passageway and down a ladder to the *Enterprise*'s expansive hangar deck. Planes cluttered the aft end of the space, near the rear elevator, and mechanics crawled over and under each one, completing their last-minute preparations. Kleiss noticed that all fourteen of the TBD

Devastators were fitted with Mark-13 torpedoes under their fuselages, and it upset him. He knew from firsthand experience that the fish were faulty and that the pilots had, after the strikes in the Marshalls, "cursed them . . . for failing so spectacularly."[28] Admiral Halsey had even demanded earlier that year that a torpedo-laden TBD never leave one of his hangar decks again, as he knew of their frequent malfunctions.

Kleiss spotted his best friend Tom Eversole watching the sailors as they pushed a Devastator onto the rear elevator. He walked over to his Academy classmate. "Tom, why the hell are the TBDs armed with torpedoes? Do the admirals expect them to go into battle?"[29]

Eversole, unable to mask his worry, nodded and told Kleiss that his unit, Torpedo Six, had been ordered to accompany the air strike. Kleiss then asked if any of the SBDs had been equipped with smoke bombs to cover the torpedo planes as they attacked. Eversole shook his head and looked away. Kleiss was genuinely confused. Why were the torpedo squadrons being sent in again? Had no one told Admirals Fletcher and Spruance about the torpedoes' deficiencies? Had Halsey's directive not been conveyed? Had the pilots of the torpedo squadrons not complained loudly enough?

Kleiss and Eversole shook hands. For Kleiss, the goodbye was gut-wrenching. He knew this was "likely farewell forever," and as he wished his friend good luck, a strange thing happened to him.

> Tom's image started to blur. I was on the verge of tears! I always did my best to hold my emotions in check. I vowed never to show sadness or grief. This was the one moment during the war when I just couldn't hold it back. A flood of memories washed through me as I recalled the wonderful times Tom and I had shared together. I remembered all the high jinx we'd perpetrated at the Naval Academy. I thought of the days we'd spent together as aviation students at Pensacola. . . . There is nothing quite so dark and terrifying as knowing your friend is about to be killed and being utterly unable to help him. All we could do was put on a brave face and try not to think about it.[30]

Before first light, combat air patrols took off from the carriers to buzz in circles around the task forces and scout bombers were sent north to fly search patterns. But sighting the Japanese fleet would really be up to scouts from Midway Island. Nothing would happen until they found the enemy, as Fletcher wanted another definite sighting report before committing his main strike forces—scheduled to comprise 221 operational planes across the three carriers, including 79 fighters, 101 dive-bombers, and 41 torpedo planes. Conditions for flying were expected to be ideal: excellent visibility on a tranquil sea and a gentle, southeasterly five-knot wind. In the predawn, stars peeked through the high clouds.

Just as they had at Pearl Harbor, the Japanese Kido Butai steaming off to the southwest had planned on launching the attack on Midway Island as the sun rose. Nagumo and his admirals readied for their assault, still believing the Americans had no idea where they were, potentially even no idea they were coming. They would launch search planes to scan the sea around them, but these efforts would be haphazard, almost desultory. In the morning darkness, loudspeakers blared on the decks of the four Japanese carriers ordering the aviators to assemble, and air crews made final preparations to the planes. Engines coughed and started, then settled into throaty roars, steady and strong. The Japanese that morning mustered 228 operational aircraft: 73 Zero fighters, 74 carrier bombers, and 81 carrier attack planes. The aviators settling into the cockpits in brown suits and helmets were the best fliers the Japanese navy had. Nagumo gave the order: "Launch the air attack force."[31] Floodlights lit up, and the carriers formed into a box formation on the sea and increased their speed into the wind. Green signal lanterns were swung in wide circles, and the first plane took off at 0430. Within fifteen minutes the entire Midway attacking force was airborne and winging away to the southeast. Soon after, dawn broke brilliantly.

Fletcher and Spruance, even then narrowing the range to where they thought the Japanese would be, anticipated that the enemy's attack on Midway would occur at dawn. Their intelligence indicated as much. Their plan was to strike the lightly defended Japanese carriers as they busied themselves with their Midway attack. The timing had to be precise, but if it all went to plan, and if their intelligence was right, and if their attack caught the Japanese by surprise, the results could be monumental. As historian Stephen Moore described it, the fight would be a battle of flight decks: who had more, and whose could be shut down first. The Japanese had the four carriers in Nagumo's carrier striking force. The Americans had four flight decks as well: the *Enterprise*, *Yorktown*, *Hornet*, and the airstrip on Midway.[32] For everything to work for the U.S. Navy, the first requirement was to find the Japanese carrier force.

Across the three American carriers that pretty morning, fliers from the Naval Academy's Class of 1938 were spread throughout the various ready rooms and flight decks. In addition to Bill Leonard and Dick Crommelin flying with Fighting Three under Jimmy Thach on board the *Yorktown* and Dusty Kleiss with Scouting Six on the *Enterprise*, there was Lieutenant Andy Anderson, assigned to Bombing Six under Lieutenant Dick Best, and, also on the Big E, Rhonald "Buster" Hoyle, still with VF-6 under Lieutenant James Gray, and Lieutenant (jg) Tom Eversole, flying with Torpedo Six. Osborne Wiseman would fly that day with Bombing Three, part of the *Yorktown*'s complement, and Wil Rawie was flying an SBD as part of Scouting Six. Lieutenant (jg) Curtis Howard was set to fly a Devastator with Torpedo Three. They were a long way from the Yard and their bunks in Bancroft Hall but perhaps took some solace in knowing they were together.

At 0530 Lieutenant Howard P. Ady, piloting a PBY Catalina, sent back to Midway Island a report of an enemy carrier bearing 320 degrees, distance 180 miles. Spruance received the report on board the *Enterprise* four minutes later. He was frustrated at the vagueness of Ady's message but perked up when, at 0545, another report from a Catalina west of the island piloted by Lieutenant (jg) William A. Chase arrived: "Many planes heading Midway."[33] This was the strike force he and Fletcher had been anticipating. Then Ady, as he turned his plane around, saw through a break in the clouds a truly "awe-inspiring sight": there were not one but two carriers as well as main body ships crowding the sea on a course of 135 degrees, speed thirty-five knots.[34]

When at 0603 word of this second, bigger sighting reached Fletcher on the *Yorktown*, still sailing ten miles away from his other two carriers, he ordered Spruance to "proceed southwesterly and attack enemy carriers as soon as definitely located."[35] He would follow with his own strike force once he had recovered his scout planes. More than that, though, Fletcher wanted to keep his options open. He sent Spruance with the *Enterprise* and *Hornet* charging southwestward toward the sighting while he hung back.

Spruance, on the other hand, had no compunction about launching a full strike at the targets his scouts had sighted. "I figured that if I was going to hit the Japanese, I should hit them with everything I had. . . . We couldn't afford to wait. We had to strike, strike swiftly, and strike in great force."[36] He and his staff debated when they would be close enough to launch—they were eager to get the planes in the air but knew that if they launched too soon many would not be able to make the return flight. Regardless, they could get the men in their planes and ready to go, and quickly the orders bellowed through the loudspeakers on the two carriers: "Pilots, man your planes!"[37] The pilots stood, shook hands, and filed out of their ready rooms.

As the sun began its creep above the horizon, the air was cool, the sea an indigo blue, the sky clear with patches of clouds aloft but otherwise providing perfect visibility. TF 16 turned into the wind and sped up while Kleiss and the other pilots on board the *Enterprise* and nearby *Hornet* hit the starter switches to their engines. Spruance's staff estimated that the Japanese attack on its way to bomb Midway Island would have finished their task and returned to their carriers by 0900, and they figured that Nagumo would maintain his heading until that time. The window to hit the Japanese fleet while it was vulnerable was closing, but the range to the target was still uncomfortably long. It was, according to Spruance, one of the most difficult decisions he would ever have to make. Launching at such an extreme range would place enormous challenges on his pilots and their crews; the danger for the slow Devastator torpedo bombers would be especially high. Fatefully, aware of both the risks involved and the desperate urgency, Spruance decided he would launch his planes at 0700. Anderson, Eversole, Hoyle, Kleiss, and the other pilots on the two carriers remained in their cockpits, "gloved and garbed," the carriers now "cocked like loaded pistols."[38]

The attack by the Japanese on Midway, which began a little after 0600, was intended to soften up the island for the amphibious assault to follow, and in that regard it was ruthlessly effective. Virtually every American fighter sent aloft was shot down in the swirling dogfights that preceded the Japanese bombing runs. Destroyed were the island's power plant, its mess hall, the fuel tanks, a seaplane hangar, the Navy dispensary, and numerous other buildings. Bomb craters were left from one end of the sandy, scrubby island to the other save the island's runway, which, anticipating they would take Midway later in the day, the Japanese left undamaged for immediate future use. By 0645 the IJN pilots reassembled to the west of Midway and set off on their return flight to the carriers. But Lieutenant Joichi Tomonaga, the strike's leader, did not feel his force had fully accomplished its mission. There were still targets to be had on Midway, so he radioed Nagumo that they were homeward bound but that a second strike on the island was needed.

Tomonaga's message presented a quandary for Nagumo: Should he send in the second strike as Tomonaga had requested, or should he wait to receive the reports from his scout planes as to the location of any possible American fleet? His decisions were monumental; the entire war hinged on them, yet he had very little time to assess the information at hand and discuss the various scenarios with his senior staff. He had to act quickly. Nagumo gave the order for the remaining planes he had kept in reserve on his carriers to switch from antiship torpedoes to Type 80 land bombs. They would be launched when ready to attack Midway in a follow-up raid. But the switch entailed hard and time-consuming work, so his armorers and plane handlers set to it.

At 0728, however, Nagumo received a message from one of his floatplanes reporting what appeared to be ten enemy surface ships 240 miles northeast of Midway. Unfortunately for Nagumo, the message did not include anything more specific. It was frustratingly vague, yet it rattled the senior Japanese admiral. The pilot had not reported any aircraft carriers, and a mere surface fleet at that range could pose no danger, but if the enemy fleet did in fact contain carriers, then that changed everything. To be safe Nagumo halted the switching of his planes' ordnance, which by that point was about half completed. He then snapped at the scout to maintain contact with the American ships and provide more details.

A few minutes prior, at 0700, the blue planes of the *Hornet* had begun their launches cleanly and in good order. They were all aloft by 0740. The strike formation flew off almost due west. The *Enterprise* launched her dive-bombers well, but the deck crew was slow to get the subsequent torpedo planes and Wildcat fighters in the air, forcing the SBDs to circle the fleet and burn precious fuel. Dusty Kleiss, again with his gunner John Snowden in the rear seat, had been one of the first fifteen SBDs to take off from the *Enterprise*'s deck. Next off were the fifteen SBDs of Bombing Six, including Lieutenant Edward "Andy" Anderson, USNA '38, who rose from the deck second to last. His dive-bomber was weighted with a 1,000-pound bomb and full tanks of fuel, and his gunner, Aviation Radioman Second Class (ARM2c) Stewart Mason Jr., breathed a sigh of relief when Anderson got the heavy plane aloft in the wind.

Spruance, frustrated that the launch was taking so long, went ahead and sent his dive-bombers on without waiting for the other planes, doctrine be damned. The carrier signaled the circling planes by blinker light at 0745, and Lieutenant Commander Clarence "Mac" McClusky pulled the SBD dive-bombers, including Kleiss and Anderson, into a single formation of stepped-down V-shaped sections, the highest planes at 20,000 feet, and set off in a direction that took them farther southwest than the *Hornet*'s strike force. Their orders were to find and attack the enemy carriers. The torpedo planes and fighters would set off piecemeal when they were able. It would prove a key decision as it meant each carrier's strike forces would be departing and eventually attacking independently of each other and that most of the units would be without their fighter escorts. The last elements of the *Enterprise*'s group to take off were the fourteen Devastators of Torpedo Six, flying low and slow on a heading of 240 degrees. Among them was Tom Eversole. When all the launches were completed, 116 bombers, torpedo planes, and fighters from the two carriers were heading toward the estimated Japanese position. It had been a long, chaotic, and poorly executed process, resulting in two American strike forces that were uncoordinated, acting independently, and heading in different directions, but at least the planes were in the air. It was not yet 0800.

As Nagumo, his mood sour, waited for more information from his scout, he was kept busy. Beginning at 0749 another flight of sixteen SBD-2 Dauntless dive-bombers flown by Marines from Midway (they had gotten away just before the first wave of Japanese planes attacked the island) arrived over his fleet and dropped their bombs on the *Hiryu* and *Kaga*. None hit. Half of the American dive-bombers were shot down in the attack. A few minutes later, fourteen American B-17s arrived over the fleet and dropped their bomb loads on the Japanese carriers *Hiryu* and *Soryu*. They were too high for effective antiaircraft fire and so were able to line up their bombing runs unmolested, but again, none caused any real damage to the flattops. The Japanese sailors were left unimpressed by the Americans' offensive tactics, but the attacks did hinder Nagumo's flight operations at a crucial time during the day's action.

Finally, at 0758, another message from his scout was placed in Nagumo's hand. This new sighting reported that the American ships had changed course sharply. There was no reason for a fleet to change course like that except to launch planes into the wind, yet that telling detail seems to have been ignored or overlooked by Nagumo and his officers. They simply wanted the pilot to confirm the types of ships he was seeing, which the scout did not do. Nagumo, now fuming, again demanded that the scout advise him of the ship types below him. The pilot replied, "Enemy is composed of five cruisers and five destroyers."[39] The new message did not meaningfully allay Nagumo's fears. Surely, he believed, it was some sort of escort force protecting something bigger, something as yet unseen, something potentially far more dangerous.

1938
USNA

JOHN THOMAS EVERSOLE

Pocatello, Idaho

It took a brilliant pep talk by a commander to persuade Tom to leave the wilds of Idaho. He came not with bowed legs and Western drawl, but with a pleasing smile and attractive personality. While he claims to have denied this to the femmes back home, he is no novice snake. However, he manages to hold them off long enough to show his hand at sports. Buoyant of mind but not of body, his one plague was the sub squad. But nothing so small could stop Tom. For four years he's been a fine roommate and in life he'll make an excellent shipmate—on land, at sea, or in the air. His one ambition is to fly and already he is sprouting wings. May his flight through life be a smooth one.

The Lucky Bag, 1938

Chapter Seventeen

SIX MINUTES

At 0820 on the morning of June 4, 1942, two things happened to the Japanese carrier strike force steaming eastward in the central Pacific that forced Admiral Chuichi Nagumo to adjust to the actions of his enemy rather than dictate the flow of affairs, an unfamiliar feeling for any Japanese admiral up to that point. The first was the arrival of yet another flight of land-based American bombers from Midway sweeping in to harass his fleet. The second was the receipt of a new message from his scout plane then flying over the American ships to the northeast. The message was considerably more worrisome to Nagumo than the slow American planes overhead. It read, "Enemy force accompanied by what appears to be [an] aircraft carrier bringing up the rear."[1]

Shocked that the Americans had ambushed him, Nagumo and his staff huddled, for they faced a serious problem. Many of the carrier attack planes arrayed below them on the *Akagi*'s deck and across the water in the *Kaga*'s hangar were parked and in the middle of being rearmed. To attack the American carrier, those planes now already lugging land bombs would need to be refitted once again with torpedoes, causing a delay in Nagumo's ability to launch. That was bad enough, but what was even worse for the Japanese senior staff was the status of their fighters, necessary to protect any strike force that could be assembled.

Only six Zeros were ready to be launched. Most of the remaining fighters were already aloft on combat air patrol and would have to land and refuel before they could escort any dive-bombers and torpedo planes sent to attack this new American threat. But even this was a moot point at the moment.

No strike forces could be launched, no fighters landed and refueled, until the last of the Americans' nettlesome Midway-based planes had been chased off. Planes could not land while the carriers twisted and turned to avoid falling bombs. What Nagumo faced, after he received the sighting of the American aircraft carrier, was a series of obstacles preventing him from responding as he had been trained to. He was forced into a position to which he was unaccustomed, and by which he was much disturbed: he was forced to wait.

Where he could, Nagumo acted decisively. He ordered the decks of his four carriers cleared and his planes carrying land bombs rearmed immediately. On the flattops around him, his armorers rapidly set to their work, sweating through their tropical shirts, though in their haste they left fuel lines and munitions littering the decks and the hangars below. As the last of the American bombers were finally chased away, once again without inflicting damage on the Kido Butai, Nagumo paced the *Akagi*'s bridge and scanned the skies for planes. Time was precious. Landing operations commenced, and almost as soon as a recovered plane's tires struck one of the flight decks of the carriers, occurring in twenty-five- to forty-five-second intervals, they were shuffled off to the elevators and dropped down to the hangar decks while fueled and armed planes were brought up from below and pulled into launch positions. Nagumo's men were working frantically, but painful minutes passed. Before long, he was ready to launch a partial attack against the Americans, but he decided—surprisingly, given his anxiety and consternation—to wait until the full strike force was rearmed, refueled, and ready. The work continued while the fleet plowed through the water at a blistering thirty knots. He blinked a message to his ships: "After completing homing operations, proceed northward. We plan to contact and destroy the enemy task force." Then he sent a message back to Yamamoto: "Enemy composed of 1 carrier, 5 cruisers, and 5 destroyers sighted. . . . We are heading for it."[2] He did not yet know that the all-important first punch of the battle was even then winging his way.

Prominent World War II historian Gordon Prange judged Nagumo's decision to recover and rearm all of his planes and then send out a fully formed strike force rather than piecemeal formations launched in a panic a "theoretically impeccable command decision."[3] He acted reasonably, given the information at hand. Yet he was losing the initiative as each second passed.

With the squadrons from the *Enterprise* and *Hornet* already aloft and winging toward the suspected positions of the Japanese fleet, the *Yorktown*, some distance northeast of Spruance's TF 16, positioned her planes for launch beginning at 0820. Neither Fletcher nor Spruance was fully aware of exactly how many carriers steamed with the Japanese fleet to the southwest, but their intelligence had suggested it was more than one, so Fletcher was finally compelled to add some of his own squadrons to the attack. Lieutenant Commander Lem Massey's twelve TBD Devastators of Torpedo Three (whose pilots included Lieutenant [jg] Curtis Howard, USNA '38) and the seventeen SBD-3 Dauntless dive-bombers of Max Leslie's Bombing Three (including Lieutenant [jg] Osborne Wiseman, USNA '38) were spotted on the *Yorktown*'s deck. Fletcher would keep the rest of his air forces in reserve. Just after 0830 the *Yorktown* began to launch her planes into a light southeasterly wind, beginning with the slow Devastators. Once aloft, Osborne Wiseman in plane 3-B-16 formed up with Leslie's formation. That day he and his rear gunner, ARM3c Grant U. Dawn from Tennessee, were assigned as second section leader in the 3rd Division, and after circling for a bit to allow the torpedo planes to get out ahead of them, VB-3 set off. The cruiser *Astoria* below them blinked a farewell message: "Good hunting and safe return."[4]

Visibility was excellent as the *Yorktown* receded over the horizon behind them. The ceiling was unlimited, with only a scattering of clouds at three thousand feet. The dive-bombers climbed, letting the Devastators lumber down below near the water. Leslie signaled Wiseman and the planes around him to arm their bombs. They flew straight through the clear morning air, eighty minutes behind the planes from the *Enterprise*.

The leaders of the *Yorktown*'s strike had been ordered to keep to the east of the last reported enemy position and, if they found nothing, then assume the enemy fleet was retiring and make a starboard turn before flying a reverse course to the northwest. It was believed the Japanese carriers would be no more than eighty or ninety miles west of Midway. These instructions, formulated by the *Yorktown*'s air officer, Commander Murray E. Arnold, were well considered and, according to the U.S. Navy's official report of the battle, led to "the most important decision of the entire action."[5]

A Grumman F4F-4 Wildcat during the Battle of Midway, June 4, 1942

After the *Yorktown* strike force set off, Fletcher launched a relief combat air patrol (CAP) of six Wildcats, including Bill Leonard's 3rd Division. Leonard had scheduled himself in that time slot, expecting the enemy counterattack to come at that moment. He wanted to be in the air with primed machine guns when it arrived. After this, seventeen dive-bombers of VS-5 were spotted for launch but held on deck and kept ready to take part in any follow-up attack. Assigned to escort these dive-bombers would be the six F4Fs of Dick Crommelin's section.

At 0855 the Japanese scout, putting in yeoman's work that morning, radioed Nagumo with one final update before departing the area. The pilot had spotted ten American torpedo bombers on a heading that would take them directly to the Japanese fleet.

The battle started poorly for the *Hornet*'s air groups and would get no better as the morning passed. After they launched, the planes flew away on a heading that brought them too far to the west. All they found out there were scattered clouds and an empty ocean. Lacking creativity, the air group's commander, Stanhope Ring, kept his squadrons pointed westward, their fuel gauges falling as they flew onward. Eventually his planes were all forced to turn back home. They would play no role in the day's battles.

Except for one group. Earlier, Lieutenant Commander John C. Waldron, the commanding officer of *Hornet*'s Torpedo Squadron Eight, had turned his fifteen Devastators away from Ring's formations and pointed them west-southwest. He did not believe Ring was headed in the right direction and, rather than fly aimlessly out into an empty sea, he took his squadron to search on their own. They flew away at one hundred knots, just 1,500 feet above the wave tops, the planes spread out in a wide scouting line. The men all thought they were alone, but unbeknown to them, they had company. Lieutenant Jimmy Gray's fighters from VF-6 cruised well above the Devastators at 22,000 feet, swinging from side to side in wide S-turns to maintain station over the slow torpedo bombers below. Gray assumed Waldron knew where he was going and so did not break radio silence, concentrating instead on scanning the skies around him for enemy fighters. They liked to come out of the sun, and they could be difficult to spot.

Away to the southeast, Lieutenant Commander C. Wade McClusky, with the thirty-two SBD dive-bombers of Scouting Six and Bombing Six around him (including Andy Anderson and Dusty Kleiss), flew at 20,000 feet and had an unlimited view from one horizon to the other. In a manner similar to Ring's planes, the dive-bombers from the *Enterprise* had arrived at a point on the sea expecting to find a Japanese fleet steaming on the surface but found nothing save sunlit water. Unlike Ring, McClusky had a contingency plan in mind. Knowing Midway and its atolls lay just beyond his port horizon and reckoning that he had probably passed beyond the line of Nagumo's advance, he made a starboard turn and took his group west, then northwest on a reciprocal bearing to the Japanese fleet's last known course. It was a gamble, McClusky knew, because the Japanese could just as easily be between him and Midway, unseen but frightfully close by, and he would be heading in the opposite direction, but McClusky was a gifted commander and an intelligent flier, and he wasted no time debating it. His formation had a mere fifteen minutes, about thirty-five miles, to spot something on their heading before their planes' fuel limitations would force them to return to the *Enterprise*, so he could not dawdle. McClusky's decision would prove monumental.

Thirty minutes later there was still no sign of the Japanese fleet. The veterans in McClusky's formation worried about the nerves, surely jangled, of the younger pilots—very soon none of the planes would make it back to the carrier if they did not start their return flight, and they all knew it. Every pilot and his gunner scanned the sea, searching for anything, any sign of a Japanese ship. Reaching the end of his thirty-five-mile course, McClusky obstinately chose to fly on, swinging to starboard and heading northwest in a box search. He would turn home after five more minutes, he decided. Anderson and Kleiss shivered in their own cockpits behind him. Ice began accumulating on the pilots' oxygen masks.

John Waldron's flight was uneventful for an hour, though at one point he and his *Hornet*-based torpedo squadron crossed the path of a lone Japanese scout plane who spotted them in the air: it was the floatplane that had been reporting the location of the American fleet all morning. Above VT-8, at 0910, Jimmy Gray's 2nd Division leader, Lieutenant (jg) Jack C. Kelley, cut in over the radio: "There they are at one o'clock down, skipper."[6] Directly in front of them, on the other side of a wide cloud bank, white wakes cut across the blue ocean. Gray twisted his head, searching every quadrant of the sky for more American planes or for diving Japanese Zeros. "Our necks were working overtime."[7] Waldron, always highly aggressive, soon spotted the fleet himself—the course he had chosen after flying away from Stanhope Ring's group had proven to be superbly accurate, and he led his Devastators into a shallow dive to close the distance with the Japanese flattops. Theirs would be the first attack that morning to originate from an American carrier deck.

A Douglas TBD-1 Devastator at Midway

Ahead of Waldron, the Japanese flattops were finishing up their recovery operations when Nagumo was alerted by spotters on the *Chikuma* to the arrival of enemy planes, first seen as tiny specks low to starboard. Then Gray's fighters were spotted up high. In the instant before his antiaircraft guns opened up, Nagumo pieced together that there were too many planes out there to come from one single American carrier. There must be more than one, sailing beyond the horizon somewhere unseen. His previous assumptions unraveled. His heretofore meticulous planning fell to nothing. Nagumo was now fighting a different sort of battle than he had anticipated.[8] He must counterattack, and immediately. Desperately he issued his next order: "Speed preparations for immediate takeoff." It was an order impossible to follow, though, for by then his carriers were independently beginning their sharp turns and zags away from the approaching American planes.[9]

As Waldron began his dive, Jimmy Gray and his fighters momentarily lost sight of their charges. When Gray spotted them again, several dozen Zeros (perhaps as many as twenty-nine) had already set upon the slow Devastators, attacking VT-8 from both sides at once, hitting the lead planes first like "wolves ripping into a herd of deer."[10] Waldron's squadron, slow and unwieldy and skimming the wave tops with nowhere to maneuver, could do little, and one by one they belched smoke or caught fire or flipped out of control and dropped into the water. Waldron was one of the first to die, his plane hit in the left gas tank. Some of the Devastators in his squadron were able to launch their torpedoes before they were shot down, but the Japanese fleet easily dodged them, as they were dropped from too far a distance. Ensign Gray, flying above it all, had been slow to react but pragmatic when he saw that the Japanese fighters had already pounced on the torpedo planes and were finishing them off quickly. He stayed above the melee, opting to use his fighters now as scout planes, and tried to contact McClusky but got no reply. Waldron had never even known Gray and his intended fighter escort were there. Of fifteen planes and thirty men, only one American from VT-8 survived the attack: Ensign George Gay, who had brought up the rear during the dive in, launched his torpedo at the *Soryu* (it missed), flew low over her flight deck, and was then shot down by no fewer than five Zeros in the midst of the Japanese task force. Famously, he would escape his sinking plane and hide in the water under a floating seat cushion, where he watched the epic battle unfold as the fleet ranged to the north of him. VT-8 was lost, with nothing to show for it. Yet as Captain Marc Mitscher, commanding officer of the *Hornet*, would later write in his official report of the battle, "No higher praise nor traditions of the service could possibly be cited that gallant band."[11]

Thirty miles away to the southeast, Lieutenant Commander Gene Lindsey's Torpedo Six squadron off the *Enterprise* was flying on a heading of 240 degrees when they sighted smoke in the distance. Among the formation was Lieutenant (jg) Tom Eversole. Lindsey led his squadron in a starboard turn and came upon the Kido Butai just as Waldron's ill-fated initial attack was winding down. He spotted three of the carriers all sailing at high speed to the northeast and aimed his men at the nearest of them, the *Kaga*. As they flew in, Lindsey split his squadron, sending 2nd Division around to the north. The distance to the carrier narrowed, but only slowly. Scouts on board the Japanese cruiser *Tone* saw them, black specks to the south, and the ship fired its main battery to direct the busy Zeros over to the American planes. It was 0945. Flying not much faster than the carriers themselves, over Japanese destroyers, cruisers, and battleships, VT-6's chase took time, but they were afforded it because the bulk of the Zeros flying combat air patrol that morning had been pulled to the north of the task force to fight off Waldron's torpedo planes, and many of those that were nearby had empty ammunition belts. Still, as was already painfully obvious, the Devastators were vulnerable, clumsy, slow, and ultimately of little use in carrier warfare. Nine Zeros arrived to dive down on the planes, and antiaircraft fire barked at them throughout their long pursuit, and though some of the pilots managed to drop their fish, once again none hit. Because of their slow speeds, the Japanese carrier handlers had been able to keep the planes on their quarters, refusing the Americans any advantageous angles. Ten of the planes would be lost, harried murderously after dropping their torpedoes as they tried to get away, including those of Gene Lindsey and Tom Eversole. Eversole had been Dusty Kleiss' best friend at Annapolis, a fair-haired fencer and footballer with a strong nose, rounded chin, and diminutive ears. He had had one burning ambition since leaving his hometown in Idaho: to fly. Eversole's Navy Cross citation captured the bravery of his and VT-6's attack: "The unprecedented conditions under which his squadron launched its offensive were so exceptional that it is highly improbable the occasion may ever recur where other pilots of the service will be called upon to demonstrate an equal degree of gallantry and fortitude."[12]

The opening attacks by the two torpedo squadrons produced no strikes, only dead American airmen. But they did result in distracted Japanese fighter pilots, gunners, and carrier captains. Though it was unintentional, by pressing their attacks when they did, Waldron and Lindsey had occupied the attention of the Japanese at a critical time, sacrificing themselves so that the succeeding waves of dive-bombers approaching the area could make their runs virtually unopposed. Jimmy Gray still circled above the action with his ten fighters. He did not see Lindsey's attack, far off on the wide sea below him, nor did he hear anything from him on the radio. He spotted no other Zeros to attack and heard no distress calls from any torpedo planes asking him to come to their assistance, so he kept his squadron at 22,000 feet and circled the area, then radioed back that he was still over the target, running short of fuel, and would need to return soon.

As the few survivors of VT-6 flew off, many Japanese sailors and officers undoubtedly stood back in relief. Thus far that morning they had beaten off wave after wave of American planes launched from both Midway and the enemy's carriers. They had been "level-bombed, glide-bombed, and torpedo-bombed."[13] Yet for all the Americans' efforts, no ship in the Kido Butai had been damaged. On the flight decks of the carriers and behind the deck guns of the screening ships, sailors had whistled and cheered as the torpedo planes crashed in plumes of seawater. But on the *Akagi* Nagumo remained anxious. His ship formations had been broken up and his flight operations continuously disrupted. His attack planes were still being rearmed and refueled in the hangars below, his decks were crowded, much of his CAP would need to be retrieved and new fighters cycled up, and he had not yet seen any of the Americans' dive-bombers, the most lethal bullets the enemy carriers had to fire and the only enemy aircraft the Japanese truly feared.[14] American planes had been destroyed and his ships were still unscratched, but Nagumo's situation was becoming increasingly precarious, and he knew it.

At 0955, south of Nagumo and his fleet, Lieutenant Commander Wade McClusky spotted through his binoculars something on the surface of the sea beneath him, a long white wake cutting the blue water at almost a right angle to the direction in which he was headed. McClusky rightly deduced that the lone vessel producing that deep wake must be trying to catch up to the rest of the Japanese fleet, wherever it was. He immediately changed course to the north-northeast and followed the Japanese destroyer that was carving through the water at flank speed. Before long, McClusky spied a net of crisscrossing wakes, "chalk white" and thin, ahead of him—the carrier strike force he had been struggling to find, unkempt and scattered.[15] Among the ships, McClusky and his men could see multiple yellow rectangles with red circles painted boldly in their middles, the telltale shapes and symbols and colors of Japanese aircraft carriers. They could see two in the foreground and a third off in the distance. McClusky radioed his sighting back to the *Enterprise* and then waited, taking his formations on a long detour to the northeast around the enemy fleet. He wanted the sun behind him, hoping it would hinder the aim of the antiaircraft gunners below. They flew over the screening destroyers, over George Gay under his cushion, through scattered clouds, the fleet below as yet unaware of their presence due to the distractions caused by VTs-6 and -8.

Meanwhile, Ensign Gray, still in the area with his fighters and unaware of McClusky's arrival, considered making a strafing run but changed his mind. He radioed another sighting report back to TF 16 at 1000, then said, "We are returning to ship due to lack of gas."[16]

At about the same time that McClusky arrived on the scene, Jimmy Thach, in a fighter escorting VT-3, spotted smoke and wakes roughly twenty-five miles distant. The two air formations, with no communication between them, had launched two hours apart and taken separate and circuitous routes to the Japanese fleet, yet they had arrived within moments of each other. To the Japanese it must have seemed like a precisely coordinated and professional attack. In reality it was sheer circumstance, the dumbest of luck.

Lem Massey, leading the *Yorktown*'s VT-3 squadron below Thach's six fighters, was one of the most combat-experienced torpedo pilots in the American Navy, and he led his planes on a shallow climb to gain a bit more speed as they closed low to the water. Balls of black antiaircraft smoke erupted in front of them. Orange tracers streamed in all directions. It was 1003. Then, in a blink, the sky around Massey's Devastators erupted in Zeros, fifteen of them. Thach and his five fighter pilots flying slightly behind Massey's formation rose to engage them. Massey, still ten miles short of his target, poured on whatever extra speed his Devastator had, the twelve torpedo planes behind him doing the same as the enemy ships grew larger through their canopies. They aimed their attack at the *Hiryu*'s starboard beam. Thach did not believe any of his fighters would survive, but they fought tenaciously, employing dogfighting tactics of his own design, and their weaving and unexpected turns knocked the Zero pilots off balance. The Japanese airmen were used to having their way with American planes, but Thach and his men started machine-gunning Zeros from the sky, allowing Massey's torpedo planes to drone on in toward the *Hiryu*. The six fighters could only distract the Japanese fighter pilots for so long, however, and soon the relentless Zeros recovered and set upon Massey's Devastators anew, attacking in a string formation with high-side and above-rear runs that sent bullets around the armor of the American planes, and they were soon knocking Massey's men down in bunches. Ten of twelve Devastators would be destroyed, including Massey's. Five managed to drop their torpedoes six to eight hundred yards out but, almost inevitably it seems, they too scored no hits.

One of the VT-3 planes shot down in the attack was that of Curtis "Punchy" Howard, USNA '38. He had been born in 1917 on the Pacific island of Guam, where his father was stationed while with the U.S. Navy's Medical Corps. He received his appointment to the Naval Academy from the state of California in 1934 and earned his nickname while a member of the boxing team. After flight training in Pensacola, Howard joined Torpedo Squadron 3 on board the *Saratoga* in January 1941. He was killed in the attack on the *Hiryu* with his gunner, ARM3c Charles L. Moore.

Just as McClusky was nearing his pushover point, more American planes arrived. They were the seventeen SBDs of *Yorktown*'s Bombing Three, Lieutenant Commander Max Leslie leading, with Osborne Wiseman, USNA '38, in tow. They arrived from the east, miles away, on the far side of the Japanese fleet from McClusky. Again, the setup was perfect. The Americans were in the process of launching a triple-pronged attack that could not have been better coordinated. The carriers below were in a ragged line, two below McClusky, a third out toward the east and a fourth off to the north, each having maneuvered independently during the morning's attacks, and the American dive-bombers now had them boxed in just when they were at their most vulnerable. The Zeros had been kept distracted by the torpedo planes and were, because of it, low to the water and spread out.

Dusty Kleiss, flying with McClusky that morning, noted the enemy fleet's longitude and latitude as well as his altitude and the time on his plotting board, then ordered his rear gunner to change radio coils to the Zed Baker device and manually armed his bombs, choosing to bypass the sometimes unreliable electric arming button. Behind him his gunner stowed his weapon and faced forward, ready to plummet. McClusky and his division leaders then signaled their men by kicking their rudders back and forth, wagging their tails, and quickly the lead SBDs nosed up, opened their flaps, and pushed over into 70-degree angles, steep, fast, and out of the sun. It was 1020. The planes emitted shrill wails as they dove through intermittent clouds toward the *Kaga* and Nagumo's *Akagi*, both flight decks cluttered with planes and the small figures of men.

Just as the *Akagi* raised aloft the signal to begin the launch of her planes, lookouts finally spotted dive-bombers in the air dropping on the nearby *Kaga* to port. They watched the carrier across the water heel into a sharp clockwise turn, but at 1022 the first bomb of the morning struck, a 500-pounder dropped from 1,800 feet by Lieutenant Earl Gallaher, the fourth plane in the line of dive-bombers dropping down on the carrier. The bomb exploded on the aft end of the *Kaga*'s flight deck, blowing planes that had just moments before been massing for takeoff into the sea and igniting a maelstrom of fire that trapped much of the crew belowdecks. Located three planes behind Gallaher was Dusty Kleiss. He watched the explosion from Gallaher's bomb mushroom up beneath him and opted to aim for the undamaged forward section of the deck, right at the big red circle the Japanese had painted there. Peering through his sites, keeping the pipper aligned squarely to point his plane, Kleiss tried to gauge where the carrier was going to be, not where it was at the moment. He kept the carrier in his sights the whole way down, letting nothing distract him.

Flames from Gallaher's strike towered more than 50 feet in the air, the smoke much higher than that. Still falling, 150 feet behind the plane in front of him, Kleiss yanked a handle and released his big bomb at 1,500 feet, then, moments later and another few hundred feet farther down, he toggled his hundred-pound incendiary wing bombs. Desperate to secure a hit, he stayed in his dive longer than he should have, not pulling up until he was a mere one thousand feet above the water. He barely missed the ocean, the 9 g's pulling viciously at his body. Bullets sliced into his plane, but it was durable and tough and remained flyable. As he zipped over the waves, Kleiss managed to look back at the *Kaga*, something they had been trained not to do, and he watched an explosion bloom from her deck where he had been aiming. His 500-pounder had smashed through the flight deck, on the rear edge of the red circle painted there, and detonated in the hangar. A third bomb dropped after his then hit a fuel cart just forward of the island, blowing out the bridge windows and engulfing the ship's captain and everyone else around him in a firestorm. A fourth bomb then landed amidships, shattering the already roiling ship's innards. The results of the four hits were cataclysmic. Soon those men who could fled to the flight deck and open air while fuel tanks and munitions continued to explode below, sending columns of flames up into the sky. The flames that pierced the *Kaga*'s flight deck were pink and blue. The fire mains were destroyed, the damage control men cut down before they could be put to use. The ship was quickly in its death throes.

Second to last in the line of planes diving on the *Kaga* was Andy Anderson, USNA '38. After his run he pulled up but took grievous fire from the antiaircraft guns scattered around the water in the screen, shrapnel and machine-gun fire striking the plane from every angle.[17] Then Zeros took passes at him, sending bullets into his fuselage and shredding the fabric. Anderson's gunner, Stuart J. Mason Jr., took shrapnel in the face and legs, his goggles covered in blood, yet, in tremendous pain, he continued to fire his twin-mount guns at the fighters as Anderson did his best to shake them. When Mason finished with one ammunition canister, he threw it over the side and loaded another. Anderson and Mason successfully ran away from the Zeros and headed back to their carrier. As he flew Anderson handed Mason his dirty windshield rag, which the gunner used to wipe his face.

Dusty Kleiss also tried to clear the area amid murderous antiaircraft fire and tracers that flashed by his plane. He jinked right and left, never changing altitude and never flying in the same direction for more than a few seconds. A Zero dove on him as he flew low to the water, and Kleiss' gunner opened fire and beat the fighter back.

In what could have been a serious mistake, only three of McClusky's dive-bombers aimed for the nearby *Akagi*, but they were effective. Led by Lieutenant Dick Best, the three planes attacked in a shallower dive angle than was prudent, but they maintained their V formation and were well spaced. The antiaircraft fire from the carrier was wildly off-target. Captain Taijiro Aoki put the carrier into a hard starboard turn when the planes were spotted, but it was far too late for that. Sailors on board reported hearing the "metallic scream of the Dauntlesses' dive breaks, then a mighty explosion."[18] The first bomb was a near miss, drenching the bridge (and Nagumo) as it exploded just meters off the carrier's port bow. The second, however, struck near the amidships elevator, in the middle of a pack of Kate torpedo planes waiting to take off with their propellers spinning. The blast wrenched the elevator loose and dropped it into the hangar. The third bomb landed near the port flight deck. Ordinarily these twin blasts would not have been fatal, but, like the *Kaga*, the *Akagi* had been in the middle of flight operations, and her deck was stacked with planes that blew apart and added their fuel tanks, bombs, and torpedoes to the hurricane of fire. Deck plates were twisted and burned. The radio room and antenna were destroyed. The ship lost steerage as the rudder jammed. The engines stopped. Smaller explosions then wracked the carrier's insides.

At almost the exact moment that the *Kaga* and *Akagi* were struck, explosions blossomed from the *Soryu* across the water astern, three hits in quick succession. The *Soryu* had just made a turn to begin launching Zeros when Leslie and his dive-bombers, including Ozzie Wiseman, tipped their planes over to begin their attacks at 1022. The dive-bombers had plummeted down unmolested by antiaircraft fire; the Japanese gunners had not seen them. They were cheering on their fighters down near the water's surface, and their guns were depressed horizontally because of it. VB-3's dive through a hole in the clouds was "schoolbook perfect," and the damage done to the *Soryu* was the most "prompt" and "intensified" of the carriers hit that morning.[19] The three 1,000-pound bombs that struck her landed with blinding flashes in a line down the carrier's side, blowing men off the deck and starting hellish fires that were fed when the flames penetrated nearby bomb and torpedo storage rooms, ammunition lockers, and fuel tanks. Fires soon ranged across the length of the ship, and her engines cut out. Her captain would be the first to give the order to abandon ship that morning. Lieutenant Wiseman, one of the last planes in, could tell before he reached his release point that the ship was damaged beyond repair, so he saved his bombs, pulled up from the carrier, and went after a nearby battleship. The Dauntlesses of VB-3 then withdrew to the northeast and headed for home. There were no Zeros around to trouble them as they left.

Nagumo watched the *Akagi* burn to death around him. Initially he refused to leave the bridge, resigned to a captain's fate, but after being scolded by his senior officers, Nagumo tearfully relented and was led to a rope and a waiting lifeboat, which, at 1046, he used to transfer his flag to the nearby cruiser *Nagara*.

What had happened over the span of six minutes, between 1022 and 1028, would change the course of the war in the Pacific. By 1028 all three carriers were suffering horribly and mortally damaged. All were destined for the sea bottom after being scuttled by ships from their screens. But off to the north, one carrier still steamed on the waves, seemingly undamaged. Already on the *Hiryu*, which was ahead of the other three carriers at the tip of a rough diamond formation, Rear Admiral Tamon Yamaguchi had assumed command of air operations and begun to organize a hasty return strike on the Americans, their one chance to salvage something from the day. Earlier he had watched incredulously as columns of black smoke rose over the three carriers to his south. Yamaguchi himself briefed his air crews on deck, then eighteen Val dive-bombers and a half dozen Zeros, all that could be cobbled together without delay, were positioned for launch. They took off between 1050 and 1058, unaware until they were airborne that the American fleets were less than one hundred miles away.

The surviving American dive-bombers, fighters, and torpedo planes retreated singly or in small packs scattered across the water, flying toward the northeast and home. Most were dangerously low on fuel and flew by dead reckoning over the wave tops, trying their best to account for the many variables they had to consider in order to find the *Yorktown* and *Enterprise* again. They knew full well that any wrong calculations would send them careening into the water with empty fuel tanks. Dusty Kleiss and his gunner had enough fuel to climb to a higher altitude to search for the Zed Baker homing signal. A Zero prowling the skies emerged from a nearby cloud bank, and Kleiss turned toward him, ready for one last dogfight, but the two planes lost each other in more clouds, so Kleiss, after a brief search, turned away. In order to extract the most miles per gallon from his dwindling fuel supply, he kept his plane's speed at 110 knots and slowly worked his way back home.

Yamamoto and his main body sailed six hundred miles to the west that morning, in a dense fog that shrouded his ships and prompted a cacophony of horns to bellow through the soup. Confidence remained high throughout the morning until, at 1050, Yamamoto was handed a radio message from the commander of the Kido Butai's screening force: "Fires raging on board *Kaga*, *Soryu*, and *Akagi* resulting from attacks by enemy carrier and land-based planes. We plan to have *Hiryu* engage enemy carriers."[20] Yamamoto groaned, dumbstruck. Then he sank into despair, as did his officers. Heartsick, he began scratching together the workings of a plan that involved taking his ships in and engaging the American carriers in a surface battle. He then sent an order to the smaller carriers far to the north covering the Aleutian landings and instructed them to run south to help, and he radioed the troop transports steaming for Midway to turn north and get away.

News of the great success achieved by their aviators reached Spruance and Fletcher haphazardly, and it was impossible to put together what was really happening with any certainty: the battle was too spread out and happening too fast. They could not be sure how many carriers had been hit and whether or not they were fully out of action, but what they heard was encouraging, even stunning.

Ensign Jimmy Gray's VF-6 fighter escorts were the first planes to arrive back over the *Enterprise*, cruising into the landing circle at 1050. Their early arrival was understandable, as they had left the battle before it started after losing sight of Waldron's torpedo squadron and circling over the Japanese fleet. Air staff personnel were keen to interview Gray when he landed, but all he could tell them was where he had sighted the fleet an hour earlier. He knew nothing about the results of the strikes and could not confirm the tremendously exciting snatches of radio transmissions Spruance had been picking up, transmissions hinting at something big going on over the southwestern horizon. Then four torpedo planes landed, all shot up. One of the badly shaken pilots was so furious at the lack of fighter protection his squadron had received that, once out of his cockpit, he drew his pistol on Gray and had to be physically restrained. Meanwhile, many of the *Enterprise*'s SBDs, after smashing two Japanese carriers, dropped into the water trying to find their way back to her deck. She was not at her expected location but was, in fact, forty-four miles farther northeast. Of the thirty-three dive-bombers she had launched that morning, sixteen failed to return. Those that did emerged from their planes sweaty and tired, but jubilant and shouting. When Kleiss landed, he had only 10 gallons of fuel remaining of an original 310.

Once on deck the pilots went below looking for coffee and sandwiches, telling their stories to each other, slowly beginning to piece together a more complete picture of what they had all done. Kleiss rushed into the ready room of Torpedo Six looking for Tom Eversole. The squadron's survivors, only a few crewmen, lay resting in their chairs, all of them stunned, "heads hung low, eyes glassy and remote."[21] Kleiss was shaken by the sight of so many empty chairs and coaxed the story of what had happened from the men there. They had barreled into their attack runs with no fighter cover and defective torpedoes, and in moments, nine of their planes had been shot down. One more ditched into the sea on the return trip. Kleiss asked the surviving men about his friend, and they told him Tom had been lost. "The news hit me like a thunderclap," Kleiss wrote.[22] He would mourn for the rest of his life.

Andy Anderson approached the *Enterprise* around 1210, one of the last of her group to return. He and the injured Mason had managed to get their Zed Baker homing equipment working and, as he began his approach, nervous antiaircraft gunners on the carrier opened fire on him, forcing him to detour and make a recognition approach despite his critically low fuel state. On his second approach, Anderson was given a wave-off by the landing signal officer, so he flew past the carrier's island and chopped his throttle a few times, the signal to the command staff on the bridge that he had an emergency and needed to land right away. The *Enterprise* turned into the wind and allowed him to bring his plane in. He knew just how lucky he had been.[23] The air crewmen who attended to him on deck found a rear cockpit that was in shambles, absolutely torn up by machine-gun and .20-mm bullets. A pharmacist's mate helped Stuart Mason from the plane, the gunner's uniform covered in bright red blood, his face filled with shrapnel. Anderson's plane would prove too badly damaged to be flown again during the battle.

The *Yorktown* had not initiated her flight operations until well after the *Enterprise*, so her planes did not begin returning until 1100. The first of her planes to return were the seventeen SBDs of Bombing Three, none the worse for wear after turning the *Soryu* into a mass of burning steel and teak. Jimmy Thach and his fighters landed back on board at 1130, and Thach raced up to flag plot to report to Admiral Fletcher that three enemy carriers were out of action. Thach could not say what happened to the fourth, so Fletcher, after conferring with Spruance across the water, quickly turned his carrier into the wind and launched another scouting mission to find this last carrier. He was understandably anxious about the havoc it could wreak. At 1034 the radar on board the *Enterprise* had detected a spotter twenty miles in the distance, and the fighter section of Rhonald "Buster" Hoyle, USNA '38, had been sent up to deal with the interloper, arrowing out from the carrier on a heading of 295 degrees. "Step on it!," he was told. Hoyle led his planes through the overcast sky, but he and his fighters could not find the bogey in the cloud banks, and at 1045 a radioman in the *Chikuma*'s No. 5 scout plane successfully tapped out a sighting report.

As the morning stretched on, those on board the ships of TF 16 and 17 waited for the Japanese attack to come. They knew that they had been spotted and that it would only be a matter of time before they were hit. After Fletcher launched his scouting force, he sent a dozen Wildcats into the air as a combat air patrol, including Dick Crommelin, leading the 2nd Division of Fighting Three, while Bill Leonard, who had been flying CAP all morning with five other fighters, was brought back on board at 1150. It was while these rotations were underway and the new CAP was forming up that the expected incoming Japanese strike force was spotted by the *Yorktown*'s radarmen, forty-five miles out, climbing slightly in the distant high clouds and bearing down on TF 17 from out of the sun. Reports of the sighting were shouted through loudspeakers, and the vessels in the screen moved into Victor formation, defensive positions off the carrier's port and starboard bows, the cruisers closer in with the destroyers beyond. With no other options, the fighters aloft were sent out to do battle in individual sections, some even without wingmen, rather than as a coordinated force. It would be "every man of every section for himself."[24]

Dick Crommelin and the other American Wildcat pilots hauled back on their sticks to gain altitude. Crommelin remembered well how poorly the combat air patrol had performed earlier that spring at the Battle of the Coral Sea due to their inability to gain altitude quickly enough, and he and his wingman, Ensign John Bain, desperately climbed to put themselves above the approaching Vals. They pounced on the Japanese dive-bombers at ten thousand feet while they were still fifteen miles out from the *Yorktown*. As they attacked, nearby Japanese Zeros flashed in to beat them off. Crommelin and Bain pulled into a long high-side run on a group of the approaching bombers, gaining speed as they flew and firing at the enemy planes as they passed. Before they had taken off, Crommelin had told Bain to stay with him at all times, and the young ensign did just that. The two pilots recovered and turned back for a second run. Three Zeros then turned Crommelin's way and he sent round after round at the first, then turned and fired at the second, watching it fall toward the sea. The third Japanese fighter popped up behind him, so Crommelin, now with his machine guns dry, dove to escape. The American attack into the heart of the Japanese formation caused it to break apart and scatter left and right, yet the dog-fighting planes, American and Japanese, flipping about in tight rolls and turns, firing at point-blank range, still winged en masse ever closer to the carrier, and soon the gunners in the ships of the screen opened up, adding their shell bursts to the melee.

Ten Japanese planes were ultimately shot down, but at least seven of the dive-bombers got through, and they curved into their dives, the *Yorktown*'s gunners firing furiously. Under Captain Elliott Buckmaster's direction, the carrier heeled into sharp port and starboard turns and speared through the water at better than thirty knots. Though an austere and distant man, Buckmaster had won the hearts of his crew at the Battle of the Coral Sea for his expert conning, and his talents were on display yet again. The sharp turns he made were effective, but not fully. After multiple misses, one of the Japanese planes plunged steeply off the carrier's stern and sent a bomb into the *Yorktown*'s deck at 1214 in the afternoon, fifteen feet inboard, just aft of the island near mounts 3 and 4, killing seventeen men in a reddish sheet of flame.[25] The bomb dropped into the hangar deck and lit three planes on fire. Then another Val dropped a bomb with a delayed fuse that exploded down in the heart of the carrier, crippling its boilers and slashing the *Yorktown*'s speed to zero. A third bomb started a fire next to the ammunition and gasoline storage areas. Bill Leonard, USNA '38, stranded by the enemy attack and with nothing better to do, stood on deck and fired his .45-caliber automatic pistol at the enemy planes as they dove. After the bomb blasts, black smoke and acrid fumes penetrated the bridge, forcing Fletcher and his staff out into the fresh air. A column of the stuff billowed from the hole in her flight deck. Yet save for the blast near the magazines, which could have exploded and shredded the ship, none of the hits were particularly serious, and the fires were promptly brought under control. The *Enterprise* and *Hornet*, twenty miles away, were unseen and thus untouched by the Japanese strike force.

Ozzie Wiseman, USNA '38, his guns empty, had been circling the *Yorktown* waiting to land as the Japanese finished their attack. Once it was over and the five surviving Japanese dive-bombers had departed, he knew the carrier's deck was too damaged to retrieve any planes, so he flew across the water to the *Enterprise* and landed there at 1238. Thirteen more SBDs from Bombing Three and half a dozen Wildcats from VF-3 also flew over from the damaged *Yorktown* and came in after him.

After his dogfight, Crommelin set down on the *Hornet* with Bain. They, along with the other pilots who had come back on board, were met by the carrier's air officer, who worked hard to provide the pilots with food and drink back in their ready rooms, even going so far as to raid the admiral's pantry. The men gulped lemonade from paper cups and took bites of sandwiches while they "yammered and gesticulated" about their own adventures from the morning.[26] Their faces were smeared with dirt and their flight suits were stiff with sweat, but those who had found the enemy and fought (of which there were fewer on the *Hornet* than on the other carriers) were high on the exhilaration of their survival, and all they wanted to do was "go right out and fight again."[27] For his actions during the battle, Dick Crommelin would receive the Navy Cross.

At 1320 the *Hiryu* prepared a second strike on the American fleet. By then her commanders had learned that there were three American carriers to the north, not two. After their first launch at noon, the *Hiryu* had sailed with her screen farther north, cutting the distance to the American flattops. Now, as the pilots received their briefing, everyone on board the last remaining aircraft carrier in the Kido Butai knew this strike force had little chance of returning, yet the pilots climbed into their cockpits with smiles on their faces. They were well aware that the hopes of the entire Japanese navy rested on them. Ten Kate torpedo bombers lifted into the air, followed by six Zeros to escort them. The American carriers were not far; it would take barely an hour to get there.

On board the *Yorktown* crews worked frantically to repair the damage caused by the three bomb strikes, putting out the fires, clearing debris, and patching the wide hole in the flight deck, but by then Fletcher had already transferred his flag to the nearby heavy cruiser *Astoria.*

Soon, *Enterprise*'s radar detected a lone bogey flying at high altitude, forty-five miles distant. Operators alerted Red 26, two fighters already in the air serving as CAP, including Buster Hoyle, USNA '38. Hoyle and his wingman William H. Warden, turned south and climbed to 14,500 feet at 1344 to intercept. After twenty minutes they spotted their prey, a twin-float seaplane cruising at two hundred feet, well below the two Grummans. It was the bothersome No. 5 scout plane from the Japanese cruiser *Chikuma*, which had been tailing the American fleet for over three hours and steadily reporting back its position to the Kido Butai. The plane turned once it realized it had been spotted, but Warden made a run at it. Hoyle screamed in from the opposite side off the floatplane's nose and fired furiously once he had narrowed the distance to one hundred yards. As Hoyle roared past, flames erupted from the floatplane, and it dipped toward the water.

Effectively trapped on board the *Yorktown* while she waited for another Japanese attack were Jimmy Thach, Bill Leonard, and other fighter pilots from VF-3. There was little they could do while the flight deck was being repaired except check the status of their fighters. Eight were ready to go and they were spotted on the center of the flight deck. Leonard walked with the others down the length of the carrier's deck, checking for and making note of the damaged sections they would have to avoid when they took off. By 1350 the carrier's boilers had been relit and she could make twenty knots. Once underway again, Captain Buckmaster unfurled a huge American battle ensign. Sailors from the screening ships cheered heartily, and Thach, Leonard, and six other fighter pilots climbed on board their Wildcats in a freshening breeze. Thach would take off first, Leonard second. They waited for the last little bit of fuel to be pumped into their aircraft. Forty miles to the west, the *Enterprise* and *Hornet* also readied planes on their decks.

The *Yorktown*'s radar picked up the *Hiryu*'s second strike thirty-three miles out, and the six fighters circling above were vectored over, including Hoyle and Wil Rawie, USNA '38, who was also in the air flying CAP. Leonard heard the bullhorn announcing an incoming raid and screamed down the deck fifteen seconds after Thach, his fuel tank not yet fully topped. Once airborne, he banked left to clear his slipstream away from the flight deck, cranked up his landing gear, charged and tested his guns, gained speed and altitude, and searched for a target. Dogfights swirled anew over the Pacific blue. Three of the raid's six Zeros fell quickly, as did five of the Japanese torpedo planes and two American Grummans. The remaining Kates, desperate for some results, separated to conduct an anvil attack on the *Yorktown*, which to them looked undamaged and which they therefore believed was one of the carriers they had not yet attacked that day. Bill Leonard spotted a Kate crossing the *Yorktown*'s bow and slowly descending toward the carrier, and it released its torpedo before he could line up the plane in his sights. He made a flat-side beam pass just above the destroyer *Balch*'s decks and splashed the enemy plane as it tried to pull away, his .50-caliber shell casings raining down on the destroyer's forecastle, the plane falling toward the water with bright flames blazing from its fuselage. Leonard turned sharply to pick out another enemy plane. Black flecks of smoke peppered the sky as the screen's antiaircraft gunners opened up, but other surviving Japanese torpedo bombers were able to launch their fish as well, and two 800-kilogram torpedoes with yellow noses slammed into the just-repaired *Yorktown* at 1443, both striking her port side amidships as Buckmaster made a starboard turn to evade. Over his shoulder Leonard saw a "great upside-down Niagara" of water blow from the ship's side where the torpedo struck.[28] There were thuds and aftershocks, and the big ship trembled and the lights winked out and the carrier went dead in the water and listed to port at a sickening angle. The rudder was jammed, power connections were cut, and portside fuel tanks ruptured. Because of his dwindling fuel supply, Leonard could not pursue the surviving Japanese planes (five torpedo bombers and four Zeros) as they flew away sending incorrect reports that a second American carrier had been hit. He circled the carrier protectively with three other Wildcats, certain that, as he looked at her sloping deck, he would need to find another place to land.

Wil Rawie was flying high and almost missed the retreating Japanese planes that hugged the wave tops beneath him, but he heard over the radio that there were bogeys below, so he dove toward the water, catching sight of a lone enemy torpedo plane at three hundred feet. He and his wingman Ralph Rich moved to box the plane in and attack from both sides, the two fighters making simultaneous high side runs from abeam that, despite heavy fire from the plane's rear seat gunner, soon caused smoke to pop from the Kate. It splashed into the water a moment later. The kill was credited to Rich.

As he circled the *Yorktown*, Leonard's fuel status went from bad to worse. Over his radio he was told, "When it gets bad, go down and land beside [a] destroyer."[29] Leonard was not yet ready for that. At 1500 he keyed his radio and asked for the correct vector to Spruance's carriers, now to the southeast. When he arrived over the *Enterprise*, he was told to circle and wait, as the carrier's flight deck was unusable while a squadron of SBDs was being respotted for launch. It was not until 1542 that the *Enterprise* finally allowed circling fighters to line up and land. Leonard was among the first to touch down, just before his fuel ran out. As the most senior VF-3 pilot on board, he was ordered to report to the bridge for a meeting with Spruance himself. Once there the lean fifty-five-year-old admiral asked Leonard for a firsthand report on the *Yorktown*'s condition and his personal assessment of the situation. Leonard thought the *Yorktown* could be saved and told Spruance as much. What he did not yet know was that roughly fifty minutes earlier Captain Buckmaster had reluctantly ordered his crew to abandon ship. The *Yorktown*'s list had become so severe there were concerns the carrier would roll over, and it could not be corrected, as there was no power. Men were even then sliding down knotted lines into a sea coated with gasoline to be picked up by whaleboats and destroyers from the task force nearby.

Just after the second attack on the *Yorktown*, Fletcher and Spruance received the information they had been waiting for—the fourth Japanese carrier had been found, bearing 279 degrees, only 110 miles to the east, a course that was taking her directly to the *Enterprise* and *Hornet*. Immediately Spruance and Marc Mitscher, the captain of the *Hornet*, both acting independently, readied their strike forces, including whatever remaining dive-bombers were still airworthy. Loaded with 500- and 1,000-pound bombs, a force of bombers cobbled together from VS-6, VB-6, VB-5, and VB-3 were launched, a "mixed bag" of the most experienced men and planes available, including Dusty Kleiss (who was "chomping at the bit" to get airborne again) and Ozzie Wiseman.[30] Andy Anderson was in the strike force as well, with a new gunner in the seat behind him. No fighters from the *Enterprise* were sent to escort them; Spruance held them back to protect his task forces. The planes began launching from the *Enterprise*'s deck at 1525 and had all left the area by 1550.

When the American planes arrived over the *Hiryu*, the pilots swung wide to the southwest to approach from out of the sun and downwind. Visibility was excellent, with low scattered clouds, and the last undamaged Japanese carrier was spotted easily on the smooth sea at 1645, the columns of smoke from the three burning carriers still visible over the horizon to the south. Lieutenant Earl Gallaher led Kleiss and VS-6 into a climb to gain altitude, expecting a CAP of Zeros that surely must be aloft to slice into them at any moment. Yet they reached their attack altitude of 19,000 feet untroubled except for heavy antiaircraft fire, and Gallaher looked back to make sure his squadron was in order. They were all tucked in behind him. The enemy carrier steamed below them in the hot sun. Gallaher dove at 70 degrees, steep and fast, aiming for the red circle on the *Hiryu*'s yellow deck, and just as the planes behind him followed, ten Zeros slashed into them from the rear, their 20-mm cannon spitting bullets.

But it was already too late for the *Hiryu*, known in Japan as the "Flying Dragon."[31] The carrier seemed to successfully avoid the Dauntlesses' first string of bombs (including Gallaher's), but the Americans' line of falling ordnance eventually caught up to her. The first bomb to hit into the flattop's forward elevator and passed through the flight deck before exploding. A second landed as well, dropped by Dusty Kleiss, diving fourth in the line of planes. He had noted the carrier's sharp port turn while in his dive and aimed his 1,000-pound bomb ahead of the ship, anticipating she would sail right into it. It was, Kleiss thought, his toughest dive yet. As he wrote in his diary later that night, "I don't know where mine landed, because of the flames from the bomb hit ahead of me."[32] Two more strikes followed in quick succession, slamming into her bow and leaving the *Hiryu* a pile of exploding gasoline and flaming steel. As Kleiss looked over his shoulder, the sight of the carrier with its deck peeled away and its burning innards open to the air seared itself into his memory. Nineteen Zero fighters parked in the hangar deck directly below the bomb strikes added to the eruptions of flame. Her captain, at least initially able to keep speed, continued to maneuver his carrier at thirty knots to avoid additional bombs, but the speed served only to fan the flames that soon engulfed the ship's flight deck. The buzzing Zeros claimed three of the American dive-bombers but could do no more. They would have nowhere to land and were in effect "marooned in the air."[33] The *Hiryu* was lost.

One of the dive-bombers shot down by these Zeros was flown by Osborne Wiseman, Class of '38. A strikingly handsome aviator with fair hair, clear blue eyes, and the look and bearing of an earnest young Navy man, he had grown up in Zanesville, Ohio, a mining town seventy miles east of Columbus, with a fierce determination to fly that had drawn him to Annapolis. A photographer and rower, Wiseman had also been a member of the Glee Club and was known up and down the decks of Bancroft Hall as the "crooner of room 1343," who preferred the old classics to anything more modern.[34] After graduation he married his wife, June, and the young couple lived with her sister and brother-in-law in a house in Kennett Square, Pennsylvania. He received his training in Pensacola, earning his gold wings in May 1941 and an assignment to VB-3 on the *Saratoga*. He had not seen June since prior to the Pearl Harbor attack. It is believed Wiseman was able to release his bomb on the *Hiryu* before he was then picked out and set upon as he pulled up from his dive. He and his gunner were last seen being chased by multiple Zeros as he tried to leave the area. He too was awarded a Navy Cross for his actions that day.

Dusty Kleiss was also attacked as he pulled up and tried to depart. Johnny Snowden behind him unleashed a heavy barrage of machine-gun fire at a Zero that sliced in at them, and his accurate aiming sent smoke belching from the fighter's engine. That Japanese pilot pulled away but was quickly replaced by another, and Kleiss pushed his bomber forward, screaming as fast as he could go, keeping the Zero well behind him. He soon joined up with several other SBDs and cleared the area for the short hop home.

At 1700 that evening, Bill Leonard was launched as a relief CAP with seven other fighters and sent to patrol over the stricken *Yorktown*. Seeing the forlorn carrier drifting on the sea, her canted flight deck barren and freakish, was a sad experience for the 1938 First Classman. The sight was altogether too familiar to him. "I had watched the same scene less than a month before as we CAPPED *Lexington* for the last time in the

Coral Sea," he remembered later.[35] As Fletcher pulled the rest of his task force away from the wounded lady, leaving only one destroyer behind to stand guard, Leonard turned circles in the darkening sky, flying "around and around the old warrior, waiting for the worst."[36] He and the other few pilots keeping up the patrol waited until sundown, then sped across her deck one more time before banking away back toward the *Enterprise*, leaving the carrier to the darkness.

While Nagumo watched his fourth carrier burn that late afternoon, he seemed unable or unwilling to grasp reality. In addition to 2,181 men, he had lost almost three hundred aircraft and thus command of the air; he had also lost both the ability to affect offensive action and the mystique of invulnerability that his fleet had enjoyed since Pearl Harbor. At 1755 he sent a most unwelcome report of the day's happenings to Yamamoto, still sailing impotently out to the west. All four of his strike force's carriers were wrecked. The battle was over. It had been, in the words of historian Stephen Moore, a "decisive day of retribution."[37] Gordon Prange called the remnants of the IJN's Kido Butai a "panorama of death and destruction such as Yamamoto [and Nagumo] had never dreamed possible."[38] Official Japanese policy in the days and weeks to come would be to play down the results and impacts of the Midway battle, and press reports in Japan even touted it as a grand victory to keep up morale at home, but to the surviving officers and sailors and airmen of the Japanese fleet aware of what had happened, the results were clear. There was no downplaying a 47 percent reduction in their Navy's front-line carrier tonnage, the destruction of so many airplanes, and the loss of so many first-class pilots.

As the sun set, Spruance faced a different problem. He was not certain the *Hiryu* had been sunk, and the only options available to him that evening were complicated. He could steam westward after the battered remnants of the Japanese carrier fleet, but he had no wish to engage the Japanese in a night action and risk the health of the *Enterprise* and *Hornet*. He also worried about Midway, still his primary mission, and could not be sure the Japanese navy would not attempt an invasion even with the loss of their carrier fleet. So Spruance collected Fletcher's remaining task force (overloaded with crewmen from the *Yorktown*) and turned eastward, opting not to pursue Nagumo's forces but rather to put himself in a holding position from which he could easily move wherever the next day's action required him to be. It was a wise decision, though an unconventional one, and would be roundly criticized later for its seeming timidity. The Japanese hoped for, indeed craved, a westward turn by the Americans. The IJN was far superior in nighttime actions, enjoyed the more effective torpedoes, and could field more battleships than the Americans (four to zero). Spruance's turn away threw the Japanese admirals for a "total loss," closing their bitterly painful day with even more demoralization.[39]

The four Japanese carriers burned through the night, each suffering their own version of a fiery denouement with acrid smoke, periodic explosions, final crew evacuations, and last measures taken to send the stricken flattops to the depths. The *Kaga* and *Soryu* were scuttled by Japanese destroyers between 1915 and 1930. The *Soryu* went down amid "banzai" cries from the sailors in her screen. The *Hiryu*, by then a "floating blast furnace," was scuttled at 0510 the following morning.[40] The *Akagi*, smoldering through the night on a fog-shrouded sea, was torpedoed and sunk not long after. As the ships slipped under, Yamamoto, still to the west, canceled the Midway operation and ordered the remnants of Nagumo's fleet, the screening force, the transport group, and his own main body to pull back. It was an admission of defeat. His attempts to bring about the Final Battle he so craved had resulted in a general retreat toward home. He believed that it must have been five or six American carriers that had beaten him and that his forces had sunk two of them. He was, of course, wrong on both counts.

Exhausted after the battle, Kleiss slipped away to his bunk to get some sleep. Before retiring, he took a slug of whiskey. The catalogue of the dead was grievous, and he was heartbroken. He had lost too many of his best friends and classmates that day. There was some elation among the airmen in general over the battle's end—they were alive, and thankful for it—but for the most part their joy was tempered by the "uncertainty, disorientation, sorrow, and exhaustion" of the battle.[41] Kleiss wrote in his journal, "Now, oh Lord, won't you please take care of those Wonderful Ones who loved us so much. They were willing to die for us without hesitation."[42] Before falling asleep, he wrote another letter to Jean: "I'm okay, but am tired to the dickens. Have been wearing your nice soft sweater and it keeps me warm way up thar' and keeps me safe way down below. If anything should get me now, I just want you to know and Dad to know that recently I've had more than my share of luck and [Japanese prime minister Hideki] Tojo is most unhappy about it all."[43]

Andy Anderson captured in his diary some inkling of what he and his fellow aviators had accomplished: "I believe that the Japanese losses were so great that this will be a turning point in our favor for a final victory."[44]

By daylight on June 5, Spruance received confirmation of the massive damage his men had wrought the previous day. His relief was indescribable, he would say later, but he could not be truly satisfied or fully stand down until final confirmation of the fourth carrier's sinking was obtained. Unfortunately for his peace of mind, the *Hiryu* would sink out of sight of any American scouts and would thus cause confusion throughout the day for Spruance and his staff. He sent a makeshift collection of Dauntlesses, including Anderson and Kleiss, on a long flight westward after some damaged Japanese vessels later that afternoon, but the attack group found bombing a zagging cruiser and destroyer much harder than hitting aircraft carriers, and they returned without scoring a hit. The aviators on the day after the battle were in no mood for more unreasonable sacrifices, and most resented the mission. But the next day, June 6, Spruance launched another raid—one last all-out attempt to finish off any straggling Japanese ships still within range. A morning attack by eighteen Dauntlesses was sent after the Japanese ships *Mikuma* and *Mogami*, and among the complement of SBDs were, once again, Anderson and Kleiss. The two damaged ships were easily tracked by the oil slicks they left on the sea's surface and were pummeled. Kleiss believed he put a bomb squarely near the *Mogami*'s stack. They left her dead in the water, burning fiercely. The *Mikuma* was put in a similar condition.

With his mission accomplished beyond his or anyone else's wildest expectations, Spruance suspended his air operations at 1900 on the evening of the 6th. He turned away to the east to rendezvous with his oilers and then set a course for Oahu. The lessons of the battle were neatly summarized by Spruance in his postbattle report to Admiral Nimitz, delivered two weeks later. Among his assessments were that whichever side's carriers were able to attack first would win and that aircraft carriers were most vulnerable to fire, especially when their planes were on deck. Early and accurate scouting reports were essential for carrier operations to be successful, as was operating at least two carriers together. He also reported, in a statement that perhaps did not give the tough old Wildcats (or their pilots) enough credit, that the F4Fs were still "greatly inferior" to the Japanese Zeros. His report's most obvious finding was that the TBD Devastators needed to be replaced "as soon as possible."[45] Some of their fellow aviators felt that all of the Devastator pilots of Torpedo Eight, Torpedo Six, and Torpedo Three who flew during the Battle of Midway deserved Medals of Honor. Their sacrifices and their courage had been extraordinary. They had cleared the skies for the approach of the dive-bombers, and though it was unintended, they had done so magnificently. Of the forty-one torpedo planes launched that June 4 morning, only four returned to their carriers.

As the American task forces sailed eastward, the personal effects of the dead and missing pilots were collected to be shipped home to families as yet blissfully ignorant of the losses they had just suffered. Nearly 110 American carrier aircraft overall were lost during the Battle of Midway, about half of the total complement that had departed Pearl Harbor. Some of the downed crewmen were even then still alive, but adrift on the open ocean, a terrifying fate from which they would not be saved.

The *Yorktown* had its own final story to tell. As the Japanese retreated westward in the predawn darkness of June 5, one solitary vessel stayed behind with orders to find a disabled American carrier in the region and sink her. The vessel was the *I-168*, a Japanese submarine cruising the waters off Midway.

By daylight only a small flotilla of destroyers sailed alongside the *Yorktown*, which, despite a dangerous list, continued to drift obstinately on the quiet sea. Captain Buckmaster, assessing his carrier in the daylight, was soon eager to take a salvage party back on board, and by early afternoon he had gathered a group of volunteers on the nearby destroyer *Hammann.* The ship transferred the 170-man crew to the blacked-out carrier early the morning of the 6th and was instructed to stand to just off the *Yorktown*'s bow in order to provide hoses, Foamite, and water to the salvage party. The volunteers then set to work extinguishing fires, restoring what power they could, salvaging any sensitive material, and trying to correct her severe list. By early afternoon there was real hope the carrier could be towed back to Pearl Harbor.

But the *I-168*'s captain, Lieutenant Commander Yahachi Tanabe, had spotted her column of smoke and was stalking ever closer. His presence had been undetected by the seven destroyers arrayed around the *Yorktown*, and the captain sailed in close and saw in his periscope the carrier's entire silhouette, lined up beautifully in his sights and unmoving. At a range of twelve hundred yards, Tanabe sent four torpedoes at the carrier in two tightly packed groupings, aiming at the same point for maximum explosive power. Less than a minute later, the captain and his crew heard the explosions.

The four torpedoes were spotted slicing through the smooth sea, and the *Hammann*, which sat on the water directly between the carrier and the onrushing torpedoes, sounded her general alarm and fired away at them with her 20-mm alarm gun in hopes of exploding the fish before they struck. It missed, and the destroyer had no time to get clear. The first torpedo was running shallow and smacked into the *Hammann* amidships in the No. 2 fireroom, one more passed away off target, and the next two exploded into the *Yorktown*, punching a large hole in her hull. The *Hammann*, her back broken, settled into the water on an even keel before sliding down into the murk. She went under in five minutes, disappearing at 1339. Remarkably, a sizable portion of her crew managed to escape into the water, but many who had not yet climbed into lifeboats were killed when the depth charges on board her exploded in a tremendous blast once the ship sank far enough for them to reach their set points. Elsewhere, the *Yorktown*, buried under an explosion of "fire, oil, water, and metal" that caused rivets in the foremast to shear and threw men in every direction, settled more deeply into the sea.[46] Another nearby destroyer pulled alongside immediately to remove her salvage crew. Buckmaster, still clinging to hope, planned to return at first

The *Hammann* sinking, as seen from the USS *Yorktown*, June 6, 1942

light the following day to continue his salvage work. The *I-168*, after dodging over sixty depth charges from flailing and furious American destroyers, managed to escape back toward Kure.

Among the survivors of the *Hammann* that day was Charles Hartigan Jr., also from the Naval Academy's Class of 1938. A naval officer's son who had spent his childhood in Brazil, China, and France, "Connie" played soccer when he reached Annapolis, earning multiple N-Stars in the process. Relaxed, competent, a born storyteller, and a natural leader, Hartigan had been very well respected on the Yard and beloved by his classmates. When the four torpedo tracks appeared five hundred yards off the starboard beam, Hartigan was on the bridge, and he ran to the gun director as General Quarters sounded. He brought his 20-mm guns to bear on the tracks and was trying to get his 5-inch guns sighted when the blast from the explosion threw him from the director to the lookout platform. When he regained his senses, he saw that the forecastle deck was awash, and he ordered his director crew and lookouts to put on their life jackets and abandon the area. He then joined the captain on the bridge, and together the two men inspected the pilothouse, chart house, and radar room to ensure that all had been abandoned. Once in the water, injured and without a life jacket, Hartigan spotted a mess attendant still on board who had been wounded and was holding onto the forecastle lifeline. He swam back through the fuel oil to the rapidly sinking vessel and pulled the man free. Hartigan was eventually brought on board the *Yorktown*.

The following morning, June 7, before a brilliant dawn, the grand *Yorktown* was given up for lost. All of the crewmen on the destroyers arrayed around her lined their decks and stood at attention as she rolled onto her beam ends, exposing the huge holes in her hull where the *I-168*'s torpedoes had struck, and went under by the stern. It would be a three-mile journey to the ocean's bottom.

No one at Pearl Harbor initially knew or felt that Midway had just won them the war against the Japanese. They were well aware that a hard slog still remained. But whatever doubts they may have had about the battle's immediate and long-term impacts were promptly put to rest by Nimitz in his first communique about the battle, released not long after, which read, in part:

> Through the skill and devotion to duty of our armed forces of all branches in the Midway area, our citizens can now rejoice that a momentous victory is in the making. It was on a Sunday just six months ago that the Japanese made their peacetime attack on our fleet and army activities on Oahu. . . . Pearl Harbor has now been partially avenged. Vengeance will not be complete until Japanese sea power has been reduced to impotence. We have made substantial progress in that direction. Perhaps we will be forgiven if we claim we are about midway to our objective.[47]

Nimitz's missive was well put. As Gordon Prange wrote, "At Midway, the United States laid aside the shield and picked up the sword, and through all the engagements to follow, never again yielded the strategic offensive."[48]

The victorious American task forces sailed back into Pearl Harbor on June 13, preceded by a massive fly-in of the surviving aircraft from the *Enterprise* and *Hornet*. Navy Yard workers and other base personnel lined the shores and docks of the harbor and cheered. When Andy Anderson landed his plane at Kaneohe Air Station, Stuart Mason, his face and legs heavily bandaged, once again rode in the rear seat. As each plane taxied to a stop, a pair of Marines stepped up to award each pilot a few cans of beer. There was a grand celebration awaiting the pilots at Kaneohe, including a Navy band. Bill Leonard led his surviving VF-42 personnel in to Ewa Field and took part in a personal homecoming with other squadron mates at the hangar. After Dusty Kleiss landed, he scribbled in his diary, "Seems as though a big Saturday night is in the offing."[49] The pilots checked into the Royal Hawaiian or the Moana Hotel on Waikiki Beach and committed vigorously to their all-night parties and bacchanals, but these were marked, in the words of Ian Toll, by an "anguished carousing" rather than a joyful one.[50] Many wept openly for their dead friends. Others turned to their fists and fought whomever they could. Hotel property was vandalized and broken. MPs and shore patrolmen trying to keep the peace were ignored or openly insulted. The traumatized pilots tramped from room to room and drank whatever they could find. Some went looking for girls, but most released their pent-up tension and rage and exhilaration by drinking, shouting, arguing, crying, fighting, and breaking anything and everything.

The Battle of Midway would be Dusty Kleiss' last combat action. In the following days he was sent back stateside via a transport ship to a new posting as an instructor of rookie dive-bomber pilots. He would be awarded the Navy Cross and a Distinguished Flying Cross for his heroics. Once back home, Kleiss wasted no time in starting a new life. From San Francisco he took the first train he could find to Los Angeles, where he reunited in the station with Jean Mochon. They piled into a car with her sister and brother-in-law and drove through the desert to Las Vegas, where, in a chapel whose marquee advertised "speedy weddings," the two were married on July 3, not yet a month after the Battle of Midway. He vowed then and there never to be apart from her again.

ERNEST DEWITT CODY

Mayville, Michigan

Six years ago Ernie said: "Mom, I think I'll be a sailor." Appointments happened to be scarce just then out thar in Michigan, so he enlisted with the Academy as his goal. After serving aboard the USS Tennessee, he crashed the Fleet's picked "prep" class and directly joined '38. Ol' Dewey, as the folks at home call him, was plenty salty when we got him and he's kept right on getting more so. Now and then his views have not coincided with those of the Academic Departments, but he's always beaten them to the punch. Through four years we've found Ernie like his name, earnest and sincere, and moreover a true friend. He doesn't wear any stars, but they will get a mighty fine man and a good officer when he goes back to the Fleet.

The Lucky Bag, 1938

Chapter Eighteen

STANDBY

The contemporary traveler, historian, and writer Simon Winchester once wrote, "The Pacific is an ocean of secrets."[1] Undoubtedly the most mysterious fate to befall a member of the Naval Academy's Class of 1938 was that of Ernest Dewitt Cody. What happened to him is a secret the Pacific has yet to reveal.

Ernie Cody was an enlisted sailor who had gained admittance to the Naval Academy after four years in the Fleet. It was a difficult way to get onto the Yard, but, for many, the only avenue available. Many applicants were denied admittance even after years of honorable service.

Upon graduating with the Class of 1938, Cody became an aviator but flew a different sort of aircraft altogether. After flight school he had been assigned in March 1942 to Airship Patrol Squadron 32, part of Fleet Air Wing Five, where he flew the *L-8*, a blimp built by the Goodyear Tire & Rubber Company in 1940. The unit was based out of Moffett Field, Treasure Island Naval Air Facility, located in the middle of San Francisco Bay. With his sharp black hair, steely penetrating gaze, and tight mustache, Cody affected the look of a matinee idol. He had arrived at Moffett Field with his young wife Helen and assumed command of the blimp after being promoted to lieutenant (jg). He was known as a level-headed, unexcitable young man and a highly competent and reliable officer, one who could be depended on to use his wits in any sort of emergency, and, early in the war, Cody returned home with plenty of stories to tell. On April 11, 1942, he took part in a mission crucial to the ultimate success of the Doolittle raid on Japan when he rendezvoused with the aircraft carrier USS *Hornet* off the California coast to deliver a three-hundred-pound load of spare parts that were desperately needed by the sixteen B-25 bombers scattered across the carrier's deck. He hovered over the *Hornet* with the load dangling beneath him and carefully maneuvered his blimp in the ocean gusts to set the parts down in an open spot.

By the late summer of 1942, after the Doolittle raid and after the Americans' resounding victory at the Battle of Midway, a key priority for the U.S. Navy was the protection of America's West Coast against Japanese submarines, and critical to that strategy was its dirigible force. Blimps were ideal for antisubmarine duty because they could easily hover in one spot for long periods and could fly for up to twelve hours without refueling.[2] They were thus perfect for watching for any signs of Japanese U-boats, which had been known to surface just offshore and shell American oil refineries and coastal defense installations.

The early morning of Sunday, August 16, 1942, was cool and foggy on Treasure Island, a typical late summer day in the Bay Area. By then Cody, now twenty-seven, had accumulated 758 flight hours as a blimp pilot, the majority in the L types, and was one of the squadron's more senior airmen. As he and his copilot prepared for their flight, the ground crew was kept busy addressing the moisture the cool fog had built up on the blimp's coverings, moisture that added crucial weight to the aircraft. As a result, the blimp's third crewman, Aviation Machinist's Mate 3rd Class James R. Hill, was told to stay behind.

Designated Patrol Flight 101, the mission was to be a routine one. Cody and his copilot, newly commissioned Ensign Charles E. Adams, were to take the *L-8* off the California coast and conduct a simple antisubmarine patrol out to the Farallones, a small chain of rocky islands thirty miles due west of San Francisco. They would then head north to Point Reyes before swinging southeast again and returning to Moffett Field.

At 0603 Cody lifted the craft into the air and swung the silver dirigible out toward open water. The two men were reportedly in good spirits. Though a brand-new officer, the thirty-eight-year-old Ensign Adams had decades of enlisted experience as a boatswain with lighter-than-air vehicles and had grown up in, of all places, Lakehurst, New Jersey, site of none other than the *Hindenburg* airship explosion in May 1937, which Adams had witnessed and in whose rescue efforts he had participated. The mission that morning, however, would be Adams' first time piloting a blimp.

The first hour and a half of the flight progressed normally, but at 0742 Cody radioed Moffett Field that he had spotted an oil slick on the water and was taking the blimp down to investigate. "Stand by," he said.[3]

It was the last transmission ever received from the dirigible.

Three and a half hours later, at 1115, swimmers and fishermen enjoying the Sunday wind and surf on the beach near the Lakeside golf course at the Olympic Club saw the *L-8* disappear behind a pair of distant hills, then rise again after briefly becoming ensnared on a cliff face near Ocean Beach. The blimp flew crazily on the stiff breezes, its starboard engine packed with dirt, the propeller blades bent. A 325-pound Mark 17 depth charge broke free from its rack and tumbled onto the golf course. Members of San Francisco's Shore Patrol called the Navy to report the blimp's collision and the release of the ordnance.

The *L-8*, now partially deflated and sporting an obvious and ungainly sag down its middle, rose again and drifted beyond the hills. Its motors were off. It rode the breezes silently. It flew low over Mussel Rock Park, its shroud lines nearly dragging across the hilltops. As the blimp continued its descent, it scraped the rooftops of houses in Daly City, a quiet suburb, and dragged across telephone lines, sending sparks blossoming down onto Bellevue Avenue. Crowds of citizens, rescue personnel, and the merely curious tracked the *L-8* until it came to rest in the middle of the avenue's 400 block, just south of the San Francisco–San Mateo county line. The *L-8*'s gondola stood almost vertically in the street, leaning against a telephone pole, its bow pointed to the sky, its engines resting in the dirt just off the sidewalk. Gasoline drained onto the pavement. The blimp's shroud draped over power lines, across the road, and on top of a car parked at the curb. One of the aircraft's doors was latched fully open. Soon hundreds of spectators began to encircle the crash site and photographers arrived to snap pictures.

The first person to reach the *L-8* was a volunteer fireman named William Morris, in whose front yard the blimp had crashed. Worried the crew was in distress, he rushed to the gondola, noticed the open door, and looked inside. The blimp was empty. Other firefighters soon arrived and, believing the crew must be trapped, began to tear the blimp's envelope open with their axes. They found no one.

Salvagers from the Navy pulled up within the hour. They discovered the parachutes properly stowed and undisturbed, as was the life raft. The radio was in good working order. The rifles in the gondola were untouched. The crew compartment's two lifebelts, however, were gone (regulations required the men to wear the lifebelts throughout the flight). A confidential file containing classified information had not been destroyed, as per procedure when crew were abandoning the airship, but sat undamaged in its locked briefcase. One of the crew member's caps rested on the controls. A microphone used for the external loudspeaker dangled out the open door. The safety bar on the door of the gondola was missing. Though the engines of the blimp were still switched on, most of its gas had been dumped, presumably out at sea, thus the eerie quiet as the blimp floated over the hills. The helium gas valves were set as they should have been and aside from the damage suffered during the crash the blimp was, and had been, perfectly airworthy. There was simply no obvious explanation for why Cody and Adams had abandoned her, why they had not radioed if they were in distress, or where they had gone.

Immediately the surrounding coastline was searched by rescue personnel, and the Navy sent aircraft out to scan the sea while asking all planes in the area to be on the lookout for anything that might explain what had happened, but no clue as to the whereabouts of Cody and Adams was found. Commander Donald M. Mackey, the commanding officer of Moffett Field, declared a few days later that "the Navy is positive it has covered all the ground area covered by the blimp. It is positive the men were not in the ship at any time it traveled over land."[4] In the Navy's view, the two officers had evacuated the airship out over the water. The question was why. Upon hearing the news of the incident, Cody's wife Helen suffered a bad case of shock and took ill.

A subsequent board of inquiry found the most compelling evidence of what happened in the eyewitness accounts of the crews from a pair of fishing boats in the area at the time the *L-8* investigated the oil slick.

The fishermen, too, observed the slick on the water and watched the *L-8* descend to about three hundred feet above it. One crewman on the *Albert Gallatin* reported seeing the blimp descend even farther than that, to just above the waves, briefly almost sitting on top of the water. The two ships expected the blimp to drop depth charges over the oil, so they hauled in their nets and cleared the area, but no charges fell. Instead, the blimp merely circled the oil slick for about an hour, dropping one flare in the process, and then rose skyward into the clouds, heading back toward San Francisco instead of the Farallon Islands as its mission plan dictated. Aside from the flare no one on the fishing boats ever witnessed anything fall or drop from the airship while it was at sea, including any crewmen.

Ultimately, the board concluded that the sudden increase in the blimp's elevation over the oil slick had been caused by the loss of ballast when Cody and Adams, for whatever reason, evacuated the gondola. As the blimp rose higher into the sky, automatic relief valves opened, jettisoning the helium gas, which would have then caused the *L-8* to lose altitude and float back down in whichever direction the winds were blowing. The V-shaped sag in the blimp as it floated toward Daly City was caused by the weight of the gondola pulling down the dirigible's center section, now free of the gas that in normal operation maintained the fabric's shape. In the board of inquiry's report, investigators stated that whatever occurred to cause the disappearance of the two officers happened in the hour between 0750 and 0850. Their investigation ruled out fire, attack, bad weather, and a technical malfunction. The bodies of Cody and Adams were never found. According to the board's official statement, "Nothing the Navy knows now has given a satisfactory explanation of what happened."[5] It remains "one of the most enduring and perplexing missing-persons cases to come out of World War II."[6]

Rumors naturally proliferated among the public. Some claimed the men fell; others that one man fell, either intentionally or accidentally, and that the other pilot left the airship as it first crossed over land on the beach near the Grand Highway. A librarian passing by on the highway at the time reported seeing two men struggling with the deflating blimp in the ocean surf just off the beach. She assumed they were the dirigible's crew, though others reported they were simply two men swimming in the water that morning. A telephone operator out riding her horse near the beach watched the blimp through a pair of binoculars and stated she was quite certain she saw three men in the gondola rather than two. Other stories emerged that the Japanese had somehow captured the two men; that Cody and Adams had perpetrated an elaborate scheme to go AWOL; and that a stray bullet had put a hole in the gas bag; or that a stowaway had been on board, overpowered the two men, and disposed of their bodies. Some posited that the two pilots had somehow engaged a sub crew that had captured them, or that one had been a spy rendezvousing with the submarine. The Navy proffered the theory that the gondola door had malfunctioned during Cody's and Adams' investigation of the oil slick, causing one of the men to fall out, and that, hoping to rescue him quickly, the second crewmember had brought the *L-8* down close to the water, where he also fell overboard. They both died in the accident. Though the theory seemed to fit the circumstances, without evidence or bodies all the Navy could officially do was declare the two men "missing" in the immediate aftermath of the accident, and "dead" the following year. After its refurbishing, the *L-8* was put back into service.

In the months and years after the two men's disappearance, the mystery of their fate only deepened. After the war, in a letter dated August 22, 1947, Helen Cody, by then remarried, wrote to the Bureau of Naval Personnel to inform them that her mother claimed to have seen Lieutenant Cody alive after the crash, in Phoenix, Arizona. His eyes looked peculiar, "as though he were suffering from shock, or a mental illness."[7] In her letter Helen stated that she believed her husband was alive but suffering from amnesia due to a head injury. It was her belief that her mother, who knew Cody well and loved him dearly, "would not make a mistake any more than I, should I see him."[8] She asked for the bureau's help in investigating the matter, though there is no indication they ever did so.

The incident remains unsolved to this day.

By the late summer of 1944, Brink Bass, USNA '38, was stationed in the Atlantic Ocean on board the escort carrier USS *Kasaan Bay*, flying F6F Hellcat fighters and serving as the new commander of VF-74. Two years earlier Bass had won a pair of Navy Crosses during the Battle of the Coral Sea and survived the sinking of the aircraft carrier *Lexington*. He had missed the Battle of Midway after being sent home for furlough that summer and been reassigned to the Atlantic theater upon his return to duty. Now twenty-eight and a veteran airman, Bass was a hard worker who possessed boundless energy and drive and pushed the men of his new squadron relentlessly toward combat readiness. He was a good leader. Though driven, businesslike, and demanding, he was sympathetic to his men, and they respected his efficiency and his work ethic.

As the *Kasaan Bay* sailed to the Mediterranean to support General Dwight Eisenhower's operation to push the Germans out of southern France, Bass and his squadron spent their time in between missions studying maps and models of the shorelines and the targets they would be attacking. Their first month on station off Algeria, the men flew anti-submarine patrols over the water and trained for the air support role they would fill during the coming invasion. By this time the men of VF-74 were worn out and showing some strain. Bass, in particular, was long overdue for a shore leave. Pictures of him at the time show a man seemingly wizened by his work, but also exhausted. He looked in much need of a break.

On August 15, the *Kasaan Bay* arrived off the French Riviera, and Bass led VF-72's first mission. Their role was to disrupt and destroy German transportation lines and defensive positions, and he took off from the carrier at 0602 with three other Hellcats. Together they dropped their loads of 1,000-pound bombs on gun emplacements around St. Tropez. Four days later, Brink was leading his division on an armed reconnaissance mission along the Rhone Valley when they happened upon a lone German Junker 88 bomber and sent it down in flames near Valence. It was the first "kill" scored by U.S. Navy fighters in Europe.

On August 20, a Sunday, Bass was back in the air, taking off from the carrier with seven other Hellcats in the early afternoon and heading north at seven thousand feet toward the French coastline near Marseille. The

Hellcat formations were armed with 500-pound bombs and toted belly tanks filled with 150 gallons of gas. They cut west toward Montpellier before turning inland and flying northward to reconnoiter and patrol the valley country there and attack any targets of opportunity they might find. The Hellcats made strafing runs on a truck that was approaching Alais, then shot at a nearby locomotive hauling a freight train, then dropped bombs on a highway bridge near Le Puy. Afterward they flew through the sun to the village of St. Bonnet le Froid.

Targets were hard to spot in the light, so at approximately 1300 Bass took his division of three planes in low, to a height of five hundred feet, in hopes of surprising any Germans before they could abandon their trucks and trains. The other four Hellcats stayed high to cover their runs. As Bass took his planes east toward Rhone, still low to the ground, he gave the lead to his wingman, Lieutenant J. C. Forney, and flipped over to make a flat, low dive on a target he had apparently seen. He strafed a road, his bullets kicking up dust, and Forney fired too, not sure what he was shooting at (some thought it was a motorcyclist, presumably a German). Bass began to pull out, but his left wing kept dropping as if he was performing a slow roll, and his plane flipped too far onto its back. It nosed down and crashed into a field just short of two farmhouses, where it exploded in a ball of bright flame.

The men of his squadron, shocked at the death of their leader, eventually flew away back down the valley, leaving Bass' plane to smoke and burn.

Forney believed some German nearby got off a lucky shot at Bass' Hellcat. He thought Bass had been hit by a bullet at some point as he reached the bottom of his strafing run, but there were no tracer bullets visible. French civilians in the area said he had been sniped at and shot down by rogue elements of the French Resistance, for reasons unknown, possibly for spoils, but it would have been extremely difficult for rifles or machine guns to shoot down such a durable aircraft as a Hellcat. Others who watched the crash say Bass had been flying too low and his droppable fuel tank was torn away, possibly by a tree, which prevented him from regaining proper altitude before he plummeted to earth. Mechanical failure caused by damage from antiaircraft fire sustained earlier in the day was another possibility. He could have passed out on his descent, which was steep. Official reports of the U.S. Navy attribute Bass' crash to antiaircraft fire.

As the other men in his squadron winged away back to the *Kasaan Bay*, a local priest, a Fr. August Fayard, walked to the crash site and said a prayer over the dead pilot in the Hellcat's fiery wreckage. Bass' remains were eventually recovered by U.S. Army troops when they entered the area later that year. His body was completely burned, but a positive identification was made through his Naval Academy ring and his dog tags. Lieutenant Commander Brink Bass was buried in the nearby church cemetery in Vanosc.

After news of his death reached his family back in Texas, an editorial appeared in the *Beaumont Enterprise*:

> With the thousands of American boys who are sacrificing their lives for their country in this war, perhaps there is no reason to single out one for editorial mention. The sacrifice of each one is just as great as the other. He has given all he has for his country, he will be mourned by his family just as sincerely whether he has been a hero or has just gone about his duties without creating any special mention. But news of the death of Lieutenant Commander Brinkley Bass in action ends a career that has been spectacular for all his brief 28 years. . . . Brink Bass is mentioned here because he typifies the best in American youth, the kind that is winning this war for our country. For one who never met him, but has followed his activity since youth in news stories, it is hard to think of Brink as having been counted out in life's battle.[9]

1938
US NA

Part Four

BELOW THE WAVES

ELI VINOCK

Beaumont, Texas

You can take it from his "wives," Eli should have come from the North Pole instead of Texas. His yen for fresh air nearly froze us every winter for four years. Although he came back from Plebe Christmas with a very pessimistic attitude concerning his naval future, he became one of the "vicious system's" staunchest supporters. Living with radicals left him as he came to us, an idealist who preserved the proper balance in the room. Every spring found Eli out for track, where, in spite of his fourth-platoon legs, he succeeded in getting over the low hurdles. We hesitate to predict the future but think our roommate capable of making his way anywhere.

The Lucky Bag, 1938

Chapter Nineteen

CHANCES TAKEN

In the fall of 1940, while serving in the communication room on board the small carrier *Wasp* in the Atlantic, Herb Mandel, USNA '38, spotted a message that had come in from the Bureau of Navigation requesting volunteers for the next class of the U.S. Navy's Submarine School, set to convene on January 2, 1941, in New London, Connecticut. Mandel had met a few submariners before during his time in the Navy and had been impressed by them. He also knew that several of his classmates had already opted to volunteer for such duty, including many of the men who lined up alongside him on the Academy's 1938 lacrosse team. Mandel thought about the carrier under his feet and about the huge tanks filled with aviation gasoline that hunkered down there in its depths. Somewhat impulsively, he sat down to type a letter requesting reassignment. He wanted in.

Mandel did not have to wait long for a reply. He was selected, was quickly detached from the *Wasp* in Norfolk, Virginia, and in December was ordered to proceed to Connecticut for instruction. The Submarine School, on the banks of the Thames River, served as the World War II Navy's main center for submarine training and selection. Established in December 1915, it had become one of the finest technical schools in the world. Practically every submariner in the U.S. Navy had walked through its halls and been schooled in its diesel and sound laboratories, its torpedo shops, compression chamber, and escape tank.

To volunteer for submarine service was to volunteer for a long, hard, and quite rigorous course of training. Just to be selected was an accomplishment. When Mandel arrived in New London, he joined a class of forty-one trainees, all regular Navy officers and all Academy graduates from the Classes of '36, '37, '38, and '39. Each trainee selected for the service was an experienced professional in the surface fleet and already rated as either a deck or engineering watch officer. For three months the young men were taught the principles of diesel and electrical engineering, radio, navigation, gunnery, torpedo overhaul and repair, attack tactics, and undersea warfare. They practiced submerged approaches and torpedo attacks using miniature models of Japanese vessels and before long could recognize the enemy's various ship types and classes quite easily. They copied Morse code and read flashing lights and were told about the submarine disasters that filled the young service's history books, including the *S-51*, the *S-4*, and the *Squalus*, which had sunk off the coast of New Hampshire on a test dive in 1939, taking twenty-six sailors with it. Yet as one World War II submariner wrote, "Sound mind in sound body [were] not the whole requirement, for blended with these attributes must be a cooperative, democratic spirit, an ability to get along with one's fellow man in weeks of confined association. . . . Officer or man, the submariner must be a 'right guy.' . . . [At the same time], the submariner [must be] an individualist, a man who can think . . . for himself. No 'his-not-to-reason-why' mentality will do for the submersible operator whose intelligence must be energized by imagination and initiative."[1]

The Sub School had expanded when the war began and suffered that winter from an acute lack of classroom space, textbooks, and new equipment, including training boats: the trainees learned their business on board old O-type submarines that had been mothballed after service in World War I and recommissioned to satisfy the school's needs. Though many other volunteers washed out, Mandel successfully completed the training without too much hardship and was assigned to one such small, antique 186-foot "school boat" dubbed the *R-13*, on which he was given the duties of navigator, torpedoes, and gunnery, as well as first lieutenant and commissary officer.

At the end of May 1941, the *R-13* was ordered south to Key West to provide target services for the Navy's newly opened Fleet Sonar School. Mandel and the crew were thoroughly worn out by the long journey down at a paltry nine knots, the *R-13*'s cruising speed. However, the slow sail south gave Mandel and the other new submariners time to familiarize themselves with their boat, and they promptly learned every valve, gear, pipe, switch, hatch, and gauge from bow to stern. They were required to draw complete and accurate diagrams of the more than thirty principal systems on board, its "complex entrails" as Mandel described them, and every sailor had to know by heart his own specialty and that of another man as well.[2] Mere graduation from Sub School did not earn Mandel or anyone else the coveted silver dolphin insignia of the Submarine Force. Only after these initial trials at sea, and only after sufficiently convincing both his section chief and his captain that he could do, and had done, his job well, was a new submariner awarded his dolphins.

According to historian Theodore Roscoe, submarines contained "as many compartments and cubicles as a fighting ship two or three times its size."[3] Tucked into its steel hull were living accommodations, a control room, diesel engines, electric motors, fuel and water tanks, and hundreds of heavy battery cells. Jammed into crannies and compartments and bolted to every inch of space were air compressors and high-pressure air banks, navigational instruments, fire control panels, radio and radar and sonar gear and, snaking around them all, oil, air, and water lines and electric cables. There were torpedo tubes, storage spaces, refrigerated and dry foodstuffs, stills for making fresh water, air-conditioning equipment, ice machines, showers, main ballast tanks, electrical gear, periscope wells, chain lockers, and ammunition magazines. It was not a pleasant place to work, or a particularly safe one.

In July 1941 the aged *R-13* developed a problem with its electric storage battery, so orders arrived sending the sub back to New London and Mandel to a new posting. As soon as the submarine moored at the Key West pier to prepare for its homeward journey, Mandel found a base telephone and called his girlfriend. Happily, eighteen-year-old Gloria Kaufman accepted his marriage proposal. Mandel was granted leave, took a four-hour bus ride to Miami, and caught a plane for New York. He and Gloria were married in New London on August 26 with his parents, sisters, and rabbi in attendance, as well as USNA classmates Connie Zimmer and Howard Berry. After the "colorful" and "beautiful" wedding and a honeymoon involving a long automobile trip back down to Key West in a new Buick Mandel's father-in-law had given them, the young couple settled into quarters on base.[4]

When the Japanese attacked Pearl Harbor that December, the U.S. Navy's submarines were widely dispersed, and of widely varying quality. At the time the entire submarine service comprised just twenty-two boats, of which only sixteen were modern fleet-type submarines (the jewels were the 1,500-ton *Tambor*-class submarines, considered the finest in the world). Six were old S- and R-class varieties, and five of these submarines were in various stages of overhaul and repair at Pearl Harbor when the Japanese flew over. Submarines were viewed as a sort of "second cousin" in the U.S. Navy at the time, well below the battleships and carriers and cruisers in importance and prestige.[5] That is not to say they were disrespected, only that they were considered novel, odd, even radical. Plans for the Submarine Force had yet to evolve in the years leading up to Pearl Harbor, and the U.S. submarine fleet's movements and missions in the early 1940s were governed by out-of-date 1930s-era doctrine, which regarded the submarines as mere support boats for the bigger ships of the fleet. As such, submariners in the Pacific theater had trained only for scouting and support assignments, the occasional surface engagement, and minelaying operations. But as with most things in the American Navy immediately after the Pearl Harbor raid, change came quickly, and once the war started, the fleet submarines were promptly given new orders and new roles. In fact, only six hours after the Japanese attacked, the Chief of Naval Operations issued a fighting directive to all of his submarines: "Execute unrestricted air and submarine warfare against Japan."[6]

This directive was, to many in the sub service, "as startling as the Japanese attack" itself, for it called for "total war," a type of conflict in which everything, every enemy fishing boat and freighter, trawler and tugboat, was to be considered "as legitimate as an enemy battleship."[7] The commanders of the U.S. Submarine Force well knew that their boat captains and crews had not been fully schooled in such operations. They would have a great deal of on-the-job training to do.

There were also unique ethical matters to be addressed in the days after this directive was announced. Before the outbreak of hostilities with Japan, submariners had been taught to expect an "orthodox" war in which they would practice "ethical" tactics.[8] Due to the nature of the warfare they engaged in and the advantages they could bring to bear, the U.S. Navy's prewar submarines were subject to myriad legal considerations and limitations, and any crew guilty of violating these protocols could legally be sunk as pirates. The Pearl Harbor attack effectively and instantly removed these strictures: "The polite little law book went overboard."[9] They were now pirates indeed, and every ship afloat flying a Japanese flag was a fair target for plunder. Most submariners, enraged by Pearl Harbor, felt no compunction about carrying out the order, and carry it out they did. As historian Keith Wheeler wrote, "Composed of no more than 1.6 percent of the Navy's personnel, [U.S. submarines] accounted for 73 percent of Japanese ship losses from all causes during the first two years of the Pacific War."[10]

Four days after the Pearl Harbor raid, Herb Mandel received new orders detaching him to the USS *Finback.* Though it meant the beginning of a prolonged separation from Gloria, he was "overjoyed to be off to the newest ship in the Navy and to get off the 1919 relic."[11] He and his new bride loaded their Buick once again and pointed the car north. After a long trip, they pulled into New Castle, New Hampshire, and rented a small artist's studio overlooking the Piscataqua River. Upon his arrival Mandel learned that the *Finback* was part of Submarine Squadron 10 (SubRon 10) alongside a host of his Academy classmates, including Steve Mann and Ned Beach on board the *Trigger,* Mike Rindskopf on the *Drum*, and Walt Small on the *Flying Fish.*

Finback was commissioned on January 31, 1942, under the command of Lieutenant Commander Jesse Hull, USNA '26, and, after a brief period of sea trials, the submarine was ordered through the Panama Canal and into the Pacific. She arrived at Pearl Harbor on May 29 and anchored in the still-oily water near the overturned battleships. The *Trigger* was also in port that day, and Mandel's classmate Steve Mann, his teammate on the lacrosse team, came on board to greet him. Both *Finback* and

Trigger then sailed out to distant Midway Island and "participated" in the Battle of Midway, though their involvement was limited to long patrols through empty blue seas.

Mandel and his crewmates set out on their first official war patrol from Pearl Harbor on June 9, heading north with three other submarines through the northern Pacific for patrol stations around the windswept and lonely Aleutian Islands. They sighted land through their periscope on July 5, spotting the southwestern tip of Kiska, one of the Rat Islands group. Though they searched, no enemy targets were spotted in the island's bays or coves until 1510, when pinging was heard. Hull ordered the scope up and, his face pressed to the eyesights, described the tripod masts and gun mounts of two Japanese destroyers, range 6,500 yards, heading right for them "as if they knew we were there."[12]

"Pass the word. Battle Stations. Do not sound the alarm," Hull ordered.[13]

When the range fell to 1,200 yards, the *Finback* fired three torpedoes at the first ship in line, then shifted targets and fired three more at the trailing vessel. Sonar reported all fish running "hot, straight, and normal."[14] After thirty-five seconds, the captain ordered "Up scope!" followed by, just as quickly, "Down scope! 180 feet!"

The submarine had descended to 110 feet when the first depth charge exploded. It was accurately placed, so Hull shouted out for 300 feet. Five more depth charges blew in the water around the *Finback* and Mandel and the crew could hear one of the destroyer's screws through the hull as it turned around and dropped six more. It turned around again and dropped another spread of six. After an unpleasant jostling, the men escaped the area and were eventually credited with one hit on the second destroyer, their first strike of the war.

On August 9 the *Finback* was ordered to proceed east to Nazan Bay, off the island of Atka. At 0400 that morning, with the submarine sailing on the foggy surface of a cold sea, Mandel was relieved of the midwatch and turned in. An hour and a half later, at 0538, he was awakened by the diving alarm and felt the sub tilt downward. On the bridge the aft lookout had screamed "Plane!" and Mandel's replacement had instantly yelled, "Clear the bridge!

Dive! Dive!"[15] The klaxon moaned, and the crew sprinted to their stations. It was a two-engine flying boat, and it had cut down from out of the fog at high speed and picked out the submarine's wake on the sea surface. In the cold northern climes around the Aleutians, the Pacific's water is luminescent, and wakes stay visible for longer periods of time than they do in the warmer seas to the south. The plane, guided by the wake, dropped its bomb on the *Finback*, and it exploded as the submarine crossed below one hundred feet. Paint chips shook loose from the sub's overhead. Water rained from damaged lines, short-circuiting the trim, drain, and water pumps and wrecking the depth gauge in the conning tower. They survived, however, and, though wounded, the sub continued its mission, entering Nazan Bay in the darkness and rendezvousing with a seaplane tender, the cold, black, and sheer cliffs of Atka Island surrounding the bay on all sides, Mount Kliuchef in the distance. The submarine took on a party of surveyors and a dozen Marines whose mission had been to surveil nearby Tanaga Island and ascertain whether it had been occupied by the Japanese. They would find that it had not.

The following day, August 12, the *Finback*'s quite eventful first patrol was terminated, and the submarine was ordered back to Hawaii.

The *Finback* sailed into Pearl Harbor on August 23, and once ashore, Mandel stumbled across another of his Academy classmates, Eli Vinock, from Beaumont, Texas, who was serving on board a destroyer docked in the harbor. According to Mandel, Vinock was "walking around Waikiki with his gas mask and no place to go."[16] Submariners were entitled to stay at the Royal Hawaiian alongside the naval aviators, but Destroyer Command had made no similar arrangements for its crews, nor had they prepared a rest camp on Oahu. The destroyermen could bunk on their ships, but most understandably chose that option only as a last resort.

Boyish-looking, with thick black hair, light-colored eyes, and a wide chin, Vinock had run track for four years at Annapolis, though if *The Lucky Bag* was to be believed, he possessed "fourth platoon" legs.[17] Mandel took the poor man up to his room at the hotel, poured him whiskey from one of the bottles Submarine Command had provided him, let Vinock take a hot shower, and told him to get some rest. Vinock slumbered "like a baby" for twelve hours straight.[18] Mandel appreciated the role his classmate played in the service, escorting the convoys and battle groups, keeping them protected from the enemy's bombers and submarines. He knew the dangers destroyer duty entailed and the difficulties of antisubmarine warfare. And it was grueling work. As Mandel wrote, "[Vinock and his fellow destroyermen] would no sooner arrive in port than they would be immediately turned around and ordered to sea again."[19] To Mandel's way of thinking, Vinock's lot in the service was not substantially easier than his own just because he sailed on the waves rather than below them. He too deserved a good room, a good drink, and a good bed.

The *Finback* set off on her second war patrol a few weeks later, on September 23, exiting Pearl Harbor and setting a course for the distant Straits of Formosa, far to the southwest in the South China Sea. It was monsoon season, and the seas were thrashing, but Lieutenant Commander Hull eased her through the forty- to sixty-foot waves and around the Hoka Sho light and then held his submarine off the Formosan port of Keelung, just seaward of the channel buoy marking the port's entrance. Through the periscope the officers could see the masts of anchored ships. After a long week of lying in wait, watching for but spotting no worthwhile prey, a convoy of destroyers and the three heavy merchantmen they were escorting sailed through the channel at ten knots, their bows pointed westward, their stacks dumping black smoke into the sky. The *Finback* waited for darkness, then set off at eighteen knots to pursue, pulling ahead of the ships in two short hours and hitting two of the vessels with torpedoes when they sailed again across her periscope. Knowing destroyers from the nearby Japanese base at Takao would quickly be hunting for them, the *Finback* turned south toward the shallow waters off China, rigged for silent running, and waited out the Japanese ships searching with their antisubmarine sonars. After sinking two more large freighters in the South China Sea, the *Finback* was ordered back to Pearl Harbor in late October.

A few days before Christmas, the *Finback* and her crew were out to sea again on their third patrol, this time to the Japanese Home Islands and the southeastern coast of Kyushu. After a two-week sail, the men glimpsed the enemy's homeland for the first time, spying gigantic mountain ranges that reared up from the sea. Targets, expected to be heavily laden freighters leaving Japan with supplies, were few and far between. One evening, Mandel and the *Finback*'s crew heard through the water distant explosions to the north, later learning through intercepted radio traffic that the USS *Pike*, another submarine hunting in the area, had been depth-charged and seriously damaged, forcing her to withdraw. Mandel knew his good friend Pat Callahan, USNA '38, a fellow member of Fourth Battalion during their time at Annapolis, was on board.

The *Finback* would have her own excitement a few days later. As dawn broke and the *Finback* cruised on the surface, Mandel was serving as officer of the deck when Hull stepped onto the bridge for a last look around before retiring and said, "Herb, go below and take the dive."[20]

Mandel assumed his position as diving officer, then quickly heard a shouted order, "Clear the bridge! Dive! Dive!," followed by two blasts from the klaxon. The main ballast tanks were flooded, the diesel engines were shut down, and the main air induction valve was closed; however, the hatch to the conning tower had not been sealed properly, and as Mandel took a step to the ladder to investigate, "the Pacific Ocean poured in on [him]."[21] Mandel shouted, "Blow safety!," and immediately the vents on all main ballast tanks were shut and main ballast was blown. Still, the pump room just below the bridge flooded rapidly, the water rising past ankles and knees to the men's waists. Slowly, the submarine regained positive buoyancy at a keel depth of forty-six feet and inched back up to the surface. Once in open air, in the semi-light, the flooded compartments were drained, and the captain assessed the damage the water had caused: the gyro was out and the air compressors in the pump room were sopping wet, as were several motor generator sets. The submarine was soggy, but still sound.

Despite the near disaster, the *Finback* completed her patrol before setting a course for Midway Island and a refit in February 1943. There Lieutenant Commander Hull received new orders and John Tyree, the *Finback*'s executive officer, was given command of the boat. Tyree asked Mandel to assume the role of his senior watch officer. Mandel was hoping to get home to see Gloria but, as required, he replied, "John, if that's the way you want it, that's the way it will be."[22]

Tyree replied, "I will write to Gloria and tell her that you'll be home after the next patrol."

The patrol area for the *Finback*'s fourth mission was expansive. They were to sail from Midway and patrol the sea between the Japanese Home Islands and New Guinea. The submarine headed first to the island of Truk, a major Japanese naval base whose entrance was protected by a handful of smaller islands. Tyree held her off the North Pass, where the sea was glassy smooth and air patrols were frequent and where the sub was limited to short periscope exposures because of them. Matters grew immensely dull for the men. They saw nothing for days, no puffs of smoke nor mastheads on the horizon. With everyone wearing down, finally, late one night, three ships escorted by destroyers popped up in the distance, and Tyree brought the sub on a long end-around to get ahead of them. They were well positioned for an attack the following afternoon when, at almost the last moment, the convoy zagged away from them. The *Finback* chased the ships on the surface and reeled them in until they were seven thousand yards away off her starboard quarter. It was night again, Mandel had the deck, and the ships were plainly in sight when a thunderous boom erupted on the sea and the air turned bright with light. One of the destroyers had fired a star shell, exposing the submarine on the surface.

"Clear the bridge! Dive! Dive!" Mandel shouted.[23]

With the three lookouts and the quartermaster, Mandel hurried down into the submarine, which was already slipping beneath the waves. While they were held under the water by the destroyers, the convoy slipped away over the horizon. But Tyree was determined, and he ordered Mandel to catch an hour's worth of sleep and then get back after them. At around 0400 the next morning, Mandel did just that, and the *Finback* scored hits on two of the ships with its torpedoes. The ships in the convoy turned out to be troopships bound for New Guinea, each carrying over five thousand infantrymen to the jungle battle raging there. Hours later, General Douglas MacArthur himself heard about what the *Finback* had done and sent the sub a message. "Your picture is on the piano," he told them.[24]

After the patrol Tyree was true to his word, and Mandel was granted a thirty-day leave and told to proceed to the Cramp Shipyard on the

Delaware River in Philadelphia for duty as prospective executive officer of a new submarine under construction there. He caught passage on a ship leaving Pearl Harbor bound for San Francisco and then took a commercial flight to New York City, where his parents, his in-laws, and Gloria were waiting for him. He had been gone from her for a year and a half.

The couple spent a week at Lake Tarleton in New Hampshire and then headed down to Pennsylvania, where they rented an apartment in Bryn Mawr and where, for a few months, life moved leisurely. But eventually Mandel grew restless and eager to "get back out there and sink more ships."[25]

Mandel's father had other ideas in mind for him. For his service on the *Finback*'s war patrols, Mandel had been awarded a Silver Star, and his father believed that he could ask for and receive a public relations assignment at Third Naval District in New York City. But Mandel thought of his friends from the Academy out there fighting and he thought about how useful he could be, given his experience as a key member of the Submarine Force in combat.

"You might not be so lucky this time," his dad told him after he demurred.

"Dad, I love you," Mandel replied. "But I will take my chances."[26]

CARL REDMOND DWYER

Ponca City, Oklahoma

"Supposin' I had continued my early-planned career as a petroleum engineer—I might not be the proud owner of a '31 Model A Ford now." Looking in the direction from which this familiar line comes, one sees Ponca philosophizing over a piece of Reef Points stationery. The truth will out; the fellow will succeed wherever he is. In the same logical way that he attacks all academic problems does he manage everything that he undertakes. His principal fault is his good-natured teasing of other people, a sport in which he delights. Being very careful with his financial affairs, he'll be a man of means some day if the Navy doesn't keep him. If he stays in the Navy you can rest assured that his particular duty will always be efficiently carried out. Golden slippers someday, Ponca.

The Lucky Bag, 1938

Chapter Twenty

THE END OF EXISTENCE

Before setting out on their submarine's first patrol of the war in September 1943, the officers and crew of the USS *Puffer* were allowed into the Lennon Hotel in Brisbane, Australia, to enjoy the amenities of the establishment, the top floor of which served as General Douglas MacArthur's offices. After a month long journey from the United States, their submarine was undergoing some rather quick but necessary repairs in the nearby harbor, and the crew had been billeted in the small cottages of a rest camp in the quiet town of Toowoomba, about seventy-five miles inland of Brisbane. Local Australian authorities wished to keep the American submariners out of the city and, more to the point, away from the Australian soldiers there, fearing more of the bloody brawls that frequently occurred between the two nations' troops and sailors. The *Puffer*'s crew had occupied themselves at the camp with pickup softball and football games, horseback riding trips, hours of gambling, beers at local pubs, even dinners at the homes of some of the more accommodating locals. But nothing could match the luxury of the Lennon, and as their week's worth of fun wound down, the men crowded into the hotel's dining room and set to work on plates of chicken sandwiches and pitchers of beer.

The *Puffer*'s gunnery officer, Carl Dwyer, USNA '38, was born in June 1915 in Edgerton, Kansas, and raised in Osage County's Ponca City, Oklahoma. He attended Oklahoma State for a spell before graduating from Oklahoma University Junior College and entering the Naval Academy in 1934, where, as a member of Ninth Company, he ran track and cross-country, joined the Reception Committee, and was on the staff of both *The Log* and *The Lucky Bag*. After graduating Dwyer served on the cruiser *Louisville* and the battleship *Texas*, then studied at the Naval Gun Factory before earning acceptance into New London's Submarine School, from which he graduated in December 1940.

The keel of the *Puffer*, a *Gato*-class submarine, had been officially laid on February 16, 1942, in a covered shed at the Manitowoc Shipbuilding Company in Wisconsin. She had been commissioned in late April 1943, 316 days ahead of schedule. Dwyer, by then a lieutenant, had been appointed the ship's gunnery officer and was on hand for the ceremony. The sixty-three-man crew had then brought the submarine on a cruise from Lake Michigan's chilly shores to Australia, halfway around the world, and, after their week of relaxation, were at sea again on August 28, practicing approach maneuvers and crash-dive evasive tactics and testing their sound equipment. The submarine's first war patrol officially began on September 7.

The *Puffer*'s assigned area of operations was the ocean south of Ambon, a mountainous island in the Dutch East Indies and a hub of Japanese shipping. The island, a mere 4 degrees south of the equator, was hot and humid, with air temperatures averaging over 100 degrees Fahrenheit during the day, and its tropical waters offshore were as warm as a bath, which served to keep the interior of the *Puffer*'s steel hull "like a sauna" when she sailed on the surface.[1] Temperatures inside the submarine ranged from 110 to 125 degrees Fahrenheit; the humidity could, and often did, spike to a positively sodden 100 percent. Such conditions for a submarine crew were more than merely uncomfortable; they could be outright deadly. As historian Craig McDonald wrote, "Without some loss of body heat a person in such conditions for an extended period of time would literally be pressure cooked."[2]

On September 16 the submarine's captain, Lieutenant Commander M. J. Jensen, sighted a medium freighter emerging from the fog near Ambon's harbor entrance, and he initiated an approach while tubes 1 through 4 were made ready. Ultimately it was determined that what the captain had seen through his scope was a camouflaged "Q ship," a tug designed specifically to lure American submarines in close, so the *Puffer* prudently canceled its attack run and steered away to cover the island's western approaches.

Early the next morning, at 0227, a Japanese auxiliary ship and an accompanying freighter were sighted in the bright moonlight roughly five thousand yards distant, zigzagging sharply every few minutes. Jensen submerged the *Puffer* and began his approach, firing his first salvo of three torpedoes from his bow tubes at 0240. He then switched to the freighter as Dwyer plotted the solution, and the second spread of torpedoes was launched two minutes later from a range of nineteen hundred yards. No explosions were heard, so, reacting hastily, Jensen brought the submarine around to line up his stern tubes for a shot when a series of six explosions suddenly echoed through the water. The crew cheered, and the damaged auxiliary vessel was seen limping away toward Ambon. Jensen scanned the sea a few seconds more before spotting the freighter sinking rapidly into the black water. But something else caught his eye too: a sub chaser on their port side, aiming a red searchlight in their direction. The *Puffer*'s sound crew then picked up fast screws and two depth charges, far off. Jensen ordered the sub to go deep, under a thermocline layer at 260 feet which he hoped would bounce the enemy ship's sonar waves back at her. An hour later the Japanese vessel sailed away, its search efforts unproductive, and Jensen brought his submarine back up to periscope depth and cleared the area at high speed as daybreak neared.

Morale on the submarine was high after their successful attack, but Jensen, Dwyer, and the rest of the crew wanted more, so the captain set a course for the northern approaches to the nearby Maluku Islands. For four days, however, as they traversed the Molucca Sea and slipped by the northeastern corner of the Celebes, they spied nothing on the water. The men kept busy with surface patrols and training dives, and Jensen positioned the *Puffer* along the known tanker shipping routes between Balikpapan and Palau. Still nothing. They moved on westward into the Makassar Strait, spotting only sailboats on the sea, undoubtedly with Japanese spotters and radios on board. Jensen guessed the convoys and shipping traffic that normally would be plying through these sea-lanes were being routed away. The weather worsened, a strong current pushed the submarine northward, and there were few sightings to be had during the long days of late September and early October.

Things changed on the night of October 6, when, sailing on the surface at nine knots, the submarine struck a reef in water the onboard charts indicated was 1,350 fathoms deep. The sudden collision tossed men from their bunks and hurled unsecured objects through the passageways, and the *Puffer* came to a dead stop. She was hung up on a pinnacle just forward of the conning tower. Thinking quickly, the officer of the deck backed emergency and blew the ballast tanks with high-pressure air, but the sub failed to move. The men tried everything they could think of for the next ninety minutes. All ballast and variable tanks were blown. Torpedoes were disarmed and made ready for jettisoning to lighten the boat. Thousands of tons of fuel were blown from the tank near the bow of the submarine. The towing pendant was thrown overboard. Fresh water was shifted aft, along with most of the crew, and all the while the sub's engines were reversed and throttled forward repeatedly in efforts to dislodge her. Jensen made plans to scuttle the boat as nervous crew armed themselves with knives and guns to fend off any Japanese who happened by and decided to board the *Puffer*. But just as he was about to jettison the forward torpedoes and haul the anchor aft for use as a kedge, the falling tide and a final try at reversing the engines jarred the submarine free "as though catapulted."[3] She escaped the area at high speed as Dwyer and her crew smiled in relief, and dawn broke the horizon.[4]

By 0648 on October 8, the submarine lay submerged off the north entrance to the Makassar Strait, waiting for any ships headed for Balikpapan or Tarakan, and on the morning of the 9th, the sub's sound operators reported a pinging to the north. Jensen pointed the boat in that direction, and soon a mast was spotted, churning by on a steady course at fourteen knots—an escort. The captain wanted whatever was behind the torpedo boat, so he steered in the opposite direction of the ship and at 1040 spotted a maru, a quite large merchantman. For half an hour Jensen brought the submarine up close, less than two thousand yards, and as it passed directly across his bow, he fired a spread of four torpedoes. Dwyer and the other officers monitored their stopwatches, waiting expectantly, and then two torpedoes struck the Japanese vessel just aft of the bridge and inside the stern and it went dead in the water, puffed smoke, and listed 50 degrees. Jensen fired two more fish to send her to the bottom, but one torpedo exploded prematurely and the other turned out to be a dud. Dwyer by this time was concerned about the location of the escort, and he urged Jensen to check for her. She was spotted closing fast and firing her small-caliber guns, and at 1125 she dropped three depth charges that exploded harmlessly. The *Puffer*, by now submerged, commenced clearing the area, but the Japanese torpedo boat launched six more depth charges, and they "rocked the boat like a sailboat in a typhoon."[5] Water leaked in through the hatches and down through the conning tower door and poured into the after torpedo room. Jensen went deep, but the accurate depth charging continued—four more exploded directly above them.

As Jensen tried to flee, the escort seemed to stay with them, directly astern, matching each turn they took and attacking from overhead. The *Puffer* was apparently leaving behind a trail of something on the surface, an oil slick or a wake of bubbles, for the Japanese spotters to follow. Furthermore, the sharp currents were making evasive maneuvering difficult—the submarine lost its agility as the sea pushed back heavily against her planes and beams. At 1345 five more depth charges exploded, again above them, again very close. Two more blew through the sea at 1525. Wrote Jensen, "It is impossible to shake this fellow. The manner in which he keeps on us is uncanny."[6] Another six charges blew near them at 1625, and by the evening a second antisubmarine vessel had arrived in the area and five more depth charges exploded, blasting the hull, shaking the submarine, and tossing the men across the passageways. It became extremely difficult to maintain depth. At 2240, six more depth charges exploded, and though the trim pump broke and the electric motors in the bilges flooded out, the hull remained intact, a credit to the welders back in the sheds at Manitowoc.

But the depth charging continued. The *Puffer* sprang a rudder. The starboard sound head was thrown out of alignment. Gaskets were blown out of the engine air induction, and water continued to leak down through the conning tower door, wetting Dwyer's back as he manned his controls. The power went out, and Jensen struggled to keep the submarine deep, between 350 and 400 feet. Men were forced to manually control the rudder and dive planes whenever Jensen wished to change directions—an order for right or left full rudder to evade the depth charges totally exhausted a man, as each turn required thirty revolutions of the wheel.

For the next thirty hours, the *Puffer* stayed submerged. To conserve his batteries Jensen shut off the air-conditioning, and the ship's corpsman, "Doc" Spalding, had a devilish time preventing dehydration, heat stroke, and mental malaise among the crew. He walked through the ship passing out teaspoons of whiskey or brandy to brace the men, but every few minutes it seemed the physical environment deteriorated further. Sweat glazed everyone in an oily diesel film. Sleep, when men tried it, was almost impossible in the heat and stifling air, made even more challenging by the constant anxiety and by the slippery and damp and soon stinking vinyl-covered bunks. Depth charges continued to blow through the water at staggered depths just above them. Even though the submarine lay deep and quiet, the escorts stayed close, continuing to track them somehow. Glass bulbs blew from the shockwaves, and soon the only light on the submarine was from the battery-operated lanterns. The noise inside the boat when the charges blew was horrific. At one point, something rolled or was dragged loudly across the sub's deck, perhaps a dud depth charge or a grappling hook tossed down by one of the Japanese warships. The escorts above sounded like "fast trains passing . . . at a crossing."[7] The nerves of the men grew increasingly strained. In between blasts was a silence, hard and heavy in the half-light and the heat. Over time carbon dioxide began to accrue in the darkness, and men found Spalding and reported headaches. But there was little he could do, and little Jensen could do but keep the submarine deep and make sharp turns to avoid the charges. The temperature in the maneuvering room reached 125 degrees Fahrenheit. Flooding by twelve tons of seawater eventually caused the *Puffer* to tilt with a 12-degree up angle. The excess water also pushed the submarine even deeper, more than five hundred feet, which was two hundred feet greater than her test depth. The external pressure worsened the leaks, which sent more water into the submarine and pushed her down deeper.

The last six depth charges were dropped by the Japanese at 0115 on October 10. The antisubmarine ships stayed in the area for another eleven hours, making dry runs that served only to unnerve the crew of the *Puffer* even further, and the men became physically and mentally debilitated as the heat and humidity climbed and, for some, hypoxia set in. Breathing grew labored and the headaches increasingly severe. An officer making his rounds from the control room to the aft torpedo room had to stop and rest several times. In stupors, many of the men started to collapse at their dials and switches. Those asleep became impossible to rouse. There was so little air, and what there was had grown so bad, that it was difficult to light a match. Ensign William Pugh stumbled through each compartment releasing oxygen into the room from a small set of tanks intended to charge the sub's set of Momsen lungs. The levels of hydrogen in the air from the discharged batteries approached explosive levels, but an eruption was avoided, probably because of the low levels of oxygen in the submarine. What air there was reeked: men vomited throughout the compartments, and the heads filled with accumulated human waste. They were impossible to flush due to the external noise and the bubbles they would create. According to historian Craig McDonald, the submarine soon smelled like a sewer pipe.[8]

The most critical problem to their health continued to be the increasing levels of carbon dioxide. The little available oxygen became extremely uncomfortable to breathe. Headaches behind the eyes worsened as the slow hours passed. According to Frank Golay, an officer on the *Puffer*, "The throbbing pain spread through [one's] head until to be able to surface and gulp in the fresh air seem[ed] to be the end of existence."[9]

Perhaps the biggest mental reaction of the men on board was anger. They grew mad at everything and anyone. Their chief frustration was that they were being attacked but could not fight back, could not, in fact, do anything at all to fix or change the situation. In the silence all they could do was wait for the next click of a depth charge and think. Some men lost their wits. They grew hopeless. One crewman climbed the escape hatch ladder in an attempt to exit the submarine. He hit his head, fell down, pulled himself back up, and tried again. Others, in fits of insanity, tried to exit through the hatch in the crew's quarters. One man walked stiffly across his compartment acting as if he was chasing chickens back on his family's farm. Another man threatened others with a wrench if they made even the slightest noise, and he had to be wrestled down and restrained with ropes. Power in the batteries faded.

Eventually the pinging of the Japanese warships above on the surface died away and contact with the vessels was lost. Jensen could not immediately surface the ship for a look, however, since the safety and negative tanks had been blown dry, so it was decided they would remain submerged and hang on until darkness. Finally, gloriously, the *Puffer* broke the surface at 1910, the water silvered by a bright moon. No enemy ships were in sight. The *Puffer* had stayed submerged for thirty-eight hours. It would be the longest submergence of any American submarine in World War II. After repairing the boat and recharging the batteries and plugging the leaks and getting his exhausted crew some air and rest, Jensen decided the boat was too worn down for another attack, so he plotted a course back to Fremantle and turned the boat south.

1938
USNA

FRANK CURTIS LYNCH JR.

Kansas City, Missouri

Fine things are better appreciated than described. To draw a picture of a young fellow, however, blessed with a grand physique, immense vitality, and plenty of poise, coupled with a keenly analytical and well-developed mental organ, would be to outline substantially this character, Frank. He is of the fortunate with whom the briefest acquaintance is a pleasurable memory; the longest friendship, an unforgettable chapter. Native to Kansas, Frank is not conspicuously a Kansan. On the gridiron or the basketball court he handles his opponents as deftly as a teacup, and he twirls a wicked teacup! Track completes his year-round tour of the sports, for he excels in that, too. For a frolic or a fray, the lad is a best bet.

The Lucky Bag, 1938

Chapter Twenty-One

THE HIT 'EM *HARDER*

The fifth war patrol of the USS *Harder*, which occurred from May 26 through June 21, 1944, has been called "the most brilliant . . . of the entire war."[1] Over the course of four days spent in the seas around Borneo and the Japanese-held port of Tawi-Tawi, an island province in the Philippines, the *Harder* sank four sleek enemy destroyers and damaged another. Even more importantly, by the sheer volume and audacity of her attacks, the submarine convinced the local Japanese admiral, Soemu Toyoda, that multiple American subs must be swarming through the area and that his fleet should leave its anchorage early, thereby fouling his battle plans and ultimately "contributing to the Japanese defeat in the Battle of the Philippine Sea."[2] In command of the *Harder* during this famous patrol was a legendary submarine captain, Commander Samuel Dealey. Serving as his executive officer was Lieutenant Commander Frank Lynch, USNA '38, hero of the Naval Academy for his exploits on the football field and the basketball court, and soon to be hero of the submarine service.

During the month of May 1944, Admiral Chester Nimitz had completed plans for the American invasion of the Marianas, an archipelago in the western Pacific key to control of the region. From three major islands in the chain—Saipan, Tinian, and Guam—the Japanese could launch attacks almost anywhere in the Southwest Pacific, so the islands needed to be captured promptly. The American assault on the Marianas was scheduled for June, and the Japanese Imperial Navy, well aware of the importance of the archipelago's bases, eyed the approaching American fleet eagerly, anticipating an opportunity to destroy Carrier Task Force 58 and the 128,000 Marine and Army troops sailing with it. In preparation for that attack, Toyoda had ordered major elements of his Combined Fleet to assemble in Tawi-Tawi. Lynch and the USS *Harder* were part of a nest of twenty-eight submarines sent to patrol the waters through which the Combined Fleet was expected to pass on its way to do battle with the Americans.

By that time the *Harder* was already a well-known submarine: it had earned the nickname "Hit 'Em *Harder*" for Captain Sam Dealey's aggressive leadership during its previous war patrols, and Lynch, on whom Dealey depended greatly, had been on the sub for all of them, having joined the *Harder* at its commissioning.[3] When describing Lynch and Sam Logan, another officer on board, Dealey would say, "With these two madmen pushing me all the time, there was nothing I could do but go along."[4]

Frank Lynch Jr. was born in Benedict, Kansas, and grew to be a stout, imposing man, well over six feet tall and two hundred pounds. When he graduated from the Naval Academy with the Class of 1938, his accolades and accomplishments were lengthy. In addition to the N-Stars and athletic records he had accrued, Lynch earned the rank of a "five-striper," a regimental commander. There was no higher rank a midshipman could attain. While serving as the *Harder*'s prospective executive officer during its construction, "Tiny" Lynch had hand-selected and recruited the crew he would go to sea with, and his accomplishments and reputation encouraged the best to accept his offer. On board, while serving under Dealey during the *Harder*'s early wartime patrols, Lynch had been recognized for his cool efficiency, his fearlessness, his intelligence, his work ethic, and his easygoing manner. Many believed that he was in line for big things, perhaps a starring role in the Navy's hierarchy after the war, or even Chief of Naval Operations someday.[5]

For its fifth mission the submarine departed Fremantle, Australia, bound for the Celebes Sea just after noon on May 26, in company with the submarine *Redfin* and under the escort of the HMAS *Adelaide*. After a few days spent practicing periscope approaches, training new officers in sighting at different ranges, holding night surface radar exercises, and conducting dry battle surface drills, the *Harder* and *Redfin* hunkered for a night in Western Australia's Exmouth Gulf before proceeding independently toward their assigned areas via a bombing restriction lane on May 30. By 2200 on June 1, the *Harder* was thirty-five miles off Sumbawa Island.

After midnight Dealey brought the surfaced submarine slowly through Alas Strait, the bright moonlight making the navigation easy. Throughout the next day, sailing vessels with triangular mainsails and jibs of the type used by the natives were spotted in the distance, and Dealey gave them wide berths. The following night he zigzagged the submarine through a fleet of small fishing boats, perhaps as many as a hundred, sailing in a pack on a northbound course with lighted lanterns casting eerie glows across their sails. The submarine closed to within five thousand yards of Hoek Mandar, on Celebes' western coast, before following its line of beaches northward past Cape William, where they sighted and avoided a trio of medium-sized Japanese patrol craft.

On June 5 Cape Mangkalihat on Borneo was sighted, seventeen miles in the distance. The skies were overcast and the sea glassy, and the *Harder* set a course for nearby Tarakan Island, avoiding more fishing fleets that cluttered the water and complicated the transit, but Dealey and Lynch hid in rain squalls while on the surface and managed to approach the southern entrance of Sibutu Passage unseen.

On the night of June 6, a flurry of pips was spotted on the radar indicating a convoy ahead, steaming south through the passage on a course that would bring them directly to the *Harder*. Dealey sent the crew to their stations, surfaced the submarine to gain speed, and spotted the ships at 18,000 yards—three large oil tankers steaming at fifteen knots with three destroyers alongside, all high-priority targets. Dealey began his end-around. As he wrapped up his long turn, intending to dive ahead of the convoy and maneuver halfway between the escorts and the tankers so that he could fire almost simultaneously on both sets of ships, the night moon poked through the low cumulus clouds overhead and cast the submarine in light. It was pale, but it was enough. At once the nearest Japanese destroyer, now dead astern and 12,000 yards away, revved her engines to top speed and turned for them. The destroyer could make twenty-four knots, the *Harder* only nineteen, and she scratched a white wake in the water to boot.

She would not be able to escape while surfaced. Dealey gave the order to submerge, and as the *Harder* cleaved through the water and slipped beneath the sea, he ordered a turn hard left to bring her stern tubes to bear. With the range closing to 1,150 yards and the destroyer still barreling straight for them, Dealey fired a three-torpedo spread. Two hit—one under the Japanese ship's bow and the other under her bridge. It had been an easy fire-control problem for Lynch; the Japanese captain was overeager, and his vessel paid for it. Her bow went under, her stern rose in the air, and soon the explosions cooked off her depth charges, still in their racks, and she sank minutes later. The second destroyer escorting the convoy turned now to chase them, and Dealey again waited for the vessel to cross astern before firing six torpedoes, but these all missed. For several hours the Japanese destroyer dropped depth charges over and around the *Harder*, but the submarine, though shaken, survived. Dealey opted to withdraw southward.

The next night, while still chasing the convoy, a third Japanese destroyer spotted the *Harder*'s periscope on the water and gave chase, but Dealey again kept his calm, waited until the enemy ship was a mere 650 yards away, and fired three torpedoes "straight down [her] throat."[6] A massive explosion resulted when the destroyer's magazine went up, and the ship sank tail first minutes later, at 2159. Dealey and a few of the bridge lookouts watched her go under from a thousand yards away, then he brought the *Harder* over to where she had sunk. All that was left of the enemy ship was a black oil slick and a lone life buoy on the water. There were no survivors of the *Hayanami* to be seen.

Dealey did not linger long. At 2204 he put the four engines on propulsion and sailed after the escaping Japanese tankers at full speed. As Dealey wrote in his report, "From here it would be a race to see who could get to Tarakan first!"[7] The IJN, however, had still more resources to bring to bear to protect its convoy of tankers, and at 2217 the *Harder*'s radar picked up another enemy destroyer at 14,000 yards making high speed and heading straight for them. As one of his men put it, "The *Harder* seemed to have a monopoly on the whole Pacific War this date."[8] Dealey again sounded battle stations and took the submerged sub to radar depth. At 8,000 yards he brought the *Harder* up for a look through his periscope, but the cloud cover and lack of sufficient moonlight made accurate range finding difficult. At 2242, from 1,250 yards away, on an 80-degree port track angle and with a target speed of twelve knots, Lynch plotted his solution, Dealey gave the order, and eight torpedoes leapt from the bow tubes on a diverging spread. They all missed as the destroyer made a “figure S” maneuver, and once the torpedoes were past, the enemy vessel turned and headed toward the American submarine. Dealey rigged the boat for silent running and took her down to three hundred feet as, quickly, five depth charges exploded nearby. A new stern planesman, believing incorrectly that the submarine had suddenly lost power during the attack, switched the controls to hand operation and then inadvertently put the planes on “dive” instead of “rise.” Instantly the *Harder* tilted into a 15-degree down angle and passed four hundred feet, below her test depth. Dealey shouted for all available men to run into the aft part of the ship to right her. The depth charging continued until midnight, when the *Harder* was finally able to use temperature gradients in the water to wriggle free of the destroyer’s search grid. By then, however, the tanker convoy was too far distant to chase any further, so the *Harder* turned once more for the Sibutu Passage. Dealey, as pugnacious a captain as the sub service had at the time, felt the need to explain his decision to withdraw in the boat’s war report. He wrote that by that time the *Harder*’s battery was low and the air in the boat was poor, and the crew were fatigued by the seemingly constant attacks and depth charging, and their position on the sea amid a slew of narrow straits and unknown reefs was not accurately known, so Dealey, Lynch, and the crew sailed off through stiff currents under a full, bright moon.

The haggard men were granted little relief when, at 0532 the next morning, they were abruptly bombed awake. As the sub ran along the surface of the sea, it was spotted by the pilots of a Japanese floatplane droning nearby, which dove quickly and dropped a bomb on the *Harder* as it submerged and went deep. The bomb shook the boat severely, jolting the men in their racks. Though the sub was underwater and somewhat safe, the glassy smooth sea and the persistent buzz of airplanes in the sky forced the *Harder* to stay below and remain quiet for another few hours.

Dealey's feistiness remained, however. On the night of June 9, lookouts spotted the silhouettes of two Japanese destroyers sailing patrol patterns along the narrow northern neck of Sibutu Passage. The sightings were "just what the doctor ordered for the *Harder*," Dealey later wrote.[9] He fired four torpedoes when the destroyers zagged back toward him, and though the first slid underneath the lead enemy destroyer, the next two struck her bow and beneath her captain's bridge. The fourth torpedo smashed into the second enemy vessel, and it erupted in a heavy explosion when its boiler blew, a blast so massive the sub keeled over from the concussion. Dealey surfaced, and he and Lynch stared through the periscope at what they had done: the second destroyer's tail end pointed out of the water as the first disappeared beneath the sea. No more screws were audible, so Dealey sailed again to the spot where the ships went down, finding only steam and vapor drifting along the water and a lighted buoy aflame nearby. The *Harder* then turned and left the area at high speed before any aircraft arrived. Dealey took them deep and rigged for silent running to give his exhausted crew some rest.

On the afternoon of the 10th, while patrolling at periscope depth just off the Tawi-Tawi entrance at 1700, the sound crew heard both light and heavy screws, and more enemy ships popped up in the *Harder*'s periscope, this time a large, dangerous force of three battleships, four cruisers, and a half-dozen destroyers heading southward and sailing under a protective formation of escorting float planes. The *Harder* was roughly eight miles from the closest ship, one of the heavily armed battleships of the *Musashi* class. As Dealey studied the group, the nearest battleship suddenly made black smoke, and a destroyer turned toward the American submarine. They had been spotted in the clear, smooth sea by one of the planes flying over the convoy, and the pilot had alertly dropped a smoke float near the battleship. The onrushing destroyer flashed through the water at thirty-five knots, echo ranging steadily, and dropped a trio of depth charges meant to scare the *Harder* away. According to Dealey, "We had to hit him, or else!"[10]

When the destroyer was fifteen hundred yards distant and Dealey had swung the submarine's bow tubes around, Lynch plotted his solution, and the captain ordered a three-torpedo spread straight ahead. As Dealey wrote in his after action report, "Two torpedoes struck with a detonation that was far worse than depth-charging. By this time, we were just passing eighty feet and were soon almost beneath the destroyer when all Hell broke loose . . . a deafening series of progressive rumblings that seemed almost to blend with each other. Either his boilers or magazines, or both, had exploded and it's a lucky thing that ship explosions are vented upward and not down."[11]

Another destroyer moved in from starboard and lay depth charge barrages as the *Harder* passed two hundred feet, but the charges all fell astern, and aside from being loud and adding to the submarine's jolting, they did no damage. More explosions continued to rock the boat, however—bombs dropped by the floatplanes, leading to, as Dealey put it, "the most uncomfortable five minutes yet experienced during the *Harder*'s five War Patrols."[12] A barometer was knocked loose from its fittings. Men were thrown off their feet. A chain was lifted off its hook and hit a man, knocking him unconscious. Between twenty and thirty depth charges and bombs were counted. For the next two hours, Dealey worked the submarine away from the area as explosion after explosion tore through the water, clearly audible rumblings through the steel hull. Earlier in its patrol the *Harder* had secretly picked up a crew of British soldiers from an island beach, and as the submarine shook and rocked and bounced from the blasts, one of the men turned to Dealey and asked, "I say, old man, would you mind taking us back to Borneo?"[13] Dealey and his officers were amazed the submarine held together, given the pounding and jolting it endured. "Our fervent thanks go to the workmen and designers at the Electric Boat Company for building such a fine ship," he wrote in his official report of the incident.[14]

By June 11, Dealey, Lynch, their onboard guests, and the rest of the officers and crew of the *Harder* had cleared the area and were on their way back to Darwin, Australia. It had been a historic week for the submarine. For six days, from June 6 through 12, the *Harder* had been almost continuously engaged in combat operations. The crew had completed a special mission (picking up the British agents) and made six separate attacks against enemy combat ships, during which they sank five destroyers, endured multiple bombings by enemy aircraft, and survived three separate and prolonged depth charge attacks. The men needed sleep and the submarine needed repairs, including to her ice cream maker, the loss of which caused considerable disappointment to the crew as they sailed home.

Upon their return to Australia, Dealey was recommended for the Medal of Honor for his command of the submarine during the patrol, and Lynch was awarded a Navy Cross. The aggressiveness and courage and sheer endurance that the crew of the *Harder* had displayed was astounding, but it took its toll, on Dealey in particular. He had seen what the Japanese antisubmarine destroyers and float planes could deliver, and he had survived their worst. As a result, he grew overly cavalier and dismissive of the enemy's tactics. He was also suffering from a case of shock, undoubtedly post-traumatic stress, but when it was suggested that he stay behind and not command the *Harder*'s next patrol, he was insistent, demanding that he take his place on board. Lynch was transferred away to assume command of his own submarine and was therefore not on board the *Harder* when she set out late the following month for her sixth patrol to the sea around Dasol Bay in the Philippines. On August 24, in company with the USS *Hake*, the *Harder* went deep to evade a Japanese minesweeper pinging the area with its sonar, and fifteen depth charges were dropped on her. The *Hake* survived, but the *Harder* and her crew were never seen again. Japanese records tell of a great deal of oil, wood chips, and cork floating in the water after the depth charge barrage, all that remained of the legendary *Harder* and her captain and crew. Dealey would be awarded his Medal of Honor posthumously.

1938
USNA

WOODROW WILSON McCRORY

Waelder, Texas

Life begins at 6:20 for Mac, and it's always a busy day when The Lucky Bag's miser-in-chief swings into action. Characteristic of those strong, silent men of the southwest he says little, but his golden silence is often pierced by humorous take-offs on the unbeatable system. An ideal roommate, Mac; he repays borrowed stamps and fans the dying spark of social interest in our room but won't drag blind for his best friend. We wonder at the time-worn phrase, "You can't win," for Mac has been consistent in throwing the Academic Department for a loss, at the same time proving his athletic ability at pole-vaulting. His will be smooth sailing, and with his likable qualities and warm disposition it's bound to be sunny. We know him as more than an officer and a gentleman—a friend.

The Lucky Bag, 1938

Chapter Twenty-Two

THE *PARCHE'S* MELEE

By the summer of 1944, the U.S. Navy's submarines had evolved from a meager collection of older boats with disrespected crews using outdated tactics to a well-supplied and well-led force of lethal killers. The submarines delivered by the Navy's shipbuilders as the war progressed bore increasingly sophisticated and effective equipment and arms, and the commanders of these new submarines were skippers who, as historian Keith Wheeler wrote, "had learned their trade in a far harder school than peacetime exercises." The result was an "undersea [fighting force] of awesome efficiency," one that would by year's end sink over five hundred Japanese merchant ships totaling an astounding 2.3 million tons, half of the war-long total.[1] And what they were sinking were shiploads of critical supplies: oil, rice, rubber, coal, iron ore, asbestos, bauxite, and nickel. To put it in perspective, loads of much-needed oil from the Dutch East Indies declined from 1.5 million barrels a month in the middle of 1943 to a mere 300,000 barrels by the autumn of 1944, a "trickle."[2] It was primarily the Submarine Force that caused these crippling losses. And it was not solely the merchant fleet that was suffering at the hands of the American submariners. In 1944 Sam Dealey and his fellow submarine commanders would sink one Japanese battleship, seven aircraft carriers, two heavy cruisers, seven light cruisers, thirty destroyers, and seven submarines.

On June 17, 1944, the submarine *Parche* slipped away from her moorings on Midway Island and set out to sea on her second war patrol, reaching her station off Babuyan Island in the Luzon Strait later that month. The *Parche*, named for a small butterfly fish found in and around the world's coral reefs, was among the newer *Balao*-class submarines and thus sported a relatively thick hull made of high-tensile steel, which afforded her a test depth of 412 feet, deeper than most other American subs at the time. She also featured four 1,600-horsepower Fairbanks Morse 10-cylinder diesel engines in her power plant and could do slightly better than twenty knots on the surface, and eight and a half knots submerged.

The captain of the *Parche* was Commander Lawson P. Ramage, nicknamed "Captain Red." It was an apt name, for Ramage was fiery, impatient, and brash, but he also possessed in spades the qualities star submarine captains were made of: aggression, courage, coolness under pressure, and a rare and devious cunning. He had taken command of the *Parche* upon her commissioning earlier in the war at the Portsmouth Navy Yard and immediately set about putting together a hand-picked crew of exceptional officers, as well as a nucleus of veteran enlisted men who knew their business. One of the officers he chose was Woodrow Wilson McCrory, USNA '38, who would serve as his executive officer and assistant approach officer on board.

Born in Waelder, Texas, in rural Gonzales County on June 21, 1914, McCrory had been blessed from a young age with uncommon intelligence and leadership ability and was valedictorian of his high school class. Square-jawed, muscular, and fierce-looking, McCrory was a member of the pole-vault team at the Academy, studied mechanical engineering, and, most notably, graduated sixth in the Class of 1938. After two years of prewar service on board the cruiser *Concord*, he volunteered for submarine duty.

During his time in the Silent Service, McCrory had been regarded by his sub crews as serious, strict, and no-nonsense. His enlisted men were initially afraid of the young Texan but grew to respect and admire him for his courage and his integrity. Called "Mac" by the officers he served with, McCrory's first assignment was to the *S-48*, where he learned and then taught submarine battle tactics from 1941 until 1943, quickly developing a reputation as one of the smartest officers in the submarine fleet.

After twenty-nine days patrolling the Luzon Strait and chasing radar sightings through rough seas marred by forty-foot waves, driving rain, little visibility, and heavy force 12 winds that, at times, rolled the submarine 13 degrees (the remnants of a typhoon south of them), the *Parche* had nothing to show for her efforts but dead time and a full complement of torpedoes. Periscope patrols in such turbulent seas were impossible, and there was little for the men to do but endure, pray for improved weather, and hope for better luck. Several targets had been spotted over the weeks, including an aircraft carrier, but each time the ships had slipped away from them over the horizon before the *Parche* could run them down. Ramage was growing increasingly impatient.

But they were in the right spot, so the *Parche* continued to wait and watch. That July, with the Marianas and the bulk of New Guinea in American hands, the Japanese were rushing troopships loaded with reinforcements to various islands in the Philippines, and waiting for them were packs of American submarines, including Ramage's. The table was set for what would become "one of the Pacific war's wildest melees."[3]

Early on the morning of July 30, hours before dawn, the nearby American submarine *Hammerhead* sent the *Parche* a report of a seven-ship convoy with three escorts sailing on a heading of 175 degrees about thirty miles north of her position. Ramage, like a hound to the hunt, set a course to intercept and sped after the ships.

By midmorning a contact was finally spotted. The *Parche*'s lookouts reported smoke in the far distance, moving left to right across the horizon. Quickly, one column morphed into five, with at least three planes circling overhead protectively, an umbrella of aircraft lethal to any submarine trying to attack. The convoy itself soon came into view, heading southeast toward the Babuyan Islands. The *Parche* followed at full speed, with another American submarine, the *Steelhead*, close by. It took the rest of the afternoon and evening to close the convoy, but by 0240 on the morning of July 31 the *Parche* picked up radar interference dead ahead at a distance of 34,000 yards. The moon was settling on the black surface of the ocean as Ramage ordered battle stations and commenced to close the convoy's track. By 0313 he had brought the *Parche* in close—so close, in fact, that a Japanese escort lay just off her starboard bow at 6,000 yards. Ramage's radar crew were now reporting ten targets out there on the dark water, some beyond the escort and just visible to the lookouts. The sky was overcast, with scattered rain clouds moving across the sea, and soon two more escorts appeared menacingly nearby. Though the *Parche* had not yet been spotted, her position on the sea was becoming untenable, and her officers and crew knew it. Ramage quickly chose to reverse the field and close in astern of the second of the escorts that were out there, an extremely audacious move, but before long the *Parche* was inside the escorts with the ships of the convoy dead ahead, six thousand yards distant. Ramage commenced his approach on the nearest target and made ready his tubes. In the rain and the darkness, the *Parche* lost the target, so Ramage swung full starboard and quite suddenly slid down the side of a merchant ship that appeared out of the night, just two hundred yards away. He circled back around for another run at the Japanese vessel and, at 0359, prepared to fire his bow tubes. Spotters saw the *Parche*, however, and the merchantman's captain turned the vessel away. Seeing that he was going to miss, Ramage checked his fire. Two Japanese rockets arced into the night, an alarm for the rest of the convoy. Quickly, Ramage spotted two more large tankers off his starboard bow, so he swung right to close on them at almost full speed. The submarine's plotters were still tracking the first vessel, however, and the merchant ship, now behind the *Parche*, suddenly reemerged in what was a good firing position for the sub, so Ramage fired his No. 7 tube, and the men on the submarine heard an explosion through the water not two minutes later. Then he turned his attention back to the two tankers in front of him and at 0407 fired on the lead ship with his four bow tubes from fifteen hundred yards. His first torpedo struck a tanker's bow, disintegrating it, while the following three blew apart the ship's bridge, quarter, and stern. The tanker sank fast, leaving behind only a small oil fire on the water.

In the middle of a thrashing convoy now, with escorts searching for him but blocked by the tankers they were trying to protect, Ramage came hard right to bring his stern tubes to bear on the second merchant ship and fired three more torpedoes from just twelve hundred yards away. His torpedomen raced to load their tubes as fast as they were able. Ramage's first shot missed, but the second two hit forward of the tanker's superstructure, slowing it down. Desperate to destroy the American submarine and end its destructive rampage, the Japanese escort vessels opened up with machine guns and flares, firing indiscriminately, their bullets kicking up spray on the sea as they sent tracers zipping over the water and shell bursts and flares flaming through the dark, but the *Parche* still had not been damaged, and Ramage would not be dissuaded from bagging more ships. Shells screamed around him "with the din of an exploding fireworks factory."[4] The flares hovering above the water silhouetted the transports and tankers nicely. At 0412 Ramage commenced a run on yet another target, one with a sizable superstructure that, as he wrote in his report, was "just asking for trouble."[5] Still on the surface, he veered left, then right. Below him McCrory and his men sweated and grunted and tried to keep track of the information pouring in and of Ramage's shouted commands. The forward torpedo room reported that two reloads were ready to fire, and Ramage sent them on their way four minutes later. As close as he was, he could hardly miss, and both fish hit another Japanese vessel squarely amidships, breaking her in two and sending her under in minutes. Ramage avoided a nearby escort and closed on yet another tanker, one with her deck guns manned. He sailed in close and the tanker "opened up with everything he had," but the *Parche* was too close; the shells soared above them as the Japanese gun crews were unable to depress their tubes far enough.[6] Ramage sent all of his extra lookouts below and fired three stern tubes at the ship, sinking her. Again, only a small oil fire was left to mark where she had gone down.

Two of the convoy's escorts off the *Parche*'s port quarter now caught sight of the submarine and concentrated their machine-gun fire on the Americans, but Ramage still refused to flee the area. He turned to follow the "prize of the evening," a large transport in the distance, when, off the starboard bow, he spotted a small, fast-moving escort tearing in to ram them.[7] He called for the engine room to pour on the oil and turned sharply to starboard when halfway across the small ship's bow, and he was able to swing the stern clear, the Japanese screaming not more than fifty feet away as he slid past. They had escaped immediate destruction but still found themselves boxed in. Straight ahead was a large escort, so Ramage decided to fire down her throat, and at 0429 he commenced once again launching his bow tubes. Two were right in the groove and exploded. While passing the wounded ship, which had slowed "as if she had run her bow into a mud bank," Ramage fired one more torpedo from his stern: a direct hit, it blasted into the stricken transport squarely amidships.[8]

Ramage appraised the situation. The escort vessels were still tearing through the water after him, firing at the *Parche* and at each other in the confusion. Eight pips filled his radar screen. In the distance the large tanker he had struck earlier was down by the bow and smoking but did not appear to be otherwise sinking, so, refusing to leave well enough alone, Ramage resolved to go back and "deliver the coup-de-grace."[9] Before he could reach her, though, the ship turned up and sank head first. According to his radarmen, the rest of the contacts on the water were small, at ranges between 2,000 and 12,000 yards, so Ramage sailed cleanly away as dawn broke.

Ramage, McCrory, and the *Parche* left the area forty-six minutes after the attack began. In that time, they had fired all nineteen of their torpedoes and scored fifteen hits, and would be credited with sinking a large 10,200-ton tanker, a 4,400-ton passenger-cargo vessel, and a transport. As Ramage wrote, after weeks of disappointing patrols and bad weather, he and the *Parche* had "hit the jackpot with a vengeance."[10] It had been "the maddest surface action yet fought by a submarine in the Pacific."[11] He would be awarded the Medal of Honor, as historian Keith Wheeler wrote, "less for what he had done than for the way he had done it."[12] As the monograph recommending Ramage for the medal described it, "The commanding officer in his series of attacks against a large heavily escorted enemy convoy ... [conducted] one of the outstanding attacks in submarine warfare to date.... Attaining the ultimate in aggressiveness, exceptional courage, personal heroism, and bearing, the Commanding Officer sagaciously and with consummate skill ... [obtained] 14 or 15 hits in this brilliant night surface attack."[13]

When asked why he had rushed headlong through a string of escorts into the middle of a large convoy, Ramage shrugged and replied simply, "I got mad."[14]

Later that year, on December 11, McCrory took over command of the *Parche* from Ramage and set out with her on the submarine's fourth war patrol off the Ryukyu Islands. He would lead her safely on two additional patrols, during which the *Parche* would sink two cargo ships, three minesweepers, a guard boat, and other small enemy vessels around the Japanese home islands in the war's dying months. McCrory brought the submarine back into Pearl Harbor for the last time on July 28, 1945. The *Parche* ended her service as one of the most highly decorated ships in World War II's Pacific Submarine Force, earning five battle stars and two Presidential Unit Citation awards during her six patrols. McCrory had been on board for all of them.

By early January 1945, Japan's ability to keep its factories supplied and its people fed had been fatally crippled as the Submarine Force allowed almost nothing to reach the Home Islands. According to Keith Wheeler, "The US submarines had [by that time] worked themselves out of a job—at least so far as their primary mission of sinking enemy ships was concerned."[15] With an economy enormously dependent on fuel, oil, and raw materials shipped on the sea from China, Malaya, and the Netherlands East Indies, the damage inflicted by America's submarines on the Empire of Japan was insurmountable. While the Navy's surface ships, carrier fleets, and naval aviators progressively destroyed the Japanese navy's combat strength, the "undersea flotilla" of submarines progressively destroyed Japan's very ability to wage war.[16] Eminent historian Max Hastings called the U.S. Navy's Submarine Force "the most critical single contribution to the American defeat of Japan."[17]

Yet despite its triumphs, the Navy's Submarine Force suffered heavy losses of its own during the war in the Pacific. Of the 288 American submarines in service in the Pacific Theater, 52 were lost, almost 1 in 5.[18] These numbers were certainly fewer than those of the Axis navies—the Imperial Japanese Navy lost 128 submarines, and the German Kriegsmarine an astonishing 781—but they were terribly high nonetheless.[19]

By the late spring of 1945, General Douglas MacArthur had successfully taken Manila, and American heavy bombers were continuing lethal campaigns against lingering Japanese-held territories and cities across the Home Islands. On March 10, a firebombing raid on Tokyo by over 275 B-29 Superfortresses killed over 80,000 people. In response to these bombing attacks, the Japanese continued to deploy their feared kamikazes. Operation Iceberg, the American invasion of Okinawa, began on April 6, involving 548,000 Army,

Navy, and Marine personnel, 320 combat vessels, and over 1,000 support ships. President Franklin D. Roosevelt passed away on April 12, and Harry S. Truman was sworn in as the nation's thirty-third president that same day. Two days later, Tokyo was bombed again, and ten square miles of the city were wiped clean by a firestorm started by 2,139 tons of incendiaries filled with jellied fuel. Whole swaths of the city burned until there was nothing left for the flames to consume. Australian troops landed on the east coast of Borneo on May 1, the first moves by the Allies to free the Dutch East Indies from Japanese occupation. Ten days later, after a bitterly slow and bloody advance across the island, U.S. Marines launched an assault on Okinawa's capital city, Naha. Casualties had been severe throughout the campaign, among them those caused by the continuing kamikaze attacks against Navy ships supporting the attacks offshore, including, on May 12, six major strikes by 1,092 of the *kikusui*, or "floating chrysanthemums." As June approached, the battle for Okinawa neared its conclusion, with the last Japanese troops clinging to positions along a defensive line on the south side of the island.

On May 15, the submarine *Whale* set off on her eleventh war patrol for enemy-controlled waters off Japan's coastline. The captain of the submarine was Commander Freeland Carde, USNA '38, and his mission was to bring his sub into the waters off Japan and conduct lifeguard patrols involving the rescue of downed American airmen. The *Whale* was on station and had begun her patrolling by late July.

A vast armada of three hundred American planes droned across the sky above the *Whale* and her crew on the morning on July 24. The submarine waited for reports of downed planes to arrive, and before long lookouts spotted an aircraft ditching fifteen miles ahead. Then, not thirty minutes later, a damaged Grumman Avenger ditched alongside the submarine, about three hundred yards off her starboard bow, and reports were received of a third plane down in the area. It was clear that the pilots had been briefed on the submarine's location and, if they were in danger, told to crash-land into the sea nearby. Carde turned to the nearest plane and sailed over as the pilot climbed out onto the Avenger's wing before slipping and falling into the sea. Lookouts on the sub noticed that the man's plane had been punctured by flak and that his rubber raft had been opened but not inflated. Sailors on the submarine's deck tossed the man a life ring, but he made no effort to reach for it. He seemed to be barely floating, his uninflated Mae West life preserver uselessly flapping in the waves. Before a diver could jump in, the aviator disappeared beneath the sea, never to reappear. Carde quickly headed for another of the downed planes at flank speed. One plane still in the air orbited the crash site, while another vectored the *Whale* to the correct location where her pilots floated in a life raft. As the submarine approached, the circling plane dropped smoke on the water near the raft, and Carde flooded the aft section of the submarine a bit so that the pilots were able to paddle their boat onto the deck, sodden but safe. As Carde turned quickly at right full rudder to rescue more airmen in the water nearby, the *Whale* slid by a floating mine, not five feet away from the sub's hull. Carde wrote in his boat's war report, "Many stomachs sank to the deck" at the sight of it.[20]

Over the next few days, the *Whale* received reports on the positions of twelve downed planes, spread out over a sixty-mile area. Five of these men were so far into the Bungo Suido, the strait between the Japanese islands of Kyushu and Shikoku, that they were beyond the submarine's reach, but Carde was committed to saving as many as he could. On the afternoon of July 29, he directed the rescue of Second Lieutenant James C. Brechtbill, USAAF, from a life raft bobbing on the sea in a restricted area off the Japanese coast. An hour later the *Whale* brought on board George S. Lomas, an Army Air Corps pilot with a dislocated shoulder.

The survivors in the water knew to hoist red flags as high as possible atop their rafts. Doing so doubled the ranges at which lookouts on friendly submarines could spot them. One pilot in a life raft was spotted by the sub's lookouts as the airman jumped up and down to attract attention. Not every man could be found, however. Carde turned his submarine every which way on the sea for six hours trying to find one man, aided by as many as seven planes in the area, but the man was never seen. He brought on board several members of a B-29 crew who had lost a propeller while returning from a raid and had floated on the sea for two days. By determining where the men were picked up and in what order they had jumped from the plane, Carde and his officers were able to make a fair estimate of the course of the plane and where the others might be found.

On August 9 the *Whale*, now fairly crowded with its extra passengers, transferred the sixteen pilots it had saved from the water to another submarine, the USS *Blackfish*, and then headed for Pearl Harbor and some rest. On the way eastward across the Pacific, on August 15, Carde and his officers were alerted to President Harry Truman's declaration announcing that the final Japanese capitulation had been received and that all offensive operations against Japan should cease. The war had ended.

Etched in marble on the walls of Memorial Hall at the Naval Academy are the names of each year's graduates who have died in combat around the world, in battles large and small, in wars and conflicts both gloried still and quickly unremembered. The roster of those from the Class of 1938 killed in World War II is a long one, sixty-eight names, listed in the order in which they died. Inscribed near the top is Ensign Harry Howell, a "fair-haired son of steel mills and railroads" from Ben Avon, Pennsylvania, who broke many a drag's heart on hop weekends and knew even on the Yard that the sky was his calling, and an aviator's life his avocation.[21] Ohio's John Black, nicknamed "Blacky," was an indefatigably cheerful man, an avid amateur radio enthusiast and fan of both classical and swing music who kept the Navy football team near and dear to his heart. Big Samuel Hunter from Pittsburgh, black-haired and square-jawed, described himself as "rough, tough and ugly," but to his classmates he was big-hearted, easygoing, and kind, and a first-class fighting man.[22]

Oswald Zink from Ghent, New York, often entertained his classmates with renditions of "The Old Pine Tree" at full-dress parades, and John Woodruff, or "Woof Woof," won N-Stars with the track team. The list includes the names of six pilots from the Class of 1938 who were killed during the Battle of Midway. Their names are clustered together, about halfway down the list: Howard F. Clark, Roy O. Hale Jr., J. Thomas Eversole, Leonard W. Thornhill, Osborne B. Wiseman, and Curtis W. Howard. The cheerful and much-liked southerner Jep Jonson's *Lucky Bag* biography includes the lines "You don't have to ask him if he's having a grand time in life. It's in his face and every action." The thinking was that

Washington, DC's, Jimmy Ray would be a four-star someday, and David Nickerson had spent time in the Army before falling away and seeking out an appointment to the Naval Academy. Don Hamilton from Roswell, New Mexico, had wanted to attend the Naval Academy since he was a boy, and once there was a talented boxer and football player. Generous, savvy, and loyal, he was captured early in the war by the Japanese after his ship went down in the South Pacific, and he died of malnutrition while languishing in their cruel POW camps.

Pete Blauvelt and Al Sbisa were submariners who disappeared with their boats in early 1943, Blauvelt on board the *Amberjack* and Sbisa on the *Grampus*. As with so many submarines that failed to return, the details of these sinkings remain a mystery. John MacLaughlin played soccer and lacrosse at the Academy before becoming a pilot in the U.S. Marine Corps, eventually attaining the rank of major and assuming command of a Marine fighter squadron. In January 1944 he and his men flew their planes into a typhoon in the Pacific, and twenty-one of the twenty-three aircraft were forced down by the storm. MacLaughin, one of those forced to ditch, was never seen again, leaving behind a wife and their nine-month-old son. Keene Hammond survived two crash landings during the war while serving with VF-4 in the Atlantic on board the USS *Ranger*. By June 1944 Hammond, now a captain, and his squadron were transferred to the Pacific and assigned to the USS *Essex*. On January 6, 1945, Hammond led a dozen Hellcats on a mission to bomb enemy ships in harbor on the northwestern coast of Luzon, in the Philippines, and while dropping in amid heavy ship- and shore-based antiaircraft fire, Hammond's plane was hit. He was able to pilot the stricken aircraft out to sea, but his oil pressure was falling, and about eight miles southwest of Vigan City, Hammond turned his plane into the wind for a water landing. His pilots who watched him hit the sea reported a flash believed to be caused by the explosion of the belly tank, and the plane cartwheeled over the wave tops before coming to rest and sinking in seconds. Planes circled the area for twenty minutes, but nothing was found.

These men and scores of others joined Eric Allen, Brink Bass, and Ernest Cody as men lost to the sea during the century's mightiest conflagration, their lives achingly short, their glories everlasting.

1938
US NA

EPILOGUE

Lodwick Alford returned from the Far East in January 1943 before heading back to war on board the USS *Mobile* and participating in the Gilberts, Marshalls, and Solomons Campaigns. He later took part in the invasions of Iwo Jima and Okinawa on board the USS *Bennington*, and, after the war, continued to serve on destroyers during the Korean War. He retired as a captain in 1967, moving to Sea Island, Georgia. Alford passed away on December 19, 2007, in his hometown of Sylvester, Georgia.

Marion Buaas, who served with Alford on board the yacht *Isabel*, sailed home in 1943 and went into lighter-than-air aviation for a time before returning to surface ships later in his career. He retired from the Navy in July 1968 as a captain, worked for several years in the defense industry, and died in 1999.

Ben Pickett stayed in the Navy and was captain of the USS *Albany* when the ship fired three antiaircraft missiles simultaneously, launching the Navy into the modern era of missile warfare; eventually he became an admiral. Upon his retirement after thirty-three years in the service, Pickett settled in Gloucester, Virginia, where he was visited often by his old friends from his days on the *St. Louis*. He was later diagnosed with prostate and lung cancers but never let his spirit waver, weathering the treatments in a steady and uncomplaining way. He died on October 24, 2000.

Bill Spears, who was on the destroyer USS *Pope* when it was sunk by the IJN in the Java Sea in early 1942, spent the rest of World War II in POW camps on the island of Celebes, and survived. After the war, while visiting the families of prisoners who did not make it, he met and married the widow of Don Hamilton, a classmate of his at the Naval Academy who had also been captured by the Japanese and died in captivity. As historian Gavan Daws wrote regarding World War II prisoners, "Every POW saw men like himself die horribly. . . . Those who survived had to struggle to keep themselves alive in the camps, and then struggle to live with themselves afterward back in the world. They were branded by the experience."[1] Spears also served during the Korean War and commanded a refueling ship on blockade duty during the Cuban Missile Crisis. He retired from the service in 1969 and lived the rest of his life in Alexandria, Virginia. He died of a heart attack on April 10, 1995.

After surviving his long years in captivity, Hal Hamlin returned to active duty after the war and retired as a captain in 1961. He passed away in 1978.

Immediately after the war ended, Ray Calhoun brought the *Dewey* up to New York City, where she was decommissioned at the Brooklyn Navy Yard on October 19, 1945. He continued to serve, taking command of the destroyer USS *Moale* and then Destroyer Squadron Six during the Cuban Missile Crisis. He was then deputy chief of staff for U.S. Naval Forces Europe and director of research at the National War College. In private life Calhoun served as vice chancellor of the Minnesota state university system from 1968 to 1978, when he retired to Wilmington, North Carolina, with his wife, Betsy. He passed away at the age of 101 on August 29, 2015.

Jim Marks, captain of the ill-fated destroyer *Hull*, returned to duty after the inquiry into his ship's sinking during Typhoon Cobra and was present for the Japanese surrender on board the battleship *Missouri* in Tokyo Bay on September 2, 1945. After the war he held several commands during the Korean War and the Cuban Missile Crisis. He ended his career as commanding officer of Clarksville Base, the Navy's facility at Ft. Campbell, Kentucky, that housed nuclear weapons. Marks retired in 1968 and moved with his family to Winter Park, Florida. Sadly, his health declined in his later years, and he died by suicide in 1986.

The naval aviators from the Class of 1938 likely suffered a higher percentage of losses than any other Naval Academy class before or after.[2] They had graduated from Pensacola just months before the war started and were therefore assigned immediately to combat squadrons with very little training or experience. It showed in the long and sad roster of pilots from that class who did not return from combat missions.

Norman Jack "Dusty" Kleiss was married to Jean Mochon for sixty-four years. Together they would raise five children. After twenty-eight years in the Navy, he retired as a captain in 1962 and enjoyed a second career working in the aerospace industry. His beloved Jean died in 2006. When asked in 2012 how he had managed to survive the war and live such a long life, the still sharp-minded Kleiss said from his apartment in San Antonio, "The only thing I can presume is that He has not yet found me worthy to reach all those other saints above us."[3] On his one hundredth birthday in 2016, Kleiss received phone calls and letters from Senator John McCain, former president George H. W. Bush, and President Barack Obama, among others. "I'm anything but a hero," he told a CNN reporter late in his life. "I was only doing what at the time was the proper thing to do."[4] In his memoirs, written shortly before his death, he wrote, "In the end, I'm just a lucky fool, blessed with a long life and lasting love. Fortune favors me, but I have yet to comprehend why."[5] He passed away in his sleep on April 22, 2016.

Marion Dufilho, whose guns had jammed during Butch O'Hare's legendary dogfight over the USS *Lexington* on February 20, 1942, would be killed a few months later, on August 24, when he was shot down during the Battle of the Eastern Solomons while serving as a section leader with Fighting Squadron Five (VF-5) off the USS *Saratoga*. He and his squadron flew to intercept an onrushing formation of eleven Japanese bombers before they were set upon by an "overwhelming force" of Zeros.[6] Dufilho, flying through fire from his own antiaircraft guns below, personally destroyed two of the enemy planes and damaged a third before being shot down and killed. He was awarded a posthumous Navy Cross for his actions, along with a Distinguished Flying Cross and a Purple Heart. The destroyer escort USS *Dufilho* (DE - 423), launched in 1944, was commissioned in his honor. A memory marker inscribed with his name stands in Arlington National Cemetery, and he is today considered a local hero back home in Opelousas, Louisiana.

Richard "Dick" Crommelin fought in both the Battles of the Coral Sea and Midway while assigned to the carrier *Yorktown* in the war's first year. He was awarded two Navy Crosses for his actions. As the war dragged on, Crommelin was promoted to senior squadron commander of VF-88. He was killed in a midair collision with his wingman while flying an F6F on July 14, 1945.

William "Bill" Leonard, who also participated in the Coral Sea and Midway battles as well as Guadalcanal and the Solomon Islands, became a fighter ace early in the war. After surviving these actions that claimed so many of his fellow aviators, Leonard was attached to the staff of the Commander Fleet Air, West Coast, where, as part of his duties, he flew the first captured Japanese Zero fighter, as well as the experimental Ryan XFR-1 Fireball; trained new pilots; and helped advance Navy fighter doctrine and tactics. He returned to combat operations as part of Admiral John S. McCain Sr.'s TF 38 during the final push to victory in the Pacific. Leonard ultimately flew 170 combat missions during World War II, was credited with shooting down six enemy aircraft in aerial combat, and won two Navy Crosses. After the war he attained the rank of rear admiral before retiring in July 1971 to Virginia Beach, Virginia. Bill Leonard died after a brief illness on August 21, 2005.

The metal gondola of the mysterious *L-8*, the blimp Ernest Cody had been piloting when he disappeared off the coast of California, was stored for many years at Wingfoot Lake before being rebuilt in 1968 as the Goodyear blimp *America*, which was used to televise sporting events around the nation for over a decade. In 2003 the gondola was donated by the Goodyear company to the National Museum of Naval Aviation, where it resides today.

Almost 1,300 vessels were sunk by American submariners during World War II, totaling 6.1 million tons. Fatalities among the officers and crew of these American submarines totaled 3,131—22 percent of all U.S. Navy sailors who experienced submarine operations—and the highest loss of any branch of the wartime U.S. armed forces. Their contributions to the overall war effort were indispensable.

Frank "Tiny" Lynch enjoyed a truly distinguished career in World War II as the executive officer on board the *Harder* and then earned two Navy Crosses while commanding officer of the *Haddo* on her eighth and ninth war patrols. He served in the Navy until July 1954. His last assignment was as the commanding officer of the USS *Sumner*, a destroyer. He was bringing his ship to Korea for service in the war when, as she was moored in Colombo, Ceylon (now Sri Lanka) on May 25, 1953, he was seriously injured in an automobile accident while riding in a taxi. He awoke weeks later on a hospital ship in Manila Bay to discover he had lost the use of one eye, ending his naval career. Lynch retired as a captain and died from congestive heart failure in Carson City, Nevada, on May 3, 2002.

After the war, Woodrow Wilson "Mac" McCrory went on to command one of the Navy's first snorkel-equipped submarines, the USS *Halfbeak*, followed by a radar picket submarine division and a series of surface ships. McCrory's last submarine duty was as officer-in-charge of the Submarine School in New London. He retired from the Navy in his mid-fifties as a rear admiral after suffering a pair of heart attacks and returned to Texas, settling in Austin with his wife, Dort. McCrory died in the fall of 1977 and was buried in Arlington National Cemetery. The conning tower and periscopes of the USS *Parche* are on permanent display at the Bowfin Submarine Museum at Pearl Harbor.

Herb Mandel commanded the submarine *Medregal* after the war and then enjoyed a series of assignments: operations officer for Amphibious Group 4 in Little Creek, Virginia; command of the antisubmarine destroyer USS *Douglas H. Fox* during the Cold War's early years; and command of Destroyer Division 252 out of Pearl Harbor. He was later appointed Chief of Navy-Marine Military Assistance Planning, a prestigious staff position, and commanded the USS *Maury*, the Navy's largest hydrographic survey ship. While he was serving with the *Maury* his beloved wife Gloria became ill and, to care for her, Mandel retired from active service. Gloria died on February 20, 1962. Mandel spent his post-Navy career with the Electric Boat Company and the stock brokerage firm Advest. He passed away on February 4, 2016, in Lenox, Massachusetts.

Carl Dwyer was sent back to the Naval Academy after the war's end to serve as an instructor in electrical engineering. He then commanded the destroyers *Fiske* and *Rooks*, then Destroyer Division 132 and Destroyer Squadron 23. Ashore, he served for several years in the Office of the Chief of Naval Operations until his retirement from the Navy in 1967 as a full captain. He and his wife Katherine were married for fifty-eight years, until her death in 2002. He followed her on May 6, 2004, passing away quietly in Rockville, Maryland. He was buried with full military honors in Arlington Cemetery.

Of the 438 midshipmen who graduated that June day in 1938, 86 served through World War II, Korea, and Vietnam, and 78 served thirty years or more in the United States Navy.

ACKNOWLEDGMENTS

I would first like to thank my grandfather, Alden J. Laborde, USNA Class of '38, who was the principal motivation for this book and a man of uncommon faith, kindness, and integrity. It was his copy of *The Lucky Bag* that sparked an idea and set me on a path of research and writing that has been tremendous fun over the last seven years. I only wish he had lived to see the finished product.

I would also like to thank my parents, Karen and Monroe Laborde, for their constant love and support, and my siblings, Cregan, Jeffrey, and Sarah. My in-laws Eric Ehrensing, Jennifer Laborde, and Blair Laborde also provided a great deal of encouragement, as well as some much-appreciated advice (and research material).

My editor at the Naval Institute Press, Steve Catalano, graciously took on a first-time author and was an indispensable source of wisdom and guidance throughout the process. Without Steve, Jessica Sparks, Brennan Knight, Christi Stanforth, Claire Noble, Sam Caggiula, Elena Pelton, Adam Kane, and the rest of the staff at the Naval Institute Press, this project would never have seen the light of day. Thank you! I would also like to extend my gratitude to Dr. Stan Fisher at the U.S. Naval Academy for reviewing an early version of the manuscript and providing much valuable advice.

I also wish to thank my friends and colleagues at The Futures Company / Kantar, past and present, including Don Abraham, Nneka Anozie, Aarti Asrani, David Bersoff, Charlie Billings, Jonathan Brimfield, Michelle Brisson, Kevin Brown, Lauren Caddick, Chris Carbone, Andrew Cardman, Mike Carlucci, John Catlett, Sage Catlett, Ann Clurman, Gayle

Davey, Manny Davis, Kathy Duan, Callie Edwards, Casey Ferrell, Sam Golub, Bryan Gordon, Mary Kay Harrity, Callie Henson, Jeff Howanek, Elsa Irby, Anushkaa Jain, Aishwarya Jaiswal, Jennifer James, Patrick Kalgreen, Simon Kaplan, Liz Katsadouros, Carlyn Kelly, Maura Kolkmeyer, Steve Kulp, Deanna Leedberg, Rebecca Lin, Ryan McConnell, Stephanie McDonald, Tom Morley, Heather Mosser, Sara Nettesheim, Alexa Noorigian, Cathy Ortiz, Mary Panks-Holmes, Carrie Parker, Valeria Piaggio, Jon Prevett, Adrienne Pulido, Jeanne Riek, Peter Rose, Anna Ross, Emily Ross, Colleen Sharp, J. Walker Smith, Kara Sundby, Daphane Tan, Steve Travers, Michelle Trayne, Craig Wood, Andrew Yohanan, Kelly Zeller, and Graham Zimmerman. Their support, wise counsel, and good cheer over the years was indispensable.

The staffs and digital archivists at the USNA's Nimitz Library, the Naval History & Heritage Command, and Fold3.com were extremely helpful and provided material that was absolutely critical to the telling of this book's stories.

Finally, I would like to thank my children, Anna Lily, Lucy, and Lawson, for their love and enthusiasm, and my wife, Amanda. Her faith in me, her encouragement during the days when things did not go smoothly, and her constant love were the wind in my sails.

NOTES

Prologue

1. Bob Drury and Tom Clavin, *Halsey's Typhoon: The True Story of a Fighting Admiral, an Epic Storm, and an Untold Rescue* (New York: Grove, 2007), 137–38.
2. Drury and Clavin, *Halsey's Typhoon*, 137–38.
3. C. Raymond Calhoun, *Typhoon: The Other Enemy. The Third Fleet and the Pacific Storm of December 1944* (Annapolis: Naval Institute Press, 1981), 76.
4. Calhoun, *Typhoon*, 55.
5. Calhoun, 57.
6. Calhoun, 57.
7. Calhoun, 58.
8. Calhoun, 76–77.
9. Drury and Clavin, *Halsey's Typhoon*, 170.
10. Drury and Clavin, 170.
11. Calhoun, *Typhoon*, 76–77.
12. Theodore Roscoe, *United States Destroyer Operations in World War II* (Annapolis: Naval Institute Press, 1953), 449.

Chapter One. On the Yard

1. Alden J. Laborde, *My Life and Times* (New Orleans: Laborde Printing, 1996), 61.
2. Kendall Banning, *Annapolis Today: A Guide to the United States Naval Academy* (New York: Funk & Wagnalls, 1938), 4.
3. Ian Toll, *Pacific Crucible: War at Sea in the Pacific, 1941–1942* (New York: W. W. Norton, 2012), xiv.

4. Banning, *Annapolis Today*, 3–4.
5. Toll, *Pacific Crucible,* 4.
6. Toll, 5.
7. *The Lucky Bag* (Rochester, NY: DuBois Press, 1938), 27.
8. Robert Sleight, *1600 Men: A Personal Remembrance, United States Naval Academy, 1932–1936* (White Stone, VA: Brandylane, 1998), 9.
9. Herbert Mandel, *Submarine Captain and Command at Sea* (Naples, FL: Collage Books, 2005), 205.
10. Glenn Cummings, *Trailing a Texas Eagle: The Life and Legacy of Lt. Commander Harry Brinkley Bass* (Virginia Beach: Donning, 2010), 10.
11. Cummings, *Trailing a Texas Eagle,* 44.
12. Descriptions of Memorial Hall are based on Banning's *Annapolis Today*, Arthur Trader and Henry Sturdy's *Seeing Annapolis and the Naval Academy* (Annapolis: Capital-Gazette Press, 1938); Arthur Middleton's *Annapolis on the Chesapeake* (Annapolis: Historic Annapolis, 1988); and Linda Foster's *United States Naval Academy Annapolis* (Baltimore: Image Publishing, 2002), as well as my own observations.
13. Banning, *Annapolis Today*, 13.
14. Banning, 14.
15. Statistics from the class of 1938 are available online through the U.S. Naval Academy Leadership Conference, https://www.usna.edu/LeadershipConference/Sponsors/Class_of_38.php.
16. Banning, *Annapolis Today*, 14.
17. Mandel, *Submarine Captain and Command at Sea*, 209.
18. *Reef Points: 1936–1937* (Annapolis: U.S. Naval Academy, 1936), 19.
19. *Reef Points*, 75.
20. *Reef Points*, 75.
21. Ronald Spector, *Eagle against the Sun: The American War with Japan* (New York: Vintage Books, 1985), 18.
22. *Lucky Bag,* 363, Sleight, *1600 Men*, 85.
23. *Reef Points*, 5.
24. Toll, *Pacific Crucible*, xvi.
25. *Lucky Bag*, 358.
26. *Lucky Bag*, 361.
27. *Lucky Bag*, 363.
28. Mandel, *Submarine Captain and Command at Sea*, 224.
29. Sleight, *1600 Men*, 45–46.

30. Mandel, *Submarine Captain and Command at Sea*, 224.
31. Banning, *Annapolis Today*, 99–100.
32. *The Log*, February 25, 1938, 18.
33. *The Log*, March 18, 1938, 22.
34. *The Log*, 22.
35. Banning, *Annapolis Today*, 302.
36. Banning, 302.
37. Sleight, *1600 Men*, 132–33.
38. Banning, *Annapolis Today*, 302.
39. Banning, 302.
40. Franklin D. Roosevelt, "Address at the United States Naval Academy Graduation," June 2, 1938, in Gerhard Peters and John T. Woolley, *The American Presidency Project*, https://www.presidency.ucsb.edu/documents/address-the-united-states-naval-academy-graduation.
41. Roosevelt.
42. Roosevelt.
43. Toll, *Pacific Crucible*, xxiii.
44. Sleight, *1600 Men*, 144.
45. Banning, *Annapolis Today*, 317.
46. Laborde, *My Life and Times*, 79.
47. Lewis Carroll, *Through the Looking-Glass and What Alice Found There*, cited in *The Lucky Bag*, 1938, 26–27.
48. *Lucky Bag*, 1938, 26–27.

Chapter Two. Fuses

1. *The Log*, May 6, 1938, 1.
2. Derek Mercer, *Chronicle of the Second World War* (London: Longman Group UK, 1990), 12.
3. Alden Laborde, *My Life and Times* (New Orleans: Laborde Printing, 1996), 83.
4. Terry Hughes and John Costello, *The Battle of the Atlantic: The First Complete Account of the Origins and Outcome of the Longest and Most Crucial Campaign of World War II* (New York: Dial Press, 1977), 54.
5. Hughes and Costello, *Battle of the Atlantic*, 54.
6. Laborde, *My Life and Times*, 82–83.
7. Laborde, 83.

8. Ian Toll, *Pacific Crucible: War at Sea in the Pacific, 1941–1942* (New York: W. W. Norton, 2012), 137.
9. David Sears, *Pacific Air: How Fearless Flyboys, Peerless Aircraft and Fast Flattops Conquered the Skies in the War with Japan* (Cambridge, MA: Da Capo, 2011), 60.
10. Sears, *Pacific Air*, 60.
11. Glenn Cummings, *Trailing a Texas Eagle: The Life and Legacy of Lt. Commander Harry Brinkley Bass* (Virginia Beach: Donning, 2010), 144.
12. Cummings, *Trailing a Texas Eagle,* 141.
13. Cummings, 141.
14. Cummings, 144–45.
15. Interview with C. Raymond Calhoun, University of North Carolina Wilmington (UNCW), Transcript No. 33.
16. Raymond Calhoun, *Tin Can Sailor: Life Aboard the USS* Sterett, *1939–1945* (Annapolis: Naval Institute Press, 1993), 3–4.
17. Calhoun, *Tin Can Sailor*, 3–4.
18. Calhoun interview, UNCW, Transcript No. 33.
19. Calhoun interview, UNCW, Transcript No. 33.
20. Calhoun interview, UNCW, Transcript No. 33.
21. Calhoun interview, UNCW, Transcript No. 33.
22. Calhoun interview, UNCW, Transcript No. 33.
23. Calhoun, *Tin Can Sailor*, 11.
24. Calhoun, *Tin Can Sailor*, 13.
25. Lodwick Alford, *Playing for Time: War on an Asiatic Fleet Destroyer* (Bennington, VT: Merriam Press, 2006), 11–12.
26. Alford, *Playing for Time*, 21.
27. Alford, 21.
28. Alford, 20.
29. Alford, 22.
30. Alford, 27.
31. Alford, 30–31.
32. Alford, 31.
33. Hughes and Costello, *The Battle of the Atlantic*, 70.
34. Hughes and Costello, 84.

35. Hughes and Costello, 94.
36. Hughes and Costello, 113.
37. Hughes and Costello, 122.
38. George Waller, *Pearl Harbor: Roosevelt and the Coming of the War* (Boston: D. C. Heath, 1965), 5.
39. Barrie Pitt and the Editors of Time-Life Books, *The Battle of the Atlantic* (New York: Time-Life Books, 1977), 151–52.
40. Barrie Pitt and the Editors of Time-Life Books, *Battle of the Atlantic*, 176.
41. Barrie Pitt and the Editors of Time-Life Books, 176.
42. Hughes and Costello, *Battle of the Atlantic,* 176.
43. Hughes and Costello, 176.
44. Hughes and Costello, 185.
45. Francis Miller, *History of World War II: Armed Services Memorial Edition* (Washington: Esperanto, 1945), 293.
46. Ronald Spector, *Eagle against the Sun: The American War with Japan* (New York: Vintage Books, 1985), 63.
47. Spector, *Eagle against the Sun*, 63.
48. Spector, 314–15.
49. Spector, 315–16.
50. Dan Van der Vat, *Pearl Harbor: The Day of Infamy—An Illustrated History* (New York: Basic Books, 2001), 23.
51. Theodore Roscoe, *United States Destroyer Operations in World War II* (Annapolis: Naval Institute Press, 1953), 43.
52. Steve Twomey, *Countdown to Pearl Harbor: The 12 Days to the Attack* (New York: Simon & Schuster, 2016), 28.
53. Miller, *History of World War II*, 320.
54. Spector, *Eagle against the Sun*, 77.
55. Hughes and Costello, *Battle of the Atlantic*, 187.
56. Gordon Prange, with Donald M. Goldstein and Katherine V. Dillon, *Dec. 7, 1941: The Day the Japanese Attacked Pearl Harbor* (New York: Warner Books, 1988), 3.
57. Walter Lord, *Day of Infamy* (New York: Bantam Books, 1957), 14.
58. Robert Sullivan, ed., *Pearl Harbor: America's Call to Arms* (New York: Time-Life, 2001), 53.

Chapter Three. Suicide Missions and Other Routine Duties

1. Ronald Spector, *Eagle against the Sun: The American War with Japan* (New York: Vintage Books, 1985), 87–88; Stanley Weintraub, *Long Day's Journey into War: Dec. 7, 1941* (New York: Truman Talley Books, 1991), 44.
2. Lodwick Alford, *Playing for Time: War on an Asiatic Fleet Destroyer* (Bennington, VT: Merriam Press, 2006), 44–45.
3. Alford, *Playing for Time*, 44–45.
4. The other ship chosen for the mission was the 75-ton *Lanikai*, with a top speed of six knots, sails, and a very old engine.
5. Robert Sullivan, ed., *Pearl Harbor: America's Call to Arms* (New York: Time-Life, 2001), 46.
6. Sullivan, *Pearl Harbor*, 56.
7. Spector, *Eagle against the Sun*, 89.
8. Gordon Prange, with Donald M. Goldstein and Katherine V. Dillon, *Dec. 7, 1941: The Day the Japanese Attacked Pearl Harbor* (New York: Warner Books, 1988), 42.
9. Sullivan, *Pearl Harbor*, 51.

Chapter Four. Tiger, Tiger, Tiger

1. Steve Twomey, "Countdown to Infamy: The High Stakes Gamble and False Assumptions That Detonated Pearl Harbor 75 Years Ago," *Smithsonian*, December 2016, 98.
2. Dan Van der Vat, *Pearl Harbor: The Day of Infamy—An Illustrated History* (New York: Basic Books, 2001), 64.
3. Stanley Weintraub, *Long Day's Journey into War: Dec. 7, 1941* (New York: Truman Talley Books, 1991), 244.
4. Van der Vat, *Pearl Harbor*, 106.
5. Gordon Prange, with Donald M. Goldstein and Katherine V. Dillon, *December 7, 1941: The Day the Japanese Attacked Pearl Harbor* (New York: Warner Books, 1988), 272–73.
6. USS *St. Louis*—War Diary, December 1941, micro serial no. 40683, reel A27, Fold3.com, 1–2.

Chapter Five. The Lucky Lou

1. Ian Toll, *Pacific Crucible: War at Sea in the Pacific, 1941–1942* (New York: W. W. Norton, 2012), xxxvi.
2. Gordon Prange, with Donald M. Goldstein and Katherine V. Dillon, *Dec. 7, 1941: The Day the Japanese Attacked Pearl Harbor* (New York: Warner Books, 1988), 259–60.
3. Walter Lord, *Day of Infamy* (New York: Bantam Books, 1957), 125.
4. Dan Van der Vat, *Pearl Harbor: The Day of Infamy—An Illustrated History* (New York: Basic Books, 1988), 131.
5. Prange, *Dec. 7, 1941*, 311.
6. Prange, 312.
7. Included in a description of the attack found at https://www.ussstlouis.net. The two-man submarine that fired at the *St. Louis* was believed to have been sunk by the USS *Blue* shortly after its attack. The *Blue* dropped two depth charges and subsequently spotted a large oil slick on the surface of the water.
8. The "he" here is the pilot of the Midget-E submarine, Sub-Lieutenant Masaharu Yokoyama.
9. *USS* St. Louis—*War Diary*, December 1941, micro serial no. 40683, reel A27, https://www.fold3.com/, 4.
10. Prange, *Dec. 7, 1941*, 339.
11. R. O. Hudgins, "My Journal," https://www.ussstlouis.net.
12. Lord, *Day of Infamy*, 182.
13. Lord, 182.
14. Paul Casdorph, *Let the Good Times Roll: Life at Home in America during WWII* (New York: Paragon House, 1989), 2.
15. Glenn Cummings, *Trailing a Texas Eagle: The Life and Legacy of Lt. Commander Harry Brinkley Bass* (Virginia Beach: Donning, 2010), 159–60.

Chapter Six. Friendly Fire

1. John Lundstrom, *The First Team: Pacific Naval Air Combat from Pearl Harbor to Midway* (Annapolis: Naval Institute Press, 1984), 9.
2. David Sears, *Pacific Air: How Fearless Flyboys, Peerless Aircraft, and Fast Flattops Conquered the Skies in the War with Japan* (Cambridge, MA: Da Capo, 2011), 13–14.
3. Sears, *Pacific Air*, 14.

4. One of VB-6's SBDs had reported the sighting of the Japanese carrier and accompanying cruiser. What he saw, however, were friendly forces he had misidentified.
5. Sears, *Pacific Air*, 14.
6. Sears, 15. The top-secret YE-ZB homing radio beacon (nicknamed the "Zed Baker") had been developed by the U.S. Navy in 1938 and would serve as the primary aircraft-carrier homing beacon for the next two decades. A line-of-sight continuous-wave directional Morse code signal, it saved countless American lives during the war and was never discovered by the Japanese during the war.
7. This description of the aftermath of Pearl Harbor is found in Ian Toll, *Pacific Crucible: War at Sea in the Pacific, 1941–1942* (New York: W. W. Norton, 2012), 39.
8. Sears, *Pacific Air*, 16.
9. From "The Past Is Another Country," posted online to *Air and Naval Weapons* on June 17, 2015.
10. From the Pearl Harbor blog, https://www.pacificaviationmuseum.org/.
11. Lundstrom, *First Team*, 11.
12. Attributed to James Daniels in the *Honolulu Advertiser* at thehonoluluadvertiser.com/specials/pearlharbor60.com.
13. Toll, *Pacific Crucible*, 32–33.
14. Toll, 33.

Chapter Seven. Opening Onslaughts

1. Stanley Weintraub, *Long Day's Journey into War: Dec. 7, 1941* (New York: Truman Talley Books, 1991), 256.
2. Weintraub, *Long Day's Journey*, 256.
3. Lodwick Alford, *Playing for Time: War on an Asiatic Fleet Destroyer* (Bennington, VT: Merriam Press, 2006), 7–8.
4. Alford, *Playing for Time*, 7–8.
5. Alford, 46.
6. Alford, 34.
7. Alford, 35–36.
8. Alford, 50.
9. Alford, 53–54.

10. Ronald Spector, *Eagle against the Sun: The American War with Japan* (New York: Vintage Books, 1985), 129.
11. Ian Toll, *Pacific Crucible: War at Sea in the Pacific, 1941–1942* (New York: W. W. Norton, 2012), 236.
12. Alford, *Playing for Time*, 80.
13. Alford, 84.
14. Alford, 85.
15. Alford, 92–93.
16. Alford, 94.
17. Alford, 99.
18. Alford, 101–3.
19. Theodore Roscoe, *United States Destroyer Operations in World War II* (Annapolis: Naval Institute Press, 1953), 98.
20. Alford, *Playing for Time*, 105.
21. Alford, 106–7.
22. Alford, 107.
23. Alford, 107.
24. Paul Dull, *A Brief History of the Imperial Japanese Navy (1941–1945)* (Annapolis: Naval Institute Press, 1978), 64.
25. Alford, *Playing for Time*, 112.
26. Alford, 113.
27. Alford, 145.
28. Alford, 146.
29. Alford, 147.
30. Alford, 146.
31. Alford, 150–51.

Chapter Eight. A Matter of Survival

1. Theodore Roscoe, *United States Destroyer Operations in World War II* (Annapolis: Naval Institute Press, 1953), 102.
2. Roscoe, *United States Destroyer Operations*, 102.
3. Commander Walter Winslow, “Nightmare Night USS *Houston* Went Down,” USNI, August 22, 2014.
4. Roscoe, *United States Destroyer Operations*, 102.
5. Winslow, “Nightmare Night.”

6. Lodwick Alford, *Playing for Time: War on an Asiatic Fleet Destroyer* (Bennington, VT: Merriam Press, 2006), 158.
7. Alford, *Playing for Time*, 160.
8. Alford, 164.
9. Ian Toll, *Pacific Crucible: War at Sea in the Pacific, 1941–1942* (New York: W. W. Norton, 2012), 258.
10. Alford, *Playing for Time*, 164.
11. Alford, 165.
12. *The USS* Houston *Sinking: War Diary*, 1942, https://www.fold3.com/.
13. Toll, *Pacific Crucible*, 259.
14. Toll, 260.
15. *USS* Houston—*Action Report, on the Battle of Sunda Strait*, March 13, 1942, file no. FF6/A16-3, micro serial no. 40219, reel A12, https://www.fold3.com/, 2.
16. Winslow, "Nightmare Night."
17. Winslow.
18. *USS* Houston—*Action Report, on the Battle of Sunda Strait*, 2.
19. *USS* Houston—*Action Report, on the Battle of Sunda Strait*, 7–8.
20. Statement by Harold S. Hamlin, USN, https://www.ibiblio.org/.
21. Statement by Leon Rogers, USN, https://www.ibiblio.org/.
22. Statement by Rogers, https://www.ibiblio.org/.
23. Statement by Rogers, https://www.ibiblio.org/.
24. Statement by Rogers, https://www.ibiblio.org/.
25. Letter from Leon Rogers to his parents, September 15, 1941, https://www.usshouston.org/bluebonnetfiles.com.

Chapter Nine. Guardian Angels

1. From William Penninger's account of the USS *Pope*'s last action (ed. Clay Ramsey) at https://www.navsource.org.
2. Paul Dull, *A Brief History of the Imperial Japanese Navy (1941–1945)* (Annapolis: Naval Institute Press, 1978), 90; and *USS* Pope—*Action Report*, March 1, 1942, file no. FF6/A16-3, micro serial no. 40247, reel A14, https://www.fold3.com/.
3. Theodore Roscoe, *United States Destroyer Operations in World War II* (Annapolis: Naval Institute Press, 1949), 108.
4. Roscoe, *United States Destroyer Operations*, 108.

5. Roscoe, 109.
6. Roscoe, 109.
7. *USS* Pope—*Action Report*, March 1, 1942, 6.
8. Roscoe, *United States Destroyer Operations in World War II*, 109.
9. Roscoe, 109.
10. Lodwick Alford, *Playing for Time: War on an Asiatic Fleet Destroyer* (Bennington, VT: Merriam Press, 2006), 155.
11. Alford, *Playing for Time*, 188.
12. Alford, 191.
13. Alford, 192.
14. Alford, 192.
15. Alford, 192–93.
16. Alford, 193.
17. Alford, 186.

Chapter Ten. In Irons

1. Bob Drury and Tom Clavin, *Halsey's Typhoon: The True Story of a Fighting Admiral, an Epic Storm, and an Untold Rescue* (New York: Grove, 2007), 45–46.
2. Drury and Clavin, *Halsey's Typhoon*, 125.
3. Drury and Clavin, 125.
4. Drury and Clavin, 82.
5. Drury and Clavin, 110.
6. Drury and Clavin, 111.
7. *The Lucky Bag* (Rochester: DuBois Press, 1938), 151.
8. Drury and Clavin, *Halsey's Typhoon*, 134.
9. Drury and Clavin, 88.
10. Raymond Calhoun, *Typhoon: The Other Enemy. The Third Fleet and the Pacific Storm of December 1944* (Annapolis: Naval Institute Press, 1981), 153.
11. Drury and Clavin, *Halsey's Typhoon,* 92.
12. Calhoun, *Typhoon*, 17–18.
13. Drury and Clavin, *Halsey's Typhoon*, 103.
14. Drury and Clavin, 103.
15. Calhoun, *Typhoon*, 32.

16. Interview with C. Raymond Calhoun, University of North Carolina Wilmington (UNCW), transcript no. 272.
17. Drury and Clavin, *Halsey's Typhoon*, 105–6.
18. Drury and Clavin, 105–6.
19. Calhoun, *Typhoon*, 36.
20. Drury and Clavin, *Halsey's Typhoon*, 123.
21. Drury and Clavin, 122.
22. Drury and Clavin, 121–22.
23. Drury and Clavin, 145.
24. Drury and Clavin, 127.
25. Drury and Clavin, 130.
26. Calhoun, *Typhoon*, 51.
27. Calhoun, 17.
28. Calhoun, 52.
29. Calhoun, 46.
30. Calhoun, 46.
31. Calhoun, 54–55.
32. Calhoun interview, UNCW, transcript no. 272.
33. Calhoun, *Typhoon*, 76.
34. Calhoun, 168.
35. Calhoun, 65.
36. *USS* Hull—*War Diary*, December 1941, https://www.fold3.com/.
37. Calhoun, *Typhoon*, 65.
38. Drury and Clavin, *Halsey's Typhoon*, 166–67.
39. Calhoun, *Typhoon*, ix.
40. Calhoun, 65.
41. Drury and Clavin, *Halsey's Typhoon*, 194.
42. Calhoun, *Typhoon*, 66.
43. Theodore Roscoe, *United States Destroyer Operations in World War II* (Annapolis: Naval Institute Press, 1953), 448.
44. Drury and Clavin, *Halsey's Typhoon*, 204.
45. Drury and Clavin, 204.
46. Calhoun, *Typhoon*, 71.
47. Calhoun, 67.
48. Drury and Clavin, *Halsey's Typhoon*, 220.
49. Drury and Clavin, 220.
50. Drury and Clavin, 225.

51. Calhoun, *Typhoon*, x.
52. Calhoun, 107.
53. Calhoun, 138.
54. Calhoun, 138.
55. Interview with C. Raymond Calhoun, University of North Carolina Wilmington (UNCW), transcript no. 272.
56. Drury and Clavin, *Halsey's Typhoon*, 269–72.
57. Calhoun, *Typhoon*, 163–64.
58. Drury and Clavin, *Halsey's Typhoon*, 272.
59. Drury and Clavin, 272.

Chapter Eleven. Dusty

1. Max Hastings, *Retribution: The Battle for Japan, 1944–1945* (New York: Vintage Books, 2007), 105.
2. Hastings, *Retribution*, 105.
3. Norman Kleiss, with Timothy and Laura Orr, *Never Call Me a Hero: A Legendary American Dive-Bomber Pilot Remembers the Battle of Miday* (New York: William Morrow, 2017), 39.
4. Kleiss, *Never Call Me a Hero*, 109.
5. Kleiss, xvii; *Hastings, Retribution*, 105.
6. Kleiss, *Never Call Me a Hero,* 39.
7. Stephen Moore, *Pacific Payback: The Carrier Aviators Who Avenged Pearl Harbor at The Battle of Midway* (New York: NAL Caliber, 2014), 47.
8. Kleiss, *Never Call Me a Hero*, 47.
9. Kleiss, 48.
10. Kleiss, 52.
11. Kleiss, 54.
12. Moore, *Pacific Payback*, 47.
13. Timothy Orr and Laura Orr, "Jack 'Dusty' Kleiss and the Battle of Midway," *Daybook* 15, no. 4 (2012): 8–11.
14. Kleiss, *Never Call Me a Hero*, 65.
15. Moore, *Pacific Payback*, 48–49.
16. Kleiss, *Never Call Me a Hero*, 73.
17. Moore, *Pacific Payback*, 49.
18. Orr and Orr, "Jack 'Dusty' Kleiss and the Battle of Midway," 10.

19. Ian Toll, *Pacific Crucible: War at Sea in the Pacific, 1941–1942* (New York: W. W. Norton, 2012), 199.
20. Toll, *Pacific Crucible*, 204.
21. Toll, 208.
22. Moore, *Pacific Payback*, 75–76.
23. Kleiss, *Never Call Me a Hero*, 129.
24. Toll, *Pacific Crucible*, 213.
25. Interview with Norman Kleiss, CNN.com, April 28, 2016, https://www.cnn.com/videos/us/2016/04/28/captain-dusty-kleiss.cnn.
26. Moore, *Pacific Payback*, 93.
27. Moore, 99.
28. Kleiss, *Never Call Me a Hero*, 143.
29. Toll, *Pacific Crucible*, 219.
30. Moore, *Pacific Payback*, 14–15; Orr and Orr, "Jack 'Dusty' Kleiss and the Battle of Midway," 8–11.
31. Moore, *Pacific Payback*, 108.
32. Moore, 108.
33. Moore, 119.
34. Moore, 119.
35. Moore, 127–28.
36. Moore, 128.
37. Moore, 162.

Chapter Twelve. The Wingman

1. Descriptions of Butch O'Hare's engagement—for which he was awarded the Medal of Honor—are from John Lundstrom, *The First Team: Pacific Naval Air Combat from Pearl Harbor to Midway* (Annapolis: Naval Institute Press, 1984); David Sears, *Pacific Air: How Fearless Flyboys, Peerless Aircraft and Fast Flattops Conquered the Skies in the War with Japan* (Cambridge, MA: Da Capo, 2011); Steve Ewing and John B. Lundstrom, *Fateful Rendezvous: The Life of Butch O'Hare* (Annapolis: Naval Institute Press, 1997); Phil Keith, *Stay the Rising Sun: The True Story of USS* Lexington, *Her Valiant Crew, and Changing the Course of World War II* (Minneapolis: Quarto, 2015); and Bruce Gamble, *Fortress Rabaul: The Battle for the Southwest Pacific, January 1942–April 1943* (Minneapolis: Zenith Press, 2010).

2. From a letter written by Marion Dufilho to his parents, dated July 31, 1942, https://johnkellynightfighterpilot.wordpress.com/category/lieutenant-marion-dufilho/.
3. Sears, *Pacific Air*, 95.
4. Sears, 95.
5. Sears, 99.
6. Lundstrom, *First Team*, 116–17.
7. Lundstrom, 116–17.
8. Lundstrom, 116–17; Gamble, *Fortress Rabaul*, 88.
9. Ewing and Lundstrom, *Fateful Rendezvous*, 137.
10. Lundstrom, *First Team*, 117.

Chapter Thirteen. First Skirmishes

1. John Lundstrom, *The First Team: Pacific Naval Air Combat from Pearl Harbor to Midway* (Annapolis: Naval Institute Press, 1984), 154.
2. Glenn Cummings, *Trailing a Texas Eagle: The Life and Legacy of Lt. Commander Harry Brinkley Bass* (Virginia Beach: Donning, 2010), 170–71.
3. Stephen Moore, *Pacific Payback: The Carrier Aviators Who Avenged Pearl Harbor at the Battle of Midway* (New York: NAL Caliber, 2014), 136.
4. Lundstrom, *First Team*, 161–62.
5. Descriptions of the attacks on Lae and Salamaua from John Lundstrom's invaluable *The First Team* and Stephen Moore's *Pacific Payback.*
6. Edwin Hoyt, *How They Won the War in the Pacific: Nimitz and His Admirals* (New York: Lyons Press, 2000), 71.
7. Ian Toll, *Pacific Crucible: War at Sea in the Pacific, 1941–1942* (New York: W. W. Norton, 2012), 329.
8. *Naval Action in Coral Sea Area, May 4–8, 1942*, CINCPAC File A16(4) (0010N), May 27, 1942, micro serial number 41078, reel A39, https://www.fold3.com/, 3–4.
9. Toll, *Pacific Crucible*, 334.
10. Lundstrom, *First Team*, 218–20.
11. Ronald Spector, *Eagle against the Sun: The American War with Japan* (New York: Vintage Books, 1985), 159–60.
12. Toll, *Pacific Crucible*, 334.
13. Paul Dull, *A Brief History of the Imperial Japanese Navy (1941–1945)* (Annapolis: Naval Institute Press, 1997), 128.

14. Toll, *Pacific Crucible*, 338.
15. Toll, 338–39.
16. Toll, 338–39.
17. Lundstrom, *First Team*, 241.

Chapter Fourteen. Toots from Alabama

1. John Lundstrom, *The First Team: Pacific Naval Air Combat from Pearl Harbor to Midway* (Annapolis: Naval Institute Press, 1984), 248; Ian Toll, *Pacific Crucible: War at Sea in the Pacific, 1941–1942* (New York: W. W. Norton, 2012), 341–43; and *Naval Action in Coral Sea Area, May 4–8, 1942*, CINCPAC File A16(4) (0010N), May 27, 1942, micro serial no. 41078, reel A39, https://www.fold3.com/.
2. Lundstrom, *First Team*, 248.
3. Toll, *Pacific Crucible*, 343–44.

Chapter Fifteen. Just Gone

1. *USS* Lexington*—Report of Action, Battle of the Coral Sea, May 7–8, 1942*, https://www.fold3.com/.
2. John Lundstrom, *The First Team: Pacific Naval Combat from Pearl Harbor to Midway* (Annapolis: Naval Institute Press, 1984), 263.
3. Francis Miller, *The History of World War II: Armed Services Memorial Edition* (Washington, DC: Esperanto, 1945), 506.
4. Ian Toll, *Pacific Crucible: War at Sea in the Pacific, 1941–1942* (New York: W. W. Norton, 2012), 351.
5. Toll, *Pacific Crucible*, 352.
6. Lundstrom, *First Team*, 289.
7. Lundstrom, 291–92.
8. Lundstrom, 297.
9. Lundstrom, 297.
10. Lundstrom, 304.
11. Toll, *Pacific Crucible*, 355.
12. Toll, 356.
13. Office of Naval Intelligence, U.S. Navy, *Combat Narratives: The Battle of the Coral Sea—Consisting of the Actions at Tulagi, May 4th; off Misima, May 7th; and in the Coral Sea on May 8th, 1942*, micro serial no. 48849, reel A313, https://www.fold3.com/, 28.

14. Toll, *Pacific Crucible*, 358–59.
15. *USS* Lexington—*Report of Action, Battle of the Coral Sea, May 7–8, 1942.*
16. David Sears, *Pacific Air: How Fearless Flyboys, Peerless Aircraft and Fast Flattops Conquered the Skies in the War with Japan* (Cambridge, MA: Da Capo, 2011), 127–28.
17. Lundstrom, *First Team*, 341.
18. Lundstrom, 341.
19. Lundstrom, 341.
20. "Roy Orestus Hale," Alchetron.com, accessed November 12, 2024, https://alchetron.com/Roy-Orestus-Hale,-Jr.
21. *USS* Lexington—*Report of Action, Battle of the Coral Sea, May 7–8, 1942*; Toll, *Pacific Crucible*, 362.
22. *USS* Lexington—*Report of Action, Battle of the Coral Sea, May 7–8, 1942.*
23. Lundstrom, *The First Team*, 354.
24. *USS* Lexington—*Report of Action, Battle of the Coral Sea, May 7–8, 1942.*
25. *USS* Lexington—*Report of Action, Battle of the Coral Sea, May 7–8, 1942.*
26. *USS* Lexington—*Report of Action, Battle of the Coral Sea, May 7–8, 1942.*
27. Toll, *Pacific Crucible*, 374–75.
28. Miller, *History of World War II*, 503.
29. Office of Naval Intelligence, U.S. Navy, *Combat Narratives: The Battle of the Coral Sea*, 1.

Chapter Sixteen. Cocked Pistols

1. Gordon Prange, with David M. Goldstein and Katherine V. Dillon, *Miracle at Midway* (New York: Penguin, 1982), 271.
2. Prange, *Miracle at Midway*, 93.
3. Ian Toll, *Pacific Crucible: War at Sea in the Pacific, 1941–1942* (New York: W. W. Norton, 2012), 380.
4. Prange, *Miracle at Midway*, 64.
5. Prange, 103–4.
6. David Sears, *Pacific Air: How Fearless Flyboys, Peerless Aircraft and Fast Flattops Conquered the Skies in the War with Japan* (Minneapolis: Quarto, 2015), 137.
7. Prange, *Miracle at Midway*, 103–4.
8. Toll, *Pacific Crucible*, 390.

9. In World War II, American carriers were numbered in order of their commissioning: *Saratoga* was 3, *Yorktown* was 5, *Enterprise* was 6, and their fighter, bomber, scout, and torpedo squadrons were assigned numbers to match. The *Yorktown*'s fighter squadron, for instance, was designated VF-5.
10. Toll, *Pacific Crucible*, 390.
11. John Lundstrom, *The First Team: Pacific Naval Air Combat from Pearl Harbor to Midway* (Annapolis: Naval Institute Press, 1984), 396.
12. Lundstrom, *First Team*, 389.
13. Lundstrom, 399.
14. Norman Kleiss, *Never Call Me a Hero: A Legendary American Dive-Bomber Pilot Remembers the Battle of Midway* (New York: William Morrow, 2017), 181; Stephen L. Moore, *Pacific Payback: The Carrier Aviators Who Avenged Pearl Harbor at the Battle of Midway* (New York: NAL Caliber, 2014) 169–70.
15. Kleiss, *Never Call Me a Hero*, 181.
16. Moore, *Pacific Payback*, 169.
17. Lundstrom, *First Team*, 400; Robert Ballard and Rick Archbold, *Return to Midway: The Quest to Find the* Yorktown *and the Other Lost Ships from the Pivotal Battle of the Pacific War* (Toronto: Madison Press Books), 32.
18. Lundstrom, *First Team*, 400.
19. Prange, *Miracle at Midway*, 148.
20. Prange, 170.
21. Lundstrom, *First Team*, 412.
22. Moore, *Pacific Payback*, 174.
23. Kleiss, *Never Call Me a Hero*, 181.
24. Kleiss, 181.
25. Kleiss, 181.
26. Toll, *Pacific Crucible*, 418–19.
27. Moore, *Pacific Payback*, 176–77.
28. Moore, 184.
29. Kleiss, *Never Call Me a Hero*, 185.
30. Kleiss, 186.
31. Toll, *Pacific Crucible*, 409.
32. Moore, *Pacific Payback*, 178.

33. Lundstrom, *First Team*, 416; *Battle of Midway*, CINCPAC file no. A16, ser. 01693, June 15, 1942, micro serial no. 41273, reel A45, https://www.fold3.com/, 1.
34. Prange, *Miracle at Midway*, 190.
35. Prange, 239; Ballard and Archbold, *Return to Midway*, 72.
36. Prange, *Miracle at Midway*, 239.
37. Prange, 239.
38. Lundstrom, *First Team*, 418.
39. Ballard and Archbold, *Return to Midway*, 68–69.

Chapter Seventeen. Six Minutes

1. Ian Toll, *Pacific Crucible: War at Sea in the Pacific, 1941–1942* (New York: W. W. Norton, 2012), 424.
2. Toll, *Pacific Crucible*, 424.
3. Gordon Prange, with David M. Goldstein and Katherine V. Dillon, *Miracle at Midway* (New York: Penguin, 1982), 236.
4. Stephen Moore, *Pacific Payback: The Carrier Aviators Who Avenged Pearl Harbor at the Battle of Midway* (New York: NAL Caliber, 2014), 198.
5. *Battle of Midway*, CINCPAC file no. A16, ser. 01693, June 15, 1942, micro serial no. 41273, reel A45, https://www.fold3.com/, 2.
6. John Lundstrom, *The First Team: Pacific Naval Air Combat from Pearl Harbor to Midway* (Annapolis: Naval Institute Press, 1984), 431.
7. Lundstrom, *First Team*, 431.
8. Robert Ballard and Rick Archbold, *Return to Midway: The Quest to Find the* Yorktown *and the Other Lost Ships from the Pivotal Battle of the Pacific War* (Toronto: Madison Press Books, 1999), 76–77.
9. Ballard and Archbold, *Return to Midway*, 76–77.
10. Lundstrom, *First Team*, 432.
11. *Battle of Midway*, CINCPAC file no. A16, ser. 01693, June 15, 1942, 4.
12. See the Navy Cross citation for J. Thomas Eversole, "LTJG John Thomas Eversole," Military Hall of Honor, accessed November 14, 2024, https://militaryhallofhonor.com/honoree-record.php?id=91811.
13. Toll, *Pacific Crucible*, 425.
14. Ballard and Archbold, *Return to Midway*, 92.
15. Lundstrom, *First Team*, 428.

16. David Sears, *Pacific Air: How Fearless Flyboys, Peerless Aircraft and Fast Flattops Conquered the Skies in the War with Japan* (Cambridge, MA: Da Capo, 2011), 163.
17. *Report of Action: Bombing Squadron Six, June 4–6, 1942*, file no. FVB-6/A16, micro serial no. 41707, reel A60, https://www.fold3.com/, 4.
18. Sears, *Pacific Air*, 168–69.
19. Prange, *Miracle at Midway*, 270–72.
20. Toll, *Pacific Crucible*, 446.
21. Norman Kleiss, *Never Call Me a Hero: A Legendary American Dive-Bomber Pilot Remembers the Battle of Midway* (New York: William Morrow, 2017), 212.
22. Kleiss, *Never Call Me a Hero*, 213.
23. Lundstrom, *First Team*, 473–74.
24. Lundstrom, 474.
25. Lundstrom, 485–86.
26. Lundstrom, 492.
27. Lundstrom, 492.
28. Ballard and Archbold, *Return to Midway*, 102.
29. Lundstrom, *First Team*, 516.
30. Moore, *Pacific Payback*, 276 ; Kleiss, *Never Call Me a Hero*, 215.
31. Moore, *Pacific Payback*, 286–87.
32. Moore, 286–87.
33. Toll, *Pacific Crucible*, 455.
34. *The Lucky Bag* (Rochester, NY: DuBois Press, 1938), 79.
35. Lundstrom, *First Team*, 525.
36. Lundstrom, 525.
37. Moore, *Pacific Payback*, 298.
38. Prange, *Miracle at Midway*, 307.
39. Prange, 305.
40. Prange, 305.
41. Kleiss, *Never Call Me a Hero*, 222.
42. Kleiss, 222.
43. Moore, *Pacific Payback*, 248.
44. Moore, 248.
45. *Battle of Midway*, CINCPAC file no. A16, ser. 01693, June 15, 1942, 8.
46. Toll, *Pacific Crucible*, 469.
47. Prange, *Miracle at Midway*, 363.

48. Prange, 397.
49. Moore, *Pacific Payback*, 353–54.
50. Toll, *Pacific Crucible*, 469.

Chapter Eighteen. Standby

1. Simon Winchester, *Pacific: Silicon Chips and Surfboards, Coral Reefs and Atom Bombs, Brutal Dictators, Fading Empires and the Coming Collision of the World's Superpowers* (New York: HarperCollins, 2015), 19.
2. "The Crash of Navy Blimp *L-8*," Check-Six.com, accessed November 12, 2024, https://www.check-six.com/Crash_Sites/L-8_crash_site.htm.
3. "Crash of Navy Blimp *L-8*."
4. "Crash of Navy Blimp *L-8*."
5. Steven Ruffin, *Flights of No Return: Aviation History's Most Infamous One-Way Tickets to Immortality* (Minneapolis: Quarto, 2015), 220.
6. Ruffin, *Flights of No Return*, 213.
7. "Crash of Navy Blimp *L-8*."
8. "Crash of Navy Blimp *L-8*."
9. Glenn Cummings, *Trailing a Texas Eagle: The Life and Legacy of Lt. Commander Harry Brinkley Bass* (Bloomington, IN: iUniverse, 2011), 228.

Chapter Nineteen. Chances Taken

1. Keith Wheeler, *War under the Pacific* (Chicago: Time-Life Books, 1980), 89.
2. Herb Mandel, *Submarine Captain and Command at Sea* (Naples, FL: Collage Books, 2005), 27.
3. Theodore Roscoe, *United States Submarine Operations in World War II* (Annapolis: Naval Institute Press, 1949), 16.
4. Mandel, *Submarine Captain and Command at Sea*, 29.
5. Wheeler, *War under the Pacific*, 45.
6. Roscoe, *United States Submarine Operations in World War II*, 5.
7. Roscoe, *United States Submarine Operations*, 19.
8. Roscoe, 19.
9. Roscoe, 19.
10. Wheeler, *War under the Pacific*, 46.
11. Mandel, *Submarine Captain and Command at Sea*, 31.
12. Mandel, 49.

13. Mandel, 48–49.
14. Mandel, 49.
15. Mandel, 56.
16. Mandel, 57.
17. *The Lucky Bag* (Rochester, NY: DuBois Press, 1938), 89.
18. Mandel, *Submarine Captain and Command at Sea*, 57.
19. Mandel, 57.
20. Mandel, 67–68.
21. Mandel, 68.
22. Mandel, 70.
23. Mandel, 70.
24. Mandel, 72–73.
25. Mandel, 75–76.
26. Mandel, 76.

Chapter Twenty. The End of Existence

1. Craig McDonald, *The USS* Puffer *in World War II: A History of the Submarine and Its Wartime Crew* (Jefferson, NC: McFarland, 2008), 56.
2. McDonald, *USS* Puffer, 49–50.
3. *USS* Puffer—*Report of War Patrol Number One*, COMSUBSPAC Patrol Report, file no. A16-3, micro serial no. 59334, reel A670, https://www.fold3.com/, 10.
4. McDonald, *USS* Puffer, 60; *USS* Puffer—*Report of War Patrol Number One*, 10.
5. *USS* Puffer—*Report of War Patrol Number One*, 10.
6. *USS* Puffer—*Report of War Patrol Number One*, 10.
7. McDonald, *USS* Puffer, 68.
8. McDonald, 72.
9. McDonald, 50.

Chapter Twenty-One. The Hit 'Em *Harder*

1. "The Loss of the USS Harder," accessed July 2021 at www.ussnautilus.org; no longer accessible.
2. "Loss of the USS *Harder*."
3. Theodore Roscoe, *United States Submarine Operations in World War II* (Annapolis: Naval Institute Press, 1949), 237.

4. Michael Sturma, *Death at a Distance: The Loss of the Legendary USS* Harder (Annapolis: Naval Institute Press, 2006), 22.
5. Sturma, *Death at a Distance*, 23.
6. Keith Wheeler, *War under the Pacific* (Chicago: Time-Life Books, 1980), 171.
7. *USS* Harder—*Report of Fifth War Patrol*, COMSUBSPAC Patrol Report, micro serial no. 83281, reel A1109, https://www.fold3.com/, 9.
8. *USS* Harder—*Report of Fifth War Patrol*, 10–11.
9. Wheeler, *War under the Pacific*, 171.
10. Wheeler, 171; *USS* Harder—*Report of Fifth War Patrol*, 15–16.
11. Wheeler, *War under the Pacific*, 171.
12. *USS* Harder—*Report of Fifth War Patrol*, 15–16.
13. Roscoe, *United States Submarine Operations*, 378.
14. *USS* Harder—*Report of Fifth War Patrol*, 17.

Chapter Twenty-Two. The *Parche*'s Melee

1. Keith Wheeler, *War under the Pacific* (Chicago: Time-Life Books, 1980), 166.
2. Wheeler, *War under the Pacific*, 166.
3. Wheeler, 174.
4. Theodore Roscoe, *United States Submarine Operations in World War II* (Annapolis: Naval Institute Press, 1949), 344.
5. *USS* Parche—*Report of First War Patrol*, COMSUBSPAC Patrol Report, file no. FF12-10/A16-3(15)/(16), micro serial no. 76117, reel A16-3, https://www.fold3.com/.
6. *USS* Parche—*Report of First War Patrol.*
7. *USS* Parche—*Report of First War Patrol.*
8. Roscoe, *United States Submarine Operations*, 344.
9. *USS* Parche—*Report of First War Patrol.*
10. *USS* Parche—*Report of First War Patrol.*
11. Roscoe, *United States Submarine Operations*, 344.
12. Wheeler, *War under the Pacific*, 175–76.
13. Roscoe, *United States Submarine Operations*, 345.
14. Wheeler, *War under the Pacific*, 175.
15. Wheeler, 187.

16. Max Hastings, *Retribution: The Battle for Japan, 1944–1945* (New York: Vintage Books, 2007), 273.
17. Hastings, *Retribution*, 167.
18. Roscoe, *United States Submarine Operations*, 491.
19. Hastings, *Retribution*, 269–70.
20. *USS* Whale—*Report of War Patrol Number Eleven*, COMSUBSPAC Patrol Report, file no. FF12-10(A)/A16-3(18), micro serial no. 142360, reel A1880, https://www.fold3.com/.
21. *The Lucky Bag* (Rochester, NY: DuBois Press, 1938), 125.
22. *Lucky Bag*, 287.

Epilogue

1. Gavan Daws, *Prisoners of the Japanese: POWs of World War II in the Pacific* (New York: Quill William Morrow, 1994), 19.
2. John K. Leydon, *A Score for '38* (Annapolis: Class of 1938, 1948), 259.
3. Norman Kleiss, *Never Call Me a Hero: A Legendary American Dive-Bomber Pilot Remembers the Battle of Midway* (New York: William Morrow, 2017), x.
4. As quoted at "Dusty Kleiss: A Hero of Midway Remembered," Naval Historical Foundation, April 25, 2016, https://www.navyhistory.org/2016/04/dusty-kleiss-a-hero-of-midway-remembered/.
5. Kleiss, *Never Call Me a Hero*, xi.
6. As quoted in Dufilho's Distinguished Flying Cross citation at Hall of Valor by Military Times, accessed November 14, 2024, https://valor.militarytimes.com/recipient/recipient-20373/.

BIBLIOGRAPHY

Published Sources

Alford, Lodwick H. *Playing for Time: War on an Asiatic Fleet Destroyer.* Bennington, VT: Merriam Press, 2006.

Annual Register of the United States Naval Academy, 1937–1938. Washington, DC: Government Printing Office, 1937.

Ballard, Robert D., and Rick Archbold. *Return to Midway: The Quest to Find the* Yorktown *and the Other Lost Ships from the Pivotal Battle of the Pacific War.* Toronto: Madison Press Books, 1999.

Banning, Kendall. *Annapolis Today: A Guide to the United States Naval Academy.* New York: Funk & Wagnalls, 1938.

Calhoun, C. Raymond. *Tin Can Sailor: Life Aboard the USS* Sterett, *1939–1945.* Annapolis: Naval Institute Press, 1993.

———. *Typhoon: The Other Enemy. The Third Fleet and the Pacific Storm of December 1944.* Annapolis: Naval Institute Press, 1981.

Caren, Eric C. *Pearl Harbor Extra: A Newspaper Account of the United States' Entry into World War II.* Edison, NJ: Castle Books, 2001.

Casdorph, Paul D. *Let the Good Times Roll: Life at Home in America during WWII.* New York: Paragon House, 1989.

Cummings, Glenn J. *Trailing a Texas Eagle: The Life and Legacy of Lt. Commander Harry Brinkley Bass.* Virginia Beach, VA: Donning, 2010.

Daws, Gavan. *Prisoners of the Japanese: POWs of World War II in the Pacific.* New York: Quill William Morrow, 1994.

Drury, Bob, and Tom Clavin. *Halsey's Typhoon: The True Story of a Fighting Admiral, an Epic Storm, and an Untold Rescue.* New York: Grove, 2007.

Dry, Dan. *United States Naval Academy.* Louisville, KY: Harmony House, 1987.

Dull, Paul S. *A Brief History of the Imperial Japanese Navy (1941–1945)*. Annapolis: Naval Institute Press, 1978.

Eubank, Keith. *The Origins of World War II*. 2nd ed. Arlington Heights, IL: Harlan Davidson, 1990.

Ewing, Steve, and John B. Lundstrom. *Fateful Rendezvous: The Life of Butch O'Hare*. Annapolis: Naval Institute Press, 1997.

Foster, Linda. *United States Naval Academy Annapolis*. Baltimore: Image Publishing, 2002.

Frank, Benis M., and Henry L. Shaw. *Victory and Occupation: History of the U.S. Marine Corps Operations in World War II*. Vol. 5. Washington, DC: Historical Branch, U.S. Marine Corps, 1968.

Gamble, Bruce. *Fortress Rabaul: The Battle for the Southwest Pacific, January 1942–April 1943*. Minneapolis: Zenith Press, 2010.

Grover, David H., and Gretchen G. Grover. *Captives of Shanghai: The Story of the* President Harrison. Napa, CA: Western Maritime Press, 1989.

A Guide Book to the United States Naval Academy: Showing Buildings, Roads, Athletic Fields, Drill Grounds and Historic Monuments, 1924. New York: U.S. Navy Records Bureau, 1924.

Gunston, Bill. *American Warplanes*. New York: Crescent Books, 1986.

Hastings, Max. *Retribution: The Battle for Japan, 1944–45*. New York: Vintage Books, 2007.

Holland, Rear Admiral W. J., Jr., USN (Ret.). *The Navy*. Washington, DC: Naval Historical Foundation, 2012.

Hoyt, Edwin P. *How They Won the War in the Pacific: Nimitz and His Admirals*. New York: Lyons Press, 2000.

Hughes, Terry, and John Costello. *The Battle of the Atlantic: The First Complete Account of the Origins and Outcome of the Longest and Most Crucial Campaign of World War II*. New York: Dial Press, 1977.

Ienaga, Saburo. *The Pacific War: 1931–1945*. Tokyo: Iwanami Shoten, 1968.

Kehn, D. M., Jr. *In the Highest Degree Tragic: The Sacrifice of the U.S. Asiatic Fleet in the East Indies*. Potomac, MD: Potomac Books, 2017.

Keith, Phil. *Stay the Rising Sun: The True Story of USS* Lexington, *Her Valiant Crew, and Changing the Course of World War II*. Minneapolis: Quarto, 2015.

Kershaw, Alex. *The Few: The American "Knights of the Air" Who Risked Everything to Save Britain in the Summer of 1940*. Philadelphia: Da Capo, 2006.

Kilmer, David. *Daughters of Infamy: The Stories of the Ships That Survived Pearl Harbor*. Bloomington, IN: iUniverse, 2011.

Kinder, Gary. *Ship of Gold in the Deep Blue Sea*. New York: Atlantic Monthly Press, 1998.

Kleiss, N. Jack "Dusty," with Timothy and Laura Orr. *Never Call Me a Hero: A Legendary American Dive-Bomber Pilot Remembers the Battle of Midway*. New York: William Morrow, 2017.

Laborde, Alden J. *My Life and Times*. New Orleans: Laborde Printing, 1996.

Leydon, John K., ed. *A Score for '38*. Annapolis: Class of 1938, 1948.

Loomis, Robert D. *Great American Fighter Pilots of World War II*. New York: Landmark Books, 1961.

Lord, Walter. *Day of Infamy*. New York: Bantam Books, 1957.

The Lucky Bag. Rochester, NY: DuBois Press, 1938.

Lundstrom, John B. *The First Team: Pacific Naval Air Combat from Pearl Harbor to Midway*. Annapolis: Naval Institute Press, 1984.

Mandel, Herbert I. *Submarine Captain and Command at Sea*. Naples, FL: Collage Books, 2005.

Mason, David. *U-Boat: The Secret Menace*. New York: Ballantine Books, 1968.

McDonald, Craig R. *The USS* Puffer *in World War II: A History of the Submarine and Its Wartime Crew*. Jefferson, NC: McFarland, 2008.

Mercer, Derek, ed. *Chronicle of the Second World War*. London: Longman Group UK, 1990.

Middleton, Arthur P. *Annapolis on the Chesapeake*. Annapolis: Historic Annapolis, 1988.

Miller, Francis T. *History of World War II: Armed Services Memorial Edition*. Washington, DC: Esperanto, 1945.

Miller, Nathan. *The U.S. Navy: An Illustrated History*. New York: American Heritage Publishing, 1977.

Moore, Stephen L. *Battle Surface! Lawson P. "Red" Ramage and the War Patrols of the USS* Parche. Annapolis: Naval Institute Press, 2011.

——— *Pacific Payback: The Carrier Aviators Who Avenged Pearl Harbor at the Battle of Midway*. New York: NAL Caliber, 2014.

Morris, James. *History of the US Navy*. New York: Exeter Books, 1984.

Pitt, Barrie, and the Editors of Time-Life Books. *The Battle of the Atlantic*. New York: Time-Life Books, 1977.

Prange, Gordon W., with Donald M. Goldstein, and Katherine V. Dillon. *Dec. 7, 1941: The Day the Japanese Attacked Pearl Harbor*. New York: Warner Books, 1988.

Prange, Gordon W., Donald M. Goldstein, and Katherine V. Dillon. *Miracle at Midway*. New York: Penguin, 1982.

Reef Points: 1936–37. Annapolis: US Naval Academy, 1936.

Roscoe, Theodore. *United States Destroyer Operations in World War II*. Annapolis: Naval Institute Press, 1953.

———. *United States Submarine Operations in World War II*. Annapolis: Naval Institute Press, 1949.

Ruffin, Steven A. *Flights of No Return: Aviation History's Most Infamous One-Way Tickets to Immortality*. Minneapolis: Quarto, 2015.

Sears, David. *Pacific Air: How Fearless Flyboys, Peerless Aircraft and Fast Flattops Conquered the Skies in the War with Japan*. Cambridge, MA: Da Capo, 2011.

Shaw, Norman. *Screened Her Going Down*. Albany, NY: Fort Orange Press, 1984.

Shirer, William L. *The Rise and Fall of the Third Reich: A History of Nazi Germany*. New York: Simon & Schuster, 1960.

Sleight, Robert. *1600 Men: A Personal Remembrance, United States Naval Academy, 1932–1936*. White Stone, VA: Brandylane, 1998.

Spector, Ronald H. *Eagle against the Sun: The American War with Japan*. New York: Vintage Books, 1985.

Stavridis, Admiral James, USN (Ret.). *Sea Power: The History and Geopolitics of the World's Oceans*. New York: Penguin Press, 2017.

Sturma, Michael. *Death at a Distance: The Loss of the Legendary USS* Harder. Annapolis: Naval Institute Press, 2006.

Sullivan, Robert, ed. *Pearl Harbor: America's Call to Arms*. New York: Time-Life, 2001.

Swanston, Alexander, and Malcolm Swanston. *The Historical Atlas of World War II*. Edison, NJ: Chartwell Books, 2007.

Taylor, A. J. P. *The Second World War: An Illustrated History*. New York: G. P. Putnam's Sons, 1975.

Toll, Ian W. *Pacific Crucible: War at Sea in the Pacific, 1941–1942*. New York: W. W. Norton, 2012.

Trader, Arthur, and Henry Francis Sturdy. *Seeing Annapolis and the Naval Academy*. Annapolis: Capital-Gazette Press, 1938.

Twomey, Steve. *Countdown to Pearl Harbor: The 12 Days to the Attack*. New York: Simon & Schuster, 2016.

Van der Vat, Dan. *The Atlantic Campaign: World War II's Great Struggle at Sea*. New York: Harper & Row, 1988.

———. *Pearl Harbor: The Day of Infamy—An Illustrated History*. New York: Basic Books, 2001.

Waller, George M., ed. *Pearl Harbor: Roosevelt and the Coming of the War*. Boston: D. C. Heath, 1965.

Ward, Geoffrey C., and Ken Burns. *The War: An Intimate History, 1941–1945*. New York: Alfred A. Knopf, 2007.

Weintraub, Stanley. *Long Day's Journey into War: Dec. 7, 1941*. New York: Truman Talley Books / Plume, 1991.

Wheeler, Keith. *War under the Pacific*. Chicago: Time-Life Books, 1980.

Williams, Greg H. *The Last Days of the United States Asiatic Fleet: The Fates of the Ships and Those Aboard, Dec. 8, 1941–Feb. 5, 1942*. Jefferson, NC: McFarland, 2018.

Winchester, Kenneth, ed. *WWII: The Time-Life Books History of the Second World War*. New York: Prentice Hall, 1989.

Winchester, Simon. *Pacific: Silicon Chips and Surfboards, Coral Reefs and Atom Bombs, Brutal Dictators, Fading Empires, and the Coming Collision of the World's Superpowers*. New York: HarperCollins, 2015.

Winslow, Captain W. G., USN (Ret.). *The Fleet the Gods Forgot: The U.S. Asiatic Fleet in World War II*. Annapolis: Naval Institute Press, 1982.

Wright, Michael, ed. *The World at Arms: The Reader's Digest Illustrated History of World War II*. London: Reader's Digest Association, 1989.

Official U.S. Navy Sources

Battle of Midway. CINCPAC file no. A16, ser. 01693, June 15, 1942. Micro serial no. 41273, reel A45. https://www.fold3.com/.

History of the USS Houston. March 14, 1942. Micro serial no. 157247, reel A2060. https://www.fold3.com/.

History of the USS Stewart. Micro serial no. 158543, reel 12093. https://www.fold3.com/.

"Houston Survivors Liberated." U.S. Navy Department Press and Radio Release, September 1, 1945. Micro serial no. 157247, reel A2060. https://www.fold3.com/.

Naval Action in Coral Sea Area, May 4–8, 1942. CINCPAC File A16(4) (0010N), May 27, 1942. Micro serial no. 41078, reel A39. https://www.fold3.com/.

Navy Department Communique No. 54. U.S. Navy Department Press and Radio Release, March 14, 1942. Micro serial no. 157247, reel A2060. https://www.fold3.com/.

Night Attack of Balikpapan: Report of Executive Officer Lt. R. N. Antrim, U.S. Navy. U.S. Asiatic Fleet, Destroyer Division 59, USS *Pope*, January 25, 1942. File no. FB59/A16-3. Micro serial no. 40467, reel A21. https://www.fold3.com/.

Office of Naval Intelligence, U.S. Navy. *Combat Narratives: The Battle of the Coral Sea—Consisting of the Actions at Tulagi, May 4th; off Misima, May 7th; and in the Coral Sea on May 8th, 1942.* Micro serial no. 48849, reel A313. https://www.fold3.com/.

Report of Action: Bombing Squadron Six, June 4–6, 1942. File no. FVB-6/A16. Micro serial no. 41707, reel A60. https://www.fold3.com/.

Report of Action: Bombing Squadron Six, June 10, 1942. File no. FVB-6/A16. Micro serial no. 41707, reel A60. https://www.fold3.com/.

Report of Action: Bombing Squadron Three, June 4–6, 1942. File no. CV5/A16-3. Micro serial no. 41273, reel A45. https://www.fold3.com/.

Report of Offensive Measures during Air Raid Seven December 1941: USS St. Louis, *December 25, 1941.* File no. CL49/A16-3. Micro serial no. 40003, reel A1A. https://www.fold3.com/.

Report of the Board of Visitors to the United States Naval Academy—1938. Washington, DC: Government Printing Office, 1938.

U.S. Pacific Fleet, Minecraft, Battle Force, Mine Division One: Japanese Air Attack, December 7, 1941. File no. FF12-6/A16-3. Micro serial no. 40003, reel A1A. https://www.fold3.com/.

USS Dewey—*War Diary*, December 18, 1944. Micro serial no. 100897, reel A1328. https://www.fold3.com/.

USS Haddo—*Report of Eighth War Patrol.* COMSUBSPAC Patrol Report. File no. FF12-10/A16-3. Micro serial no. 103528, reel A1361. https://www.fold3.com/.

USS Haddo—*Report of Ninth War Patrol.* COMSUBSPAC Patrol Report. File no. FB5-341/A16. Micro serial no. 135174, reel A1781. https://www.fold3.com/.

USS Hammann—*Action Report, June 4–6, 1942.* File no. DD412/P6-1. Micro serial no. 41273, reel A45. https://www.fold3.com/.

USS Harder—*Report of Fifth War Patrol.* COMSUBSPAC Patrol Report. Micro serial no. 83281, reel A1109. https://www.fold3.com/.

USS Houston—*Action Report, on the Battle of Sunda Strait*. March 13, 1942. File no. FF6/A16-3. Micro serial no. 40219, reel A12. https://www.fold3.com/.

USS Houston—*Summary Submitted by Lt. (jg) Harold S. Hamlin, USN, and Lt. (jg) Leon W. Rogers, USN*. September 9, 1945. File no. EN3-11(CT)/A8-21. Micro serial no. 139002, reel A1843. https://www.fold3.com/.

USS Lexington—*Report of Action, Battle of the Coral Sea, May 7–8, 1942*. https://www.fold3.com/.

USS Parche—*Report of First War Patrol*. COMSUBSPAC Patrol Report. File no. FF12-10/A16-3(15)/(16). Micro serial no. 76117, reel A16-3. https://www.fold3.com/.

USS Parche—*Report of Second War Patrol*. COMSUBSPAC Patrol Report. File no. FF12-10/A16-3(15)/(16). Micro serial no. 87000, reel A1151. https://www.fold3.com/.

USS Parche—*Report of Sixth War Patrol*. COMSUBSPAC Patrol Report. File no. SS384/A16-3. Micro serial no. 137386, reel A1812. https://www.fold3.com/.

USS Patterson—*Report of Pearl Harbor Attack*. February 21, 1942. File no. DD392/A16/rhw. Micro serial no. 40203, reel A10. https://www.fold3.com/.

USS Pope—*Action Report*. March 1, 1942. File no. FF6/A16-3. Micro serial no. 40247, reel A14. https://www.fold3.com/.

USS Puffer—*Report of Fifth War Patrol*. COMSUBSPAC Patrol Report. File no. FF12-10/A16-3(15)/(16). Micro serial no. 87946, reel A1161. https://www.fold3.com/.

USS Puffer—*Report of Sixth War Patrol*. COMSUBSPAC Patrol Report. File no. FF12-10(A)/A16-3(18). Micro serial no. 106260, reel A1397. https://www.fold3.com/.

USS Puffer—*Report of War Patrol Number One*. COMSUBSPAC Patrol Report. File no. A16-3. Micro serial no. 59334, reel A670. https://www.fold3.com/.

USS St. Louis—*War Diary*. December 1941. Micro serial no. 40683, reel A27. https://www.fold3.com/.

USS Whale—*Report of War Patrol Number Eleven*. COMSUBSPAC Patrol Report. File no. FF12-10(A)/A16-3(18). Micro serial no. 142360, reel A1880. https://www.fold3.com/.

USS Zane—*Report of Pearl Harbor Attack*. December 19, 1941. File no. DMS14/A16-3(0366). Micro serial no. 40003, reel 0001. https://www.fold3.com/.

Other Sources

Allen, James A. *Memoir of a Civilian POW*. Accessed November 12, 2024. rims.k12.ca.us/pow/index.html.

Calhoun, Charles. Interview. University of North Carolina Wilmington, Transcript nos. 222, 272, 333.

"The Crash of Navy Blimp *L-8*." Check-Six.com, accessed November 12, 2024. https://www.check-six.com/Crash_Sites/L-8_crash_site.htm.

"Dusty Kleiss: A Hero of Midway Remembered." Naval Historical Foundation, April 25, 2016. https://www.navyhistory.org/2016/04/dusty-kleiss-a-hero-of-midway-remembered/.

"The Fury of the Sea: A Survivor Describes the End of the USS *Monaghan*." *Our Navy* 39, no. 21 (April 1, 1945).

Hagen, Jerome. "Pearl Harbor: Plus 60 Years." *Honolulu Advertiser*, accessed November 12, 2024. https://the.honoluluadvertiser.com/specials/pearlharbor60.

Kleiss, Dusty. Interview. CNN, April 28, 2016. https://www.cnn.com/videos/us/2016/04/28/captain-dusty-kleiss.cnn.

Kleiss, Norman J. Oral history. Digital Collections of the National World War II Museum, New Orleans, LA, accessed November 12, 2024. https://www.ww2online.org/view/norman-dusty-kleiss.

"Land Hunt for Blimp Crew Abandoned." *San Francisco California Bulletin*, August 18, 1942. http://sfmuseum.org/hist8/blimp.html.

"The Loss of the USS *Harder*." Accessed July 2021 at www.ussnautilus.org; no longer accessible.

"My Journal" (journal of Electrician's Mate R. O. Hudgins, USN, 12-7-41 to 12-10-41). Accessed November 12, 2024. https://www.ussstlouis.net/war_diary_1941-46.htm.

Nugent, CTC Edward E., USN (Ret.). "The Forgotten Blimps of World War II." *Foundation Magazine*, Spring 1995.

Orr, Timothy, and Laura Orr. "Jack 'Dusty' Kleiss and the Battle of Midway." *Daybook* 15, no. 4 (2012): 8–11.

Panko, Ray. "VF-6: The Deadly Night of December 7, 1941." Pearl Harbor Aviation Museum blog, January 14, 2013. https://www.pearlharboraviationmuseum.org/blog/vf-6-the-deadly-night-of-december-7-1941/.

"The Past Is Another Country." *Air and Naval Weapons*, June 17, 2015.

Ramsey, Clay, ed. "The USS *Pope*'s Last Action." As told by Mr. William Penninger, Ft. Worth, TX. https://www.navsource.org.

Rickard, J. "Naval Battle of Guadalcanal, 13–15 November 1942." HistoryofWar.org, June 17, 2013. www.historyofwar.org/articles/battles_naval_guadalcanal.html.

Roosevelt, Franklin D. "Address at the United States Naval Academy Graduation" (June 2, 1938). In Gerhard Peters and John T. Woolley, *The American Presidency Project*, accessed November 12, 2024. https://www.presidency.ucsb.edu/documents/address-the-united-states-naval-academy-graduation.

Stephenson, Parks. *Torpedo Attack on the USS St. Louis*. 2010. https://www.i-16tou.com/stlou/.

Twomey, Steve. "Countdown to Infamy: The High Stakes Gamble and False Assumptions That Detonated Pearl Harbor 75 Years Ago." *Smithsonian*, December 2016, 25–33, 96–102.

"U.S. Naval Academy Facts, Figures and History." Navy Sports: The Official Website of Naval Academy Varsity Athletics. https://navysports.com/sports/2018/5/23/trads-usna-facts-figures-history-html.

"U.S. Pilots Greeted by Friendly Fire." *Honolulu Star Bulletin*, December 4, 1999. https://archives.starbulletin.com/1999/12/04/editorial/special.html.

Whalen, Cdr Todd. "Remembering Family and a Tradition of Service on Pearl Harbor Day." iDriveWarships.com, December 7, 2014. idrivewarships.wordpress.com; no longer accessible.

Winslow, Commander Walter G. "The Nightmare Night USS *Houston* Went Down." USNI News, August 22, 2014. https://news.usni.org/2014/08/22/nightmare-night-uss-houston-went.

World of Warships: Official Forum of the Americas. https://worldofwarships.com.

Wright, Andy. "The 1942 Ghost Blimp That Bewildered a California Town." *Atlas Obscura*, October 17, 2016. https://www.atlasobscura.com/articles/the-1942-ghost-blimp-that-bewildered-a-california-town.

INDEX

Note: page numbers in italics refer to figures.

ABOUT THE AUTHOR

Justin Laborde, PhD, is a communications scholar, strategic consultant, and frequent speaker on consumer trends and business-growth strategies at Fortune 500 companies. He brings to this project a passion for World War II history, a researcher's training, and a unique personal connection to the Naval Academy: his grandfather, Alden Laborde, was a member of the Class of 1938. He has spent seven years gathering primary materials and researching the histories and wartime stories of this class' members. Justin was educated at Washington & Lee University and Florida State University and lives in North Carolina with his wife and three children.

The Naval Institute Press is the book-publishing arm of the U.S. Naval Institute, a private, nonprofit, membership society for sea service professionals and others who share an interest in naval and maritime affairs. Established in 1873 at the U.S. Naval Academy in Annapolis, Maryland, where its offices remain today, the Naval Institute has members worldwide.

Members of the Naval Institute support the education programs of the society and receive the influential monthly magazine *Proceedings* or the colorful bimonthly magazine *Naval History* and discounts on fine nautical prints and on ship and aircraft photos. They also have access to the transcripts of the Institute's Oral History Program and get discounted admission to any of the Institute-sponsored seminars offered around the country.

The Naval Institute's book-publishing program, begun in 1898 with basic guides to naval practices, has broadened its scope to include books of more general interest. Now the Naval Institute Press publishes about seventy titles each year, ranging from how-to books on boating and navigation to battle histories, biographies, ship and aircraft guides, and novels. Institute members receive significant discounts on the Press' more than eight hundred books in print.

Full-time students are eligible for special half-price membership rates. Life memberships are also available.

For more information about Naval Institute Press books that are currently available, visit www.usni.org/press/books. To learn about joining the U.S. Naval Institute, please write to:

Member Services
U.S. Naval Institute
291 Wood Road
Annapolis, MD 21402-5034
Telephone: (800) 233-8764
Fax: (410) 571-1703
Web address: www.usni.org